A History of Military Occupation from 1792 to 1914

A History of Military Occupation from 1792 to 1914

Peter M. R. Stirk

EDINBURGH
University Press

Edinburgh University Press is one of the leading university presses in the UK. We publish academic books and journals in our selected subject areas across the humanities and social sciences, combining cutting-edge scholarship with high editorial and production values to produce academic works of lasting importance. For more information visit our website: www.edinburghuniversitypress.com

© Peter M. R. Stirk, 2016, 2017

Edinburgh University Press Ltd
The Tun—Holyrood Road
12 (2f) Jackson's Entry
Edinburgh EH8 8PJ

First published in hardback by Edinburgh University Press 2016

Typeset in 11 on 13 Sabon by
Iolaire Typesetting, Newtonmore and
printed and bound in Great Britain by
CPI Group (UK) Ltd, Croydon CR0 4YY

A CIP record for this book is available from the British Library

ISBN 978 0 7486 7599 9 (hardback)
ISBN 978 1 4744 2841 5 (paperback)
ISBN 978 0 7486 7600 2 (webready PDF)
ISBN 978 0 7486 7602 6 (epub)

The right of Peter M. R. Stirk to be
identified as author of this work has
been asserted in accordance with the
Copyright, Designs and Patents Act 1988
and the Copyright and Related Rights Regulations 2003
(SI No. 2498).

Contents

Introduction: From Conquest to Occupation   1

1 The Era of the French Revolutionary and the
   Napoleonic Wars   39
2 European Occupations before 1870   104
3 Military Occupation and America: Expansion and
   Civil War   146
4 The Franco-German War and Occupation of France   188
5 Codification of a Law of Occupation   224
6 Occupations to the Eve of the First World War   254
7 Occupations by the United States of America and the
   Spanish-American War   287
Conclusion   319

Select Bibliography   331
Index   347

Introduction
From Conquest to Occupation

'Occupation is an ugly word, not one Americans feel comfortable with, but it is a fact'.[1] These words of Paul Bremer, the newly appointed head of the Coalition Provisional Authority in Iraq in May 2003, encapsulate common sentiments at the beginning of the twenty-first century. Military occupation engenders considerable passion and has always done so, even if the general disrepute into which the language and practice of military occupation has fallen is of more recent provenance. The passion is evident in the encounters between occupants and occupied, in the memoirs and histories that flourish in the immediate aftermath of occupation, in the memories of participants who would prefer to forget the experience of occupation, and even in the historical studies devoted to occupations. It is, therefore, not surprising that some occupations at least have generated an enormous literature, most notably those of the Second World War and its aftermath.

What is more surprising is that this has not led to any systematic comparative historical study of military occupation as a distinct phenomenon. Even within the context of multiple occupations by a single occupant, study of national experience predominates. This is true of occupations by Nazi Germany during the Second World War, where comparative analysis has gone further than in any other case.[2] Interestingly, after some initial reflections comparing Allied occupation policies in and after the same war, a national focus has almost entirely dominated attention.[3] Beyond these cases comparative study is extremely rare, though the frequency of occupation in the relations between France and Germany has induced some comparative reflection.[4] The task of beginning to write the history of military occupations in general, however, is still outstanding, despite the call for such a historiographical shift by Philippe Burrin, a noted historian of the occupation of France during the Second World War.[5]

Political scientists engaged in such study are even rarer, there being only two works of any substance, both recent and both having quite specific foci distinct from what would be required of histories of military occupation in general.[6] There are recent legal studies that have focused on international territorial administration and which have a strong comparative and historical dimension but these have separated out international territorial administration from military occupation and reach no further back than the administration of the Free City of Danzig and the Saar by the League of Nations after the First World War.[7] More widely, legal studies, at least from the late nineteenth century onwards, have naturally had a more comparative dimension but equally naturally have not been histories of occupations, focusing instead on legal issues from the proclamation of military occupations, through laws and courts to taxation and debts, and contributions and requisitions.[8] One could make a partial exception for the still invaluable work by Raymond Robin, *Des occupations militaires en dehors des occupations de guerre*, though as the title states, this is concerned with occupations beyond the realm of war.[9] While numerous legal texts give some indication of the development of the law of occupation, even in this area sustained analysis is less frequent than one might expect.[10]

The argument for responding to Burrin's call for a wider history of military occupation goes beyond the desire to fill an academic lacuna. The concept of military occupation has not been a fixed one, or even for most of the time a clear one. The experience of occupation has changed perceptions of the concept and practice of occupation. More recently there has been a tendency to avoid what the Italian general and sometime commander of the Kosovo Force Fabio Mini described as 'the "politically incorrect" word "occupation"'.[11] Against the opprobrium attendant upon military occupation Mini set his early recollections. 'I am old enough', he wrote, 'to remember the warning posters of the Occupying Powers after World War II: "Tomorrow the distribution of food will be suspended", "Public gathering is prohibited. Offenders will be arrested": signed Captain Charlie or Kurt or Martini.'[12] In earlier periods, even once the concept of military occupation had crystallised, the temptation was to deny the fact of occupation by the early assertion of sovereignty, as did the British during the Boer War of 1899–1902, eliciting 'an explosion of indignation amongst the continental press'.[13] Now, as in previous centuries, recognising military occupations and its associated obligations and rights mattered to wider publics, as well as diplomats and generals and, equally important, the inhabitants of occupied territory.

A second reason for responding to Burrin's call is that it has been argued that military occupation has undergone fundamental changes by virtue of changes in societies, notably a growth in their complexity and an increase in state involvement in the economy, and by virtue of changes in the nature of warfare. Both were taken to be at work in the supposed rupture in the practice of military occupation with the advent of total war in the First World War which, in turn, suggested the need for a reconsideration of the recently concluded agreements on the law of occupations at the Hague conferences of 1899 and 1907. The presumption was, as Ernst Feilchenfeld put it in 1942, that the 'Hague Regulations were a late codification of a body of law adopted in an atmosphere of nineteenth-century liberalism shaped by the basic philosophy of that era, and drafted for the conditions of a nineteenth century liberal world'.[14] Carl Schmitt came to a similar conclusion: 'The constitutional standard of liberal constitutionalism presupposed by both sides was the decisive factor in the development of *occupatio bellica*, as it found its classic formulations in the Brussels Conference of 1874 and the Hague land-war conventions of 1899 and 1907.'[15] Both authors, and those who have followed them, have presumed a fairly close congruence between the practice of nineteenth-century military occupation, the structure of nineteenth-century societies and constitutional principles and the Hague Regulations. To what extent that presumption, and hence the significance of the subsequent practices taken to have broken with them, is valid depends, however, upon the historical record of the nineteenth century. The latter is precisely what has been recalled in a fragmentary fashion so far as it has been recalled at all.

The third reason for responding to Burrin's call arises from the fact that recollection of previous occupations, by lawyers, generals and governments, has been partial at best and often inaccurate. Sometimes, as with the Napoleonic occupation of Spain in 1808–14, the presumed lessons of occupation, more or less accurately based on the reality of that occupation, have been invoked up until the present day. General Winfield Scott was said to have had these lessons in mind as his forces occupied Mexico in 1847.[16] Almost two centuries after Napoleon's forces were driven from Spain a French solder and historian sought inspiration from the policies of one of Napoleon's marshals, Suchet, in Aragon.[17] In both cases there was some plausibility in their choice of model and the features that impressed them were relevant to their concerns. Yet even relatively recent historical models in this area, as in others, can be misleading, as can memory of the chosen model. The latter is well illustrated by the uncertainty following General Archibald Wavell's request for guidance at the end of 1940 in the light of impending occupation of Italian territory in East Africa. Amidst the various suggestions that followed, the deputy undersecretary of state in the War Office proposed that 'civil authorities' should have prime responsibility under the guidance of the Colonial Office, 'who did similar work in German East Africa in the last war'. F. S. V. Donnison, who recounts this episode, observed that: 'This was totally untrue of Palestine, only partially true of Tanganyika, more nearly correct of the Cameroons. There was no mention at all of Mesopotamia which was really the leading case on the respective responsibilities of civil and military authorities.'[18] The British War Office could not even accurately recall practice, including its own, a mere two decades earlier. Even more woeful was an apparently commonplace assumption amongst American officials in the occupation of Iraq from 2003. Seated on a military transport plane, a constitutional adviser to the American authorities, Noah Feldman,

> glanced around at my new colleagues. Those who were awake were reading intently. When I saw what they were reading, though, a chill crept over me, too. Not one seemed to need a refresher on Iraq or the Gulf region. Without exception, they were reading new books on the American occupation and reconstruction of Germany and Japan.[19]

It was not the most appropriate analogy.

Delimiting and Defining Military Occupation

In order to begin drawing together some of the relevant material for a history of military occupation the current volume is restricted to the period from the outbreak of the French Revolutionary Wars through to the eve of the First World War. It covers the long nineteenth century.[20] The starting point is based on the claim that it was only with the Revolutionary and Napoleonic Wars, and the reactions they induced, that an understanding of military occupation as a distinct phenomenon began to gain widespread currency. This is not an undisputed claim, though it enjoys support from some of those who have concerned themselves with the question.[21] Exactly why and how this happened is part of the account. It ends on the eve of the First World War not because of any necessary agreement with the presumption of a rupture in the history of the practice of occupation, noted above, but simply because the first wave of codification ended close to the outbreak of the war and for the simple practical reason that incorporation of the wealth of material relating to the First World War would unbalance the narrative.

Chronological constraints are but one of the choices that have to be made. Two others are worth emphasising at the outset. First, this volume does not elide military occupation and colonialism. Such elision is commonplace today. In the long nineteenth century occupants often resorted to the language of empire and colonialism. Yet the difference is important. Military occupation as a distinct phenomenon presumes recognition that the occupant is not sovereign. Imperial powers asserted sovereignty over the territories they claimed as colonial possessions. Indeed, they often justified their assertion of sovereignty on the grounds that there were no sovereign authorities in the territories they claimed. That this has subsequently been seen as immoral, manifestly based on distortion or even inconsistent with aspects of their own practices makes no difference.[22] As Eyal Benvenisti has put it, because the concept of military occupation

> was meant to safeguard national sovereignty, it could not apply to regions whose sovereignty was not recognized. The prevailing view among the mainly European powers was that sovereignty, as a 'gift of civilization', did not extend beyond the circle of self-defined 'civilized', mainly Christian nations.[23]

European nations did extend the concept of military occupation to some non-European and non-Christian territory, notably in some areas of the decaying Ottoman Empire, including French occupation of Syria and British occupation of Egypt, and Japan adopted the European concept of occupation in its occupations during the Chinese–Japanese War and the Russo-Japanese War. Both Japan and European nations deployed the concept and practices during their occupation of Peking. These were, however, exceptions bound up with the status of the Ottoman Empire and Japan in the predominantly European legal community. The term occupation was deployed extensively within the context of empire, as was the refinement 'effective occupation', especially towards the end of the nineteenth century, but with the very different purpose of asserting title to sovereignty.[24]

Second, the account of military occupations given below is mainly driven by the view from above. It does not purport to be a social history of occupied societies or to be a history of resistance to occupation, still less to be justification of resistance to occupation.[25] Even histories of specific occupations often make such choices.[26] An account seeking to cover over a century of occupations has no alternative to making such choices.[27] The choice of the view from above is made in the light of the definition of military occupation given below. This choice does not mean, of course, that the view from below is wholly ignored. How occupants have behaved, and even how they have understood themselves, is shaped by the reactions of the occupied. To see oneself as a 'liberator' becomes increasingly difficult if the occupied reject that perception and resort to violent resistance. That has been illustrated recently in the occupation of Iraq. The dilemma was evident from the beginning of the occupations by the armies of Revolutionary France.

An even more important choice concerns the definition of military occupation and indeed the very choice of the term military occupation rather than simply occupation or belligerent occupation. It has become commonplace here to refer to the lament by August Wilhelm Heffter in his *Das europäische Völkerrecht der Gegenwart* of 1844 of insufficient clarity in distinguishing between conquest and occupation. Sometimes he has been said to have been the first to clearly draw the distinction.[28] Strictly speaking that is not true. The distinction had been clearly drawn much earlier but Heffter was the first widely cited and respected author of a text on international law to insist on consistent use of the distinction.[29] The distinction between conquest and occupation, often qualified as 'mere military occupation', is the starting point for a definition of military occupation.[30] It signifies that the occupant is not the sovereign. Quite how the relationship between the occupant and the sovereign or sovereignty is to be expressed has proven to be one of the most intractable aspects of the understanding of military occupation.[31] However expressed, the distinction appears in all key texts. It is evident in the opening clause of article 43 of the Hague Regulations of 1907: 'The authority of the legitimate power having in fact passed into the hands of the occupant . . .'.[32] It follows from this, of course, that authority is ascribed to the occupant. The occupant is seen as enjoying a legal status and having authority, not merely the capacity to exercise brute force.[33] The implications of that for any obedience owed by the occupied to the occupant had been, and would remain, unclear, save in certain limited respects, notably whether the occupant was entitled to impose an oath upon the occupied.[34] The incompatibility of an oath of allegiance follows logically from the non-sovereign status of the occupant.[35]

The second key element in the definition is that military occupation is a form of government. Again this is recognised in the Hague Regulations, though it is expressed in the context of concern about the territorial extent of military occupation rather than directly in terms of the nature of military occupation: 'Territory is considered occupied when it is actually placed under the authority of the hostile army. The occupation extends only to the territory where such authority has been established and can be exercised.'[36] Both elements of the term military government are worth emphasis. First it is a form of government. This was put succinctly by the German lawyer Karl Heyland in 1925: 'The centre of gravity of the activity of the occupant lies in administration.'[37] Second it is military in nature, irrespective of whether the administration is carried out by military personnel or civilian officials of the occupant. This is clearly illustrated by the American *Rules of Land Warfare*:

> It is immaterial whether the government established over an enemy's territory be called a military or civil government. Its character is the same and the source of its authority is the same. It is a government imposed by force, and the legality of its acts are determined by the laws of war.[38]

The dual character of military occupation as a form of government which is military in nature is in some ways brought out even more clearly by the attempt at the end of the nineteenth century in America to distinguish between the authority exercised by military forces over their own citizens in times of emergency, for which the term martial law was reserved, and the authority exercised by military forces over citizens of other states, for which the term military government was preferred.[39] Military government is now so widely used to designate authority exercised by military forces over their own societies that it would be misleading to attempt to revert to the late nineteenth-century American distinction, nor is it necessary to do so. The term military occupation suffices to recall the essential features of the government of alien citizens imposed by force, or threat thereof, but claiming to exercise authority and not mere brute force. Those features are still discernible in recent cases where the occupant has fought shy of the term occupation. They show through in the exercise of authority, if only in the accompanying embarrassment about it.

The term military occupation has another advantage which serves to illustrate a third important element of a definition. For most of the period in which military occupation has been subject to study, mostly in the form of legal analyses of one kind or another, the preferred term has been belligerent occupation. According to Arnold McNair, the latter term 'is clearly better than "military occupation", which can occur in times of peace'. McNair specified that his article 'is not concerned with the military occupation of foreign territory which may occur in time of peace or in pursuance of an agreement for an armistice'.[40] Even at the time of writing, 1941, McNair's preference was misguided. Ironically, it would be instances of occupation continued or begun under the conditions of the Second World War which led the negotiators of the Geneva Conventions of 1949 to explicitly exclude the requirement for belligerency. Common article 2 provides that 'The Convention shall apply to all cases of partial or total occupation of the territory of a high Contracting Party, even if said occupation meets with no armed resistance'. As Jean Pictet's commentary makes clear, 'the wording adopted was based on the experience of the Second World War, which saw territories occupied without hostilities, the Government of the occupied territory considering that armed resistance was useless.'[41] From the viewpoint of a historical survey of military occupations, however, that development has a potentially even more misleading implication, suggesting that chronologically and possibly conceptually non-belligerent occupation was secondary or derivative. Such impressions should have been avoidable in the light of Robin's *Des occupations militaires en dehors des occupations de guerre* of 1913. As will be shown below, there is a case for considering occupations beyond the realm of war as central to the development of the understanding of military occupation. The latter term has the advantage of avoiding the possible implications of McNair's preference.

Military occupation understood as a form of government is, however, a concept that brings with it problems of its own. As with all forms of government it is not omnipresent, at least not in any obtrusive sense. The government within the context of military occupation is more likely to be obtrusive, coloured by the force on which it ultimately rests, but is often even less visible to most inhabitants. Especially in the case of most nineteenth-century occupations the personnel of the occupant were thinly spread in relation to the population and the territory of the occupied. It was precisely for this reason that at the Brussels Conference of 1874 General Voigts-Rhetz opposed a requirement that occupation should be recognised only where the military power of the occupant is visible.[42] No such requirement was included in the draft agreed by the conference. The underlying problem was not thereby resolved. Much later the United States Military Tribunal considered the case of the German occupation of Greece and Yugoslavia. It conceded that 'it is true that the partisans were able to control sections of these countries at various times' but denied that this signified that these areas constituted unoccupied territory. The immediate reason was that 'the Germans could at any time they desired assume physical control of any part of the country'.[43] This is consistent with the established doctrine that insurrection does not deprive the occupant of his status. The rationale was that 'occupation indicates the exercise of governmental authority to the exclusion of the established government. This presupposes the destruction of organised resistance and the establishment of an administration to preserve law and order.'[44] This clearly leaves a grey area in the sense that the absence of German administration of certain areas was what was at issue. The tribunal followed established practice in arguing that countries as a whole were considered to be occupied following the capitulation of their governments or armed forces, that is, the 'exclusion of the established government', regardless of the temporary absence of German administration in certain areas. This does not necessarily create any more difficulty than in recognising that the exercise of administration by a legitimate government may be weak or even absent in certain parts of its territory. Both cases, however, indicate the existence of a grey area.[45] It is a grey area that has continued to haunt courts. In one case the defence argued that absence of effective occupation signified the absence of occupation. The court accepted the logic of this argument in line with the definition of occupation in the Hague Regulations. It then invoked Jean Pictet's *Commentary* on the Geneva Conventions of 1949.⁴⁶ According to the *Commentary*, as quoted by the court, in the Convention

> the word 'occupation' ... has a wider meaning than it has in Article 42 of the Regulations annexed to the Fourth Hague Convention of 1907. *So far as individuals are concerned*, the application of the Fourth Geneva Convention does not depend upon the existence of a state of occupation within the meaning of Article 42.⁴⁷

The court's gloss on this was that

> The Chamber accepts this to mean that the application of the law of occupation as it affects 'individuals' as civilians protected under Geneva Convention IV does not require that the occupying power have actual authority. For the purposes of those individuals' rights, a state of occupation exists upon their 'falling into the hands of the occupying power'.⁴⁸

The significance of this and similar judgements here is less their greater or lesser success in resolving legal issues of liability under certain laws than their exposure of the grey zone experienced by both occupants and occupied. Whether the uncertainty is created by insurrection, by the existence of a phase of invasion before occupation is established, by raiding, or by the gradual diminution of the authority of an occupant that makes it difficult to even determine when the occupation might have ended, military occupation is surrounded by a penumbra of uncertainty that forms part of the experience of occupation by both occupants and occupied.⁴⁹

Occupation and Conquest

That uncertainty extends to the core elements of the definition of occupation. As already noted, in 1844, Heffter had complained about insufficient clarity in distinguishing between conquest and occupation. To later lawyers the distinction seemed clear and reflective of the progress of international law. From their perspective the change in both law and the practice of invaders could hardly be starker. According to William Hall in 1909:

An invader on entering a hostile country was considered to have rights explicable only on the assumption that ownership and sovereignty are attendant upon the bare fact of possession. Occupation, which is the momentary detention of property, was confused with conquest, which is the definitive appropriation of it. Territory, in common with all other property, was supposed, in accordance with Roman Law, to become *terra nullius* on passing out of the hands of its owner in war; it belonged to any person choosing to seize it for so long as he could keep it. The temporary possession of territory therefore was regarded as a conquest which the subsequent hazards of war might render transient, but which while it lasted was supposed to be permanent. It followed from this that an occupying sovereign was able to deal with occupied territory as his own, and that during his occupation he was the legitimate ruler of its inhabitants.

Down to the middle of the eighteenth century practice conformed itself to this theory. The inhabitants of occupied territory were required to acknowledge their subjection by taking an oath, sometimes of fidelity, but more generally of allegiance; and they were compelled, not merely to behave peaceably, but to render to the invader the active services which are due to the legitimate sovereign of a state.[50]

Lassa Oppenheim was briefer but if anything more extreme in his account of earlier doctrine and practice, published in 1906:

> In former times enemy territory that was occupied by a belligerent was in every point considered his State property, with which and with the inhabitants therein he could do what he liked. He could devastate the country with fire and sword, appropriate all public and private property therein, kill the inhabitants, or take them away into captivity, or make them take an oath of allegiance ... That an occupant could force the inhabitants of occupied territory to serve in his own army against their legitimate sovereign, was indubitable.[51]

Both agreed that attitudes began to change in the second half of the eighteenth century though neither gave much indication of why.[52]

Looking back on such claims, which he characterised as the 'orthodox doctrine', from the viewpoint of the mid-1920s, Thomas Baty, under the subheading 'was an invader ever sovereign', concluded that they were exaggerated. The practices they reported had 'fallen into desuetude' long before the Seven Years War and had never been anything more than 'mere abuses of force, reprobated by all authorities'.[53] Which, if either, of these sets of views is the more accurate, has considerable significance for understanding the emergence of a concept of military occupation resembling the definition given above. If Hall and Oppenheim are right the conceptual distance and changes in practice required are enormous. If Baty is right then it would seem that the distance is far less; so much less that it might be supposed that something resembling military occupation was already evident much earlier than has been supposed here. Baty had ended his critique of the 'orthodox doctrine' by quoting an extract from the correspondence between the Spanish General DeVillene and the French Marshal de Noailles in 1694, in which it was asserted that 'people conquered by force of arms should be considered as subjects of the prince who has the domination of their country only in the case of a veritable cession following the conclusion of a peace'.[54] This was the principle that should prevail according to late nineteenth- and early twentieth-century lawyers, including those who ascribed very different principles to the era before the mid to late eighteenth century. More recently serious consideration has been given to the possibility that not only was bare possession seen as insufficient to establish sovereignty but that bare possession entailed something resembling military occupation.[55] Before turning to the meaning and practice of conquest before 1789 and the possibility of military occupation before 1789 it is useful to consider attitudes to conquest more generally.

This is important because, although principled objections to conquest had emerged, conquest had not acquired the opprobrium which attaches to it in the twenty-first-century mind. To classically educated minds, conquest, as recorded in Greek and Roman history and poetry, could still seem admirable. That was evident in a late eighteenth-century tract which acknowledged that conquest could not be reconciled with prevailing understanding of law and morality yet whose author proclaimed

> when I examine my own feelings, and, as far as I can learn, the feelings and sentiments of Mankind in general, I find that a Conqueror is not the object of our detestation; I find that our moral sense of right and wrong is not offended, at his conduct; but that, on the contrary, he becomes by it the object of universal praise and admiration.[56]

It was only in the wake of the Charter of the League of Nations, the Kellogg–Briand Pact of 1929, renouncing war as an instrument of policy, the United Nations Charter and other declarations, that conquest fell into general disrepute.[57] In the latter half of the nineteenth century and the early decades of the twentieth century there were, to be sure, several authors, predominantly French, who denied that conquest as an act of force could give birth to any right.[58] Rejection of conquest could be abrupt, as when Pasquale Fiore denied that conquest 'in itself could be considered as juridically effective for the acquisition of territory', or polemical, as when Frantz Despagnet, associated it with 'mystical tendencies' to invoke divine providence.[59] Even these writers, however, more or less reluctantly admitted some qualified acceptance of conquest.[60] In this they were not quite as far removed from those who adopted a more affirmative attitude towards conquest than at first seems to be the case. Those who took the more affirmative attitude often reserved the term conquest to the subjugation of an enemy state, setting it alongside cession in a treaty as a mode of acquiring territory. Alphonse Rivier was relatively clear on this point: 'Not all annexation of territory as a consequence of war is conquest. If it is consented to in a treaty of peace by the defeated state [*l'état vaincu*], it takes place by virtue of a cession.'[61] Conquest in the technical sense of the term meant subjugation:

> There is subjugation, *debellatio*, when the war ends by the complete defeat of one of the belligerents such that all its territory is seized, that the authority of its government is suppressed and that, consequently it ceases to exist as a state.[62]

Conquest here could be justified by the 'juridical construction' that 'the subjugated state has ceased to exist; its territory is *res nullius*; the conqueror [*le vainqueur*] is therefore master by virtue of occupation'.[63] However phrased, and whether explicitly contrasted with acquisition of territory at the end of a war by cession in a treaty or not, conquest in the sense of subjugation was generally accepted. So too conquest, even if denied the name, could be legitimated by cession in a treaty.[64] The difference, of course, was that the latter made room for a period when, short of subjugation, territory was occupied by one party but the other remained in the field, there was some prospect of it recovering the territory, and the occupant was not considered to be the sovereign. Statesmen, generals, publicists and publics naturally often used terminology in a less precise sense, though the level of clarity attained by the lawyers should not be exaggerated. The main point is that a doctrine of conquest still existed; it was most clearly and forcefully articulated in the case of subjugation;

it was consistent with, and to some extent facilitated, identification of a distinct phase of military occupation.

Turning to the concept and practice of conquest before 1789, it is desirable to distinguish between certain levels of analysis: namely, between the doctrines as expressed in what came to be recognised as the major texts of an incipient international law; the arguments used by statesmen and sovereigns in making their claims against each other; and the practices and concepts deployed by invaders and inhabitants, especially in the context of the occupation of specific towns and provinces.[65] Separating out here conquest and occupation is not strictly speaking possible for that presumes a conceptual clarification that was not available in this era. Even the etymology of the word occupation militated against such a distinction. The Latin word *occupare* originally meant to seize, especially in a chase or hunt.[66] Carried over into the context of warfare it still meant taking possession, a significance that was all the more natural when the acquisition of property was a prime purpose of warfare.[67] As Jacob Connor explained, according to the Roman understanding of the term: 'the property of the enemy was in Roman law *res nullius*, inasmuch as it was the property of persons whom that law regarded as nobodies, and who, if captured, themselves became *res nullius*.'[68] The concept of postliminium, also taken over from Latin and Roman law, reinforced this meaning, for postliminium referred to the right to what was retaken into possession.[69] Once extended to matters of public authority it retained this significance of seizure. When Samuel Pufendorf in the seventeenth century referred to the violent acquisition of authority he noted that this was often called *occupatio*.[70] Rather than signifying any contrast between seizure and rightful possession or conquest, the very word signified precisely seizure and rightful possession or conquest.

Use of the term occupation more widely to justify the existence of private property in the context of a Christian supposition that the earth had been given to mankind in common may have given a somewhat different direction to the development of the Roman term but did nothing to move it towards the meaning of occupation in the context of military occupation. That can be seen as late as 1813 in a French repertoire of judicial terminology where the entry devoted to occupation focused primarily on the notion of a right of first occupancy. It did briefly note that

The law of nations introduced however a new means to acquire property, not by the right of first occupant, but by right of occupation or invasion. Thus, every nation that makes war for a just cause has the right to appropriate things it seizes from the enemy. One calls this *conquest* for towns and lands taken from the enemy, and *booty* for moveable things.[71]

This, of course, confirms the persistence of the equation, or here the partial equation, of occupation and conquest.

In terms of the development of international law Grotius is an important reference point for several reasons: the general reputation of his *The Rights of War and Peace*; his role in popularising the use of the term *occupatio bellica*; and the frequency with which much later authors invoked Grotius when wishing to illustrate the extremity of earlier conceptions of conquest.[72] There is indeed no doubt about the licence that Grotius extended to the exercise of violence in warfare: '*in war the Guilty and Innocent fall alike*'. He added that 'how far this Licence extends itself, will hence appear, in that the Slaughter of Infants and Women is allowed, and included by the Right of War.'[73] It was from this right of killing enemies that Grotius derived the right to enslave enemies and to acquire all the rights that they had possessed. Continuing this line of argument Grotius proclaimed:

> No wonder that he who can bring into Slavery every particular person of the Enemies Party, that falls into his Hands . . . may also impose a Subjection upon the whole Body, whether it be a State, or part of a State.[74]

Even at this stage in the argument Grotius allowed some limitation in the case where sovereignty is acquired 'so far as it was in the King, or another Governor, and then all Power he had passes to the Conqueror, and no more'.[75] Later on, when considering what ought to be done in the light of 'Justice', 'other Vertues' and might make actions 'more commendable in the Opinion of good Men', Grotius referred to a much wider range of outcomes in consequence of conquest.[76] These included leaving 'to the Conquered . . . their own Government'; 'that their own Sovereignty should be left to the Vanquished is not only agreeable to Humanity, but often also to Policy'; 'that some Part of the Government may be left to them, or their Kings'; that they be allowed 'the Exercise of their antient Religion'; that even 'when all Sovereignty is taken from the conquered, there may be left to them their own Laws, about their private and publick Affairs, of some small Moment, and their own Customs and Magistrates'.[77] Grotius illustrated these practices and norms as he illustrated his assertion of more extreme rights and practices primarily by reference to ancient sources, especially Roman sources. The potential latitude allowed by Grotius to conquered peoples had, however, a specific significance in the states, overwhelmingly monarchies, of his own day. These states were not the centralised states of the late nineteenth century but composite states, consisting of distinct kingdoms having in common only their subjection to the same sovereign. Their character was brought out by the seventeenth-century Spanish jurist Juan Solórzana Pereira: 'These kingdoms must be ruled and governed as if the king who holds them all together were king only of each one of them.'[78] This did not signify any diminution of the sovereignty of their king but only that sovereignty did not have the connotations ascribed to it in the late nineteenth century. Each of these kingdoms could be governed in accordance with its own institutions, laws and customs. Governing them in this way was expedient and sometimes the only way of ensuring control. It was even possible for a new sovereign to present himself as a liberator who wished to restore the ancient liberties which had been eroded by the previous ruler. Thus the Dutch while in possession of Lille from 1708 to 1713, and while insisting upon their acquisition of sovereignty by 'the right of conquest and war', claimed they were intent upon restoring the privileges and customs of Lille to their condition before 1667 when the town had been acquired by the French. They even apologised for violating customs, excusing themselves on the grounds of ignorance, and promised to abide by them in the future.[79]

The complexity of early modern European polities found reflection in another doctrinal question that was taken up by the Dutch jurist Cornelius van Bynkershoek in the eighteenth century, namely whether possession of territories and towns brought with it possession of dependent towns and territories. Bynkershoek invoked the decrees of the States General of the United Provinces and the King of Spain during the 1630s, which were issued during the prolonged war between the Dutch and the Spanish, in order to resolve the matter. He cited a decree of the Spanish king himself,

> in which the King argues that the territory that belongs to a city follows the conquest of the city. And this is the law that the States-General also with entire propriety adopted in the aforementioned edicts, because those

who rule at pleasure over a territory are considered to have occupied that territory. However, if there be some as yet unoccupied stronghold in the territory, the possession and dominium of the invader does not extend over the part dominated by the said stronghold.[80]

Although Bynkershoek did not mention it, that still left room for dispute about what relationship of dependence did or did not prevail in a particular case.

In general, however, attempts to formulate international law clarifying conquest were marked by the continuing contrast between what might be called a strong version, typically drawing on the work of Grotius with greater or lesser emphasis upon a hypothetical right of slaughter and enslavement, and moderate versions which sought to soften the implications of conquest if only by reference to considerations of humanity and prudence. Although not conducted within what were the standard reference points of early international law, it is worth noting a specific instance where uncertainty about the consequences of conquest was expressed in a wider public debate, namely justifications of the seizure of power in the English Glorious Revolution. Arguments about the rights of conquest were but one of several sets of arguments and were used by both supporters of the deposed king and supporters of the new rulers. Central to the fate of the arguments from conquest in favour of the new rulers was the idea that conquest entailed an extinction of all existing rights. Supporters of the new rulers invoking conquest faced the problem that

> 'conquest' had become the practical monopoly of the champions of royal against parliamentary power. To talk of a conquest in the early 1690s invited associations with the debates over the Norman Conquest and Tory attacks on parliamentary rights as simply the concession of conquering kings.[81]

These connotations were powerful enough to induce Parliament to put an end to the debate by having the tract *King William and Mary Conquerors*, which supported William and Mary, burned by the public hangman.[82] Although this debate was clearly coloured by the specific circumstances of England at the time and the record of and attitude to conquest in the English legal tradition, it too reflects the clash between a strong version of conquest, here seen as extinguishing existing rights, and the unsuccessful attempt to defend a moderate version in which conquest and existing rights could be reconciled.

Doctrinal attempts to resolve the problem would continue, but without becoming notably more successful. Pufendorf, for example, drawing upon his wider political theory, argued that 'since men are by nature all equal, and no one is subject to another's sovereignty, it follows that mere force and seizure are not sufficient to constitute legitimate sovereignty over men'.[83] Indeed, Pufendorf held the transition from war to peace to be inexplicable without some 'intervening pact'. This, however, only led to a rather dubious consolation: 'The only advantage the victors obtain by a just war is that they do not have to elicit the consent of the conquered by flattery or entreaties, but can extort it by the threat of extreme penalties.' The logic was Grotian, for Pufendorf claimed that the vanquished would not 'hold his consent to his victor's sovereignty a thing to his own hurt, since he can thereby escape death'.[84] There were still echoes of that logic in Vattel's *Law of Nations* though by the publication of his text in 1758 they were faint and Vattel did not dwell on them. Slavery could be justified, he conceded, in extreme cases but he soon added: 'I shall dwell no longer on the subject: and indeed this disgrace to humanity is happily banished from Europe'.[85]

Conquest had not been banished from Europe. Indeed Vattel in one sense made a stronger case for it than his predecessors, by weakening the insistence upon the acquisition of territory in a just war. The first rule of the voluntary law of nations, that is of a notion of international law distinct from other kinds of law, for which alone Vattel claimed novelty, was that *'regular war, as to its effects, is to be accounted just on both sides'*.[86] By its effects he meant 'acquisitions made by arms'.[87] Much is often made of another assertion by Vattel, namely that:

> Immovable possessions, lands, towns, provinces &c. become the property of the enemy who makes himself master of them: but it is only by the treaty of peace, or the entire submission and extinction of the state to which those towns and provinces belonged, that the acquisition is completed, and the property becomes stable and perfect.[88]

We have here the two criteria that many nineteenth-century lawyers would recognize as necessary for the perfection of conquest: cession by treaty or subjugation. It is also suggested that the intervening period before acquisition is completed heralds the emergence of the modern concept of occupation.[89] Vattel, however, illustrates the point only through the well-known risk that a third party undertakes in purchasing something possessed by a victor before the original owner had renounced all claim to it in a treaty of peace or had been subjugated. Nor should it be forgotten that even Vattel's insistence upon a peace treaty was far from universally accepted. In a prominent English legal case not long after the publication of Vattel's *Law of Nations* Lord Mansfield proclaimed that 'A cession is not necessary to a conquest; it is not necessary for the right. Jamaica never has been ceded, I believe, to this hour'.[90] There was no suggestion that this implied the least restraint upon the powers of the conqueror. To the contrary, Lord Mansfield continued:

> This is not a matter of disputed right; it has hitherto been uncontroverted that the King may change part or all of the political form of Government, over a conquered dominion . . . It is not to be wondered that an adjudged case in point is not to be found; no dispute ever was started before upon the King's legislative right over a conquest: it never was denied in a Court of Law or Equity in Westminster-Hall, never was questioned in Parliament.[91]

It is arguable, however, that Vattel's insistence on the uncertainty of acquisition until confirmation in a peace treaty is relevant to the experience identified by the second level of analysis, that is, that it reflected part of customary practice by sovereign and statesmen in making claims against each other. Conquest alone, that is, the bare fact of possession, was often held to be insufficient. That is hardly surprising for most of early modern Europe, where the territorial state was at best in its infancy. The early modern French state, for example, has been described as

> not yet, strictly speaking, territorial in nature. Its governing idiom was that of jurisdictions, including 'appurtenances, dependencies and annexes' . . . Jurisdictional sovereignty . . . meant that the crown accumulated rights to specific domains – fiefs, bailiwicks, bishoprics, seignuries, boroughs, and even villages.[92]

Even late in the eighteenth century a contemporary Frenchman could describe Lorraine as 'mixed, crossed, and filled with foreign territories and enclaves belonging with full sovereignty to the princes and states of Germany'.[93] Reference to rights was an inevitable and natural consequence of this condition, especially as dynastic intermarriage and a plethora of overlapping claims to titles made the advancement of ambition under the guise of legal claim comparatively easy, if not always entirely persuasive.[94] There was, to be sure, an important change in the eighteenth century as the language of the balance of power became increasingly prominent in diplomatic negotiation and justification, though even here this was not a mere balance of naked power but a balance that recognised legitimate claims.[95] Both languages were, of course, open to abuse and contemporaries were as prone as later commentators to assert the existence of hegemonic ambition behind the veil of the legal claims of their opponents.[96] There was, however, generally a reluctance to abandon these justificatory languages in favour of arguments from conquest alone. At the Peace of Westphalia the leading German princes rejected the right of conquest outright. French negotiators were instructed to base claims on the rights of war but were also instructed to advance French claims on the basis of ancient rights in explicit contrast to the claims of their allies, which could rely only on the right of conquest. The Spanish view was that pure conquest could engender no stability at all.[97] It was not that conquest, the fact of possession, was of no account. Thus, in 1634 France asserted possession of Lorraine and Bar on the grounds of 'very considerable and ancient claims'; 'current possession by treaties and by force of arms'; and the 'extraordinary felony of the duke', that is the Duke of Lorraine, who had violated certain obligations to the French king, according to the French account at least.[98]

Even Louis XIV and Frederick the Great, the two figures who most scandalised and alarmed the diplomatic world of the seventeenth and eighteenth centuries, provoking dangerous coalitions against their states, sought to clothe their ambitions in the garb of legitimacy. Louis deployed lawyers and historians to work up his claims to Lorraine, Rousillon and Franche-Comté.[99] It is true that in 1685 Louis instructed his ambassador to Vienna that Lorraine had become French

> as much by right of conquest and confiscation as by the treaties made with the late duke and by the refusal of the present one to subscribe to the conditions that the Imperial ministers stipulated in his favour in the Treaty of Nijmegen.[100]

This, however, followed fifteen years of propaganda and diplomacy intended to extract recognition of French claims as well as efforts to win over the elites of Lorraine. Frederick's much quoted cynicism about a justification for his seizure of Silesia in 1740 drawn up at his instruction – 'Splendid, that's the work of an excellent charlatan' – does not detract from his perceived need to offer such a justification.[101] Right of conquest alone was insufficient. It could play a part but it typically needed not only confirmation by treaty but also often elaborate claim to title offered in advance and reinforced during the negotiations intended to extract confirmation.

While acquisition of territory remained precarious until some recognition had been obtained assertion of sovereignty over the inhabitants of invaded territory was another matter. Yet this third level of analysis also reveals a much more complex picture than suggested by Hall and Oppenheim. It is true that here the right of conquest, or rather rights of conquest, did not wait for the end of war.[102] The rights of conquest covered a range of claims relating to rights over persons, rights over moveable property and rights over immoveable property. That continued to be the case in some measure in the practice and law of occupation in the long nineteenth century. What was set aside, excluded from the rights of occupation, pending subjugation or determination in a peace treaty, was claims to territorial sovereignty with all that entailed. Precisely that distinction was not clearly established before 1789. Again considerable caution is needed in making assertions about these issues. It is notable that the standard reference points are the works of Irénée Lameire, published before the First World War, and Hubert van Houtte, published in 1930.[103] Lameire specified that he was concerned in his study of the law of conquest with conquest 'independent of any treaty'.[104] More specifically he was concerned with the situation in which 'the seizure of a place is followed by the immediate displacement of sovereignty'.[105] Lameire emphasised that this displacement, defining as it did the relationship between the occupant and the occupied, could only be understood to occur where both parties considered that the occupied territory belonged to a sovereign other than the sovereign asserting the claim. Otherwise there could clearly be no displacement of sovereignty. This seemingly obvious point acquires significance in the light of the fact that sovereign statehood was not the universal norm during the Europe of the *ancien régime*. Hence, Lameire excluded German territory from his surveys given the persistence of some notion of overarching imperial sovereignty within the Holy Roman Empire and the complex relationship within it.[106]

Within these parameters Lameire discerned instances of the immediate displacement of sovereignty in the seventeenth century, for example, with what he described as striking clarity with Louuis XIV's seizure of Mons and Namur in 1691 and 1692 and in the eighteenth century, after 1744, he claimed the displacement was the easiest to follow: 'Belgium was annexed to France, town by town, *châtellenie* by *châtellenie*, royal court by royal court, in line with the victories of Maurice of Saxony'.[107] Lameire found examples across the regions of Europe he had selected. In the conflict between France and Savoy he found, for example, in 1704, during the French possession of the Italian town of Bielle, that French officials described it as 'belonging presently' to the French king, enacted new investitures of judges in the name of the French king, and prohibited communication with places owing obedience to the Duke of Savoy, thereby implying that the town of Bielle owed no such allegiance.[108] Despite, or because of his minute study of occupation Lameire, however, remained reluctant to draw general conclusions. The displacement of sovereignty was not always evident: 'To the contrary, sovereignty is often fragmented, displaced in certain respects, not displaced in others: as a result there is a curious superimposition of sovereignty.'[109]

Hubert van Houtte expressed less reservation than Lameire.[110] The normal practice was, according to van Houtte, the assertion of sovereignty upon completion of occupation, that is, upon seizure of the main administrative centres. At this point the conqueror was held to be entitled to all rights held by the previous sovereign.[111] Formal assertion of such rights could take the form of the demand for a formal act of submission, as required of the Council in Brussels in 1706, the replacement of Austrian arms in the same city by French arms in 1746, or the announcement in the same year that justice would be pronounced in the name of the French king, even though this was some months before the formal imposition of an oath of fidelity.[112] A recent account of the Dutch occupation of Lille between 1708 and 1711 reinforces van Houtte's claim that the assertion of sovereignty was the norm. Acceptance of this was facilitated by the fact that the inhabitants' identity was bound to the town and locality, not to any wider French identity.[113]

There is, then, clear evidence of the existence of an understanding and the associated practices of an immediate transfer of sovereignty in the relations between occupant and occupied, even if the extent and consistency of it is far from certain. Baty's assertion of the paucity of such evidence is not sustainable, but nor are the claims of Oppenheim which owe more to a selective reading of Grotius than to understandings of the relationship between the new sovereign of conquered territory and its inhabitants. This is in no way to deny the frequent excesses committed by invading armies as they pillaged their way across invaded territory.[114] It does mean claiming that there was no unified and clear understanding of what conquest meant. The doctrines of lawyers, the claims and counter claims of sovereigns, and of those who claimed other titles than sovereignty in anything resembling its modern sense, and the practices and understandings evident when occupant confronted occupied are probably best understood not as reflections of a single doctrine but as layers which intersected at various points but also diverged. To this must be added the complexities arising from the diversity of political regimes across the Europe of the *ancien régime*.

The precariousness of sovereignty identified by Lameire and the absence of any single model of statehood in the sense that late nineteenth-century lawyers might be said to have a model of statehood, leaves open the possibility that military occupation as defined above might be said to have existed in some instances at least during the *ancien régime*. There are, indeed, a limited number of strong cases for precisely this possibility. The most interesting concerns the occupations of territory in the Rhineland, especially the occupation of the western provinces of Prussia during the Seven Years War. Here the situation was complicated by the fact that this was a joint occupation. Although French armies invaded the territories, they did so as allies of the Habsburgs, whose commissioners were, it had been agreed, to exercise 'all the rights attaching to sovereign authority'.[115] Implementing that agreement proved to be problematic because of the complex legal situation within the Holy Roman Empire and because of concerns that the Prussian king would retaliate by imposing oaths of loyalty in territory he had occupied, potentially creating a crisis of legitimacy.[116] In the province of Ostfriesland, however, the French commander, who had not been informed of the legal complications, took possession in the name of the French king, causing tension with France's Austrian ally and the neutral United Provinces.[117] The hesitancy about asserting sovereign authority, as well as the administrative practices of the French, does indeed exhibit a striking similarity to what would come to be seen as the position of the occupant. There is some irony in this, for as the historian of these developments, Horst Carl, has suggested 'practice in the old *Reich* is more indicative of the future than the behaviour of a comparatively modern state, be it that of the Sweden of Gustavus Adolphus or the France of Louis XIV'.[118]

What general conclusions are intended to be drawn from such instances is not entirely clear.[119] Much turns on the claim to sovereignty typically made by the putative occupant, either as a direct assertion of authority over the occupied or as a claim against the former or ousted sovereign. Yet, as has been indicated, Lameire found extensive evidence of a lack of clarity, of precariousness. Given competing claims to sovereignty, especially in a political system in which the most common form of polity relied upon dynastic succession to secure state continuity, uncertainty created by the figure of the usurper or the interim ruler was a longstanding problem, raising such issues as whether obedience was owed to whoever possessed power, merely by virtue of such possession, and what validity, if any, attached to their acts, including transactions between private citizens and such rulers.[120] Moreover, uncertainty about the location of sovereignty, including in varying degrees ascription of sovereignty to what was otherwise recognised as an occupant, would persist long after the codification of a binding law of occupation.[121] Similarly, even in the *ancien régime* the dilemmas of those faced with the imposition of an oath could be recognised and even elicit sympathy.[122] Oaths of various kinds would indeed continue to be commonplace in military occupations throughout the nineteenth century.[123]

What can be safely concluded is that the emergence of military occupation as a distinct phenomenon in the shape of an abrupt and clean break with the past is a myth. It is argued below that it emerged as the accumulated experiences of the ambiguity of authority increased in frequency and intensity under the impact of the Revolutionary and Napoleonic Wars, forcing generals, administrators, occupied populations and courts, both courts of the occupant and courts of restored regimes, to try to make sense of those experiences. Innovative doctrines would play an important part in this, but as will be shown below, doctrinal innovation did not all point in the same direction. It could point to the renunciation of conquest, and open the way for the emergence of a concept of occupation, but also provide new justifications for conquest.

What is also clear is that towards the end of the Napoleonic Wars the language of military occupation and its attendant problems was being used and disputed in a way that is recognisable from the perspective of what became the codified law of occupation. This is the central perspective that informs the following history of military occupation. To the extent that occupants and the occupied used the language, recognised the problems, struggled to find solutions to military occupation, the phenomenon can be said to have existed without having to be reconstructed behind their backs. This is no perfect strategy, least of all with military occupation. Too rigid an insistence upon it excludes earlier instances. Too lax an instance upon it leads to an indiscriminate application of the concept of military occupation, which becomes more and more problematic as the term becomes commonplace and its connotations emotive. There is no substitute for making judgements, case by case, and accepting that some at least of these will be disputed. It also needs to be re-emphasised that the concept and practice of military occupation did not emerge against the backcloth of a clear concept and practice of conquest. That is the point of recalling the world of the *ancien régime*. By the same token, the concept and practice of military occupation would never acquire unequivocal clarity in the minds of those who practised it, were subject to it, or reflected on it. That, however, is also part of its history.

Notes

1. Quoted in Ivo H. Daalder and James M. Lindsay, *America Unbound* (Washington DC: Brookings, 2003), p. 154.
2. See A. Toynbee and V. Toynbee (eds), Survey of International Affairs. Hitler's Europe (London: Oxford University Press, 1954); Czeslaw Madajczyk, 'Die Besatzungssysteme der Achsenmächte', Studia Historicae Oeconomicae, 14 (1980), 105–22; Wolfgang Benz, 'Typologie der Herrschaftsformen in den Gebieten unter deutschen Einfluss', in Wolfganag Benz, Johannes Houwink ten Cate and Gerhard Otto (eds), *Die Bürokratie der Okkupation* (Berlin: Metropol, 1998), pp. 11–25; Hans Umbreit, 'Towards continental domination', in Militärgeschichtliche Forschungsamt (ed.), *Germany and the Second World War*, vol. 5, part 2 (Oxford: Clarendon Press, 2000), pp. 5–292; Mark Mazower, *Hitler's Empire: Nazi Rule in Occupied Europe* (London: Penguin, 2009). A more comparative dimension has also begun to appear in the study of occupations of the First World War. For an overview see Sophie de Schaepdrijver (ed.), *Military Occupations in First World War Europe* (Abingdon: Routledge, 2015).

3. For some comparative works see Carl J. Friedrich (ed.), *American Experiences in Military Government in World War II* (New York: Reinhart, 1948); Hajo Holborn, *American Military Government: Its Organization and Policies* (Washington DC: Infantry Journal Press, 1947); Lord Rennell of Rodd, *British Military Administration of Occupied Territories in Africa During the Years 1941–1947* (London: HMSO, 1948); F. S. V. Donnison, *Civil Affairs and Military Government: Central Organization and Planning* (London: HMSO, 1966).
4. Marc Blancpain, *La vie quotidienne dans la France du Nord sous les occupations (1814–1944)* (Paris: Hachette, 1983); Richard Cobb, *French and Germans, Germans and French: A Personal Interpretation of France under Two Occupations 1914–1918/1940–1944* (Hanover, NH: Brandeis University Press, 1983); Peter Hüttenberger and Hansgeorg Molitor (eds), *Franzosen and Deutsche am Rhein 1789–1918–1945* (Essen: Klartext, 1989).
5. Philippe Burrin, 'Writing the history of military occupations', in Sarah Fishman, Laura L. Downs, Ioannis Sinanoglou et al. (eds), *France at War: Vichy and the Historians* (Oxford: Berg, 2000), p. 78. Burrin notes that there is 'no global historical study of occupations beyond Eric Carlton's unsatisfying work, *Occupations: The Policies and Practices of Military Conquerors*' (ibid. p. 87). Given the utter lack of conceptual precision it would be more accurate to say that Carlton's book is not even about military occupation in any meaningful sense of the term.
6. My own *The Politics of Military Occupation* (Edinburgh: Edinburgh University Press, 2009) focuses on understanding military occupation as a political phenomenon and disavows any claim to be a history, p. 4). David Edelstein, *Occupational Hazards: Success and Failure in Military Occupation* (Ithaca, NY: Cornell University Press, 2008) is, as the subtitle suggests, a response to 'a simple central question: why do some military occupations succeed whereas others fail?', p. vii. It is also highly selective, though extensive justification for the selection, given the intended purpose, is given, pp. 171–92.
7. See Ralph Wilde, *International Territorial Administration: How Trusteeship and the Civilizing Mission Never Went Away* (Oxford: Oxford University Press, 2008); Carsten Stahn, *The Law and Practice of International Territorial Administration: Versailles to Iraq and Beyond* (Cambridge: Cambridge University Press, 2008); Richard Caplan, *International Governance of War-Torn Territories. Rules and Reconstruction* (Oxford: Oxford University Press, 2005); Simon Chesterman, *You, the People: The United Nations, Territorial Administration, and State-Building* (Oxford: Oxford University Press, 2004). In most cases the subtitles suffice to indicate the scope. The

reasons for separating their cases from military occupation, or at least suggesting that the analogies with military occupation are limited, vary. See Caplan, *International Governance of War-Torn Territories*, pp. 3–4; Chesterman, *You, the People*, pp. 45–6; Stahn, *The Law and Practice of International Territorial Administration*, pp. 471–4.

8. The topics are taken from the chapter headings of Gerhard von Glahn, *The Occupation of Enemy Territory* (Minneapolis: University of Minnesota Press, 1957).

9. Raymond Robin, *Des occupations militaires en dehors des occupations de guerre* (Paris: Larose, 1913). A partial English translation was published by Carnegie, under the same title, in 1942.

10. The most cited older text is Doris A. Graber, *The Development of the Law of Belligerent Occupation 1863–1914: A Historical Survey* (New York: AMS, 1949). The best modern text is Eyal Benvenisti, *The International Law of Occupation* (Princeton: Princeton University Press, 2012).

11. Fabio Mini, 'Liberation and occupation: a commander's perspective', *Israel Yearbook on Human Rights*, 35 (2005), 84.

12. Ibid. p. 72. In fact, what Mini complained about as the 'blasphemy' of military control over civil institutions was already evident in some minds in the Second World War. See the recollections of F. S. V. Donnison, *Civil Affairs and Military Government: Central Organization and Planning*, p. 19. As will be shown below, this sentiment is considerably older though this should not detract from the significance of the change in attitudes in Fabio Mini's lifetime.

13. Thus Frantz Despagnet, ' Chronique des faits internationaux: Grande-Bretagne, République Sud Africaine ou du Transvaal et État Libre d'Orange', *Droit international public*, 9 (1902), 137. See also Alexandre Mérignhac, 'Les pratiques anglaises dans la guerre terrestre', *Revue générale de droit international public*, 8 (1901), 95–6.

14. Ernst H. Feilchenfeld, *The International Economic Law of Belligerent Occupation* (Washington: Carnegie, 1942), p. 17.

15. Carl Schmitt, *The Nomos of the Earth* [1950] (New York: Telos, 2003), p. 209. The point has been reiterated ever since. See for example Benvenisti: 'Only seven years after the Hague Peace conference reconfirmed the nineteenth century concepts of belligerent occupation, their underlying assumptions proved inadequate', *The International Law of Occupation*, p. 46.

16. David Glazier, 'Ignorance is not bliss: the law of belligerent occupation and the U.S. invasion of Iraq', *Rutgers Law Review*, 58 (2005), 139. As the subtitle indicates, Glazier in some respects sought to recall the lessons through Scott that Scott had drawn from the Napoleonic occupation of Spain.

17. Jean-Louis Reynaud, *Contre-guerilla en Espagne (1808–1814): Suchet pacifie l'Aragon* (Paris: Economica, 1992).
18. Donnison, *Civil Affairs and Military Government: Central Organization and Planning*, p. 21.
19. Noah Feldman, *What We Owe Iraq* (Princeton: Princeton University Press, 2004), p. 1. According to Paul Bremer, Ahmad Chalabi claimed that the analogy between MacArthur's role in Japan and Bremer's in Iraq had occurred to the Ayatollah Sistani, but with a predictably different estimation of the significance of the analogy. See L. Paul Bremer, *My Year in Iraq* (New York: Threshold, 2006), p. 94. On the inappropriateness of the analogy see Andrew Arato, *Constitution Making Under Occupation: The Politics of Imposed Revolution in Iraq* (New York: Columbia University Press, 2009), pp. 32–7. See also the conclusion of James Dobbins, Seth G. Jones, Benjamin Runkle et al.: 'One of the administration's more serious conceptual errors was to model its efforts in Iraq on the post-World War II occupation of Germany and Japan', *Occupying Iraq: A History of the Coalition Provisional Authority* (Santa Monica: Rand, 2009), p. 330.
20. Diverging slightly from the chronology associated with Eric Hobsbawm who begins with *The Age of Revolution: Europe 1789–1848* (London: Abacus, 1977).
21. See, for example, Eyal Benvenisti, 'The origins of the concept of belligerent occupation', *Law and History Review*, 26 (2008), 622.
22. It has been argued that the very concept of sovereignty itself was formed in the process of the encounter between Europeans and non-Europeans. See Antony Anghie, *Imperialism, Sovereignty and the Making of International Law* (Cambridge: Cambridge University Press, 2004). Even if this is accepted it has no bearing on the European provenance of the concept of military occupation. I refer to manifest distortion because there are claims that the European imperial enterprise involved the destruction of what were arguably sovereign states. This point goes back to arguments about the conquest of the Americas and was in some respects widely accepted, at least in respect of pre-Colombian polities conquered by the Spanish. The vast literature is too large to cite but the obvious starting point is Francisco de Vitoria. See his *Political Writings* (Cambridge: Cambridge University Press, 1991). I refer to inconsistency because Europeans signed treaties with those they deemed to be incapable of exercising sovereignty despite the fact that capacity to sign international treaties was deemed to be a mark of sovereignty. This caused some embarrassment to lawyers at the time.
23. Benvenisti, 'The origins of the concept of belligerent occupation', p. 647.

24. Effective occupation was put on the agenda at the Berlin Conference of 1884–5, but with some reservations. See S. E. Crowe, *The Berlin West Africa Conference 1884–1885* (London, Longmans, 1942), p. 184, and Jörg Fisch, 'Africa as *terra nullius*', in Stig Förster, Wolfgang J. Mommsen and Ronald Robinson (eds), *Bismarck, Africa, and Europe* (Oxford: Oxford University Press, 1988), pp. 347–75.
25. For an example of the latter see Karma Nabulsi, *Traditions of War: Occupation, Resistance and the Law* (Oxford: Oxford University Press, 1999).
26. See the explicit decision to break 'with scholarly trends that favour social history from the bottom up' in the study of the German occupation of France. Thomas J. Laub, *After the Fall: German Policy in Occupied France 1940–1944* (Oxford: Oxford University Press, 2010), p. 21. Allan Mitchell made the same choice in *Nazi Paris: The History of an Occupation 1940–1944* (New York: Berghahn, 2008), pp. xiii–xiv.
27. Accounts that can plausibly claim to give a multi-faceted, full picture are rare. For a brilliant exception to the general constraints see John Dower, *Embracing Defeat: Japan in the Aftermath of World War II* (London: Penguin, 1999).
28. For example, by Arthur Lorriot, *De la nature de l'occupation de guerre* (Paris: Charles-Lavauzelle, 1903), p. 26. This was repeated, for example, by von Glahn, *The Occupation of Enemy Territory*, p. 8.
29. For some welcome precision about what Heffter wrote see Benvenisti, 'The origins of the concept of belligerent occupation', pp. 630–2.
30. See 'United States, Lyon, et al. v. Huckabee', *US Reports*, 83 (1872), 434.
31. See Peter Stirk, *The Politics of Military Occupation* (Edinburgh: Edinburgh University Press, 2009), pp. 148–74.
32. James Brown Scott, *The Proceedings of the Hague Peace Conferences: The Conference of 1907*, vol. 1 (New York: Oxford University Press, 1920), p. 629. It is indicative of the continuing imprecision that the official British translation presented to Parliament, despite reproducing the French text parallel with the translation, has 'The authority of the power of the State having passed *de facto* into the hands of the occupant', *Final Act of the Second Peace Conference Held at the Hague in 1907*, Cd. 4715 (London: HMSO, 1908), p. 58. The inaccurate translation was reproduced in the British War Office, *Manual of Military Law* (London: HMSO, 1914), p. 343. The American translation was accurate, see War Department, *Rules of Land Warfare* (Washington DC: Government Printing Office, 1917), p. 163.
33. According to Yoram Dinstein, the 'second (by no means secondary)

myth surrounding the legal regime of belligerent occupation is that it is, or becomes in time, inherently illegal under international law', *The International Law of Belligerent Occupation* (Cambridge: Cambridge University Press, 2009), p. 2.
34. After the First World War principled debate about this key issue was avoided. On this, and the nature of the debates, see Stirk, *The Politics of Military Occupation*, pp. 122–49. Debate was explicit and often fierce throughout the period covered by the present volume.
35. Hence article 45 of the Hague Regulations of 1907: 'It is forbidden to compel the population of occupied territory to swear allegiance to the hostile force'.
36. Article 45, Hague Regulations of 1907.
37. Karl Heyland, 'Occupatio bellica', in Julius Hatschek and Karl Strupp (eds), *Wörterbuch des Völkerrechts und der Diplomatie*, vol. 2 (Berlin: de Gruyter, 1925), p. 162.
38. War Department, *Rules of Land Warfare*, p. 108.
39. See especially William E. Birkhimer, *Military Government and Martial Law* (Washington DC: J. J. Chapman, 1892).
40. Arnold D. McNair, 'Municipal effects of belligerent occupation', *Law Quarterly Review*, 57 (1941), 33. That preference is reflected in the title of Lorriot, *De la nature de l'occupation de guerre*, the subtitle of von Glahn, *The Occupation of Enemy Territory: A Commentary on the Law and Practice of Belligerent Occupation* and the title of Dinstein, *The International Law of Belligerent Occupation*. Interestingly Benvenisti uses *The Law of Occupation* but also 'The origins of the concept of belligerent occupation'. In contrast see Robert Kolb and Sylvain Vité, *Le droit de l'occupation militaire* (Brussels: Buylant, 2009).
41. Jean S. Pictet, *Commentary: Fourth Geneva Convention* (Geneva: ICRC, 1958), p. 21.
42. *Correspondence Respecting the Brussels Conference on the Rules of Military Warfare* (London: HMSO, 1875), p. 237.
43. 'The Hostages Trial', *Law Report of Trials of War Criminals*, 8 (1949), 56.
44. Ibid. pp. 55–6.
45. In the case of legitimate governments, absence of effective administration may be so extreme as to lead to the suggestion that they constitute quasi-states or failed states. The classic source on these is Robert Jackson, *Quasi-States: Sovereignty, International Relations and the Third World* (Cambridge: Cambridge University Press, 1990). The implied analogy between certain military occupations and quasi-states should not be pushed too far. The analogy breaks down crucially in that the governments of quasi-states are at least arguably the legitimate

power whereas the authorities of the occupant are by definition not the legitimate power.
46. Pictet's *Commentary* has acquired such an authoritative status that some have argued that it has become a substitute for the meaning of the Conventions themselves. See David John Ball, 'Toss the *travaux*? Application of the Fourth Geneva Convention to the Middle East conflict – a modern (re)assessment', *New York University Law Review*, 79 (2004), 990–1029.
47. *Prosecutor v. Naletilic*, ICTY (March 2003), para. 220.
48. Ibid. para. 221.
49. For a legal evaluation see Dinstein, *The International Law of Belligerent Occupation*, pp. 38–45. While determining the end of an occupation may be comparatively easy, even allowing the specification of a precise day, it can be notoriously difficult. For a recent example see Adam Roberts, 'The end of occupation: Iraq 2004', *International and Comparative Law Quarterly*, 54 (2005), 27–48, and Andrea Caracona, 'End of occupation in 2004?', *Journal of Conflict & Security Law*, 11 (2006), 41–66, especially the ambivalence on the last page.
50. William Edward Hall, *A Treatise on International Law*, 6th edn (Oxford: Clarendon Press, 1909), pp. 458–9.
51. Lassa Oppenheim, *International Law: A Treatise*, vol. 2 (New York: Longmans, 1906), p. 168.
52. Hall suggested that 'After the termination of the Seven Years' War these violent usages seem to have fallen into desuetude', *A Treatise on International Law*, p. 460. Oppenheim suggested that 'during the second half of the eighteenth century things gradually began to undergo a change', *International Law*, vol. 2, p. 168.
53. Thomas Baty, 'The relations of invaders to insurgents', *Yale Law Journal*, 36 (1927), 966 and 972.
54. Ibid. p. 972.
55. The literature here is limited. The most important recent works are Markus Meumann and Jörg Rogge (eds), *Die besetzte res publica: Zum Verhältnis von ziviler Obrigkeit und militärischer Herrschaft in bestetzten Gebieten vom Spätmittelalter bis zum 18. Jahrhundert* (Berlin: Lit, 2006), and Horst Carl, *Okkupation und Regionalismus: Die preussischen Westprovinzen im Siebenjährigen Krieg* (Mainz: von Zabern, 1993).
56. [Allan Ramsay], *An Essay on the Right of Conquest* ([Florence], 1783), p. 4.
57. Sharon Korman, *The Right of Conquest* (Oxford; Clarendon Press, 1996), pp. 135–248. It is important to note her conclusion: 'The point is that if the contemporary prohibition of conquest is to have a greater meaning in practice than the mere conversion of *de jure* conquests

into *de facto* conquests – until the conquests are recognized *de jure* by other states – sterner actions than mere non-recognition of conquest will have to be adopted by the international community, which would have the effect of *reversing* conquests when they occur', p. 247.
58. Paul Fauchille, *Traité de droit international public*, vol. 1, part 2 (Paris: Rousseau, 1925), lists Henri Bonfils, Franzt Despagnet, Pasquale Fiore, L. A. de Montluc and P. Tradier-Fodéré, p. 768. Korman, *The Right of Conquest*, produces the same list, p. 94. See also, however, Franz von Holtzendorff, *Eroberungen und Eroberungsrecht* (Berlin: Lüderitz, 1871) who, despite his evident desire to justify German acquisition of Alsace-Lorraine, is critical of most justifications of conquest.
59. Pasquale Fiore, *Le droit international codifié* (Paris: Pedone, 1911), p. 514; Frantz Despagnet, *Cours de droit international public* (Paris: Larose, 1894), p. 106.
60. Despagnet introduces his polemic against conquest in the context of partial conquest, having earlier noted, without such protest, cases of total annexation, *Cours de droit international public*, pp. 96–102. Fiore allows prescription and the necessity of the inhabitants to adjust to the new order to slowly legitimate the acquisition, *Le droit international codifié*, p. 515.
61. Alphonse Rivier, *Principes de droit des gens*, vol. 1 (Paris: Rousseau, 1896), p. 181.
62. Alphonse Rivier, *Principes de droit des gens*, vol. 2 (Paris: Rousseau, 1896), p. 436.
63. Rivier, *Principes de droit des gens*, vol. 1, p. 182. Strictly Rivier said this constriction was admissible but not necessary. Oppenheim took great exception to the notion that the territory became *res nullius*, a doctrine he ascribed to German authors. The difference between, for example, Oppenheim's phrasing and that of Heimburger's, who does indeed say that *debellatio* is a 'sub-species of occupation', is less significant than Oppenheim claims or Heimburger implies. See Oppenheim, *International Law*, vol. 1, p. 288; Karl Heimburger, *Der Erwerb der Gebietshoheit* (Karlsruhe: Bruan'schen Hofbuchdruckerei, 1888), p. 128.
64. The nuances and precise use of language are of some interest but cannot be followed further here.
65. Heinhard Steiger, '"Occupatio bellica" in der Literatur des Völkerrechts der Christenheit (Spätmittelalter bis 18. Jahrhundert)', in Meumann and Rogge (eds), *Die besetzte res publica*, distinguishes between the practices specific to the occupations of territories, fortresses, town or even complete states; the general rules provided by individual states for their armies; the international law texts, pp. 202–3. Given the

undeveloped nature of the research on this topic, Steiger restricts himself to the latter. The reason for deploying a somewhat different tripartite division will become clear below.

66. Peter Haggenmacher, 'L'occupation militaire en droit international: genèse et profil d'une institution juridique', *Relations internationals*, no. 79 (1994), 286–7.
67. Ibid. p. 289; Kolb and Vité, *Le droit de l'occupation militaire*, pp. 9–10.
68. Jacob Elen Connor, *The Development of Belligerent Occupation* (Iowa: Iowa University Press, 1912), p. 15.
69. Haggenmacher, 'L'occupation militaire en droit international', p. 29. On the need for caution about conflating the Roman postliminium with modern understanding of occupation see Connor, *The Development of Belligerent Occupation*, p. 19.
70. Samuel Pufendorf, *De Officio Hominis et Civis Juxta legem Naturalem Libri Duo*, vol. 1 (New York: Oxford University Press, 1927), p. 132. The difficulties here are evident in divergent translations. Frank Gardner Moore translated the opening clause of Pufendorf's sentence as: 'The violent method of acquiring authority is usually called seizure', Samuel Pufendorf, *De Officio Hominis et Civis Juxta legem Naturalem Libri Duo*, vol. 2 (New York: Oxford University Press, 1927), p. 132. A more recent translation gives: 'Acquisition of authority by military force, which is usually called conquest [*occupatio*]', James Tully (ed.), *On the Duty of Man and Citizen According to Natural Law* (Cambridge: Cambridge University Press, 1991), p. 148.
71. Philippe-Antoine Merlin, *Repertoire de jurisprudence*, vol. 8 (Paris: Garney, 1813), p. 688.
72. On his popularisation of *occupatio bellica* see Steiger, '"Occupatio bellica" in der Literatur des Völkerrechts der Christenheit', pp. 215–16; for an example of later references to Grotius see Korman, *The Right of Conquest*, pp. 29–30, citing Grotius, Oppenheim, *International Law*, 1st edn, and H. W. Halleck, *International Law* (San Francisco: Bancroft, 1861).
73. Hugo Grotius, *The Rights of War and Peace*, vol. 3 (Indianapolis: Liberty Fund, 2005), pp. 1279 and 1283. Though the point cannot be developed here, it is important to recall that Grotius developed a multilayered approach to law. At this stage in his argument he did 'not mean a Permission that renders the Action of killing the Enemy entirely innocent, but an Impunity', p. 1279.
74. Ibid. p. 1374.
75. Ibid. p. 1376.
76. Ibid. p. 1411.
77. Ibid. pp. 1501, 1504, 1507, 1509, 1510.

78. Quoted in J. H. Elliott, 'A Europe of composite monarchies', *Past and Present*, no. 137 (1992), 53.
79. Catherine Denys, 'L'occupation hollandaise à Lille de 1708 à 1713', in Meumann and Rogge (eds), *Die besetzte res publica*, pp. 329–30.
80. Cornelius van Bynkershoek, *Quaestionum Juris Publici Libri Duo*, vol. 2 (Oxford: Clarendon Press, 1930), p. 47.
81. M. P. Thompson, 'The idea of conquest in controversies over the 1688 Revolution', *Journal of the History of Ideas*, 38 (1977), 43.
82. Ibid. p. 45.
83. Samuel Pufendorf, *De Jure Naturae et Gentium Libro Octo*, vol. 2 (Oxford: Clarendon Press, 1934), p. 1085.
84. Ibid. p. 1086. Pufendorf does not go into much detail here, observing simply: 'the way in which sovereignty is acquired over conquered peoples is set forth by Grotius, Bk. III, chap. viii', ibid. p. 1314.
85. Emer de Vattel, *The Law of Nations* (Indianapolis: Liberty Fund, 2008), p. 556.
86. Ibid. p. 591.
87. Ibid. p. 591.
88. Ibid. p. 596.
89. Benvenisti,'The origins of the concept of belligerent occupation', p. 622.
90. 'Campbell v. Hall', *English Reports*, 98 (1774), 893.
91. Ibid. pp. 896–7.
92. Peter Sahlins, 'Natural frontiers revisited: France's boundaries since the seventeenth century', *American Historical Review*, 95 (1990), 1427.
93. Ibid. p. 1428.
94. For the predominance of the language of rights see the comment of Andreas Osiander on the negotiations leading to the Peace of Westphalia: 'Significantly, the peacemakers spoke of "rights" when they meant territories', *The States System of Europe* (Oxford: Clarendon Press, 1994), p. 69. An influential eighteenth-century guide to diplomatic practice warned: 'The point of honour, rank, precedence, are the most delicate article of the political faith. Princes cede towns, even provinces, but it is not possible with all the skill of the most adroit negotiators to persuade them to cede a rank which they believe they are due', Jean Rousset de Missy, *Mémoires sur le rang et la préséance entre les souverains de l'Europe* (Amsterdam: L'Honoré, 1746), p. 3.
95. See Osiander, *The States System of Europe*, pp. 90–165; Richard Little, 'Deconstructing the balance of power: two traditions of thought', *Review of International Studies*, 15 (1989), 87–100; M. S. Anderson, *The Rise of Modern Diplomacy 1450–1919* (London: Longman, 1993), pp. 163–80.

96. In at least one instance later commentators have arguably been more prone to accept such accusations at face value. See the observation of Andreas Osiander on anti-Habsburg propaganda during the Thirty Years War ascribing hegemonic ambitions to the Habsburgs: 'While its original addressees were thus relatively impervious to the anti-Habsburg propaganda, posterity has proved more amenable'. 'Sovereignty, international relations, and the Westphalian myth', *International Organization*, 55 (2001), 264.
97. Osiander, *The States System of Europe*, pp. 50–1.
98. Philip McCluskey, 'From regime change to *réunion*: Louis XIV's quest for legitimacy in Lorraine, 1670–97', *English Historical Review*, 126 (2011), 1393.
99. Ibid. p. 1394.
100. Quoted in ibid. p. 1404.
101. Quoted in Korman, *The Right of Conquest*, p. 71. This is not the place to assess Frederick but the interpretation offered by Friedrich Meinecke is worth mentioning: 'He was giving himself moral reassurance by invoking these "rights" and ... was using them to cover up the motive which really impelled him and which he himself described as *droit de bienséance*', *Machiavellism* (New Brunswick: Transaction, 1998), p. 99.
102. As emphasised by Steiger, '"Occupatio bellica" in der Literatur des Völkerrechts der Christenheit', p. 223.
103. The works of Irénée Lameire are *Théorie et pratique de la conquête dans l'ancien droit* (Paris: Rousseau, 1902); *Les occupations militaires en Italie pendant les guerres de Louis XIV* (Paris: Rousseau, 1903); *Les occupations militaires en Espagne pendant les guerres de l'ancien droit* (Paris: Rousseau, 1905); *Les occupations militaires de l'ile de Minorque pendant les guerres de l'ancien droit* (Paris: Rousseau, 1908); and *Les déplacements de souveraineté en Italie pendant les guerres du XVIIIe siècle* (Paris: Rousseaue, 1911). The works of Hubert van Houtte are *Les occupations étrangères en Belgique sous l'Ancien Régime*, 3 vols (Ghent: Van Rysselberghe and Rambaut, 1930).
104. Lameire, *Théorie et pratique de la conquête dans l'ancien droit*, p. 7. He noted that the French Council of State 'generally calls territory annexed following a diplomatic convention , *pays d'ancienne conquête*: territory occupied during war are territories *de nouvelle conquête*', ibid.
105. Ibid. p. 33.
106. Ibid. p. 8. Most of International Relations as a discipline and much of modern international law works on the misguided assumption that from the Peace of Westphalia Europe was essentially a world of equal

sovereign states and is blind to these problems. The myth of the birth of the Westphalian model of sovereign statehood has been exposed by Osiander, 'Sovereignty, international relations, and the Westphalian myth'. See also Peter Stirk, 'The Westphalian model and sovereign equality', *Review of International Studies*, 38 (2012), 641–60.
107. Lameire, *Théorie et pratique de la conquête dans l'ancien droit*, pp. 48 and 61.
108. Lameire, *Les occupations militaires en Italie pendant les guerres de Louis XIV*, pp. 165, 167, 173.
109. Ibid. p. 380. See also his description of 'precariousness' as the 'most important element of this entire period' in *Les déplacements de souveraineté en Italie pendant les guerres du XVIIIe siècle*, pp. 516–17.
110. In part this seems to have been because Houtte saw Lameire as a jurist seizing on any diminution of the rights of the occupant as progress, *Les occupations étrangères en Belgique sous l'Ancien Régime*, vol. 1, p. 278. Houtte's attitude seems also to be bound up with his development of a three-stage model, distinguishing between a phase in which territory was regarded as a *pays de contribution*, a second stage of incomplete occupation and a final stage of complete occupation, associated with seizure of major administrative centres in which full sovereignty was asserted. For a concise summary see Carl, *Okkupation und Regionalismus*, pp. 13–14. Since the second phase was by far the most onerous for the population, transition to the third phase with the consequence of no longer being treated as enemies was preferable, Houtte, *Les occupations étrangères en Belgique sous l'Ancien Régime*, vol. 1, pp. 278 and 308.
111. Ibid. p. 263. See his reference to a memoir drawn up by an official at Ypres in 1752 envisaging this scenario, p. 261.
112. Ibid. pp. 306, 309, 328.
113. Denys, 'L'occupation hollandaise à Lille de 1708 à 1713', pp. 317–18. See also van Houtte's warning against ascribing modern sentiments of loyalty to the period and his specific warning that 'Fear of punishment on the return of the legitimate government is the only consideration which impeded the majority of the inhabitants, even the notables, from immediately recognizing the sovereignty of the occupant', *Les occupations étrangères en Belgique sous l'Ancien Régime*, vol. 1, p. 279. See also the case of Cambrai in 1597 where the inhabitants denied that they had been subjugated by the Spanish on the grounds that, although under siege, they had voluntarily placed themselves under the sovereignty of the Spanish king, José Ibáñez, 'Théorie et pratiques de la souveraineté dans la monarchie hispanique', *Annales, Histoire, Scienes Sociales*, 55 (2000), 623–44.
114. Pillage was practised even on the territory of the army's own state. On

this, and efforts to restrain it, see Jon Lynn, 'How war fed war: the tax of violence and contributions during the *Grand Siècle*', *Journal of Modern History*, 65 (1993), 286–310.
115. Quoted in Gh. De Boom, 'L'occupation des pays du bas Rhin pendant la Guerre de Sept Ans', *Revue d'histoire modern*, 5 (1930), 401–2.
116. Carl, *Okkupation und Regionalismus*, p. 90.
117. Ibid. p. 96.
118. Horst Carl, 'Französisches Besatzungsherrschaft im Alten Reich', *Francia*, 23, no. 2 (1996), 44.
119. Elsewhere Horst Carl makes a much more wide reaching claim, despite acknowledging the tendency in the period to make claims to unlimited rights on the basis of the law of conquest. See 'Militärische Okkupation im 18. Jahrhundert', in Meumann and Rogge (eds), *Die besetzte res publica*, pp. 354–5. See also the assertion of McCluskey, that the 'laws of conquest, feudal law and dynastic right would remain the usual basis for legitimacy in occupied territory until renounced by revolutionary France' but that while the 'precise status of occupied territory would not be fully elaborated until much later . . . the experience of Lorraine demonstrates that by the seventeenth century it was already a clearly recognised feature in European international relations', 'From regime change to *réunion*', p. 1407. See also the claim of the editors of *Die besetzte res publica*, contrary to Carl's emphasis upon the significance of the old *Reich*, that 'military occupation in the strict, modern sense is tied to the existence of the sovereign state' which they then date to the seventeenth century, 'Markus Meumann and Jörg Rogge, 'Militärische Besetzung vor 1800 – Einführung und Perspektive', in Meumann and Rogge (eds), *Die besetzte res publica*, p. 24.
120. On the usurper see A. M. Honoré, 'Allegiance and the usurper', *Cambridge Law Journal*, 25 (1967), 214–33, which takes as its starting point the English Statute of Treasons of 1351. For an early example of debts due to the state, but received by an interim ruler, see the case of the French in Italy in 1495, Sherston Baker, *Halleck's International Law*, 3rd edn (London: Kegan Paul, 1893), pp. 464–5. On the importance of distinguishing between the interim ruler and occupant see Geffcken's note to Wilhelm Auguste Heffter, *Das europäische Völkerrecht der Gegenwart*, ed. Heinz Geffcken (Berlin: Müller, 1888), p. 410.
121. On the problem of sovereignty and occupation see Stirk, *The Politics of Military Occupation*, pp. 148–74.
122. In the occupation of Prussia's western provinces in the Seven Years War indigenous officials were allowed to formulate a declaration in which they managed to swear to obey the Austrians, while reaffirming

their loyalty to their king. Later, pressure on such officials elicited sympathy from the French military who agreed the officials should not have to act contrary to their oath, Carl, *Okkupation und Regionalismus*, pp. 93 and 102. When the French finally left the town of Emden they formally certified that the magistrates had fulfilled both sets of obligations, Tileman Dothias Wiarda, *Ostfriesische Geschichte*, vol. 9 (Aurich: Winter, 1798), p. 55.

123. Carl links hesitancy to impose oaths in some cases to the declining relevance of oaths in an age where authority was secured by military authority and bureaucratic efficiency, *Okkupation und Regionalismus*, pp. 90–1. While accurate in relation to the role of oaths in general it misjudges the important link between the underlying weakness of the authority of the occupant and persistent recourse to the imposition of oaths. See Stirk, *The Politics of Military Occupation*, pp. 126–7.

Chapter 1
The Era of the French Revolutionary and the Napoleonic Wars

The Provisionality of the Revolutionary and Napoleonic Order

The wars that would make military occupation a recurrent feature of the European experience for over two decades and that overturned the eighteenth-century balance of power were so often justified in terms of competing principles and constitutional orders that principle and competition of constitutions have been seen as the cause of the wars and the factor behind their continuation.[1] From the Declaration of Pillnitz of 27 August 1791, in which Frederick William II of Prussia and Leopold II of Austria declared 'that they regard the present position of His Majesty the King of France as a matter of common concern to all the sovereigns of Europe', and the inflammatory speech of Jacques-Pierre Brissot de Warville, of 20 October 1791, invoking the spectre of an anti-revolutionary conspiracy to be met by war, it readily appeared that the eventual declaration of war against Austria by the French Legislative Assembly on 20 April 1792 was an inevitability.[2] By the same token Napoleon has been seen as the heir of the Revolution, or even as a 'Robespierre on horseback', whose opponents finally set the seal on the Revolution at the Congress of Vienna, some of them at least creating a Holy Alliance to smother any revolutionary sparks that might ignite a renewed conflagration.[3]

Others have seen more traditional factors of great power rivalry at work, with the French revolutionaries and Napoleon inheriting the goals of the French monarchy, and France's opponents, and sometime allies, continuing their respective traditions. From this perspective the wars amounted not to the violent imposition of the Revolution but its betrayal and both sides were ultimately corrupted by their attempt to deal with the other. As Albert Sorel put it: 'In order to deal with the French Revolution, old Europe abdicated its principle: in order to deal with the old Europe the French Revolution falsified its own'.[4] More nuanced accounts have tried to integrate both sets of factors, adding the influence of mutual misperception and miscalculation.[5]

Revolutionary ideology and counter-ideologies of the most diverse kind as well as considerations of power, national or dynastic honour, and misperception and miscalculation continued to feed the wars after 1792. However one judges the precise combination of such factors, which varied throughout the wars and regions, it is clear that reconciling Revolutionary France or the Empire with some stable European order was difficult, and ultimately proved impossible. This outcome was itself the product of a combination of factors. The revolutionaries proclaimed as a matter of principle that treaties concluded without the consent of peoples had no validity. Philippe-Antoine Merlin de Douai put it succinctly: 'It is not the treaties of princes that regulate the rights of nations.'[6] In a Europe overwhelmingly characterised by monarchical government, that amounted to the denunciation of the entire system of international law as understood by the governments of the day. It has been argued that there was in reality no meaningful system of European law in the eighteenth century or that such law as existed entailed no constraint on the predatory ambitions of eighteenth-century international politics.[7] Ironically such interpretations were heralded by the revolutionaries themselves. Drawing on established indignation at the perceived hypocrisy of statesmen who preached international morality but were driven by the lust for conquest, Garran de Coulon proclaimed that in times of war all the ties of humanity dissolved, leaving only the reciprocity of reprisals as the law of nations.[8] Other revolutionaries drew a different contrast, pitting the Republic as the guardian of the true law of nations, which was not to be confused with the treaty law of Europe, against the hypocrisy and perfidy embodied in Austrian practice.[9] Despite the radically different principles espoused by the French revolutionaries, the outcome was the same: assertion of the profound difference between the values recognised by or embodied in the Republic and existing values.

This was not the only factor that called into question the legitimacy of established governments and opened the way to the emergence of military occupation as a recurrent feature of the turbulence that would last for over two decades. Other factors were equally important. The Republic embarked upon war without any clear strategic goals.[10] The only goal it might be said to have had was that of saving the Republic from the conspiracy it believed it faced. Thus began the pursuit of the elusive concept of security. The difficulty lay in determining where that lay, whether at the Rhine and France's other supposedly natural frontiers, a notion that had indeed become commonplace by the end of 1792, or beyond those frontiers in the shape of buffer states of indeterminate extent.[11] As the impecunious Republic turned, as it soon did, to the notion that 'war must feed war' another force for instability was added.[12] The Republic could be safeguarded only by its armies but its armies could live, in some cases literally live, only by drawing on the resources of foreign territory. The generals who led them often had their own ambitions, seeing foreign territory as potential fiefdoms over which they would exercise personal rule. General Dumouriez's ambitions in Belgium, General Hoche's in the Rhineland, and General Bonaparte's in Italy, illustrate this combination of political ambition and military strategy on all three major fronts in the early years of the wars.[13] Uncertainty about the eventual status of these territories and the extent of France's territorial ambitions would create the conditions in which military force and authority constituted *de facto* government.

Napoleon Bonaparte went on to attempt to establish new political structures across much of Europe, but at each step he embarked on new ventures in which military occupation resurfaced with varying degrees of clarity. To his military successes under the Directory which governed France from 1795 to 1799 he added the title of First Consul after the coup of 18 Brumaire (9–10 November 1799), then Emperor in May 1804 and King of Italy the following year. It would be in the name of 'His Majesty the Emperor and King' that Napoleon's generals would take possession of conquered territory, though what this seizure of possession would mean for the future of those lands was uncertain.[14] The empire over which he presided was strictly speaking pre-1789 France plus the territories formally annexed to it, though by the final years of the Empire this was very extensive. The governments of the Revolutionary Republic had begun the pattern of annexation with the papal enclaves of Avignon and the Comtat Venaissin (1791), Savoy (1792), Nice (1793), Belgium (1795) and Geneva (1798). After the 18 Brumaire the left bank of the Rhine, whose fate had already been determined, was formally incorporated. From 1805 Genoa and other minor Italian territories were added, including Rome (1810). The wave of annexations of Italian territories had only just ended when a northern expansion incorporated Holland, the Hanseatic ports and Oldenburg. A southern expansion into

Spain, namely Catalonia, was underway when Napoleon embarked upon his invasion of Russia in 1812. In addition to these formally annexed areas Napoleon's relatives ruled the Duchy of Berg and Kingdom of Westphalia in the north of Germany, the Kingdom of Naples and Spain. Holland had also been ruled by a Bonaparte as the Kingdom of Holland before its annexation. In varying degrees these territories were subject to processes of *'raillement'* and *'amalgame'*, signifying ever greater levels of integration.[15] Exactly what was understood by these terms is not entirely clear. It is clear that Napoleon himself recommended the principle of amalgamation and saw it as replicating the fusion of the nation within France on a larger scale.[16] To that extent, Napoleon's successes culminated in conquest on a scale that Louis XIV could never have realistically aspired to.

This complex edifice, however, was marked by the instability and provisionality that were to become the marks of military occupation. Even within the territories ruled by members of his family the impermanence was evident in the transfer of his brother Joseph from Naples to Spain in 1808 and his replacement by Napoleon's general and brother in law, Joachim Murat, who had been Duke of Berg. Berg, in turn, was ruled after Murat's departure by an Imperial Commissioner, Count Beugnot, nominally on behalf of Napoleon's nephew. Beugnot would later recall that 'I was in Germany what the proconsuls were in Rome'.[17] A later historian would observe in respect of the structures imposed by Napoleon in Italy that they never 'lost this aspect of impermanence, of improvisation'.[18] That was more than a retrospective gloss. The language of provisionality was the language of Napoleon and his sympathisers. It can be found from the beginning of the period of Napoleon's rule to the dying years of the Empire. Not long after he had seized power he wrote to Talleyrand, in September 1801, stating that it was not his intention to give a 'definitive organization' to the Cisalpine Republic until the conclusion of peace.[19] What had seemed stable and definitive, a kingdom no less, could turn out to have been merely provisional. Thus, in 1810, he gave instructions that the Dutch should be informed of his 'solicitude' and his desire to 'put an end to the provisional governments . . . which have tormented this part of the Empire'.[20] Equally striking is the justification offered by a Spanish official in French service for a delay in the implementation of the Napoleonic Code, namely that they should wait for the final victory of French arms.[21]

Therein lay the problem. It was not at all clear what final victory would mean for Napoleon and his empire any more than it was clear what would satisfy the Revolution's search for security. At least, in Napoleon's case it was not clear what it would mean short of the subjugation of every competing power in Europe. It is worth emphasising that this was not because the other powers had been consistently intent on destroying his empire any more than the opponents of the Revolutionary Republic had been consistently intent on strangling it at birth. The French émigrés in the German principalities had found that the monarchs to whom they appealed were willing enough to make gestures but would ignore them or even consent to their dispersal if that seemed expedient.[22] Even Britain, which only once, and then briefly, made peace with France, had an equivocal attitude to the Revolutionary government in France, leaving Edmund Burke railing against those who would make peace with regicides.[23] Peace was made, first by Prussia in the Treaty of Basel in 1795 and subsequently by every significant power in Europe, all of which save Britain became Napoleon's allies at one point or another. None of them could find a stable mode of coexistence with Napoleon's Empire.[24] That was clear in the final coalition which brought about his fall and which had been so difficult to construct because two of the parties to the coalition, Prussia and Austria, knew that the price of failure of this final gamble could well be their own destruction. Metternich put it well: 'All the calculation of Austria and other poor intermediaries must be directed at how not to be *wiped out*.'[25]

The road to the war in which Metternich gambled Austria's existence had begun at a militarily indecisive battle at Valmy on 20 September 1792 that served, however, to block a Prussian advance on Paris and was elevated by the French into a symbol of the resolve of the French nation.[26] The French could now go on the offensive which would bring them the first significant challenge of deciding how to deal with foreign territory. To the south-west a largely unopposed French army moved into Savoy and Nice in the immediate aftermath of Valmy. In the Rhineland General Custine pushed forward, on 21 October seizing Mainz, from which the French would not be dislodged until the following July. Following a decisive victory over Austrian forces at Jemappes on 6 November by General Dumouriez, French forces quickly occupied most of Belgium.[27] The following year demonstrated the fragility of the French hold on territory to the west and north. The military victories of France, abetted by revolutionary rhetoric, had, moreover, promoted the emergence of a wider anti-French coalition including the Netherlands and Britain, on whom the French declared war on 1 February 1793 in a catalogue of grievances against the supposed malevolence of Britain towards the Republic, and Spain.[28]

The year 1793 started well for the French as they pushed into the Netherlands but the tide turned with the defeat of Dumouriez's army at Neerwinden on 18 March. Following this disaster the French were driven from Belgium and the Netherlands and suffered reversals in the Rhine. The Holy Roman Empire resolved on war with France on 22 March, citing the need to combat revolutionary ideology as well as French invasion of territories of the Empire.[29] Toulon surrendered to a British fleet on 29 August, presenting the British with their own problems about how to treat occupied territory. Even the Spanish enjoyed success, occupying French territory. Paris was faced with counter-revolutionary insurgency within France itself. To add to French woes, Dumouriez, fearing that defeat would be followed by accusations of treason, having failed to rally his army behind a march on Paris to restore the authority of the French king, defected to the Allies. All of these twists and turns of war, as well as the threat to the Revolution from within, would shape the attitude of the various parties to the territory they seized, as they would shape the attitude of the inhabitants of such territory as they contemplated the possible return of former rulers or of the occupant. The prospect of the return of the occupant was made clear in the chilling warning of the representative of the National Convention with the French forces in Mainz, Antoine-Christophe Merlin de Thionville, as he responded to hostility to the departing French: 'it is not the last time that you will see me here'.[30] These sudden changes in control over significant tracts of territory heightened the sense of uncertainty and the provisionality of such control as the contending parties were able to exert.

Although the French would not return to Mainz until much later, 1794 ended well for them. Following victory at Fleurus on 26 June 1794 they reasserted their grip on Belgium. After some hesitation, linked to the uncertainty following the overthrow of Robespierre, the French resolved on another attempt to invade Holland, this time successfully.[31] Utrecht surrendered on 16 January and three days later the first French troops entered Amsterdam where the Provisional Representatives of the People of Amsterdam waited to greet them.[32] This extension of French control brought new problems. Most of the territory lay unequivocally beyond France's natural frontiers and the Dutch Patriots had more authority in their own country than the beleaguered republicans of the Rhineland. Yet, whereas the Patriots saw the French as liberators, Lazare Nicolaus Marguerite Carnot of the Committee of Public Safety saw the Dutchmen as 'so-called patriots, interested only in the expulsion of their personal enemies so that they could replace them in their turn'.[33] Conquest and annexation were not options but the viability of an independent Dutch state was far from clear.

The rapid French advance into the Netherlands had been helped by the increasing lack of coordination and resolution amongst its enemies. The same feebleness of opposition facilitated their reassertion in the Rhineland. By the end of 1794 the left bank of the Rhine was in French hands. That too presented a problem. The People's Representatives with the Army of the Moselle reported the desire of the soldiers to proclaim the Rhine as the frontier of France but Paris was so hesitant about that option that it even omitted that part of their report from the published version.[34] Wider diplomatic considerations were also at work here. They were also reflected in the Treaty of Basel with Prussia of 4 April 1795, the first significant crack in the anti-French coalition. The Treaty of Basel brought peace with Prussia and provided for, but did not formally agree, French acquisition of Prussian territory on the left bank, and explicitly referred to 'occupation' as the interim arrangement.[35]

The next wave of French military victories brought no resolution of the fate of the left bank of the Rhine, though the French National Convention had resolved upon the annexation of Belgium on 1 October 1795.[36] That French victories did not ensure annexation of the Rhineland was due primarily to the architect of those victories, Napoleon Bonaparte. Bonaparte swept through northern Italy in 1796, crushing the feeble resistance of Piedmont and driving the Austrians out of Italy. Turning south he imposed an armistice on the Pope on 23 June 1796. The following year he imposed the Treaty of Tolentino on the Pope and then moved north into Carinthia and Styria. The Austrians responded with alacrity to a proposed armistice. The negotiation of the outcome, the Preliminary Treaty of Leoben of 18 April 1797, was, on the French side, the work of Bonaparte. Here Bonaparte's agenda was different from that of the Directory in Paris. The Directory's policy was to exchange the gains in Italy for Austrian recognition of French possession of the left bank of the Rhine. Bonaparte's policy was to secure the gains in Italy. It was the latter that prevailed. The fate of the left bank of the Rhine remained unsettled, though Austria recognised French annexation of Belgium.[37] In the end only one of the directors, Reubell, voted against accepting the treaty, though another, La Revelière, protested vigorously against the proposed partition of Venice.[38] While the treaty perpetuated the uncertainty in the Rhineland, another kind of uncertainty was created as Bonaparte began reorganising northern Italy. Even before Leoben he had supported the spontaneous formation of a Cispadane Republic in 1796, though he was dissatisfied with the elections they held the following April. The republic, he told the Directory, would need a 'provisional government' for three or four years in order to diminish 'the influence of the priests'.[39] After Leoben he created a Ligurian Republic out of the former Republic of Genoa on 6 June 1797 and a Cisalpine Republic on 29 June 1797 centred on Milan, to which the Cispadane Republic was added.[40] All of these were notionally 'sister republics' following the example of the Republic of the United Provinces created in 1795 in the Netherlands.[41]

Leoben clearly entailed no end to the instability for Venice, upon which France declared war on 9 April 1797, inaugurating a period of French transformation of those parts of Venetian territory assigned to France and French occupation of the remainder until the Austrians installed themselves in the following January in accordance with the terms of the Peace of Campo Formio of October 1797.[42] Before the end of the year, with the murder of a French general accompanying the French ambassador in Rome, another pretext for war appeared. By February the papal government had been suppressed by a small French army that had occupied the city without resistance and another republic was created. Citing French treatment of the Pope, the King of Naples unwisely moved against the French, briefly dislodging them from Rome only to see his army defeated and Naples occupied by General Championnet, who created the short-lived Parthenopian Republic at the beginning of 1799. For Italy the French intervention had signified only the 'indefinite existence of provisionality'.[43] For Switzerland, where the French took advantage of internal conflict, it also entailed territorial losses to the Cisalpine Republic in 1797 and the loss of Geneva, which was annexed by France in 1798. In the now familiar pattern a sister republic, the Helvetic Republic, was established in the same year.[44]

The fragility of the structures created by Bonaparte and other French generals in Switzerland and Italy was promptly demonstrated by their collapse in the War of the Second Coalition as Allied armies swept into Italy. Bonaparte himself returned from the ill-fated expedition to Egypt he had embarked upon in 1798 and seized power in Paris in the coup of 18th Brumaire 1799, and in the following year inflicted a defeat on the Austrians at Marengo on 14 June 1800 which arguably consolidated his power in a way that the 18th Brumaire had not.[45] A truce was followed by another crushing French victory, under General Moreau at Hohenlinden in December, and Austria accepted French terms for peace in the Treaty of Lunéville in 1801. Austria now recognised French annexation of the left bank of the Rhine and the sister republics. Peace with Britain followed at Amiens in the following year. Bonaparte had consolidated French gains and his own power and arguably brought about a settlement with which both the major powers and many minor ones on the continent could live, and some were even eager to live.[46]

Bonaparte could not. The resumption of war with Britain brought an added motive for occupation: the occupation of Hanover and its Hanseatic dependencies sought to close the Elbe to British trade while the occupation of Italian ports served the same function in the south.[47] At this point Bonaparte embarked upon a veritable 'rage of organisation'.[48] This would contribute to and be reinforced by the War of the Third Coalition. On 26 May 1805 he transformed the Republic of Italy he had established in 1802 into a kingdom, crowning himself in Milan. The following month he annexed the Ligurian Republic to France. Both events antagonised Austria and Russia.[49] In the ensuing war Austria suffered heavy defeat at Ulm in October and a combined Austrian and Russian force was crushed at Austerlitz in December. With Vienna under French occupation Austria signed the humiliating Treaty of Pressburg. Prussia had remained aloof and was being encouraged by the prospect of the acquisition of Hanover, which Prussian forces had occupied as the French withdrew in 1805. Prussia, however, was not consulted in the formation of the Confederation of the Rhine in July 1806 and finally stung by news that Bonaparte had offered to return Hanover to Britain in abortive peace negotiations. In the war that followed Prussian armies were destroyed at Jena and Auerstadt in October and Berlin was occupied by French troops. French occupation returned to both Hanover and the Hanseatic ports. It was from Berlin that Napoleon issued the decree of 21 November 1806 reinforcing the attempt to exclude British trade from the continent and reinforcing that motive for occupation. Territory seized from Prussia helped to form the new duchies of Berg and Warsaw and the Kingdom of Westphalia, while French occupation of the Kingdom of Naples led to the imposition of Napoleon's bother Joseph as King of Naples.

In part in pursuit of his economic conflict with Britain, Bonaparte occupied Portugal in 1807, albeit briefly, in alliance with Spain, only to convert the alliance into an occupation during which he forced the claimants to the Spanish throne to abdicate, transferring Joseph to Madrid as the new king in 1808. From then until Wellington crossed the Pyrenees in 1814 war and occupation were constant features in the Iberian Peninsula. Indeed while the Duchy of Berg and Kingdom of Westphalia acquired sufficient stability and recognition for the rule of Napoleon's relatives to be considered as at least legitimate interim rulers, the instability of Spain and, to a lesser extent and for different reasons, Naples, readily invites the suggestion that military occupation is a better characterisation of their condition.[50] At the time the fate of Spain encouraged Austria to embark upon its gamble to take on Napoleon alone, leading to Austrian defeat at Wagram in July 1809 and the Peace of Schönbrunn, which included territorial losses in the south-east that helped form the Illyrian provinces.

At the height of French power Napoleon had still failed to build a stable system. Military occupation remained a feature. Further annexations in 1810 and the contemplated annexation of Catalonia in 1812 failed to eliminate it as Napoleon departed for his ill-fated invasion of Russia and the subsequent formation of the final coalition which would lead to his defeat. In 1814 it was the turn of the Allied victors to face the problem of military occupation, most notably in Germany, in a political landscape that had been turned upside down by Napoleon, and then in France itself. Competition between the Allies themselves, acceptance that France not only had to continue to exist but had to remain a significant European power meant that annexation offered a limited solution to the problem of how to treat these lands. Pending the determination of their fate the only solution was military occupation. Napoleon's failed bid to return to power reinforced a resort to military occupation. Indeed military occupation would form part of the provisions of the second Treaty of Paris, of 1815, which marked the final end of the Napoleonic enterprise.

Although of no comparable military or political significance, one of the consequences of the economic struggle between the British and Napoleon was the Anglo-American War of 1812, which was finally brought to an end by the Treaty of Ghent, signed at the end of 1814. The occupations it entailed, to the extent that they were understood as occupations, were brief and geographically limited. It had none of the ideological overtones or institutional innovations that complicated the European stage. Yet here too there were signs of the problems and solution that would slowly crystallise into the concept of military occupation.

In Europe it was the sheer pace and scale of events, the sweep of Revolutionary and especially Napoleonic armies, the sequence of armistices, peace treaties, conventions and then renewed war, and the persistent provisionality of the political structures left in their wake, that provided the context in which military occupation as a distinct phenomenon began to crystallise. The French Revolution and Napoleon had put an end to the old order in Europe and as a by-product of the march of their armies created a transient political and military arrangement, military occupation, that was beginning to acquire its own language, but slowly and inconsistently.

Revolutionary Doctrine: Between Liberation and Conquest

The French revolutionaries were not concerned at the outset with the language of military occupation. It was the language of conquest and liberty that first attracted, and continued to dominate, their attention. Even here their interest was engaged by specific concerns and contexts. It was the potential embroilment of France in a dispute between Spain and Britain on the other side of the Atlantic that induced the National Assembly to begin to formulate a policy relating to war and conquest.[51] The Assembly promptly discerned the wider constitutional issue at stake, that is, the relative powers of the king and his ministers and the legislative power.[52] In a protracted debate lasting several days there were repeated assertions of French respect for the rights and liberty of other nations and the associated disavowal of conquest, some even seeing this as the key to the entire debate.[53] Yet it is the constitutional question that still shone through the final version of the disavowal of conquest in article 4 of the declaration of 22 May 1790. According to this article ministers or other agents of the executive would be held guilty of a crime against the nation if they undertook a war of aggression and for this purpose the Assembly declared that the 'French nation renounces undertaking any war with a view to making conquests and that it will never use its forces against the liberty of any people'.[54] The same language appeared in the constitution of 1791.[55] No sooner had the constitution come into effect than the Assembly voted for the reunion of Avignon and the Comtat Venaissin, a step which it had been debating, and postponing ever since the insurgents in the papal enclaves had requested reunion over a year earlier.[56]

The prime argument in favour of this step, which circumvented the charge that France was engaged in conquest, was that it was a response to the freely expressed wish of the inhabitants. Underlying this doctrine, however, was a more far reaching claim that was expressed in November 1790 by Jérôme Pétion de Villeneuve:

> There is no true political union, a union engaging all the members of society, unless its conditions have been regulated by the individuals who compose it. An engagement without will is null; this truth is safe from all attack and the United States have rendered it solemn homage during the formation of their government. There is no point at which France has had a genuine political federation. Each of the provinces which compose this beautiful empire was a separate state which had its particular statutes, its privileges . . . One could perhaps say that the provinces of an empire, whatever title might be attached to it, find themselves bound together by a tacit consent . . . It is not necessary to allow oneself to be misled here by this appearance of consent; it is nothing other than the submission of weakness to the empire of force. As long as the parts of an empire do not bind themselves, do not incorporate themselves by a free vote, there is no association, there is no alliance; force alone establishes the relationship: but force violates the law instead of consecrating it.[57]

By this logic there was only one true political union in Europe: France, once it had given itself a constitution. The rest of Europe was composed only of mere agglomerations of men held together by the iron bands of tyranny. As yet, however, the French had not drawn the full consequences from Pétion's claims for the uniqueness of their country.

As French armies entered foreign territory in the wake of the Battle of Valmy the pressure to clarify the implications of the declarations of principle mounted. From Savoy, General Montesquiou wrote in September 1792 asking for guidance on how he should respond to what appeared to be sentiments 'disposed to a revolution resembling ours' and to whether to favour the idea that Savoy should become a

French department or 'a republic under its protection', and whether to replace the existing authorities or nominate a governor general.[58] The debate in the National Convention witnessed the reassertion of the renunciation of conquest but division on whether this entailed allowing the Savoyards to give themselves whatever constitution they deemed fit or whether, as Danton preferred, the French should instruct the Savoyards not to give themselves any more kings.[59] Amidst the debate on principles one contributor tried, unsuccessfully, to insist that they were confronted with two distinct issues: 'the general principle and the request that Montesquiou has put to you to give him a plan of conduct for the particular circumstances in which he finds himself'.[60] The outcome was that the Convention had to return to the matter the following month when it also condemned General Anselm for taking possession of Nice in the name of the French nation, a practice rejected as more appropriate to conquerors in the service of kings, and legislating for the territory.[61] Only in the following month did the Convention move towards reunion, though still showing great concern to distinguish this from the hated conquest and on taking precautions to assure itself that this was indeed the freely expressed wish of the inhabitants of Nice and not merely the views of a minority.[62]

The desire to unite the renunciation of conquest with the promotion of liberty became stronger in two decrees that followed these debates. By the first decree, of 19 November 1792, responding this time to pleas for guidance from General Custine in Mainz, the Convention declared

> in the name of the French nation, that it will grant fraternity and aid to all peoples who wish to recover their liberty; and it charges the executive power with giving the generals the orders necessary for bringing aid to such peoples and for defending citizens who have been, or who might be, harassed for the cause of liberty.[63]

Cursory and vague though this was, there was no sign of the earlier reluctance to intervene or to accept whatever constitution the liberated might deem fit for their particular circumstances.[64] The second decree, of 15 December 1792, sought to provide greater guidance and to respond to the problem which had emerged in Belgium, that is, of a people who seemed to lack the strength to liberate themselves. Pierre-Joseph Cambon, who proposed the decree, made clear that in such cases 'it is necessary that its liberator take its place and act in its interest, momentarily exercising the revolutionary power'.[65] Consistent with this the decree provided that 'In the territories which are or may be occupied by the armies of the Republic, the generals shall proclaim immediately, in the name of the French nation, the sovereignty of the people'.[66] Unlike the decree of 19 November, this time the implications were spelled out. Taxes and feudal rights were to be suppressed. The people was to be convoked 'in primary or communal assemblies, in order to create a provisional administration and justice', with all officials of the former government being excluded from such assemblies and ineligible for office in the administration.[67] French generals would exercise authority over public assets and resources. The French Executive Council was to despatch national commissioners to such territories. The decree also provided that France would be reimbursed for the expenses incurred in the 'common defence' and where the 'common interest requires the troops of the Republic to remain upon foreign territory' measures would be agreed for their maintenance.[68] The language was that of liberation, though the tension between the proclamation of the sovereignty of the people and the French assumption of the 'revolutionary power', that is sovereignty, did not go unnoticed.[69]

Just as it had been the implications of the presence of French armies on foreign territory that induced the Convention to clarify, and radicalise, its position so too French reverses brought about a significant change in tone. As early as April 1793, Danton, who had wished to deny the liberated the right to choose monarchical government, now lamented that the Convention had passed a decree, 'in a moment of enthusiasm', committing it to give protection to all peoples wishing to liberate themselves from tyrants.[70] The Convention then decreed that it would not 'intervene in any manner in the government of other powers but would not tolerate any inference by them in France's internal affairs.[71] This defensive tone, indicative of the threat the Convention faced from its enemies, was also evident in the constitution of 1793. It reiterated the prohibition on intervention and added that the French people 'do not make peace with an enemy who is occupying their territory'.[72] It was consistent with the perception of the threat that the Convention decreed a new law of 30 April 1793 on the Representatives on Mission, giving them a wide-ranging remit of surveillance over French armies and civil agents, including the right to dismiss both civil and military officials, and, more generally, 'unlimited powers in order to exercise the functions delegated to them'.⁷³ As the instructions of the Committee of Public Safety that followed shortly after make clear, the loyalty and commitment of French generals was a prime concern.⁷⁴

This, however, was only one direction which the reaction against the decree of 15 December 1792 took. More significant for future conduct was a decree of 15 September 1793. According to this French generals would 'henceforth renounce all philanthropic ideas' and 'conduct themselves towards the enemies of France in the same manner as the powers of the coalition conduct themselves'. This meant that they would, 'in respect of countries and individuals subjugated by their arms, exercise the ordinary rights of war'.⁷⁵ Two days later the Committee of Public Safety specified that those rights included seizing hostages, levying contributions, living off the land and transporting foodstuff, forage, animals and much else behind the French lines.⁷⁶ This meant reverting to the doctrine of conquest of the *ancien régime*, not in the sense of asserting an immediate displacement of sovereignty, but in the sense of a right of seizure of persons and moveable goods.

Just as the proclamation of liberation had not initially clarified exactly how French generals would behave towards occupied populations, so too the doctrine of conquest, although more specific from the outset, did not fully clarify how French generals would behave in pursuit of the policy of conquest. Again clarification slowly emerged in the light of experience and the need to impose some regularity on the behaviour of different armies and the host of civil agents accompanying them. Thus, on the 18 July 1794, the Committee of Public Safety issued new instructions to the Representatives of the People attached to the armies. The Representatives of the People, or in their absence the generals, were to assemble the magistrates 'in all places occupied by the armies of the Republic' and to demand a list of all civil and military officials. Military officials were to be dismissed but the Representatives were to declare that

> civil functionaries are provisionally maintained in their employment under the protection of the Republic in order to fulfil the functions which will be delegated to them; but that they [the Representatives] will dismiss and replace those they judge not to merit confidence and those who manifest sentiments opposed to the interests of the Republic.⁷⁷

Fuller clarification came at the initiative of some of those Representatives of the People, namely those attached to the armies of the North and the Sambre and Meuse. Their express purpose was to combine in a single decree all the existing provisions relating to 'the police, general administration and order which should be observed in Belgium and other countries conquered by the armies of the Republic'.[78] The result was a set of instructions of 14 August 1794, running to 34 articles marked by a desire to impose some order on French occupation policy and practice. Those, for example, who sought to levy contributions or make requisitions without due authorisation were to be punished by death.[79] The instructions repeated the provisions for the continued employment of civil functionaries made by the Committee of Public Safety. It stated, moreover, that 'The laws and particular customs of the conquered country are provisionally maintained', specifying that this included regulations affecting policing matters, regulations relating to forests and markets and taxation, unless specification derogation was made by the Representatives of the People.[80]

Revolutionary doctrine had begun with the renunciation of conquest but was from the outset based on a doctrine of legitimate power, of true political union, that effectively denied the legitimacy of all states not founded upon the kind of compact the revolutionaries believed had constituted their own nation. That this opened the road to conquest was more or less concealed by the language of reunion supposedly supported by the wish of those who were to united with the Republic. The tension, however, between the renunciation of conquest and French assumption of the 'revolutionary power' in occupied territory was evident even at the time. More importantly, the pressures of war and the reality of occupation promoted the reassertion of the language of conquest and then of instructions that did not automatically assume liberation or annexation, but rather the provisional employment of existing officials and the continuing validity of existing laws and customs. Although still formulated in terms of rights of conquest, an understanding of military occupation was beginning to emerge. There would, however, be no simple, linear development towards a distinct concept of military occupation. The tensions and ambiguities that emerged in the early years of the Republic would continue to mark the efforts of the French revolutionaries and their Napoleonic successors, especially as general principles, and general instructions, clashed and intertwined with the reality of military occupation.

Military Occupations by the Armies of the Republic

The first test of French Revolutionary principles and organisation came with the short-lived occupations of Mainz and surrounding territory which lasted from October 1792 to the surrender of the French garrison in Mainz on 23 July 1793 and in Belgium between the victory at Jemappes on 6 November 1792 and defeat at Neerwinden on 18 March 1793. In both cases the commanding generals, Custine in Mainz and Dumouriez in Belgium, clearly grasped that the reaction they would meet from populations would depend in large part upon the conduct and discipline of their soldiers. Custine, for example, reacted to initial outbreaks of plundering by his soldiers by having three soldiers arrested as ringleaders and summarily condemned and shot.[81] In Belgium, Dumouriez sought to avoid the worst of requisitioning, paying for what his troops needed wherever possible. This was not merely a pragmatic matter but was consistent with their understanding of themselves as liberators and of the superiority of the virtuous soldiers of the Revolution compared with the predatory soldiery of the *ancien régime*. In Mainz, the impact of this initially seemed equivocal. The German Jacobin Georg Forster recorded that the inhabitants received the French invaders 'in a kind of gloomy silence, without any vigorous signs of opposition, but without any applause and without any rejoicing'.[82] In fact this augured well for the French, who stood to benefit from the simple contrast between their discipline and the depredations which inhabitants of occupied towns customarily expected. What mattered here was not only the instructions of commanding generals but the behaviour of subordinate officers and even ordinary soldiers. Concrete demonstrations of the revolutionary doctrine of equality could impress people from lower social orders for whom revolutionary rhetoric had little if any meaning.[83] In Belgium the French benefited from the pre-existing conflict between the majority of the population and their Austrian rulers. In Mons, Dumouriez's soldiers were greeted with cries of 'Long live the saviours of the Belgians'.[84] The French claim to be liberators could appear to be welcome, at least insofar as this meant liberation from the Austrians. The French, of course, thought that liberation meant much more than that. In a related miscalculation the French took the relative friendliness and cooperation of the inhabitants of Mainz that emerged after the initial hesitations as evidence of revolutionary inclinations; a misperception that influenced the formation of liberation policy in Paris in November.[85] The scene was already set for disillusion on both sides.

In both cases, however, the proclamations issued by the commanding generals suggested a more tolerant approach to the future of the occupied territories than eventually emerged. In Mainz on 23 October, Custine went so far as to proclaim that although he came to offer the inhabitants liberty, a 'spontaneous wish will decide your fate' and they could choose slavery and the despot under which they preferred to live.[86] Custine repeated this offer two days later in a proclamation to the 'oppressed people of the German nation'.[87] In fact this broader proclamation, extending the promise of self-determination to all territories occupied by the French, already amounted to a commitment to support self-determination in disregard of the integrity of the German Empire within whose structures the German people lived.[88]

More significant, though, than the rhetorical flourish respecting a preference for slavery was Custine's promise to respect existing institutions until a free wish of the inhabitants decided to amend them.[89] In Belgium, Dumouriez also pronounced that he came bearing liberty but would not interfere in their choice of constitution.[90] He instructed his generals not to intervene in the administration nor in 'any political details', nor to influence the choice the Belgians made for the arrangements they deemed appropriate to maintain liberty.[91]

In reality neither general could honour these promises. In differing degrees their own convictions, the constraints emanating from Paris, either in the shape of proclamations of principle or civilian agents despatched to the occupied territory, and the dilemma faced by occupants in divided societies meant that they had to choose between different domestic factions. Indeed, even in calling for the national view of the Belgian people Dumouriez set himself on a collision course with those who defended the constitutions and rights of the distinct states that composed Belgium.[92] His claim to stand, so to speak, above the contesting parties was as fatally flawed as similar claims by later occupiers faced with divided societies, further dislocated by the impact of invasion and occupation.[93] In Mainz, Custine's assertion of neutrality was qualified not only by the rhetorical option of slavery that he offered the inhabitants but also by his avowed intent in the same proclamations to impose contributions only on those who had oppressed the people. More significant still was Custine's extension of French protection to the Jacobin club, the Society of the Friends of Freedom and Equality, in Mainz and his recruitment of revolutionary orators in Strasbourg 'to preach the French revolution'.[94] Similarly, in Belgium, immediately after Jemappes, Dumouriez welcomed the establishment of a radical club in Mons.[95] Where Dumouriez was not present other French generals, some notably more radical than Dumouriez, stood behind the clubs.[96]

Again, in both cases the French ran into significant barriers. In Belgium, in almost all cases where the election of provisional authorities was not strictly controlled it was the defenders of the traditional rights and liberties of the Belgians, enshrined in the medieval *Joyeuse Entrée*, who triumphed.[97] Alongside genuine commitment to these traditional rights lay an interesting consideration that appeared in some pamphlets. If the fortunes of war led to the return of the Austrians they would have the right to govern the country as they found it. If they found it without Belgium's traditional institutions, the inhabitants could not appeal to the rights and protections enshrined in those institutions.[98] The strident anticlericalism of many French generals, evident in General Verrière's boast of his pride in being an enemy of the 'despots of the cross and the mitre', could only provoke further opposition, strengthening in its turn the French tendency to blame all opposition on the machinations of 'priestly cabals'.[99] In Mainz, early indication of the barriers came in a carefully worded response from the guilds to Custine's proclamations. It expressed admiration for the French along with the regret that their temperament and condition made it impossible for the citizens of Mainz to imitate them. It conceded the need for constitutional reform but then minimised the actual reforms required and pleaded for time.[100] Here too conflict with a strong religious ethos, as well as different understandings of liberty and even of patriotism compounded mutual misunderstanding between the majority of the population on the one hand and the French occupants and their Jacobin sympathisers on the other.[101]

Resistance from the indigenous societies encouraged administrative reform and reliance upon the limited number who were committed to the goals of the revolution. It was this that led Custine to dissolve the existing administration and install a new body, the General Administration, in the middle of November 1792. This had the further advantage that, given its more extensive territorial remit compared with the old Mainz authorities, there was now a single administrative body for the occupied area.[102] Subordinate municipal authorities for the various towns within occupied territory followed. In general there was a clear attempt to reshape the administrative structure on the French model and to staff it with those seen as politically reliable. The shortage of such personnel meant, however, that members of the old administrative elite remained predominant in the lower echelons. The indigenous Jacobins now had administrative authority behind their programme as well as the propaganda of the Jacobin clubs.[103] Administrative reform in Belgium was more chaotic. The greater territorial extent, the diversity of indigenous opinion, the wilful behaviour of French generals, who often clashed with Dumouriez, and the impact of the revolutionary decree of 15 December 1792, all contributed to this outcome. Reaction to the decree in Belgium was hostile leading to protests that the French were acting as conquerors and were imposing change of such an extent that not even the Austrians had dared to impose.[104] French generals feared insurrection. Even the radical General Labourdonnaye, one of those who clashed with Dumouriez, counselled caution. Yet only Dumouriez protested vigorously against the decree. He even sought to avoid implication in its implementation by claiming that his soldiers lacked the requisite administrative and judicial skills to enforce it.[105] The result was administrative chaos and inconsistency. There was no uniformity in the administrative structure of the different provinces. Effective government was paralysed in any case by the suppression of existing taxes in accordance with the first article of the decree of 15 December.[106] Coordination among the various French agencies was almost nonexistent, leading to calls for the appointment of a plenipotentiary minister to supervise them, though the prospects of such a minister imposing his authority on the generals, the Representatives of the People and the national commissars were slim.[107]

Although the Representatives of the People and the national commissars, that is, the commissars of the French Executive Council, were intended to ensure the coordination and implementation of French policy, neither group had sufficient authority or coordination to impose order. The Representatives, despatched by the Convention, acted as 'ambulant dictators', while the national commissars, of whom there were only thirty for the whole of Belgium, had a broad remit covering security, registration of property placed under the protection of the Republic, the enforced circulation of the hated *assignats*, the Republic's paper currency, and requisitioning to supply the army.[108] In Mainz they worked well together and pushed General Custine into the background.[109] As Mainz was besieged in April 1793 they even played a prominent role in the war council established by the new commanding general, François d'Oyré. As Oyré recalled, their influence was enhanced by the fact that their powers had not been clearly delimited.[110] In Belgium, however, the generals continued to effectively conduct their individual occupation policies.

All of these actors, the generals, the Representatives of the People, the national commissars and the indigenous Jacobins, whether in the administration or purely the clubs, were resented and even hated not just because of their administrative reforms or their anticlerical views but above all because of requisitioning. The impact of this was clear to the French authorities. Commissar Simon reported from Mainz that the practice had 'turned the inhabitants of the countryside against the French Revolution'.[111] As discipline disintegrated, along with the shortage of food General Beurnonville lamented that the atrocities committed by his men made him shiver, threatened to have the first man he caught shot, but ended writing: 'Am I Cartouche or a general of the army?'[112] In Belgium inadequate provisioning of the army was well known. Dumouriez engaged in a vitriolic dispute with the minister of war, whom Dumouriez accused of being responsible for the disorganisation of his army. Some of those charged with provisioning the army were arrested. Broken promises and mutual recrimination became commonplace. What all agreed upon was that the condition of the army was indeed deplorable.[113] Decades later General von Moltke would claim that one of the greatest factors that had lessened the barbarity of war was 'vigilance of administration which provides for the subsistence of troops in the field'.[114] It was a vigilance that the armies of Revolutionary and Napoleonic France never attained with any consistency. Having conceived themselves as liberators, French generals and soldiers came to see themselves as conquerors even where they had no wish to act as such. It was inevitable that those who had supported the revolutionary programme, who were indeed genuinely committed to the abolition of privilege, the cause of liberty and enlightenment found themselves caught between the ill-provisioned armies and the populace they had to exploit. Georg Forster from Mainz was left asking: 'Are we only the officials and bailiffs of the army, executors of military orders dictated by necessity or whim? Are we only the blind instruments of an enemy power?'[115]

In both Belgium and Mainz in the last weeks of the occupation the French organised bodies that would proclaim the desire of the territories they claimed to represent to unite with the French Republic. In Mainz, the Rhenish-German National Convention opened on 17 March 1793. Georg Forster played a leading role in its decisions, including the resolution on 21 March requesting the incorporation of the Rhenish-German people into the French Republic. Although diverse arguments for reunion were rehearsed there was never any doubt about the outcome.[116] Forster was amongst the group that took this request to Paris. In Belgium the organisation of the call for reunion was more difficult. Meetings in the major towns had to be staggered, beginning with Mons on the 11 February 1793, in order to allow the French authorities time to arrange that the meetings could be harangued by French commissars and protected by French soldiers, who also ensured that only those disposed to vote for reunion were allowed to attend.

Military defeat promptly ensured that these requests were, as yet, meaningless. Especially in Mainz itself, French defeat had dire consequences for those who had supported the French. Although the French garrison marched out under terms of the capitulation of the city, it had failed to get agreement from the Prussian General Kalckreuth that Mainz's Jacobins could leave with it. It was not the Prussians, however, from whom the Jacobins had the most to fear. Their fellow citizens organised 'clubist hunts' to search them out. The savagery which then met them was bad enough for the Prussian commandant who took over from the French to issue, as one of his first decrees, a warning of severe punishment for those who resorted to ad hoc justice.[117] The fate of Mainz's Jacobins would weigh heavily in the minds of German revolutionaries when the French returned.

When the French swept into Belgium again following the Battle of Fleurus of June 1794, the Representatives with the armies of the North and the Sambre and Meuse asked for guidance on how to treat the country. Their request was probably motivated by the fall of Maximilien Robespierre and uncertainty about whether this would be followed by a change of policy in the Committee of Public Safety. On 3 August 1794 the Committee pointedly reaffirmed the commitment to a policy of conquest it had adopted after the reverses of the previous year: 'We have told you . . . to treat these countries as occupied territory, do not fraternise, do not municipalise, do not concern yourselves with reunion'.[118] They specified that this entailed complete disarmament of the inhabitants, prohibition of assemblies, seizing hostages, stripping Belgium of everything useful for French consumption and enforcing the circulation of the *assignats*. The only overt remnant of revolutionary principle was the injunction to 'bear down on the rich' but to respect the people, including its 'prejudices', by which they meant its religious prejudices. In reality Belgian elites proved adept at deflecting the burden of requisitions to their poorer fellow countrymen.[119] The Representatives had grasped that their new instructions entailed more coherent organisation than had been the practice in the initial French occupations of enemy territory. That awareness was evident in the general instructions of 14 August, intended for application in all occupied territory. It was reflective of the problems of coordination even between the Committee and the Representatives, that in the Committee's response approving the general instructions, the Committee expressed surprise that its own decrees relative to Belgium, which the Representatives had also requested, had not already been sent to them.[120] Awareness of the need for greater coordination was also evident in the Representatives' more specific plans for Belgium, where, as they noted, each province had its own distinctive administrative structure. Such diversity was incompatible with the need to centrally coordinate information about the available resources.[121] In order to rectify this they decreed, on 5 September, the creation of a Central Military Administration. A Committee of Surveillance in Brussels followed, with similar bodies in other major towns. Local administration was standardised throughout Belgium. Finally, in October, a General Administration was established in each province reporting to a Central Superior Administration in Brussels which was created in the following month.[122] Criminal tribunals were established, which were aided by the Committees of Surveillance, to try offences against the French army and the decrees of the Representatives.[123] Nothing, it seemed, would be allowed to stand in the way of this centralised machine. Even the radical popular societies would be swept aside if they disrupted the central purpose, as was that of Brussels on 13 September for indulging in 'incendiary declarations'.[124]

Yet despite the frenetic administrative activity the reality underlying these structures was chaotic. There was widespread pillaging by the army. Where they sought to pay in *assignats*, which exchanged on the free market at a fraction of their face value, Belgians often refused to accept the near worthless paper currency. This led to brawls, sometimes deadly, between soldiers and inhabitants.[125] Despite the large number of French troops in the country, amounting at one point to one for every ten Belgians, they could not protect areas especially in the north from organised brigandage.[126] Chronic shortage of personnel, given the scale of French ambition, meant that hordes of French agents were recruited to conduct the various forms of requisitioning with scant attention being paid to their competence or probity.[127] As early as 22 August one Representative reported that Belgian communes were often confronted with agents, or individuals calling themselves agents, demanding exactly the same goods, and that that the communes did not know whom to obey and supply.[128] Even at the heart of Brussels, chaos reigned. Another Representative deliberately deployed the word 'chaos' explaining that

> you will not find the word improper when you understand that there are ten volumes of decrees by the Representatives of the People, most of which are inconsistent with each other, independent of the ancient customs and usages that one has allowed to continue and certain laws of the Republic.[129]

It took, he added, considerable courage to undertake the task of administration 'amidst this organized anarchy'.

On the left bank of the Rhine the situation was complicated by the fact that two separate armies had occupied the region and the administrative structures, designed as they were to support the army, were not only coextensive with the areas held by the respective armies but also varied in structure.[130] In both cases, the army proved difficult to control. Coordination existed only at the highest level of the civilian and military structures. To the south, in the area between the Moselle and the Rhine, the Representatives issued a brief decree on 12 August 1794, emphasising the authority of the army but without imposing any new administrative structures.[131] Two days later a further decree specified that all war contributions and other assets seized by the Republic were to be delivered to the paymaster general of the army.[132] Over the next year little more was done to ensure effective administration in this zone. Even the French agents supposed to extract resources lacked any fixed residence and had no significant administrative apparatus. The indigenous administrative bodies that the decree of 12 August had instructed to remain in place operated only at the level of the communes.[133] A year later plans were being made for a more structured administration, though ones explicitly designed to avoid the 'multitude of administrations that had been adopted in Belgium'.[134] Those plans were effectively stifled as the Austrians pushed the French out of most of that part of the Rhineland.

In both Belgium and the Rhineland what mattered to most of the population was less the administrative structures to which they were subject and more the ruthless requisitioning. By the beginning of 1795 the Representatives in both areas were protesting that the current system could not continue. From Belgium they wrote in February that the country 'is exhausted, its inhabitants reduced to despair'.[135] They feared that in the event of a French military reverse they would be faced with a veritable 'Sicilian vespers'.[136] Another Representative responded to the imposition of another contribution in the area between the Meuse and the Rhine by writing that 'the country has been devastated by the calamities of war for three years ... What is left? Nothing, or as good as nothing'.[137] It was not just the sheer scale of contributions and requisitioning, it was the violent and often undisciplined manner in which they were imposed. Ironically, French revolutionary ideals contributed to this. Reacting against the severity and arbitrariness of systems of justice in the armies of the *ancien régime*, which they held to be incompatible with armies of citizens, they had introduced a system of military justice based on the principles of the Revolution. Custine's earlier resort to the practices of the *ancien régime*, despite its salutary effect, did not accord with the new spirit, and would indeed be one of the grounds on which he was condemned.[138] The outcome of the new spirit, as General Championnet complained, was that 'The soldier was judged by his comrades, who had an interest in betraying their conscience, because almost all of them had committed the offence they were asked to try or were ready to do so at the first opportunity'.[139] A policy of requisitioning, of treating enemy territory as conquered territory, based on the principle that war had to feed war, because the impecunious Republic could not feed it, combined with an inadequate and often corrupt supply system and an inadequate system of military justice.

In Belgium, the French, in February 1795, had sought to alleviate some of the more oppressive measures they had imposed, revoking the committees of surveillance, remitting fines imposed for non-payment of contribution, allowing payment of part of the contributions in *assignats* and releasing hostages seized to enforce payment of contributions. The following month they decided to introduce jury trails.[140] Jury trials signified a return to more normal forms of justice, though the picture of a period of bloody revolutionary justice painted by later Belgian historians was an exaggeration; only twenty-two death penalties had been imposed in the entire period by the revolutionary tribunals.[141] None of this brought about any fundamental improvement in Belgian views of the French. Belgian functionaries resigned from administrative posts in increasing numbers. By March the situation was so bad that the Representatives decreed that henceforth they would only accept resignations if they were accompanied by a medical certificate.[142] Despite, or rather precisely because of these sentiments, a mass meeting of delegates from Belgian towns, held in January 1795, had already called for reunion with France. The meeting had submitted a memorandum, headed '*remonstrances*', the term customarily used for the petitions of grievances addressed to their sovereigns.[143] The Representatives replied accusing the Belgian delegates of merely wanting to put an end to the regime of contributions, of having no sincere attachment to France, of having stood by or even betrayed the French when they were driven out of Belgium in 1793.[144] All that was true. Accepting the sovereignty of the conqueror, as the Belgians had in the *ancien régime*, was preferable to the regime of requisitioning and outright pillaging. Yet the Representatives themselves could see no viable alternative to annexation. In the French Convention which debated the issue at the end of September members were divided but finally voted for reunion.[145]

By the time the Convention decided the fate of Belgium two other decisions had been made that had considerable significance for the history of military occupation. One concerned the fate of the Dutch. The French had invaded the United Provinces in the autumn of 1794. As the momentum of the French advance gathered pace in January the Committee of Public Safety assured representatives of the Dutch Patriots on 10 January that as soon as revolution broke out and a provisional government had seized power, 'hostilities will cease and the Batavians, their persons and property will be treated not as enemies but as friends ... *in no case will the French Republic* interfere with the form of government which the Bataves wish to introduce in their own country'.[146] General Souham went further in accepting the surrender of Utrecht by the established authorities, the States of Utrecht, and giving them his assurance that existing political institutions would be respected.[147] By the time the French entered Amsterdam they were met by the Provisional Representatives of the People of Amsterdam. The old order was crumbling. Shortly before their own entry into Amsterdam the French Representatives with the Army of the North reported their first impressions, reserving final judgement, but expressing cautious optimism about the new authorities in Amsterdam.[148] They were much more decisive in matters of requisitioning. They asserted that arrangements would be made with the 'constituted authorities' and that thereby they would avoid 'that horde of agents and requisitioners whose presence, ignorance or impropriety has been so disastrous in the countries we have conquered'.[149] Their determination was evident in their assertion that Frenchmen and foreigners alike would be denied entry to the country unless they served in the army or had their passports approved by the Representatives themselves. In a fuller consideration of the options, on 17 February 1795, they listed the possibility of direct requisitioning by French agents only to conclude immediately that it did not 'merit any attention' because of the vices it had brought with it in Belgium and other conquered countries.[150]

Although they continued sometimes to use the language of conquest the Representatives expressed caution, as indeed did the Committee of Public Safety and General Pichegru. The Representatives warned against the exaggerated expectation in France about the wealth of the country, widely believed sufficient to support the 300,000 men of the French armies on the Rhine. In reality, Representative Ramel asserted, the 'public fortune is almost zero in the United Provinces'.[151] The true resources of the Provinces lay in the support which their citizens could give to the French. One could, of course, treat them as 'conquered territory' but the result would be the exhaustion of their resources in a month, after which famine would rage amongst the French army and Dutch citizens alike.[152] For its part the Committee of Public Safety repeatedly warned against allowing French troops to enter the larger towns, especially Amsterdam.[153] General Pichegru was even reluctant to disband the Dutch army because the French lacked the numbers to ensure security throughout the Provinces, and for fear that if he did disband it the large number of foreigners enlisted in the army would run riot through the countryside.[154] Not all Frenchmen, military or otherwise, were inclined to such moderation. At the beginning of February, General Sauviac expressed open contempt for the 'timid adventurers' he saw in the Dutch Patriots, asserting that they had done nothing to bring about their own liberation. There was no reason, he asserted, 'to treat it [Holland] differently from a conquered country'.[155] Even more striking was the reaction of the French Convention to news of the terms of the capitulation of the province of Zeeland. This was judged too conciliatory by many members of the Convention.[156] The Committee of Public Safety wrote anxiously to the Representatives explaining that the Convention had demanded a report on the affair, wanting to know whether 'the conquerors received law from the vanquished'; while the Committee feared that the tone of the debate would produce a dire impression amongst the Dutch.[157]

The moderation of the Committee was in fact relative. When the Dutch learned the proposed terms of the treaty, by which hostilities would formally cease and the new Dutch authorities would be formally recognised by the French Republic, they were shocked by the severity of the terms, which included territorial secessions, an indemnity and a loan.[158] From the French perspective they had little choice. Pichegru's army was on the verge of starvation. Conditions in the Rhineland were desperate. Salvation could only come from the resources of the Dutch. As the French negotiators increased the pressure in the final days before agreement was reached, Reubell and Sieyès, who had been despatched from Paris to join the French negotiating team, reported that one of the greatest outstanding difficulties was the question of military occupation by the French after the conclusion of peace.[159]

Article 1 of the Treaty of the Hague, signed on 16 May 1795, proclaimed French recognition of the Republic of the United Provinces 'as a free and independent power' whose liberty and independence was guaranteed by France.[160] The treaty did entail territorial losses by the Dutch and provision for a French garrison in the port of Flushing, which was to be treated as 'common to the two nations'.[161] Article 20 provided for the payment by the Dutch of an indemnity of 100 million florins. Vital though this was to the French war effort the prime purpose of the treaty was to ensure the loyalty of the new 'sister republic' to France. That was clear from article 17, according to which

> The French Republic will continue to militarily occupy, but by a number of troops to be determined and agreed between the two nations, the places and positions it will be useful to guard for the defence of the country, during the present war alone.[162]

The restriction of the occupation to the present war was, however, contradicted by article 3 of the Separate and Secret Articles of the treaty, which provided the continued presence of the French army after the present war.[163] The conditions and remit of this French presence were more closely specified in a Convention and set of Regulations, both signed on 27 July. Neither employed the term occupation but they did provide for the presence of an autonomous body of French troops, maintained at Dutch expense. According to the Convention the commanding French general would notify the Dutch of troop movements but article 2 stated that French troops would receive orders only from their French commander.[164] That autonomy was reflected in article 11 of the Regulations: 'All military delicts which are committed in the French army will be subject to the jurisdiction of a French tribunal, organised according to the laws of the Republic'.[165] The Convention also set out the remit of the French forces, consistent with the wider purpose of the treaty. According to article 7, 'French military personnel will not intervene in the discussion which may take place between the inhabitants of the country, as regards public affairs, save in the cases specified above'.[166] Those cases, set out in articles 5 and 6, were where the Dutch authorities requested assistance or where, by virtue of sedition or violence, the Dutch authorities were unable to convene or issue the necessary request, in which event the French could act independently in order to 'restore order and public tranquillity'.[167] No such constraints had appeared in the Treaty of Basel of 5 April 1795, though this too had explicitly referred to French occupation of foreign territory in article 5:

> The troops of the French Republic will continue to occupy the parts of the state of the King of Prussia, situated on the left bank of the Rhine. All definitive arrangements in respect of these provinces will be postponed until the general pacification between France and the German Empire.[168]

It was not war alone, but peace as well that induced the French to begin to clarify their understanding of the purpose, authority and remit of armies of occupation. The extent to which they would abide by the terms of those treaties, conventions and regulations varied. In relation to the Prussian provinces on the left bank of the Rhine they did adhere to their commitment not to annex them until a general peace was signed with the Empire. That would mean another six years of uncertainty for the inhabitants of those territories. For the Dutch, French recognition of a free and independent sister republic entailed another kind of uncertainty. What was clear was that peace and recognition had not meant the end of occupation but its indefinite prolongation. The promise not to intervene was not respected. The French were never convinced of the stability of the Dutch Republic and were involved in coups in 1798. The commitments respecting Flushing led to endless conflicts with the Dutch, who attempted to assert civil authority throughout the port, including the area occupied by the French, and denied that they had ever ceded sovereignty.[169]

When French armies under Napoleon invaded northern Italy the Directory was far from convinced that the creation of sister republics was desirable, both because of the intent to exchange gains in Italy for recognition of the French hold on Belgium and the Rhineland and because of doubts about the revolutionary potential of the Italians and increasing contempt for the radical Italian refugees.[170] Initially at least, Napoleon affected to leave the decision about the fate of Lombardy to the Directory.[171] In Milan, he satisfied himself with removing the highest authorities of the ousted Austrian rulers, and installing a three-man 'Military Agency' in their place. The rest of the existing administration was to be 'provisionally maintained' and effusive assurances were given of the supposed differences between victorious monarchist armies and those of a republic, along with promises of respect for property, persons and religion.[172] The reality was the imposition of contributions to feed the army and transfer funds to the regime in Paris. Privately, Napoleon boasted to the Directory of the sums that could be extracted from 'our prey' in Italy.[173] The mechanics of these exactions, however, left Bonaparte exasperated. The private contractor, the company Flachat, was, he wrote, 'a bunch of swindlers, devoid of real credit, devoid of money and devoid of morality'.[174] The combination of the policy of extracting as much as possible from occupied territory, aggravated by widespread corruption, contributed to a series of uprisings against the French which Napoleon and his generals suppressed with increasing brutality throughout 1796.

Nor was this the only obstacle to the management of occupied territory. The tensions between French civilian officials and the military, which had been there from the outset of the French occupations, became especially acute in Italy. Initially the civilian commissioner, Saliceti, had worked with the military to establish the Military Agency. His successor, Pinsot, however, sought to overturn Saliceti's organisation and clashed repeatedly with the military and the Italians appointed by them. This was not only a matter of disagreement about the appropriate administrative structures but also about taxation strategies and the ultimate fate of Lombardy.[175] In the end Pinsot lost the battle and was recalled. That was the prelude to dismantling the principle of direct civilian oversight of the military, which amounted to a break not only with the practices of the Revolution but also the practice of pre-Revolutionary France.[176] Although this did not mean the end to the deployment of civilians in other capacities, and although the principle of direct oversight would be reasserted in 1798, the measure did reflect the growing independence of the generals in matters of occupation policy.[177]

The autonomy of the generals was promptly demonstrated. Napoleon had been favourable to the aspirations of some Italians for the creation of a republic from the outset. Throughout 1796 and into 1797 that inclination became more pronounced. By December 1796 Bonaparte had moved to promise the Lombards a union, but without a revolution. It was to be a republic led by moderates.[178] The following May he established a committee of Italians to draft a constitution and at the end of June he issued a proclamation in which he claimed that the French Republic had succeeded to the rights of the former sovereign, Austria, 'by right of conquest', but that France was renouncing this right in favour of a 'free and independent' Cisalpine Republic within which the Cisalpine people would pass from a 'military regime' to 'a constitutional regime'.[179] In retrospect at least one member of the Directory, Jean-François Reubell, denounced Bonaparte's role in the creation the Cisalpine Republic: 'There never was a constitution accepted by the people in the Cisalpine. General Bonaparte, as a general, gave them a provisional government or constitution, as an experiment.'[180] Summarising Reubell's views, a modern historian has concluded that for Reubell the constitution of the Cisalpine Republic 'was only a military ordnance without popular legitimacy and that the provisional authorities could not be considered as a government representing the wishes of the sovereign'.[181] At the time the Directory accepted Bonaparte's *fait accompli* and also consented to the absorption of the stillborn Cispadane Republic into the Cisalpine Republic. The model of the sister republic also found favour in the case of Genoa, where the French were drawn into what amounted to a civil war. The outcome of French occupation was the imposition of a Ligurian Republic.

The same outcome seemed to be an option for the Venetian mainland territory despite the fact that Venice itself was neutral as French armies occupied Venetian territory in pursuit of the Austrians. Although French generals did not initially disarm Venetian garrisons they tolerated or actively aided declarations of independence by Venetian cities even before the declaration of war and occupation of the city of Venice. On the mainland French generals organised new administrations according to their inclinations, though all shared a dependence on French military authority. Even after moves were made to provide some wider administrative coordination stark military tutelage was unmistakeable.[182] Venice itself followed the familiar path towards the proclamation of a Republic. Concern in Paris about the increasing autonomy shown by Napoleon and his fellow generals only elicited the menacing response from Napoleon that he spoke 'in the name of 80,000 soldiers'.[183]

All of these republics also followed the Dutch model in signing treaties or conventions regulating the presence of French armies of occupation. It was in these agreements, as well as in a peace treaty with the King of Sardinia and an armistice and then a treaty with the Pope, that the French formally clarified their understanding of occupation, though this formal understanding sometimes indicated more restraint than the practice of French generals and agents actually exhibited. Indeed it is not without irony that the Convention with the Republic of Genoa of 9 October 1796 provided that French commanders would not interfere 'in any manner' in civil and political matters.[184] Within months French commanders intervened decisively in the creation of the Ligurian Republic. In June 1796 the armistice with the Pope provided that the Legations of Bologna and Ferrara were to 'remain in the possession' of France while the citadel of Ancona was to be 'placed in the hands of the French army', though the town of Ancona was 'remain under the civil government of the pope'.[185] By the treaty between France and the Republic of Venice of 16 May 1797 the latter requested 'a division of French troops in order to maintain order and the safety of persons and property and to assist the first steps of the government in all areas of its administration'.[186] By the treaty of alliance with the Cisalpine Republic of 21 February 1798 the French Republic recognised the 'free and independent' Cisalpine Republic which requested French forces 'sufficient to maintain its liberty, its independence and its public tranquillity'.[187] The sister republics were in fact dependent upon continued French occupation for their very existence. They were all consequently subject to continuing French interference and to the consequences of disagreements between Paris and the French authorities in the republics, which in turn were often divided. In the Cisalpine Republic, for example, refusal by the legislature to ratify the 1798 treaty led to the French Directory's decision to purge the legislature though General Berthier resisted full implementation. His successor, General Brune, proved to be too radical, leading to the dispatch of a civilian, Trouvé, to act as restraint upon the general and force through more conservative constitutional revision. His successor, Fouché, however, made common cause with General Brune, seeking to undo Trouvé's work until both Brune and Fouché were recalled.[188]

The recall of their self-willed proconsuls, whether military or civilian, was one of the few weapons the Directory could effectively deploy. It had already had occasion to resort to it in respect of the occupation of Rome and would do so again in the respect of the occupation of Naples. The invasion of Rome issued in the proclamation of a Republic of Rome in February 1798, although General Berthier continued to issue decrees without consulting the consuls of new republic.[189] His replacement, General Masséna, ran into a rare problem in the record of military occupation in this time, namely the revolt of his own army. The soldiers even openly posted the address to Masséna which he had refused to accept. In it they protested that they had not come to Rome to pillage the city, disavowed those who seized goods without issuing receipts, claimed that such actions dishonoured the name of France, and protested about their lack of pay.[190] Although their motives were wider even than this address reveals, the address does indicate some widespread understanding of the normative bounds within which the soldiers thought they and their fellow Frenchmen ought to operate. Masséna's position was untenable, though the civil commissioners dispatched from Rome hesitated to openly challenge his command, reflecting the deference to military authority. Only the eventual decision of the Directory transferring Masséna to Geneva alleviated their embarrassment.[191] With the restoration of order in the army under new command, the French oversaw a new constitution which reconfirmed military authority. Indeed, article 369 specified that until the conclusion of a treaty of alliance with France, all legislation by the authorities of the Roman Republic required the assent of the French general.[192] The civil commissioners sought to avoid any public display of their authority, publishing their own laws and decrees under the name of the general in order to avoid any public challenge to military authority.[193] This attempt to emphasise unity of command barely concealed the tensions between civil commissioners, the army and the various factions of the Roman Republic which variously sought allies amongst the commissioners or the generals. Nor was conflict amongst the French authorities the only problem. The commissioners reported to Paris their view of the officials of the new republic: 'it is difficult to find in history a species of government more debased ... Corruption, venality, spiteful and vindictive passions animate every discussion.'[194] It was, however, the conflict between French civil authority and French military authority, a conflict the Directory was unwilling to resolve, that paralysed French efforts to induce more order in their new creation.[195]

The tension between the generals and the civil commissioners was even more intense in the occupation of Naples that began in January 1799.[196] The commander in Naples, General Championnet, had already shown his disregard of the civil commissioners when he reoccupied Rome after the French had been briefly driven out by the Neapolitans. In Naples, however, his hostility to them, and especially to commissioner Faipoult, reached new heights. Faipoult had been charged by the Directory with rooting out corruption, though he had direct authority only over civilians, being obliged to report his suspicions about military personnel to Championnet. Nevertheless, Championnet refused to acknowledge that Faipoult and his civil commissioners had any authority and ended by expelling them from Naples. The Directory was already angered by Championnet's proclamation of the Parthenopian Republic in Naples, a creation they opposed on wider foreign policy grounds, and suspicious of the radicals with whom he surrounded himself.[197] Now forced to act by the total breakdown of relations between the military and civilian wings of the occupation administration, the Directory recalled Championnet. His fragile creation, the Parthenopian, lasted a mere five months. Those Neapolitans who had collaborated with it faced execution or long prison sentences.

A year before Championnet entered Naples, General Brune had invaded Switzerland, seizing the city of Berne and its treasury. As with

Naples, the Directory had not wanted a military invasion, hoping instead, in the case of Switzerland, to bring about internal change by a mixture of pressure and support for Swiss opponents of the existing regimes, and to secure access across the Alps for French troop movements into northern Italy. Bernese resistance to the independence of the Vaud, which the French supported, induced the French to invade. Initially the Directory was embarrassed by the bloodshed which it had hoped to avoid and uncertain what to do with its new victory, at one point ordering its generals to prepare the division of Switzerland into three separate republics.[198] After the Directory reversed its decision, General Brune proclaimed the 'Helvetic Republic, one and indivisible' on 22 March 1798.[199] Brune was not without some political skill and had closed the divisive radical clubs in Berne to the outrage of the more revolutionary elements.[200] The same could not be said for his successor, General Schauenbourg, though he had a reputation for imposing discipline upon his own soldiers and had some of those found guilty of pillaging executed. The choice of civil commissioners was especially important given that the Directory wanted to persuade the other European powers, especially the Austrians, that despite the occupation the Helvetic Republic was a genuinely independent body. The task of the commissioners was aggravated, however, by the need to extract contributions for the French war efforts, especially once the funds of the Bernese treasury were exhausted, and the need to control the corruption which as usual accompanied French requisitioning. Indeed, some members of the Directory, notably Reubell, paid detailed attention to remonstrances from the Swiss about French abuse of power.[201] Commissioner Rapinat, angered by both Swiss recourse to the authorities in Paris and recalcitrance in making financial contributions, struck out at the Swiss Directory, purging it of those he deemed most obstructive. Unfortunately, this made a mockery of the French Directory's protestations to the Austrians about the spontaneity of the Swiss revolution and the independence of the Helvetic Republic. Quite how seriously they took this was proven by their prompt dismissal of Rapinat. The limits of their concern and their scope for manoeuvre were also demonstrated by their decision to reinstate him but leaving him humiliated in the process.[202] Independent civil commissioners could be almost as troublesome as independent generals. For the Swiss commissioner, Rapinat would become the symbol of French exactions though these were probably less harsh than those suffered by the Italian states.

Once again the French had resorted to the creation of a sister republic as an alternative to annexation. Although the Treaty of Alliance between the new republic and France of 19 August 1798 did not provide for the continuation of occupation both external theatres and internal dissent would later give the French the occasion to return to the practice of occupation. The possibility of a sister republic as a solution for the Rhineland had never been a strong one. Even many German radicals had little conviction in it. It was, however, only in September 1797 that the Directory definitively informed General Hoche that reunion with France was the fate of the Rhineland. A separate republic, they argued, would be unable to support itself and would only be an embarrassment for France.[203] By then Hoche had managed to persuade the Directory to resolve at least one problem of the management of occupied territory in the Rhineland, namely its fragmentation. After ineffective administrative reform in 1796 the Directory first agreed to Hoche's argument that restoration of indigenous administrative structures would both facilitate better provisioning of the army and reduce antipathy to the French. The following month, March 1797, it extended Hoche's remit over civil administration, until then restricted to the area of operation of his own army, to the entire left bank of the Rhineland. Ironically that created a new problem in the shape of opposition from General Moreau, commander of the other French army in the region, who refused to cooperate with Hoche's agents. That problem was not resolved until Moreau's recall to Paris on grounds unconnected with the administration of occupied territory.[204] Even so, Hoche's hopes that hostility to France would diminish met with limited success. It is true that even in the Prussian provinces in the Rhineland, faltering conviction in Prussian commitment to their recovery induced some pragmatic adaptation but that failed to alter the underlying antipathy amongst the majority of the population.[205] Even pragmatists were antagonised by the demands of the French army and often fearful of the possible charge of treason that might await those too closely associated with French occupation.

The armies of the French Revolution had not been prepared for the task of military occupation. They lacked any guidance in the shape of international law or military manuals. They possessed what in retrospect inevitably looks like a rudimentary understanding of occupation, or, more in tune with their own language, were caught between the language of conquest and the language of liberation, neither of which was well-suited to capture some of the difficulties they experienced. They were hampered by the strain caused by armies whose country could not adequately provision them, aggravated as it was by rampant corruption. Frequently, they were troubled by the unresolved relationship between military and civilian agencies. Their prime alternative to annexation, the creation of sister republics, more often prolonged than ended military occupation. The triumph of military power with Napoleon's coup would simplify one of these problems but little else.

Military Occupations by Napoleonic Armies

The occupations that followed the resumption of French military successes after the reversal of 1799 exhibited considerable continuity with the occupations under the Directory. That was clear as the French re-established the provisional authorities of the Cisalpine and Ligurian republics. The requisitions, with their attendant disorder and corruption, continued. In the Ligurian Republic, Dejean, the minister extraordinary, who presided over the governing commission, was soon lamenting his inability to exercise effective control and wrote to Talleyrand pleading for his intercession with Napoleon to secure Dejean's recall.[206] For both the Ligurian and Cisalpine republics as well as for Piedmont, which had been under more or less continuous French occupation since 1796, Napoleon instructed that nothing definitive was to be agreed concerning their futures. The fate of Piedmont, however, became clear as early as April 1801 when Napoleon ordered that it was to form a 'military division' and that General Jourdan, until then French minister attached to the government of Piedmont, was to be the Administrator General of Piedmonnt. Jourdan was advised to 'apply the principle of amalgamation which has succeeded so well in France'.[207] Formal reunion with France would not come until over a year later, in September 1802. By then the Cisalpine Republic had been transformed into the Republic of Italy, with Napoleon as its president and the Italian Francesco Melzi d'Eril as its vice president. To what extent that marked the end of military occupation is questionable. The new republic continued to support a French army and Melzi's authority was weakened by conflict with the French General Joachim Murat, who even established a secret military police which operated independently of the national police force of the Republic.[208] Ironically, Joachim Murat would find his own authority subject to challenge by an occupation force when he became King of Naples in 1808. Murat had shown too much independence for Napoleon's liking, seeming to treat his kingdom as if it were an autonomous entity, even daring to replace the French flags on fortresses and Neapolitan naval vessels with the Neapolitan flag. Napoleon responded by reminding him that his kingdom was part of the French Empire and that he himself remained French. Even more significantly he instructed General Grenier, commander of the Observation Corps of Meridional Italy, that Grenier had the authority to issue orders to all Frenchmen 'regardless of the opposition of the King of Naples'.[209] In retrospect this curious situation led Raymond Robin to conclude that 'this is, in reality, the occupation of French territory by French troops'.[210] It could also be said that the existence of the satellite kingdoms served to inhibit the emergence of a clear concept of military occupation at the time.

As Napoleon's armies continued to expand across Europe, neither sister republics or satellite kingdoms ruled by Napoleon himself or his relatives or annexation were obvious options, at least not initially. In the case of the occupation of Munich in June 1800, for example, indigenous radicals were few in number and, more importantly, French strategy was to win over the Elector of Bavaria and the Palatinate as a future ally against Austria. Thus, when General Decaën was approached by a delegation from republican clubs seeking support for a rising against the elector he rebuffed them. When they turned to Decaën's superior, General Moreau, they were informed that his task had been to conquer the territory but not to transform it into a republic.[211] Indeed. Although the inhabitants of occupied Munich suffered from the usual outbreaks of indiscipline, requisitioning and inflated prices, especially of food, caused by the presence of a large French army, there was no attempt on the part of the French to bring about any change of regime.

The French initially also had limited ambitions in Hanover, which they invaded in response to the resumption of war with England. After desultory defence the Hanoverians agreed to the Convention of Sulingen of 3 June 1803. This expressly provided that 'Hanover will be occupied by the French army'.[212] Article 10 provided that 'The General and Commander in Chief reserves the right to make such changes as he deems convenient in the government and authorities established by the Elector'.[213] That provision, however, was not a prelude to revolutionary transformation but a pragmatic measure for the modification of government structures to allow the French occupiers to more effectively manage the occupation. The French commander, General Mortier, promptly proceeded to create an Executive Commission composed of Hanoverian officials, over which a French Government Commissioner, a former administrator of occupied territory in the Rhineland, Durbach, sometimes presided.[214] His prime task was to ensure that French financial demands were met, though the Hanoverians exploited the intricacies of their archaic financial system to hide at least some sums from the French. Those officials were also in contact with Hanoverian ministers who had fled to neighbouring territory, as General Bernadotte, Mortier's successor, indignantly complained. In other respects the French limited their interference in Hanover's affairs, leaving the administration of justice in place and not even interfering in civil claims made by Frenchmen against Hanoverians.[215] Both generals also sought to maintain strict discipline. The financial strain on the inhabitants, both because of French exactions and the disruption of trade with England, was considerable. Some relief came as the main French force withdrew to confront the Austrians in 1805, ceding Hanover to occupation by France's ally, Prussia.

Officially Prussia claimed that its intent was purely to ensure Hanoverian neutrality. The Prussian Administrative Commission was to supervise the existing Hanoverian administration and even cover some of the costs of the occupation force out of Prussian funds.[216] The Hanoverians were cautious. They agreed that Hanoverian judges should continue to sit but only as long as the Prussian commissioner did not interfere in their judgements or require anything incompatible with their official oaths. They also obstructed Prussian attempts to gain an accurate overview of Hanoverian finances, just as they had obstructed the French. Hanoverian suspicion of Prussian ambitions was fully justified when the Prussian king issued a Patent of 1 April 1806 in which he proclaimed the 'effective seizure of possession' of Hanover, which would henceforth be ruled in 'our name and supreme authority'.[217] Yet despite this assertion of Prussian sovereignty, the Prussian authorities were reluctant to undertake wholesale change in the administration of Hanoverian territory until their possession had been confirmed in a general peace. On the other hand they were determined to demonstrate their will to retain possession to the Hanoverians, selecting reform of the postal service as an example.[218] Most Hanoverians were convinced that the return of the French was more likely than the persistence of the Prussian hold on their territory.[219]

French withdrawal from Hanover was soon followed by occupation of Vienna in November 1805. Here too the French left the existing municipal authorities in place, including the national guard, which contributed to the maintenance of order on several occasions, sparing the French the resources that would have been needed to replace it. The predicament of Vienna did, however, lead to a direct threat to its existing authorities. The city was dependent on food supplies shipped up the Danube from Hungary. When these supplies were cut Napoleon responded by writing to the Austrian emperor, stating that he had so far not instituted changes in the administration of the city associated with his right of conquest but warning that if he was obliged to take the city under his 'protection' it would be necessary to give it a constitution more appropriate to the times. The warning, effectively to challenge the legitimacy of the institutions of Austria's capital, was effective.[220]

Vienna's occupation had been brief, a total of 62 days, but the wave of occupations that followed the war between France and Prussia were more prolonged, more extensive and more varied in their consequences than Vienna's first experience of occupation. It is clear from some of these occupations that there was no consistent set of expectations even about the simple proclamation of the occupation. Thus when General Mortier occupied Hesse he announced to the inhabitants 'I come to take possession of your country', adding that 'Your religion, your laws your customs your privileges will be respected, discipline will be maintained'.[221] In Hanover he declared 'I come to take possession of your country in the name of His Majesty the Emperor and King, my august sovereign. The revenues will be collected and justice administered in his name.'[222] This time there was no explicit guarantee of religion, laws and customs, though he did confirm that the existing local administration would be maintained. The language of possession which the Prussians used to announce a claim to sovereignty and the prospect of regime transformation elicited no apparent protest or concern, despite, in the case of Hanover, the fact that the administration of justice in the name of a power had often been construed as signifying the assertion of sovereignty. In Bremen, however, the proclamation of 'possession' by Colonel Clément was met with vigorous and prolonged protest by Bremen's Senate which demanded a new proclamation asserting only French 'occupation' of the city.[223]

In practice, however, the form in which Napoleon's generals took 'possession' of territory provides no consistent guide to the nature of the occupation they imposed or to its outcome. Much depended on the significance of the occupied territory in the wider conduct of Napoleon's wars and on the character of the general in command. Although sometimes subject to precise instruction from Napoleon himself, his generals had considerable latitude. That is strikingly illustrated by General Lagrange, who had taken over from Mortier in Hesse. In the wake of a brief unsuccessful revolt by elements of Hesse's former army, Napoleon ordered extensive and savage reprisals but Lagrange, though pushed further than his initial inclination, significantly mitigated the reprisals demanded by Napoleon.[224] Open revolt in the German territories was rare though clashes between smugglers and French customs officials on the north German coast were not uncommon. French attempts to cut off trade with England from the proclamation of the Berlin decrees of 21 November 1806 onwards forced a significant percentage of the population in the coastal cities into smuggling. Violence, however, could sometimes be avoided by the simple expedient of paying French officials, who were as intent upon enriching themselves during the occupation as most of Napoleon's generals.[225]

Inhabitants could also exploit the shortage of French personnel and French preference for relying on local officials. Hanoverian officials were adept at this, especially after the French intendant, Belleville, let slip French reluctance to take over the administration of the complex Hanoverian taxation system.[226] By the same token the French could exert pressure on the occupied by threatening to replace indigenous officials with Frenchman as they did when the Hanoverians were slow to find what the French regarded as an effective director of police.[227] French dependence on the occupied also increased whenever the main body of French military forces withdrew to take part in the ever more wide ranging manoeuvres of the French armies. Thus, in 1807, both the French gendarmerie and customs officials in the Hanseatic ports found themselves reliant upon local agents and authorities.[228] Dependence on indigenous officials also offered the opportunity to play off the different branches of the French occupation regime against each other. The conflicts between them frequently crippled the efforts of the occupation regime, even where, as in Hamburg, a special council was created precisely to ensure coordination.[229] Yet there were limits to such strategies. There were gains to be had from persuading the occupant of the willingness of officials to cooperate with the occupation regime. This was well understood by the key figure on the Government Commission in Hanover, a coordinating body of indigenous officials created by the French commander.[230] Cooperation in its turn brought with it the risk of being accused of lack of loyalty to the legitimate power, especially where indigenous officials were seen as too closely involved in the enforcement measures of exactions of the French authorities. Both sides were aware of this constraint, though the extent to which they made provisions to mitigate the risk varied.

Those pressures were especially apparent in Berlin which was occupied in October 1806 in the wake of the devastating defeat of Prussian forces by Napoleon. There both the city authorities and the head of the civil guard which helped the French maintain order were obliged to swear an oath to obey French orders, an oath that many fellow Germans found degrading as well as potentially treacherous. The attempts of the officials to mitigate the appearance of the oath by inserting the reservation 'within the limits of our employment' were rejected by the French civil intendant, Louis Bignon, who threatened those who showed an inclination to refuse the oath that they would be dismissed and their offices taken over by French officials.[231] Ironically, even French soldiers and officials could express their disdain for the lack of patriotism of those subject to their authority, especially where this involved relations between the sexes.[232] The perspective of the occupant was, however, no more uniform than the perspective of the occupied. In the second occupation of Vienna in 1809, while some Frenchman were struck by what they saw as Viennese commitment to the pleasures of life others feared an uprising analogous to the one the French had faced in their occupation of Madrid in 1808.[233] The French could also show some understanding for the predicament of those who had cooperated with them, insisting in the Peace of Tilsit that the Prussian king undertook not to punish either members of the city authorities in Berlin or the members of the Berlin civil guard.[234]

The peace had at least preserved the existence of a rump Prussia. For the Hanoverians and the inhabitants of the Hanseatic states the occupation was brought to an end only by annexation of the latter to France and the incorporation of the former into the Kingdom of Westphalia at the end of 1810. Prussia in 1807, by contrast, preserved its existence but only at the cost of prolonging the occupation until payment of a war indemnity. French control of the size of the indemnity effectively allowed Napoleon to use this provision to prolong the occupation, only agreeing to modify the terms in 1808 in response to pressure from Russia and the need to transfer forces to Spain. Even then the Treaty of September 1808 maintained French garrisons in specified fortresses. Although the treaty provided that the administration of revenues and justice in these fortresses belonged to the King of Prussia, it also provided that the police would be 'in the hands of the French commandant'.[235] Such cursory provisions, however, left considerable scope for uncertainty, even in the minds of the French, about the extent of the authority of the occupier.[236] As French troop strength increased again in preparation for the invasion of Russia in 1812, the Treaty of Alliance and associated Convention of February 1812 provided greater clarity about the supposed extent of French authority but no more certainty in practice as the French generals repeatedly exceeded the limits of what was agreed by the alliance.[237]

Occupation of Prussian territory had been complicated by the fact that part of it was used to create the Grand Duchy of Warsaw, Napoleon's concession to the idea of recreating an independent Poland. The titular head of the duchy was Napoleon's German ally the King of Saxony, but it was French authorities that dominated and ensured the existence of this political structure. When French troops entered former Polish territory this outcome had not been determined, leaving French generals and those Poles who fought with them to establish local and diverse administrations that took account of the need to avoid immediately alienating the Prussian administrators whilst acknowledging the ambitions of the Poles who saw the French as their liberators.[238] Even once a more centralised Polish authority was established in the shape of a Government Commission in 1807, it was the French army under General Davout and the French intendants, supervised from Berlin by Intendant General Daru, who exercised ultimate authority. One of those intendants became the first French Resident in Warsaw. Notionally a diplomatic office, the Resident was, as one of them put it, a 'legal intermediary' between the French army and the government of the duchy.[239] The French army also stood behind the Resident's policies when these went beyond what could be agreed with the official authorities of the duchy.[240] Even after the withdrawal of the main French force in August 1808 the Residents remained a powerful force in a duchy whose continued existence was dependent upon French military backing. Although the duchy was the most plausible instance of occupations by Napoleonic armies that could be seen by both sides in terms of liberation, the reality of occupation and mutual misunderstanding coloured attitudes on both sides. As early as September 1807 Resident Vincent was reporting that despite the orderly behaviour of French soldiers, the Poles treated them with a coldness that bordered on rudeness.[241] Of course, the behaviour of the French soldiery was not always orderly at all and French disdain for the country and culture of the Poles was frequently intense.[242]

Cultural misunderstanding and antipathy had been a frequent characteristic of the occupations since the outbreak of the wars of Revolutionary France. In the occupation of Spain they took on a violent intensity that has made that occupation the most widely referred to of all the Napoleonic occupations. Napoleon's own reflections, notably his reference to it as 'that fatal knot' which undermined his empire, contributed significantly to its prominence.[243] It was here that the term 'guerrilla' took on its modern connotations of the armed civilian fighting against the occupier, a sense clearly recognised by the British General Wellesley as early as 1809.[244] In the same year the Spanish Central Junta, the provisional authority claiming to speak in the name of the Spanish, called for resistance to the French, whom it described as 'bandits not soldiers, ferocious monsters not men'.[245] The French responded in kind, refusing to treat the guerrillas as legitimate belligerents and executing many as bandits. The cycle of violence began with a revolt against the French in Madrid in May 1808 while Napoleon, whose forces had originally entered Spain as allies, was forcing the abdication of the Spanish royal family, which he would replace with his brother Joseph as king. Although the revolt soon spread it was never uniform, much more intense in Navarre and surrounding provinces, and the character of the guerrilla remains disputed.[246] It was moreover only one factor that complicated understanding the situation in Spain.

Part of the difficulty was evident in one of first Spanish cities occupied by the French, Barcelona. There General Duhesme had taken command in February 1808. Duhesme experienced the usual difficulties in preventing pillaging by his own soldiers, lacked an adequate administrative staff or specialised services and was plagued by a chronic shortage of food in Barcelona.[247] Duhesme was also concerned about the nature and extent of his own authority, especially in relation to Spanish officials. He had received no guidance beyond the general instruction to secure Barcelona and to take hostages. Joseph made no attempt to exert or even display his authority in Barcelona. Duhesme's request in June 1808 that he be endowed explicitly with 'superior authority' elicited no response.[248] In practice Duhesme tried to rely on Spanish officials where he could and sought to preserve at least the appearance of their authority and status. They in turn did not exhibit any overt spirit of opposition but nor did they exhibit much zeal in fulfilling the tasks Duhesme bestowed on them.[249] The uneasy and ineffective cooperation was eased by Duhesme's avoidance of any attempt to impose an oath of loyalty, even to Joseph, on the Spanish functionaries. However, when Duhesme came under the command of General Gouvion Saint-Cyr, the latter insisted in April 1809 on the imposition of an oath. The result, with few exceptions, was the resignation of the Spanish officials who found themselves, quite contrary to their inclinations, elevated into heroes and martyrs by their fellow countrymen.[250] Duhesme, against his own inclinations, in turn found himself forced more and more into the role of an administrator rather than a soldier, as he understood that profession.

Not all of Napoleon's generals saw the two roles as mutually exclusive. General Suchet in Aragon realised that his task as a soldier, including establishing security, could be reinforced by political and administrative measures. He recalled in his memoirs, with an inevitable positive gloss, 'introducing a policy of justice and moderation, which he calculated would enable him, whilst he held possession of Aragon, to subdue the animosity of its population'.[251] There were, of course, limits to Suchet's moderation. Nevertheless, he skilfully exploited Aragonese provincial identity, blocking the transfer of religious plate from Saragossa to Madrid demanded by the minister of finance.[252] He rejected functionaries sent from Madrid, and made concessions to Aragonese religious authorities, while imprisoning and deporting recalcitrant priests. He also made genuine efforts to promote economic development in Aragon, even seeking authorisation to import sheep in order to avoid further depleting Aragonese flocks.[253] The comparative success of Suchet's administration of Spain did not prevent guerrilla incursions from neighbouring provinces whenever Suchet had to withdraw forces for operations elsewhere. Nor was there any central organisation for the administration of Spain as a whole.

Indeed, Napoleon contributed to the fragmentation of the

administration of Spain in February 1810. He instructed that Suchet be ordered to 'consider Aragon as a province in a state of siege' and not to tolerate any communication between the Aragonese and Madrid. Suchet was to be warned that Napoleon's interests and those of France did not necessarily coincide with those of the ministers in Madrid, that is, the minsters of the King of Spain, Napoleon's own brother. Should the latter seek to issue administrative orders Suchet was authorised to inform the king that Suchet exercised command in Aragon.[254] Similar instructions went out to several other generals in Spain. For Suchet this created the paradox, enhanced by the difficulty of communicating in a country wracked by insurrection, that whilst he understood that he had absolute authority in respect of the government of Aragon, he remained bound by an earlier regulation identifying Joseph as commander-in-chief in Spain and hence bound to obey Joseph in *'purely military* operations'.[255] Despite Suchet's confusion the outcome of Napoleon's instructions of February 1812 was to consolidate the reality of uncoordinated and fragmented military government. It was as if Napoleon's generals were in occupation of parts of the country contrary to the authority of King Joseph. Attempts to reverse this amidst Napoleon's plans for the invasion of Russia came too late to change the established practices of Napoleon's generals, as Joseph himself was painfully aware. Nor was his position enhanced by lack of consultation about the prospective annexation of Catalonia, notionally part of Joseph's kingdom, by France.[256] On the eve of the invasion which would herald the downfall of Napoleon's empire, Napoleon had reaffirmed the complete absence of any systematic approach to the problems of military occupation which had characterised his rule and had come to such striking fruition in Spain.

Allied Military Occupations

Allied occupations had occurred throughout the period of the wars of Revolutionary France and the Napoleonic Wars but until 1813 they had been brief and small in scale compared with those conducted by the French. On the other side of the Atlantic, in the war between the British and the Americans of 1812, raiding rather than occupation was the prime activity and concern.[257] Nevertheless on both sides of the Atlantic some of the problems of military occupation, including efforts to make sense of it and to apply or formulate rules governing its conduct, were evident. Early in the wars, during the brief occupation of Toulon, the British had exhibited no great inclination to engage in regime transformation and the civil commissioner had been instructed 'not to do violence to existing Prejudices'.[258] No such restraint was exercised in what the French courts would later see as the British occupation of Corsica from 1794 to 1796 but where at the time the British and their Corsican supporters saw a kingdom of Corsica headed by George III with institutions modelled on those of Britain.[259] Elsewhere the brief Allied occupations typically involved the proclamation of the return of the regime ousted by the French and similar patterns of requisitioning and excesses associated with the occupations by the French. None of these, however, compared with the challenges that the Allies faced after 1813, especially in Germany and France itself. It was here that military occupation as a clear concept and practice emerged most fully.

The driving force behind this was the Prussian reformer Baron vom Stein. It was at Stein's prompting that the Prusso-Russian Convention of Breslau in March 1813 established an Administrative Council for the administration of occupied territory, though this came to little, in part because of uncertainty about whether the sovereignty of the princes of the Confederation of the Rhine would be respected or, temporarily at least, set aside by the Council. The prospective remit of the Administrative Council soon seemed to be curtailed by the decision of the Convention of Kalisch of April 1813 to distinguish between territory subject to military occupation and territory belonging to states which would join the alliance against Napoleon.[260] However, the chaos that accompanied the Allied move into Saxony gave Stein the opportunity to revive the idea of the need for a coordinated approach to occupation. The outcome was the Leipzig Convention of 21 October 1813. According to this agreement a central administration would be created to which military governors would be subordinate. The central administration was to report to a Ministerial Council, though in practice this turned out to be relatively inactive.[261]

Stein's ambition for the central administration was extensive. In relation to the princes of the Confederation of the Rhine, Stein suggested that they should 'suspend the power of the princes until the peace by virtue of the right of conquest of the Allies' and even that the princes should be physically removed from the territories concerned.[262] When some of the princes of the smaller former Westphalian territories made claims to the restoration of their position, Stein's response was to suggest that if they sought to interfere in the government of these territories they should be arrested and deported.²⁶³ Although Stein still used the language of the rights of conquest to justify suspension of the sovereignty of these princes, it was a suspension of sovereignty, not the assertion of the sovereignty of one of the Allied powers that he sought. Indeed Stein insisted that his officials issue their decrees in the name of the Allied powers and not in the name of their own sovereign.²⁶⁴ Similar considerations, though less precisely formulated, can be found elsewhere. Thus the British Foreign Minister Castlereagh suggested that although Antwerp would be occupied by either the British or a combination of the British and Dutch, 'I do not think it prudent to hoist these colours exclusively, as all the ceded territory, of which this place forms a part, must be held in the name of the Allied Sovereigns generally'.²⁶⁵ Stein also had a clear conception of the limited authority proper to the provisional government exercised by the central administration, even if he did not always insist that his subordinates abided by it.²⁶⁶

It was Stein's intent that the central administration and the subordinate General Governments should take over the existing administration, coordinate the provisioning of the Allied armies, manage the finances of occupied territories, oversee policing and, in occupied German territories, recruit further troops for the conduct of the war against Napoleon. Much of this Stein and his subordinates achieved, though imperfectly and not without recurrent conflict with recalcitrant Allied generals jealous of their own authority, sometimes attentive to the specific interests of their own sovereigns, and unaccustomed to such restraint. Since Stein and his agents lacked any power of command of their own over the soldiers winning the cooperation of the generals was as crucial as the backing of the Allied powers themselves for his central administration. Here Stein invoked not only the principled agreements on which his authority was based but also the benefits to army commanders whose operational movements, he suggested, made it impractical for them to exercise administration over specific fixed territories.²⁶⁷

Although the remit of Stein's central administration extended into part of France as well as part of occupied German territory, it was far from being responsible for the administration of the entirety of territory nor did the brevity of the first Allied occupation of France favour the full development of Stein's plans.[268] Nor could Stein's overstretched organisation directly curtail the excesses which accompanied both the occupation of 1814 and the occupation 1815. In both there were significant differences between the attitudes of the generals of the diverse armies. Those from countries which had been humiliated and occupied by Napoleon and coerced into becoming France's allies were more prone to sanction the desire for revenge. The proclivity to resort to violence was probably also promoted by the anxieties of the occupiers. The Prussians, especially, often seen as the harshest of the occupiers, feared both an uprising by the French and that there might be attempts to poison the food the French were obliged to supply the occupants.[269] If anything, the second occupation of France was more marked by such anxieties than the first. In 1814 the official view of the Allied powers had been that they were at war with Napoleon not with the French nation. The number of Frenchmen who had rallied to Napoleon in 1815, however, gave rise to quite different sentiments.[270] Nor was this the only cause for concern. Wellington, who tried to moderate the behaviour of the Allies and exhorted his own troops to moderation but was frequently exasperated by the excesses to which all, including his own soldiers, were prone, had seen the vicious spiral of violence induced by the French occupation in Spain. That experience was reflected in his warning in July 1815 that 'we shall immediately set the whole country against us . . . if the useless . . . oppression practised on the French people, is not put a stop to'.[271]

In 1815 there was no central administration to coordinate the Allied occupation. The French had created a Requisition Commission the day after the French king returned to Paris on 8 July and somewhat later the Allies created an Administrative Council, though the conceptions behind the two were very different. The Allied Council, which evaded meaningful cooperation with the Requisitions Commission, asserted the direct authority of military governors and commanders and even refused to receive complaints channelled through the Commission.[272] Wellington did persuade the Allies to adopt a more organised dispersal of their now massive armies though their sheer size inevitably led to a catalogue of complaints about arbitrary and often violent behaviour. Nevertheless there was no outbreak of the kind of revolt Wellington feared and by late September the Allies had begun the withdrawal of the bulk of their forces even before the signature of Treaty of Paris of 20 November 1815. As with so many of the occupations by the French in the preceding years, the restoration of peace meant the continuation of occupation.

In Wellington's view occupation was a clear and preferable alternative to conquest: 'I prefer the temporary occupation of some of the strong places ... to the permanent cession of even all of the places which in my opinion ought to be occupied for a time'.[273] It was a preference which the Allied powers shared. Hence, according to the Peace, 'it has been judged indispensable to occupy ... by a corps of Allied Troops certain military positions along the frontiers of France, under the express reserve, that such occupation shall in no way prejudice the Sovereignty of His Most Christian Majesty'.[274] The French king of course could not see the continued presence of 150,000 foreign troops on his territory as anything other than a restriction of his sovereignty, and in this case, as expression of doubt about his government's ability to maintain internal security within France. Although the Convention governing the occupation specified that civil administration, the collection of taxes and the administration of justice were to remain in French hands even in the occupied fortresses, French military authority was excluded. Moreover, the ambassadors of the four powers formed a surveillance committee to monitor developments in France and were not averse to intervening in French political life.[275] Ironically, however, it was the very possibility that had induced the Allies to insist on the occupation, concern about the internal stability of France, which allowed the French to successfully argue for ending the occupation earlier than the maximum term of five years set out in the Treaty. The commander of the occupation force, Wellington, agreed that the persistence of the occupation was itself more likely to provoke the unrest it had been created to prevent than its withdrawal.[276] The ensuing Allied agreement in 1818 finally brought to an end the last occupation of the Napoleonic Wars.

The Allied occupations exhibited many of the features of their French counterparts. They were expressed as much in the language of conquest and liberation as occupation, though the language of occupation came out most clearly in the provision of occupation beyond the realm of war. Though not driven by the underlying financial constraints of Revolutionary and Napoleonic France, both logistics and the rights of the victor meant that the burden on the occupied was extremely heavy. Wilful generals and undisciplined troops exacerbated the inevitable problems. Even a strong and determined commander such as Wellington seems to have been frequently frustrated by his inability to suppress the excesses of his own troops, still more so the excesses of his Allies' troops. An able administrator such as Stein could see many of the problems but was limited by his own lack of direct authority and divided views of his political masters. Nevertheless, the Allied occupations exhibited both a clearer understanding of the distinctive nature and problems of military occupation.

Judging Military Occupation

Although legal assessment of these occupations was relatively infrequent during or in the aftermath of them compared with occupations later in the century, courts were being forced to consider the meaning of military occupation. It was in fact French courts that began to grapple more clearly with the problematic nature of military occupation. One striking case involved the prospective trial of the Italian commandant of the fortress of Barcelona and the Spanish police commissioner for the murder of a Spanish inhabitant of Barcelona during the French occupation. The Court of Cassation was troubled by the consequences of the fact that Napoleon's armies were not merely French and by the status of an indigenous inhabitant who was the police commissioner. Moreover the court specifically raised the implications of the fact that Barcelona at the time of the crime had been 'as it still is today, occupied by French troops and governed, militarily as well as politically in the name of France'.[277] It concluded that despite these facts 'the town of Barcelona is not the less foreign; it is not the less governed by foreign laws; it is not the less in the name of a foreign sovereign that justice is administered'.[278] The court thereby acknowledged French occupation, notwithstanding the fact that it was nominally ruled by one of Napoleon's relatives, who Napoleon insisted should never forget they were French, and insisted that occupation did not signify the extension of French sovereignty.[279]

The following year the Court of Cassation had to determine French attitudes to the validity of acts, in this case an amnesty which was considered to be an act of sovereignty, issued by Neapolitan authorities occupying Rome, in 1800. Here it envisaged two possibilities, either that the King of Naples had reconquered it from the French on behalf of the Pope or that he had conquered it in his own name from both the French and the Pope. In the former case it concluded that the King of Naples never exercised sovereignty. In the latter case it concluded that the King of Naples had exercised sovereignty, but that the validity of his acts ceased the moment he lost possession of Rome.[280] This was not obviously consistent with the Court of Cassation's view the previous year but still reflected awareness of the potentially problematic status of an occupant or interim ruler. There was, however, as yet no clear and consistent distinction between the status of an interim ruler who exercised sovereignty and an occupant who was not considered to be sovereign.

There was greater clarity in a decision after the wars but relating to the French occupation of Catalonia in 1811. There the court overturned the judgement of the Assize Court to the effect that 'Catalonia was occupied by French troops and administered by French authorities suffices for it be reputed an integral part of French territory'. To the contrary the Court of Cassation decided that

> this occupation and this administration by French troops and authorities had never communicated to the inhabitants of Catalonia the title of Frenchmen, nor to their territory the quality of French territory; that this communication could only have resulted from an act of reunion emanating from the public authority, which never existed.[281]

Military occupation alone did not, in this view, entail the extension of sovereignty.

The French Court of Cassation would continue to return to the occupations of the Revolutionary and Napoleonic Wars for several decades, even concluding in 1841 that the acts of the British authorities in their brief occupation of Corsica, which the British understood to be sovereign possession, but which the court assimilated to 'hostile occupation', were null and void, with retroactive effect, from the moment the British lost possession of the island.[282] By then, however, the language of occupation and the contrast between occupation and conquest was more clearly, if still inconsistently, applied. It was, however, the experience of the Revolutionary and Napoleonic Wars that had laid the foundations for the emergence of a concept of military occupation. It was not a clear or unilinear process, let alone an abrupt and decisive one. Both regime transformation and hesitancy to engage in regime transformation accompanied what looked in other respects like military occupation. In some ways occupation was more clearly defined in the provisions for military occupation beyond the realm of war, in peace treaties and conventions, than in belligerent occupation itself. While some, notably Baron vom Stein, had a relatively coherent concept of military occupation, others did not and continued to try to make sense of their experience and ambition in the language of conquest and liberation. Such confusion would in fact continue. So too would the experience evident in the Revolutionary and Napoleonic Wars of being unprepared for the challenges of occupation, of the difficulty generals experienced in controlling their own soldiers and of the tensions between military and civil authority.

Notes

1. For an early example of this see A. H. L. Heeren, *A Manual of the History of the Political System of Europe and its Colonies* (London: Bohn, 1874). The first German edition appeared in 1809.
2. For the Declaration of Pillnitz and the declaration of war see John Hall Stewart (ed.), *A Documentary Survey of the French Revolution* (Toronto: Macmillan, 1951), pp. 223–4 and 286–8; for Brissot's speech see *Archives parlementaires*, 34 (1890), 309–17.
3. The image of the Holy Alliance enjoyed an influence that exceeded the actual power of the Alliance.
4. Albert Sorel, *L'Europe et la Révolution Française*, vol. 1 (Paris: Plon, 1887), p. 3.
5. See the judgement of T. C. W. Blanning, *The Origins of the French Revolutionary Wars* (London: Longman, 1986), p. 123.
6. Quoted in André Fugier, *Histoire des relations internationales: La Révolution Française et l'Empire Napoléonien* (Paris: Hachette, 1954), p. 25.
7. Sorel, *L'Europe et la Révolution Française*, vol. 1, pp. 9–11. For a somewhat different, more recent version see James R. Sofka, 'The eighteenth century international system: parity or primacy', *Review of International Studies*, 27 (2001), 147–63. For an evaluation see David Armstrong, *Revolution and World Order: The Revolutionary State in International Society* (Oxford: Clarendon Press, 1993), pp. 79–84.
8. Marc Belissa, 'Garran de Coulon, la conquête de la Belgique et l'élaboration d'un nouveau droit public', *Revue du Nord*, 81 (1999), 553.
9. Hervé Leuwers, 'République et relations entre les peuples', *Annales historiques de la Révolution française*, no. 318 (1999), 2–4.
10. David A. Bell, *The First Total War: Napoleon's Europe and the Birth of Modern Warfare* (London: Bloomsbury, 2007), p. 126.
11. For an assessment of the debate on natural frontiers see Peter Sahlins,

'Natural frontiers revisited: France's boundaries since the seventeenth century', *American Historical Review*, 95 (1990), 1423–51. T. C. W. Blanning points out that even the natural frontiers doctrine was not as clear a guide as the name might suggest, *The French Revolutionary Wars 1787–1802* (London: Arnold, 1996), p. 92.
12. For the parlous state of French armies during the first winter see Albert Sorel, *L'Europe et la Révolution Française*, vol. 4 (Paris: Plon, 1891), pp. 245–7.
13. Jacques Godechot, *La Grande Nation: L'expansion révolutionnaire de la France dans le monde de 1789 à 1799*, 2nd edn (Paris: Montaigne, 1983), pp. 128–9. As Godechot notes, not all generals shared these expansionist ambitions, ibid. p. 128, citing General Jean-Baptiste Kléber.
14. Thus General Mortier in respect of Hanover on 12 Novemer 1806, Frignet Despréaux, *Le Maréchal Mortier*, vol. 3 (Paris: Berger-Levrault, 1920), p. 292.
15. On these terms see Stuart Woolf, *Napoleon's Integration of Europe* (London: Routledge, 1991), pp. 109–10, 166–7, 195–6, and Michael Rowe, 'Between empire and home town: Napoleonic rule on the Rhine', *Historical Journal*, 42 (1999), 649.
16. See his letter of 13 April 1801 to Talleyrand, *Correspondence de Napoléon Ier*, vol. 7 (Paris: Plon, 1861), p. 121.
17. Quoted in Herbert A. L. Fisher, *Studies in Napoleonic Statesmanship: Germany* (Oxford: Clarendon Press, 1903), p. 191.
18. Geoffrey Bruun, *Europe and the French Imperium 1799–1814* (New York: Harper & Row, 1938), p. 110.
19. J.-E. Driault, *Napoléon en Italie (1800–1812)* (Paris: Alcan, 1906), p. 53.
20. *Correspondance de Napoléon 1e*, vol. 20 (Paris: Plon, 1866), pp. 453–4.
21. Frédéric Camp, 'Des Catalans et de Napoléon', *Revue des etudes napoléoniennes*, 33 (1931), 37.
22. Blanning, *The Origins of the French Revolutionary Wars*, p. 101.
23. See Edmund Burke, *Select Works of Edmund Burke, vol. 3: Letters on a Regicide Peace* (Indianapolis: Liberty, 1999). For the equivocation see Jennifer Mori, 'The British government and the Bourbon restoration: the occupation of Toulon, 1793', *Historical Journal*, 40 (1997), 669–719.
24. See Paul Schroeder, *The Transformation of European Politics 1763–1848* (Oxford: Clarendon Press, 1994).
25. Quoted in ibid. p. 460.
26. Bell, *The First Total War*, pp. 129–36.
27. Blanning, *The French Revolutionary Wars*, pp. 88–91.

28. For the declaration see Stewart (ed.), *A Documentary Survey of the French Revolution*, pp. 398–401. The French declaration of war on Spain followed on 7 March 1793.
29. Hansgeorg Molitor, *Vom Untertan zum Administré* (Wiesbaden: Steiner, 1980), pp. 18–19.
30. Alfred Rambaud, *Les Français sur le Rhin (1792–1804)* (Paris: Perrin, 1891), p. 267.
31. For the hesitations see Simon Schama, *Patriots and Liberators: Revolution in the Netherlands 1780–1813* (London: Collins, 1977), pp. 174–5.
32. Ibid. pp. 188–91.
33. Quoted in ibid. p. 201.
34. Molitor, *Vom Untertan zum Administré*, p. 27.
35. The hesitation lay in the fact that these territories formed part of the Holy Roman Empire whose integrity the Prussian king was reluctant to openly violate. Molitor, *Vom Untertan zum Administré*, p. 28. According to the Prussian king, publication of such an agreement would be pointless and would undermine confidence in him by his fellow members of the Empire. Joseph Hansen (ed.), *Quellen zur Geschichte des Rheinlandes im Zeitalter der Französischen Revolution 1780–1801*, vol. 3 (Bonn: Hanstein, 1935), pp. 472–3.
36. M. R. Thielemans, 'Deux institutions centrales sous le régime français en Belgique', *Revue Belge de philologie et d'histoire*, 44 (1966), 518–28.
37. For the details of the manoeuvring see Raymond Guyot, *Le Directoire et la paix de l'Europe* (Paris: Alcan, 1911), pp. 356–64.
38. Ibid. pp. 366–7.
39. Driault, *Napoléon en Italie*, p. 26.
40. Blanning, *The French Revolutionary Wars*, p. 178.
41. The debate leading to the model of the sister republics had begun in relation to Belgium: Sophie Wahnich, 'Les républiques-soeurs, débat théorique et réalité historique, conquêtes et reconquêtes d'identité républicaine', *Annales historique de la Révolution française*, no. 296 (1994), 165–77.
42. Filberto Agostini, 'L'installation des municipalités républicaines et des gouvernements centraux dans la Terre Ferme vénitienne (1797)', *Annales historique de la Révolution française*, no. 313 (1998), 567–92.
43. Driault, *Napoléon en Italie*, p. 57.
44. Alexander Grab, *Napoleon and the Transformation of Europe* (Houndmills: Palgrave Macmillan, 2003), pp. 114–15.
45. Blanning, *The French Revolutionary Wars*, p. 226.
46. Schroeder, *The Transformation of European Politics*, pp. 213–16. According to Schroeder the prospect of French domination of Europe

emerged only after the settlements at Lunéville and Amiens, p. 213.
47. Charles J. Esdaille, *The Wars of Napoleon* (London: Longman, 1995), p. 22.
48. E. Chevalley, *Essai sur la droit des gens napoléonien* (Paris: Delagrave, 1912), p. 30.
49. Esdaille, *The Wars of Napoleon*, p. 24; Schroeder, *The Transformation of European Politics*, p. 264.
50. See Esdaille: 'beset by popular resistance, the operations of Spanish and Anglo-Portuguese regular armies, the intransigence of military commanders whom Napoleon purposely allowed to operate outside Joseph's authority, and growing bankruptcy, the administration of *el rey intruso* was reduced to impotent irrelevance. In consequence, Spain is perhaps better regarded as an occupied territory rather than a satellite', *The Wars of Napoleon*, p. 73. See also Stuart Woolf's reference to Napoleon's 'ultimate inability to find a definitive solution to the mechanics of occupation', and to Spain as the 'simplified, exasperated and appropriately belligerent means of resolving the issue', *Napoleon's Integration of Europe*, p. 53.
51. On the dispute see Blanning, *The Origins of the French Revolutionary Wars*, pp. 61–2, 79.
52. *Archives parlementaires*, 15 (1883), 510–11, 515–19.
53. Ibid. p. 609.
54. Ibid. p. 667.
55. Stewart (ed.), *A Documentary Survey of the French Revolution*, p. 260.
56. Blanning, *The Origins of the French Revolutionary Wars*, p. 75; Albert Sorel, *L'Europe et la Révolution Française*, vol. 2 (Paris: Plon, 1887), pp. 195–203, 293–4.
57. Quoted by Jules Basdevant, *La revolution française et la droit de la guerre continentale* (Paris: Larose and Forcel, 1901), p. 191.
58. *Archives parlementaires*, 52 (1897), 189.
59. Ibid. pp. 180, 191.
60. Ibid. p. 190.
61. Ibid. pp. 653–4.
62. *Archives parlementaires*, 53 (1898), 146–7.
63. Stewart (ed.), *A Documentary Survey of the French Revolution*, p. 381. For Custine's request see Joseph Hansen (ed.), *Quellen zur Geschichte des Rheinlandes im Zeitalter der Französischen Revolution 1780–1801*, vol. 2 (Bonn: Hanstein, 1933), pp. 601–2.
64. Franz Dumont, *Die Mainzer Republik von 1792/93* (Alzey: RDW, 1982), p. 93.
65. *Archives parlementaires*, 55 (1899), 71.
66. Stewart (ed.), *A Documentary Survey of the French Revolution*,

p. 382.
67. Ibid. p. 382.
68. Ibid. p. 383.
69. *Archives parlementaires*, 55 (1899), 74. The record notes that the protest against the violation of sovereignty was made 'with fervency'.
70. Hansen (ed.), *Quellen zur Geschichte des Rheinlandes*, vol. 2, p. 821.
71. Ibid. pp. 820–1.
72. Stewart (ed.), *A Documentary Survey of the French Revolution*, p. 468.
73. F.-A. Aulard (ed.) *Recueil des actes du Comité de Salut Public*, vol. 3 (1890), pp. 536–7.
74. F.-A. Aulard (ed.) *Recueil des actes du Comité de Salut Public*, vol. 4 (1891), pp. 25–7. Their powers would be continually expanded until the fall of Robespierre on 27 July 1794, Molitor, *Vom Untertan zum Administré*, p. 34.
75. Hansen (ed.), *Quellen zur Geschichte des Rheinlandes*, vol. 2, pp. 904–6.
76. Ibid. p. 906.
77. F.-A. Aulard (ed.) *Recueil des actes du Comité de Salut Public*, vol. 15 (1903), p. 261.
78. A. V. Daniels (ed.), *Handbuch der für die Königl. Preuss. Rheinprovinzen verküngikten Gestetze, Verordnungnen und Regierungsbechlüsse aus der Zeit der Fremdherrschaft*, vol. 6 (Cologne: Bachem, 1841), pp. 4–5.
79. Ibid. p. 10.
80. Ibid. p. 7.
81. Dumont, *Die Mainzer Republik von 1792/93*, p. 61.
82. Quoted in T. C. W. Blanning, *Reform and Revolution in Mainz 1743–1803* (Cambridge: Cambridge University Press, 1974), p. 276.
83. Dumont, *Die Mainzer Republik von 1792/93*, p. 103.
84. Henri Pirenne, *Histoire de Belgique*, vol. 6 (Brussels: Maurice Lamertin, 1926), p. 23.
85. Dumont, *Die Mainzer Republik von 1792/93*, p. 105.
86. Hansen (ed.), *Quellen zur Geschichte des Rheinlandes*, vol. 2, p. 469.
87. Ibid. pp. 510–11.
88. As pointed out by Hansen, ibid. p. 511.
89. Ibid. pp. 469, 510.
90. *Archives parlementaires*, 53 (1898), 103.
91. Arthur Chuquet, *Jemappes et la conquête de la Belgique 1792–1793* (Paris: Chailley, 1890), p. 181.
92. As pointed out by Pirenne, *Histoire de Belgique*, p. 25.
93. As noted by Ernst Fraenkel, *Military Occupation and the Rule of Law: Occupation Government in the Rhineland, 1918–1923* (Oxford:

Oxford University Press, 1944), pp. 31–2.
94. Dumont, *Die Mainzer Republik von 1792/93*, pp. 99–101.
95. Chuquet, *Jemappes et la conquête de la Belgique*, p. 181.
96. See the case of General Moreton in Brussels whose agitation induced so much trouble he had to be replaced, ibid. pp. 215–16.
97. Ibid. pp. 185–90.
98. Ibid. pp. 190–1.
99. Pirenne, *Histoire de Belgique*, pp. 30–1; Chuquet, *Jemappes at la conquête de la Belgigue*, p. 191.
100. Hansen (ed.), *Quellen zur Geschichte des Rheinlandes*, vol. 2, pp. 569–73. For the context and implications see Blanning, *Reform and Revolution in Mainz*, pp. 279, 289–92.
101. Klaus R. Scherpe, 'Der "allgemeine Freund: Das Vaterland": Patriotismus in der Literatur der Mainzer Republik 1792/93', *Monatshefte*, 81 (1989), 19–26.
102. Dumont, *Die Mainzer Republik von 1792/93*, p. 118.
103. Dumont emphasises that administrative authority was more effective in driving forward the revolutionary programme, ibid. p. 130.
104. Chuquet, *Jemappes et la conquête de la Belgique*, p. 200.
105. Ibid. pp. 200, 203–5, 207.
106. A. D. Borgnet, *Histoire des Belges a la fin du XVIIIe siècle*, vol. 2 (Brussels: Lacroix, 1861), pp. 180–1.
107. Chuquet, *Jemappes et la conquête de la Belgique*, p. 223.
108. For the description of the Representatives as '*dictateurs ambulants*' see Chuquet, ibid. p. 229, and Pirenne, *Histoire de Belgique*, p. 38. For the remit of the national commissars see Chuquet, *Jemappes et la conquête de la Belgique*, p. 234.
109. Dumont, *Die Mainzer Republik von 1792/93*, p. 322.
110. Athur Chuquet, *Mayence (1792–1793)* (Paris: Plon, 1892), p. 161.
111. Blanning, *Reform and Revolution in Mainz*, p. 299.
112. Arthur Chuquet, *L'expedition de Custine* (Paris: Plon, 1892), p. 168.
113. On the dispute see Suzanne Tassier, *Histoire de la Belgique sous l'occupation française en 1792 et 1793* (Brussels: Falk, 1934), pp. 154–61.
114. Percy Bordwell, *The Law of War Between Belligerents* (Chicago: Callaghan, 1908), p. 114.
115. Chuquet, *Mayence*, p. 79.
116. Dumont, *Die Mainzer Republik von 1792/93*, pp. 429–35.
117. Ibid. pp. 474–5.
118. Aulard (ed.) *Recueil des actes du Comité de Salut Public*, vol. 15 (1903), p. 640.
119. Robert Devleeshouwer, 'La cas de la Belgique', in Colloque de Bruxelles (ed.), *Occupants-occupés 1792–1815* (Brussels: Universite Libre

de Bruxelles, 1968), pp. 51–2.
120. Aulard (ed.) *Recueil des actes du Comité de Salut Public*, vol. 16 (1904), pp. 549–50.
121. Ibid. p. 674.
122. M. R. Thielemans, 'Deux institutions centrales sous le régime français en Belgique', *Revue Belge de philologie et d'histoire*, 41 (1963), 1102–6.
123. Xavier Rousseaux, 'De la justice révolutionnaire à la justice républicaine: le tribunal criminal de Bruxelles (1794–1795)', in Michel Vovelle (ed.), *La Révolution et l'ordre juridique privé*, vol. 2 (Paris: Presses Universitaires de France, 1988), pp. 530–1.
124. Pirenne, *Histoire de Belgique*, p. 64.
125. Michael Rapport, 'Belgium under French occupation: between collaboration and resistance, July 1794 to October 1795', *French History*, 16 (2002), 66.
126. Ibid. p. 61.
127. Pirenne, *Histoire de Belgique*, p. 63.
128. Aulard (ed.) *Recueil des actes du Comité de Salut Public*, vol. 16 (1904), p. 276.
129. Aulard (ed.) *Recueil des actes du Comité de Salut Public*, vol. 20 (1910), p. 590.
130. Molitor, *Vom Untertan zum Administré*, points out that this is typical of regimes of occupation, p. 38.
131. A. V. Daniels (ed.), *Handbuch der für die Königl. Preuss. Rheinprovinzen verkündigten Gestetze, Verordnungen und Regierungsbechlüsse aus der Zeit der Fremdherrschaft*, vol. 7 (Cologne: Bachem, 1842), pp. 352–3.
132. Ibid. pp. 354–5.
133. Molitor, *Vom Untertan zum Administré*, p. 44.
134. Hansen (ed.), *Quellen zur Geschichte des Rheinlandes*, vol. 3, p. 583.
135. Pirenne, *Histoire de Belgique*, p. 68.
136. Sorel, *L'Europe et la Révolution Française*, vol. 4, p. 245.
137. Albert Sorel, 'L'Autriche et le Comité de Salut Public, Avril 1795', *Revue historique*, 17 (1881), 35.
138. L. Hennequin, *La justice militaire et la discipline à l'Armée du Rhin et à l'Armée de Rhin-et-Moselle (1792–1798)* (Paris: Chapelot, 1909), pp. 17–19.
139. T. C. W. Blanning, *The French Revolution in Germany: Occupation and Resistance in the Rhineland 1792–1802* (Oxford: Clarendon Press, 1983), p. 94.
140. M. R. Thielemans, 'Deux institutions centrales sous le régime français en Belgique', *Revue Belge de philologie et d'histoire*, 42 (1964), 417–18.
141. Rousseaux, 'De la justice révolutionnaire à la justice républicaine',

pp. 535, 537.
142. M. R. Thielemans, 'Deux institutions centrales sous le régime français en Belgique', *Revue Belge de philologie et d'histoire*, 42 (1964), 427.
143. Ibid. pp. 403–4.
144. Ibid. pp. 404–5.
145. Ibid. pp. 518–28.
146. Schama, *Patriots and Liberators*, p. 195.
147. Ibid. p. 188.
148. H. T. Colenbrander (ed.), *Gedenkstukken der Algemeene Geschiedenis van Nederland van 1795 tot 1840*, vol. 1 ('s-Gravenhage: Martinus Nijhoff, 1905), p. 590.
149. Ibid. p. 591.
150. Aulard (ed.), *Recueil des actes du Comité de Salut Public*, vol. 20 (1910), p. 349.
151. Colenbrander (ed.), *Gedenkstukken der Algemeene Geschiedenis van Nederland*, p. 612.
152. Ibid. p. 616.
153. Ibid. p. 606.
154. Aulard (ed.), *Recueil des actes du Comité de Salut Public*, vol. 20 (1910), p. 355.
155. Colenbrander (ed.), *Gedenkstukken der Algemeene Geschiedenis van Nederland*, p. 595.
156. Aulard (ed.), *Recueil des actes du Comité de Salut Public*, vol. 20 (1910), p. 185.
157. Ibid. p. 321.
158. Schama, *Patriots and Liberators*, p. 203.
159. Colenbrander (ed.), *Gedenkstukken der Algemeene Geschiedenis van Nederland*, p. 649.
160. Alexandre De Clercq (ed.), *Recueil des traités de la France*, vol. 1 (Paris: Pedone-Lauriel, 1880), p. 236.
161. Ibid. p. 238.
162. Ibid. p. 238. On this wider purpose see Raymond Robin, *Des occupations militaires en dehors des occupations de guerre* (Paris: Larose, 1913), pp. 75–6.
163. Clercq (ed.), *Recueil des traités de la France*, vol. 1, p. 239.
164. Ibid. p. 249.
165. Ibid. p. 264.
166. Ibid. p. 250.
167. Ibid. pp. 249–50.
168. Ibid. p. 233.
169. Schama, *Patriots and Liberators*, pp. 402–3.
170. R. R. Palmer, *The Age of the Democratic Revolution*, vol. 2 (Princeton:

Princeton University Press, 1964), pp. 272–3.
171. Paul Gaffarel, *Bonaparte et les républiques italiennes (1796–1799)* (Paris: Alcan, 1895), p. 8.
172. For his Proclamation and Decrees of 19 May 1796 see *Correspondance de Napoléon 1ᵉʳ*, vol. 1 (Paris: Plon, 1858), pp. 297–301.
173. Gaffarel, *Bonaparte et les républiques italiennes*, p. 12.
174. *Correspondance de Napoléon 1ᵉʳ*, vol. 2 (Paris: Plon, 1859), p. 50.
175. Jacques Godechot, *Les commissaires aux armées sous le Directoire*, vol. 1 (Paris: Presses Universitaires de France, 1941), pp. 371–85, and Palmer, *The Age of the Democratic Revolution*, vol. 2, pp. 300–1.
176. Godechot, *Les commissaires aux armées sous le Directoire*, vol. 1, p. 650.
177. For reassertion of the principle see Jacques Godechot, *Les commissaires aux armées sous le Directoire*, vol. 2 (Paris: Presses Universitaires de France, 1941), pp. 195–203, Guyot, *Le Directoire et la paix de l'Europe*, pp. 882–3.
178. Gaffarel, *Bonaparte et les républiques italiennes*, p. 41.
179. Ibid. pp. 45–6.
180. Quoted in Bernard Nabonne, *La diplomatie du directoire et Bonaparte: D'après les papiers inédits de Reubell* (Paris: La nouvelle edition, 1951), p. 175.
181. Leuwers, 'République et relations entre les peuples', p. 9.
182. See Agostini, 'L'installation des municipalités républicaines et des gouvernements centraux dans la Terre Ferme vénitienne (1797)', pp. 467–92.
183. Gaffarel, *Bonaparte et les républiques italiennes*, p. 159.
184. Clercq (ed.), *Recueil des traités de la France*, vol. 1, p. 301. For elaboration on these agreements see Robin , *Des occupations militaires*, pp. 93–6.
185. Clercq (ed.), *Recueil des traités de la France*, vol. 1, p. 276.
186. Ibid. p. 324.
187. Ibid. p. 351.
188. Palmer, *The Age of the Democratic Revolution*, vol. 2, pp. 320–2.
189. Gaffarel, *Bonaparte et les républiques italiennes*, p. 240.
190. Albert Dufourcq, *Le régime Jacobin en Italie: Étude sur la République Romaine 1798–1799* (Paris: Perrin, 1900), pp. 127–8.
191. Ludovic Sciout, 'Le Directoire et la République Romaine', *Revue de questions historiques*, 39 (1886), 158–61.
192. Ibid. pp. 155–6.
193. Godechot, *Les commissaires aux armées sous le Directoire*, vol. 2, pp. 18–19.
194. Gaffarel, *Bonaparte et les républiques italiennes*, p. 244.

195. Dufourcq, *Le régime Jacobin en Italie*, pp. 221–4.
196. On the occupation of Naples see Guyot, *Le Directoire et la paix de l'Europe*, pp. 886–96.
197. Eugenio di Rienzo, 'Néo-jacobinisme et question italienne à travers les manuscrits de Marc-Antoine Jullien de Paris', *Annales historiques de la Révolution française*, no. 313 (1998), 493–514.
198. Guyot, *Le Directoire et la paix de l'Europe*, pp. 660–1.
199. For his proclamation see Henry Zschokke, *The History of the Invasion of Switzerland* (London: Longman, 1803), pp. 205–6.
200. Ludovic Sciout, 'Le Directoire et la République de Berne (1797–1799)', *Revue des questions historiques*, 51 (1892), 535.
201. See Reubells comments in Emile Dunant, *Les relations diplomatiques de la France et de la République Helvétique 1798–1803* (Basel: Basler Buch- und Antiquariatshandlung, 1901), pp. 81–3.
202. Guyot, *Le Directoire et la paix de l'Europe*, pp. 762–7.
203. Hansen (ed.), *Quellen zur Geschichte des Rheinlandes*, vol. 3, pp. 1212–13.
204. Molitor, *Vom Untertan zum Administré*, pp. 50–3, Hansen (ed.), *Quellen zur Geschichte des Rheinlandes*, vol. 3, pp. 1041–3, 1170–1.
205. Wilhelm Steffens, 'Die linksrheinischen Provinzen Preussens unter französischer Herrschaft 1794–1802', *Rheinische Vierteljahrsblätter*, 19 (1954), 445–6.
206. Driault, *Napoléon en Italie*, pp. 119–20.
207. Ibid. pp. 103–4.
208. Albert Pingaud, *Bonaparte: Président de la République Italienne*, vol. 2 (Paris: Perrin, 1914), p. 139.
209. Albert Sorel, *L'Europe et la Révolution Française*, vol. 7 (Paris: Plon, 1904), p. 546.
210. Robin, *Des occupations militaires*, p. 114.
211. Manfred Peter Heimers, *Die Trikolore über München* (Munich: Buchendorfer, 2000), pp. 60–1.
212. Mathieu Dumas, *Précis des événements militaires*, vol. 9 (Paris: Treuttell, 1820), p. 392. This convention was not ratified but is indicative of understanding of occupation.
213. Ibid. p. 394.
214. Friedrich Thimme, *Die inneren Zustände des Kurfürstentums Hannover unter der französisch-westfälischen Herrschaft 1806–1813* (Hanover: Hhn'sche, 1893), p. 61.
215. Ibid. pp. 70–1, 73, 82–3.
216. Ibid. pp. 136–8.
217. Leopold von Ranke (ed.), *Denkwürdigkeiten des Staatskanzlers Fürsten von Hardenberg*, vol. 2 (Leipzig: Duncker & Humblot, 1877), p. 526.
218. Thimme, *Die inneren Zustände des Kurfürstentums Hannover*,

p. 175.
219. Ibid. p. 177.
220. Anton Pfalz, *Die Franzosen in Wien im Jahre 1805* (Vienna: Deutsch-Wagram, 1905), pp. 20–1.
221. Despréaux, *Le Maréchal Mortier*, vol. 3, p. 277.
222. Ibid. p. 292.
223. Helmut Stubbe da Luz, *Okkupanten und Okkupierte*, vol. 2 (Munich: Meidenbauer, 2005), pp. 18–19; Johann Hermann Duntze, *Geschichte der freien Stadt Bremen* (Bremen: Heyse, 1851), pp. 686–8.
224. Alfred Rambaud, *L'Allemagne sous Napoléon 1er* (Paris: Didier, 1897), pp. 188–95.
225. Katherine Aalestad, 'Paying for war: experiences of Napoleonic rule in the Hanseatic cities', *Central European History*, 39 (2006), 649–53.
226. Thimme, *Die inneren Zustände des Kurfürstentums Hannover*, p. 199.
227. Ibid. p. 377.
228. Stubbe da Luz, *Okkupanten und Okkupierte*, vol. 2, p. 77.
229. Ibid. p. 51.
230. Thimme, *Die inneren Zustände des Kurfüstentums Hannover*, p. 221.
231. Frank Bauer, *Napoleon in Berlin* (Berlin: Berlin Story Verlag, 2006), pp. 143–4.
232. Ibid. p. 103. See also Robert Ouvrard, *1809: Les Français à Vienne* (Paris: Nouveau Monde, 2009), p. 109.
233. Ibid. pp. 174–5.
234. To the disgust of the Prussian officer Ludwig von Marwitz, *Aus dem Nachlasse Friedrich August Ludwig von der Marwitz* (Berlin: Mittler, 1852), p. 192.
235. De Clercq (ed.), *Recueil des traités de la France*, vol. 2 (Paris: Pedone-Lauriel, 1880), p. 272.
236. See C. de Mazade, *Correspondance du Maréchal Davout*, vol. 3 (Paris: Plon, 1885), pp. 198–9.
237. Karl Obermann, 'La situation de la Prusse sous l'occupation française 1807–1813', in Colloque de Bruxelles (ed.), *Occupants-occupés*, pp. 281–2.
238. Marcel Handelsman, *Napoléon et la Pologne 1806–1807* (Paris: Alcan, 1909), pp. 70–6.
239. Marcel Handelsman, 'Rapport du Baron Serra sur la mission à Varsovie', *Revue des etudes napoléoniennes*, 3 (1913), 413.
240. John Stanley, 'The French Residents in the Duchy of Warsaw', *Canadian Slavonic Papers*, 27 (1985), 55.
241. Marcel Handelsman (ed.), *Instructions et dépêches des Résidents de France à Varsovie 1807–1813*, vol. 1 (Cracow: L'Academie des

Sciences de Cracovie, 1914), p. 28.
242. John Stanley, 'French attitudes toward Poland in the Napoleonic period', *Canadian Slavonic Papers*, 49 (2007), 209–27.
243. John Lawrence Tone, *The Fatal Knot* (Chapel Hill, NC: University of North Carolina Press, 1994), p. 3.
244. Vittorio Douglas, 'La guerrilla espagnole dans la guerre contre l'armée napoléonienne', *Annales historiques de la Révolution française*, no. 336 (2004), 91–4.
245. Tone, *The Fatal Knot*, p. 71.
246. For a detailed judgement see Charles Esdaille, *Fighting Napoleon: Guerrillas, Bandits and Adventurers in Spain 1808–1814* (New Haven: Yale University Press, 2004).
247. John Morgan, 'War feeding war? The impact of logistics on the Napoleonic occupation of Catalonia', *Journal of Military History*, 73 (2009), 83–93.
248. Pierre Conrad, *Napoléon et la Catalogne 1808–1814* (Paris: Alcan, 1910), pp. 113–16.
249. Ibid. pp. 124–5.
250. Ibid. pp. 191–4.
251. Marshal Suchet, *Memoirs of the War in Spain*, vol. 1 (London: Colburn, 1829), p. 40.
252. Ibid. pp. 299–300.
253. Jean Louis Reynaud, *Contre-Guerrilla en Espagne (1808–1814): Suchet pacifie l'Aragon* (Paris: Economica, 1992), pp. 111, 116–17, 121, 137–44.
254. *Correspondance de Napoléon Ier*, vol. 20, pp. 234–5.
255. Suchet, *Memoirs of the War in Spain*, vol. 1, pp. 91–5.
256. A. Du Casse (ed.), *Mémoires et correspondence politique et militaire du Roi Joseph*, vol. 8 (Paris: Perrotin, 1854), pp. 165–80, 249–50; Geoffrey de Grandmaison, *L'Espagne et Napoléon*, vol. 3 (Paris: Plon, 1931), pp. 55–60. For Napoleon's logic see *The Confidential Correspondence of Napoleon Bonaparte with his Brother Joseph*, vol. 2 (London: Murray, 1855), pp. 250–2.
257. See Robin Fabel, 'The laws of war in the 1812 conflict', *Journal of American Studies*, 14 (1980), 199–218.
258. Mori, 'The British government and the Bourbon restoration', p. 706.
259. Elisa Carrilo, 'The Corsican Kingdom of George III', *Journal of Modern History*, 34 (1962), 256–7.
260. Peter Graf von Kielmansegg, *Stein und die Zentralverwaltung 1813/14* (Stuttgart: Kohlhammer, 1964), pp. 12–14.
261. Ibid. pp. 17–23.
262. Walther Hubatsch (ed.), *Freiherr vom Stein. Briefe und amtliche Schriften*, vol. 4 (Stuttgart: Kohlhammer, 1963), p. 301.

263. Ibid. p. 347.
264. Kielmansegg, *Stein und die Zentralverwaltung*, p. 83.
265. Arthur Wellington (ed.), *Supplementary Despatches, Correspondence and Memoranda of Field Marshal Arthur Duke of Wellington*, vol. 9 (London: Murray, 1862), p. 67.
266. Kielmansegg, *Stein und die Zentralverwaltung*, p. 97.
267. See his letter of 25 January 1814 to General Wrede, Hubatsch (ed.), *Freiherr vom Stein*, vol. 4, p. 476.
268. Kielmansegg, *Stein und die Zentralverwaltung*, p. 107.
269. Jacques Hantraye, *Les cosaques aux Champs-Élysées* (Paris: Belin, 2005), pp. 23–30.
270. On the contrast see Roger André, *L'occupation de la France par les alliés en 1815* (Paris: Boccard, 1924), pp. 6–29, and Hantraye, *Les cosaques aux Champs-Élysées*, pp. 152–3.
271. John Gurwood (ed.), *The Dispatches of Field Marshal the Duke of Wellington*, vol. 12 (London: Murray 1838), p. 558.
272. André, *L'occupation de la France par les alliés en 1815*, pp. 30–43.
273. Gurwood (ed.), *The Dispatches of Field Marshal the Duke of Wellington*, vol. 12, p. 599.
274. Michael Hurst (ed.), *Key Treaties of the Great Powers 1814–1914*, vol. 1 (Newton Abbot: David & Charles, 1972), p. 132.
275. Robin, *Des occupations militaires*, p. 152–3.
276. Thomas Veve, *The Duke of Wellington and the British Army of Occupation in France, 1815–1818* (Westport, CT: Greenwood, 1992), pp. 150–1.
277. Philippe-Antoine Merlin, *Recueil alphabétique de questions de droit*, vol 7 (Brussels: Tarlier, 1828), p. 42. On the details of the case see Conrad, *Napoléon et la Catalogne*, pp. 389–403.
278. Merlin, *Recueil alphabétique de questions de droit*, vol. 7, p. 42.
279. As noted above Napoleon made this point to Joachim Murat when Murat was King of Naples. See also the same point in Napoleon's proclamation of his brother Louis as King of Holland, *Correspondance de Napoléon 1er*, vol. 12 (Paris: Plon, 1858), p. 434.
280. *Recueil général des lois et des arrêts*, vol. 4 (1812–14), 90.
281. *Recueil général des lois et des arrêts*, vol. 18, part 1 (1818), 179.
282. *Recueil général des lois et des arrêts*, vol. 41, part 1 (1841), 507–9.

Chapter 2
European Occupations before 1870

Occupation and the Concert of Europe

Just as the turmoil of the Revolutionary and Napoleonic Wars had set the framework for the emergence of the concept of military occupation, so too the European settlement embodied in the Vienna Conference and the arrangements for its perpetuation set the framework for the development of the concept and practice of military occupation in Europe and to some extent beyond it. The Vienna Conference and associated alliance system not only provided for a specific territorial settlement which the negotiators intended should endure but also committed the Great Powers, as they were now recognised, to the management of that settlement through the periodic coordination of those Great Powers.[1] Initially that promise of coordination had been tied up with a commitment to the defeat of France, in the Treaty of Chaumont of March 1814. The later Quadruple Alliance of 20 November 1815 reaffirmed their will to oppose the 'Revolutionary Principles which upheld the last criminal usurpation', namely the 100 days of Napoleon Bonaparte, and 'might again, under other forms, convulse France'.[2] Yet France had regained admission to the club of the Great Powers during the Conference at Vienna, membership that was explicitly reaffirmed after Napoleon's final defeat at the time that the Allies agreed upon the early termination of the occupation of French territory, at the Conference of Aix-la-Chapelle in 1818. A British memorandum, invoking and summarising these various agreements concluded that they 'may be considered as the great Charte, by which the Territorial System of Europe, unhinged by the events of war and Revolution, has been again restored to order'.[3]

While far from entailing any principled renunciation of conquest, as the revolutionary principles of the French once had, the practical effect of these arrangements was to create a considerable predisposition against territorial change and especially territorial change by conquest entailing an immediate displacement of sovereignty. The consequence was that whereas before 1815 it was fundamental disagreement about the territorial settlement of Europe that shaped the emergence of the concept and practice of occupation, after 1815 it was the, albeit fragile, agreement about the territorial settlement that provided the framework for occupation.[4] As a matter of principle, flowing from the commitment to the territorial settlement, and diplomatic practice, and flowing from the coordination and management of the system by the Great Powers, the presence of troops, especially Great Power troops, on foreign territory could not readily and openly be justified in the language of conquest but it could be justified in the language of occupation.

This logic, of course, would last only so long as the Concert of Europe, that is the concert of the Great Powers, lasted. The longevity of the Concert of Europe as well as its basic nature, the extent to which it was held together by some normative commitment, and if so, what commitment, whether it was built upon a balance of power or a form of hegemony, have all been strongly disputed.[5] The record of occupation, as will be shown below, tends to suggest that the accounts placing more emphasis upon some form of shared understanding between the Great Powers are more useful in understanding the dynamics of occupation. Indeed one might suggest that whereas it was the great battles of the Revolutionary and Napoleonic Wars that shaped the cartography of occupation before 1815, in the wake of the Vienna settlement it was diplomatic conferences, and the constraints they imposed, that shaped the location and to some extent the duration of occupation. This reflected not only the desire to conserve the existing order, most notably associated with Prince Metternich, but also the desire to manage change, evident in the arguments of Louis Napoleon of France. France, he acknowledged, 'had always shown an inclination to murmur at the arrangements' embodied in the treaties of 1815. Others frequently suspected France of being intent upon their wholesale repudiation. Yet, Louis Napoleon expressed a willingness, indeed a desire, as a 'member of the great European Family' to cooperate, on the basis of these 'arrangements', with a view to their 'modification in connexion with the necessities of the existing generation'.[6]

The longevity of the Concert has proven as uncertain as the principles and mechanisms underlying it. For Louis Napoleon it clearly outlived the system of congresses that arose directly out of the treaties of 1814–15. At its maximum extent it is held that it 'operated intermittently across the better part of a century'.[7] Many accounts argue if not for the demise then at least the fundamental weakening of the Concert by the Crimean War, pitting, as it did, the Great Powers directly against each other for the first time since 1815. The significance of the Crimean War for the story of occupation, however, is less dramatic, for it entailed only minimal occupation of the territory of a Great Power. In that respect the occupation of Austrian territory in the war of 1866 was more significant, and reflective of the wars associated with national unification that were a fundamental challenge to the Vienna order. That war pointed forward to the much more dramatic Franco-German War of 1870–1, with its more substantial, protracted and traumatic occupation of the territory of a Great Power. It had been possible, if somewhat naive perhaps, to underestimate the significance of the Crimean War, to set it aside as another outbreak of the intractable Eastern Question. It was not as easy to underestimate the Franco-Prussian War.[8]

If the intervening period was that of the most effective operation of the European Concert, it was still a period in which its operation was intermittent. When Louis Napoleon expressed his desire for cooperation he was speaking in relation to the crisis in Rome and the Papal States arising from the revolutionary movements of 1848–9 and cooperation in relation to Rome was not forthcoming. Crisis was a recurrent feature of the period, from the faltering of re-established states in the immediate aftermath of 1815, through the revolutionary outbursts of 1830 and 1848, responses to which sometimes overlapped with the crises in the decaying Ottoman Empire. In the case of the latter, while the European powers were less solicitous of the rights of the Ottoman Empire, their mutual suspicions sufficed to exert significant restraint upon their actions.

These crises have been portrayed in terms of a conflict between 'reform', or in other accounts 'liberation' or 'revolution' and reaction, with the emphasis either upon the revolutionary or the reactionary, or as a struggle between the two.[9] It is argued, more widely, that such characterisations mislead more than they enlighten.[10] In the specific context of military occupation it is so for two specific reasons. First, as Paul Schroeder has argued,

The distinguishing characteristic of the post-Vienna era was not the zeal, rigour and united will with which conservative governments stamped out popular risings. It was instead the lax, inefficient nature of many regimes and the inhibition which almost all monarchs of this era felt about using force against their own citizens or other countries, which constantly permitted risings and conspiracies, often derived from a slender base both in power and popular support, to occur and sometimes let them succeed.[11]

By the same token, such risings then tempted external governments to either support the feeble, but partly successful rising or to support the feeble government against it. In either event, the external power could find itself in the position of an occupant. The second reason for reservation about the utility of a contest between reaction and revolution is that the record of military occupation too frequently reveals the way that a combination of the constraints of the Great Power Concert and the usually unanticipated deficiencies of would-be revolutionaries and governments confounded such simple dichotomies in the eyes of the occupants themselves. The dichotomy does retain some utility but primarily in terms of whether or not the occupant intended to aid the establishment of a new government or to prop up an existing one.

Terminologically and to some extent conceptually, the phenomenon of occupation was now firmly on the agenda, occurring with a frequency and consistency not evident earlier. Yet, 'occupation' was neither the great novelty of the era nor did it receive the most sustained discussion. That honour was reserved for the related but not synonymous term of intervention. That same preference persists in the current historiography of the twenty-first century as historians look back for the precedents of the humanitarian intervention of the late twentieth and early twenty-first centuries.[12] Its prominence as a term with the specific significance of 'interference in the internal disputes of a single state' coincides with the opening years of the Concert of Europe.[13] According to P. H. Winfield, '"intervention" did not become a technical phrase till the dozen or so years bounded by 1817–1830'.[14] Once introduced in this sense it acquired sustained attention, figuring more prominently in the major international law texts than the term occupation. In Robert Phillimore's *Commentaries upon International Law*, for example, intervention received a distinct chapter whereas occupation appeared under the heading of limitations on the doctrine of postliminium.[15] Moreover, occupation as a term was defined by its contrast with conquest, not in relation to intervention, despite the fact that the term occupation was used when discussing specific interventions.[16] The rationale for the primary definition of occupation in terms of the contrast between conquest and occupation lay not only in the provenance of the very distinction but also in the continuing proximity of occupation and conquest. Interventions could easily, so it was feared, turn into conquests by the intervening power, inviting then the reference to occupation in order to warn against the unwanted conquest. It was precisely such considerations that also led to the imposition of the constraints of occupation beyond Europe, in relation to both the non-European territories of the Ottoman Empire and the New World.

It does not follow from this, however, that, as some have supposed, the practices of intervention were held to be distinct from the practices of warfare.[17] It is true that a specific intervention could be held to not entail a state of war in order to avoid invoking all of the reciprocal rights of war, or that an intervention could be declared to entail a state of war in order to assert some of the recognised rights of war, or that intervention without formal declaration of war would be accepted as limiting the rights of a state.[18] Yet war and intervention were not discrete categories. Intervention could readily be recognised as, at the least, 'armed interventions' where armed intervention 'is virtually a *war*'.[19] All of these options, of intervention that was not formal war, or could become formal war, or was virtually a war, were variations upon the theme of 'imperfect wars', which were well known to the period.[20] Imperfect wars, like occupation, which they sometimes entailed, simply lacked the degree of formalised regulation of perfect wars.

That the fuller discussion of intervention would not bring much greater clarification in respect of the occupations that intervention sometimes entailed arose in part quite simply because arguments about intervention were largely arguments about *jus ad bellum* not the *jus in bello* of which occupation forms a part. There is a second and more significant reason for the failure of discussion of intervention to lead to any greater clarity, let alone formal regulation of the business of occupation. That can be found in the dispute in the early Congress system between the members of the Holy Alliance and the British, notably Foreign Minister Castlereagh. Although the Holy Alliance of September 1815 resulting from the initiatives of the tsar was treated with some scepticism even by its other members, it did lead to the enunciation of an important principle, embodied in the preliminary protocol of the Congress of Troppau, according to which, states

> which have undergone a change, due to revolution, in the form of their constitution (*regime intérieur*) and the results of which menace other states, *ipso facto* cease to be part of European Alliance, and remain excluded from it, until their situation gives guarantees of legal order and stability ... The Allied Powers do not limit themselves to announcing this exclusion, but ... will employ, in order to bring them back to the bosom of the Alliance, first friendly representations, secondly measures of coercion, if the employment of such coercion is indispensable.[21]

Against this declaration Castlereagh replied, in the shape of a Circular Dispatch of 19 January 1821, that

> no Government could be more prepared than the British Government is, to uphold the right of any State or States to interfere, where their own immediate security or essential interests are seriously endangered by the internal transactions of another state. But ... they regard the assumption of such a right only to be justified by the strongest necessity ... but they at the same time consider that exceptions of this description never can, without the utmost danger, be so reduced to rule, as to be incorporated into the ordinary diplomacy of States, or into the institutes of the Law of Nations.[22]

Though often invoked as the articulation of the principle of non-intervention, Castlereagh's circular was explicitly not such a principle. He opposed only the formal regulation of intervention, that is, the least step towards its codification, showing some hesitancy about the desirability of any multilateral dimension to intervention when it did occur.

Revolt and Occupation

These principles were formulated in response to the crises which confronted the Congress system at the beginning of the 1820s. Revolt broke out first in Spain in March 1820, then in July in Naples and in Piedmont in July 1821. In all three cases weak and vacillating monarchs made concessions to the inchoate opposition, adopting the 1812 constitution in the case of Spain, which was subsequently adopted as a model in Naples. Piedmont's king abdicated rather than proclaim the Spanish constitution, leaving that task to his son, who was implicated in the revolt.[23] In all three cases the monarchs appealed for external intervention, in the case of the kings of Spain and Naples while feigning loyalty to the constitutions they had been compelled to adopt.[24] Austria, the power with the strongest interest in Italy, preferred to avert intervention in Spain, and later to keep the Greek revolt which broke out in March 1821 off the agenda, while intervening unilaterally in Naples. France and above all Russia, however, forced Austria's Prince Metternich to accept a European Congress which opened at Troppau in October 1820. It was here, as a concession to Russia, that Metternich agreed to the Preliminary Protocol in exchange for support for Austrian intervention which was subsequently authorised at Laibach. The outcome was that Austrian forces entered Naples with a multilateral sanction and under the designation as the Allied forces in February 1821 and with a proclamation from the King of Naples depicting the Austrians as 'a force acting only for the true interests of our Kingdom'.[25]

Ironically, the Austrians had feared that the Neapolitan king would not be firm enough in suppressing the remnants of the revolt. The king and his supporters proved in fact to be all too vigorous in exacting revenge upon their opponents. The Austrians, while imprisoning so many people that special magistrates had to be appointed to try them, were repulsed by some of the more archaic forms of punishment imposed by the Neapolitans under the Austrian occupation regime.[26] Both the Austrians and the Neapolitans blamed the other for the excesses.[27] Austrian control was substantial: the Austrian army was the only force in the land; and the police were in the hands of the Austrians, headed by an Austrian general.[28] From May 1821 through to April 1822 an Allied committee headed by the Austrian special envoy sat in Naples overseeing everything from amnesties through to the reorganisation of the army.[29] Yet, for months the Austrians and their allies had not been able to persuade the King of Naples, whose kingdom they had saved by their occupation, to return to his own country or even to cooperate in passing off Austrian designs as those of the king and his ministers.[30] It was possible to put an end to the worst of the disorder by September but extracting themselves from the occupation and leaving behind a functioning government did not prove easy. A Convention of October 1821 provided for another three years of occupation, with a further extension by a Convention of September 1824 prolonging the final evacuation of Austrian forces until 1826. All this had been at disastrous cost to Naples, from which Metternich was under domestic pressure to recover the full costs of occupation. The king meanwhile was caught between his opposition to the costs of the occupation and his fear of being left alone with his subjects.[31]

The situation in Piedmont was nowhere near as parlous as Naples though the king also proved reluctant to return until vengeance had been exacted, despite Austrian warnings that this weakened his own authority. Despite his dependence upon the Austrians, King Charles Felix allowed his agents to cast aspersions on Austrian motives, exploiting popular animosity towards them.[32] It is notable that the Convention of July 1821 providing for some 12,000 Austrian occupation troops was more restrictive and less burdensome than its later Neapolitan equivalent. According to this Convention there was to be no interference in the civil or military jurisdiction of the country, no reinforcements without the agreement of the king and the costs of the occupation force were shared between Piedmont and Austria.[33] Nevertheless, greater confidence did not extend to willingness to do entirely without the Austrians by the initial deadline of September 1822, with a further extension of the occupation until September 1823.[34] Austria's exaggerated fear of revolution, compounded by the pusillanimity, vengefulness and unwillingness to reform even in the moderate direction favoured by the Allied powers, combined to make these occupations more difficult than anticipated. But that it was to be a matter of occupation not conquest was not in question: the general commitments of the Vienna system and the watchfulness of the Allies ensured that it would be a matter of occupation.

Concerns in relation to Spain were different. Metternich was anxious to prevent any intervention at all while preserving the facade of Allied unity. The tsar periodically favoured genuine multilateral action with Russia at the head of an intervention force. England favoured no intervention and believed itself cruelly deceived at the last moment by a newly appointed French Foreign Minister Chateaubriand, while France sought to maximise its own freedom of action.[35] Pressure for some response increased as royalists in the north proclaimed a regency and called for intervention to free the king from the control of the liberal constitutionalists while the king himself had directly appealed to the tsar in April 1822. Finally the French king declared war and announced a French invasion, promising that the war would end once the king was free and could give his people institutions which would bring them peace.[36] Herein lay part of the problem: the French had no precise idea of what they wanted beyond the idea of rescuing the king, the necessity of some reform and of an amnesty as part of a process of reconciliation. Chateuabriand misguidedly believed that the Spanish king would willingly modify the Spanish constitution.[37] It was more indicative of the reality of Spanish attitudes that while the French commander, the duc d'Angoulême, wrote to the Spanish king urging an amnesty, the royalist junta in the north issued a proclamation ordering the arrest and trial of anyone directly or indirectly involved in supporting the constitutional system.[38] Although the French had evaded any formal multilateral supervision, the duc d'Angoulême was effectively constrained by the conferences of the Russian, Prussian and Austrian ambassadors, who insisted that France abide by its own commitment to enforce nothing on the Spanish and only to set the king at liberty. Lurking behind this supervision was the suspicion that the French, though under a monarchical government, were too infected with liberal principles and would make common cause with the constitutionalists. Indeed, d'Angoulême did believe in the necessity of more liberal reforms but was inhibited both by the conference of ambassadors, to whom the Spanish royalist factions complained at every step, and his own government in Paris.[39] Managing the Spanish factions put d'Angoulême at odds with his own civil commissioner, Martignac, who had been appointed especially for this purpose of dealing with the royalist factions.[40] It was consistent with such constraints that once he reached Madrid, instead of nominating a regency government himself, as he had wished, d'Angoulême felt constrained to act through existing institutions, turning to the Council of the Indies and the Council of Castille to nominate one for him, though both of these bodies lacked confidence in their own authority.[41]

It was not only in matters of high politics that the French were constrained. Royalists sought revenge on their political opponents, including those taken prisoner during the French invasion. General Alphonse d'Hautpoul recalled that he had been able to protect his prisoners from the 'popular fury' only with difficulty, while another commander had resorted to confining his prisoners in a church in the hope of saving their lives.[42] French forces found themselves escorting the generals of the constitutionalist army, the very men they had come to defeat, to the French frontier in order that they might seek refuge.

In many places, however, the French were numerically too weak to prevent arbitrary arrests and the pillaging of the houses of constitutionalists.[43] Frustrated with the vengefulness and arbitrariness of the restored Spanish authorities and mob violence, d'Angoulême issued the Ordinance of Andujar of 8 August 1823 forbidding any further arrests by Spanish authorities without authorisation by French commanders, ordering the setting free of political detainees, prescribing the arrest of Spanish officials contravening these orders and submitting Spanish newspapers to French censorship.[44] The reaction was immediate. The Spanish regency threatened to resign and protested to the ambassadors. Spanish forces that had aided the French now proclaimed that they would not tolerate being governed by a 'foreign military authority'.[45] D'Anougoulême was forced to back down.[46]

The eventual liberation of King Ferdinand VII at the end of September brought no relief from these tensions as the king promptly violated his promise of safety for the participants in the revolution. Unable to exert direct authority to consistently block the royalist excesses, the French could only exercise indirect pressure or utilise local superiority to contain the more arbitrary excesses. The underlying weakness of the French was evident in the negotiations surrounding the Convention that would prolong the occupation with the formal agreement of the Spanish. Here, in December 1923, Foreign Minister Chateaubriand wrote to the French ambassador that 'the only sure means we have of influencing the king and the Spanish government is to fix a very short occupation and constantly threaten to withdraw'.[47] Nevertheless, the Convention of 9 February 1824, an unusually detailed and extensive text of its kind, provided extensive authority for the French force of occupation. Not only were French personnel subject exclusively to French judicial authority, but the French gendarmerie, by article 5, had authority over French camps, neighbouring areas and miscellaneous lines of communication.[48] The scheduled brevity of the occupation, however, provided limited leverage. The difficulty of withdrawing in view of the fragility of the Spanish government was compounded by British intervention in Portugal, itself prolonged by Spanish support for Portuguese insurgents. Eventually, French troops departed in November 1828, three and a half years after the initial date of withdrawal of July 1824.[49] The intervention and occupation were officially celebrated as great triumphs. France had returned to the world stage in a military role. The occupation could even be later cited as a 'successful' intervention, in explicit contrast to 1808, in favour of a further French intervention in Spain, albeit one that did not take place.[50] That reputation required ignoring the frustrations and bitter disappointments of the occupants.

At the beginning of the revolts that led to occupations in Italy and the Iberian peninsula the British Foreign Minister Castlereagh had warned Tsar Alexander against the problems of occupation, or at least military occupation in the 'Turkish State', by which he meant the Greek areas of the Ottoman Empire, then in revolt, where, Castlereagh pleaded,

> Your Imperial Majesty . . . must wait for the moment of returning reason and reflection, unless you are prepared, Sire, to charge yourself with the perils and burthens of a military occupation, to be effectuated not amongst a Christian and tractable, but amongst a bigoted, revengeful, and uncivilized population.[51]

Although Castlereagh conceded that the atrocities being committed there warranted concern, his prime interest, and that of succeeding British governments, was to restrain Russian advances in the eastern Mediterranean. Humanitarian concerns, outrage at the 'massacres', 'atrocities', 'horrors' and 'war of extermination' invoked in the context of the Ottoman suppression of the Greek revolt played an increasing role in influencing the minds, and even more the rhetoric, of political leaders.[52] It was, however, the competing interests, their mutual suspicions, which often went further than their interests, and the interlocking of multiple crises that served to exert constraints upon the deployment of military occupation as a strategy. That was particularly clear in the case of Greece. The Great Powers had moved towards intervention with the 1827 Treaty of London and its commitment to indeterminate 'ulterior means' if necessary to bring about Greek autonomy. By the time, in July 1828, they agreed to the deployment of a French occupation force to ensure the removal from Morea, and only from that part of Greece, of Ottoman forces, Russia, ostensibly to exert pressure on the Ottomans in respect of Greece, had declared war on Turkey, in April 1828, preparing the way for Russian occupation of the Danubian Principalities.[53] Although the troops in question in Greece were purely French the Protocol authorising their operations specified that they were to act 'in the name of the three Courts and in the common interest'.[54] The purpose of the French occupation force had largely been conceded by Ottoman forces even before it disembarked in August. Plans of its commander, General Maison, to deploy his forces to expel Ottoman forces from other areas of Greece were explicitly rejected by both Britain and Russia.[55]

In the absence of any serious military purpose and given the parlous condition of the country, the French troops, as the historian George Finlay put it, 'transformed themselves into an army of pioneers'.[56] This was indeed to become a common experience of occupying forces in the nineteenth century. So too were the failure to withdraw once the initial purpose had been achieved, increasing animosity between the occupying force and parts at least of the indigenous population, and the insufficiency of the force available for wider purposes. As early as November 1828 the main force departed, leaving a much smaller force of little over 5,000 men. The Protocol authorising this merely conceded that a force could be retained if France judged it necessary. The occupying troops had not in fact been popular, and were even less so once it became clear they would not aid in the wider liberation of Greece.[57] The French were sufficiently concerned to hand over certain fortifications to the Greeks in order to demonstrate their lack of self-interest and to fend off suspicions fuelled, they thought, by Russian agents.[58] They could do little, though, to stop the slide into civil war. The small number of men, concentrated in a few places, could exert little influence on wider Greek society.[59] Following the assassination of the first President of Greece, Capodistrias, in 1831, the country slid towards anarchy. The new government appealed for French aid against its opponents. The London Conference of 7 March 1832 called on the French military commanders to 'interpose' themselves between the contending parties and impose a cessation of hostilities.[60] Where they did intervene it was with the effect of making those they aided appear as instruments of the French.[61] Animosity between the French troops and some of the Greek forces was now so great that in January 1833, towards the end of the occupation, conflict between the two sides left several hundred dead in the capital.[62] As an occupying force the French contingent had never been large enough or given a wide enough remit to do more than intervene episodically and with limited effect while the London Conference worked its way slowly to selecting a monarch for Greece, whose arrival was the signal for the departure of the French.

The French were arguably more successful in Belgium while they were struggling to extract themselves from Greece. Greater success, however, signified in large part merely that much less was expected of them and they did not need to rely on the Christian tractability of the Belgian population. Indeed French interventions in Belgium in 1831 and again in 1832 seemed in retrospect to be little more than 'simple military expeditions' entailing no practical displacement of the existing authorities.[63] That was true. Yet these interventions were significant for their wider importance for the order established at Vienna and for the legal complications connected with some of them. Both considerations arose from developments occasioned by a revolt in Brussels against the Dutch monarch, beginning in August 1830 following the July overthrow of the Bourbon monarchy in Paris. Although the Belgians proclaimed their independence in October, some Belgians speculated on the possibility of reunion with France, while there were calls for annexation in the French Chamber of Deputies and British Foreign Minister Palmerston was convinced the French thought only of recovering the frontier lost in 1815.[64] In fact the new French government recognised the futility of such schemes and worked through the London Conference to sanction the independence of the Belgian lands. As the newly designated King of Belgium took his oath, however, the Dutch invaded, prompting a swift French countermove. Initially the new Belgian king asked that France suspend its action: his foreign minister had drawn attention to article 121 of the Belgian constitution prohibiting occupation of Belgian territory save in accordance with the provisions of a law.[65] Faced with the dilemma of violating the constitution of the county of which he had just assumed the throne or losing the country, the king allowed the Belgian army to confront the Dutch alone, then invoked dire necessity as the Belgian army recoiled in disarray and appealed for the French to advance. The Dutch were ousted with little effort but though the French were then willing to withdraw the Belgian king called for French forces to remain to protect his defenceless kingdom. The British, less charitably, thought the Belgians were keen to retain the French army in order to extort better terms from the Dutch.[66] French withdrawal was eventually secured, only for them to return, this time under the provisions of a Convention, to enforce Dutch relinquishment of the citadel of Anvers in accordance with the decision of the Great Powers.[67] French occupation of Belgium was one of several occupations associated with the unrest sparked off by the July events in France. In central Italy, Austrian occupation suppressed revolt and the French occupied Anconna as a counterweight to Austrian moves, while the Papacy, the sovereign of Anconna, sought to constrain French occupation by, amongst other things, insisting in a Convention that the French military be under the command of the French ambassador or a political agent.[68]

Russian Occupation of the Danubian Principalities

There was much less prospect of imposing restraint in the Danubian Principalities that Russia occupied in 1828 in the course of its war with Turkey and continued to occupy under the Treaty of Adrianople of 14 September 1829. Provisions of that treaty included occupation of the Principalities and of Bulgarian territory as guarantee of the payment of an indemnity. It was obvious, however, that the Ottoman Empire was not capable of raising the sums specified, fuelling the suspicion that Russia, which already enjoyed some authority over the Principalities in its role as a protective power, was in fact intent on annexing them.[69] Suspicion of Russian motives would endure in fact throughout the occupation, with Britain's Palmerston still believing in 1834 that Russia was intent on the dismemberment of the Ottoman Empire and the annexation of the occupied territories.[70] Annexation was indeed favoured by at least two of the Russian generals who headed the civil administration of the Principalities, who also argued for prolonged occupation in the hope that this would amount to a *de facto* annexation to which the other powers would become accustomed.[71] That this was the Russian intent and that Russia would not retreat after a prolonged occupation was also mistakenly believed by the Austrian Chancellor Metternich.[72] Yet at the beginning of the occupation the Russian chancellor had written that it was preferable to forego annexation, for then they could do what they wanted with the Principalities without having to come to an arrangement with Austria.[73] That was consistent with article 11 of the Treaty of Adrianople which stated that 'until the complete evacuation' the Ottoman government could have no impact on the 'administration or order of things' or the 'influence of the Imperial Court'.[74] Whether or not they preferred annexation, the Russians shared the ambition to shape the country in such a way that it might serve as a base for future military operations against the Ottoman Empire and that it should be brought closer to Russia and weaned away from Turkish culture and influence, and weaned away from economic dependence on Austria.[75]

In the early phases of the occupation under Count Pahlen and General Zheltuken Russian influence was distorted by the need to levy requisitions for the substantial Russian army, a need that was aggravated by Pahlen's resort to the *ispravniki*, the unpopular and notoriously corrupt tax collectors, and by Zheltuken's aggressive manner and frequent resort to insult. The major reforming impulse came, however, under the rule of General Kiselev. Kiselev took care to ensure that he enjoyed not only civil authority but also military authority, retaining his military functions at the same time, though this did not prevent a clash between Kiselev and his military superior General Diebitsch over non-military matters.[76] Kiselev worked not only on a new constitution, the *Règlement Organique*, but also on wider ranging socio-economic reform intended to win over the peasantry to the Russian cause and weaken the power of the indigenous elite, the boyars, and their attachment to what he saw as Turkish culture.[77] He also embarked on the introduction of systematic statistical analyses and urban reconstruction, including the building of Bucharest's first theatre, as part of a wider process of enlightened modernisation.[78] Especially in relation to the introduction of representative institutions, the irony of their promotion by the armed forces of an autocratic state did not go unnoticed. As the British consul put it:

> The Russian officers here have been not a little scandalised at the apparent predilection shown by the government of St Petersburg towards the Wallachians (in general despised by them) who are to a certain degree assimilated with nations enjoying a constitutional and representative government, while themselves and their countrymen continue to be ruled by an administration of a different character.[79]

Although Kiselev's reforms were clearly intended to serve Russian interests they were also motivated by a concern to promote the interests of the peasantry and to at least mitigate their exploitation by the predatory boyars and hospodars, the governors of the provinces. The Moldavian boyars, 'assuredly the most turbulent intriguers' as Kiselev put it, proved the most problematic.[80] Opposition from the boyars was significant enough for Kiselev to deliberately push through his reform programme prior to the formation of governments drawn from indigenous circles. Yet opposition was not restricted to the boyars. The introduction of a compulsory militia, intended to be the basis of an army and ally of Russia, provoked more than one revolt. Ultimately, despite the extensive powers and influence that Russia enjoyed as a protective power after the occupation and despite the power exercised during the occupation by the 'the enlightened representative of a repressive power', the efficacy of the reforms was far from certain.[81] The Russian officer Liprandi was sceptical:

> In a word, there, where not one class has matured sufficiently to accept any European institution whatsoever, even those of the most salutary of design ... in this land ... it is almost impossible, without exceptional effort, to introduce such institutions and even more difficult to implant them securely for ever. Does not Greece, which has received the constitution of the educated Swiss, serve as an example of this?[82]

This was a lament which many other occupants echoed in the nineteenth century, both in relation to those they regarded as non-European and those who were most definitely European.

The Revolutions of 1848

Rome and the Papal States of central Italy were unequivocally European but not notably more tractable for an occupant, especially one less clear about its ambitions than the Russians had been in the Danubian Principalities. Several powers were drawn to a strategy of occupation as a result of the upheavals of 1848, which affected the major intervening states dramatically as well. Louis Napoleon, still struggling to secure his political hold on France, had preferred a collective response to the crisis provoked by revolution in Rome and the rejection of the Pope's temporal authority by the Roman republicans in February 1849.[83] Unable to secure collective action, Louis Napoleon reluctantly moved towards intervention and occupation, though France then became wary of proposals for common action, preferring loose coordination between the French and the Austrians, Spanish and Neapolitans, all of whom occupied papal territory in varying degrees.[84] The assumptions on which the French occupation was based were similar to and at least as ill-founded, vague and inconsistent as those underlying the French intervention in Spain in 1823. This time the inconsistency was even more striking, for French policy was presided over by a president who presented himself as the defender of nationalities, a Voltairian President of the Council, a Foreign Minister, Alexis de Tocqueville, who was opposed to the temporal power of the Pope and a republican French Assembly, yet French policy led to the restoration of absolutist papal authority.[85]

When French forces under General Oudinot arrived at Civita-Vecchio on the coast on 25 April 1849 they had vague and conflicting instructions. As Reyneval, Toqueville's successor, put it, they were to support both the independence of the Pope and the liberties of the Roman people.[86] Oudinot's small force had expected to be welcomed as fellow republicans and liberators by the Roman republicans but found instead that they were firmly opposed, and indeed repulsed. While the French still occupied little more than Civita-Vecchio, where they had declared a state of siege, the French government decided to appoint a 'diplomatic agent' alongside the military commander to negotiate with the Roman republicans. The instruction given to Ferdinand de Lesseps in this role was that French policy was 'to deliver the States of the Church from the anarchy which prevails in them, and to ensure that that the re-establishment of a regular power is not darkened, not to say imperilled, in future by reactionary fury'.[87] Although dividing authority between military commanders and diplomatic agents proved problematic once again, and though Lesseps would subsequently castigate General Oudinot who had indeed repudiated an agreement reached between Lesseps and the Roman republicans, Lesseps' task was in fact impossible.[88] Now reinforced, Oudinot seized the city of Rome on 3 July. His proclamation of that day blamed 'factious and misled men' and then asserted that 'all power is vested in the hands of the military authorities', the existing institutions of government were suppressed, 'clubs and political associations' closed and newspapers prohibited.[89] Nothing was said about the restoration of the temporal authority of the Pope.[90] Despite what were now recognised as 'the regulations usual with armies in a conquered city', even the Italian radical Luigi Farini conceded that French behaviour was initially relatively mild.[91] Leading republicans, with one exception, were even allowed to depart under cover of British and American passports.

Ironically, it was precisely a lack of willingness to exercise authority that facilitated the reassertion of papal authority. The French had pressed the Pope to make concessions including a manifesto promising at least moderate government but the Pope availed himself of the fact of occupation to decline on the grounds that such a manifesto would not appear as 'the spontaneous provision of a free and independent Sovereign, but a condition imposed by his protectors'.[92] The French found the papal authorities recalcitrant, especially in matters of the exercise of police powers where they directly opposed French claims to authority. Despite this resistance the French proclaimed the reassertion of the Pope's temporal authority on 15 July and at the end of the month transferred civil authority to a commission of cardinals. Within days a French agent reported that 'we pass from the primary to the secondary level, from the role of active power to the role of counsellor, participating more or less in authority to the extent of the influence we are able to retain'.[93] President of the Council Barrot recalled that Oudinot soon regretted the haste with which he had divested himself of authority. Yet Barrot was also dissatisfied with what he saw as the lack of vigour of France's representatives in Rome, and recalled Oudinot.[94] The replacement of Oudinot made no substantial difference. Louis Napoleon, irate at the frustration of his liberal preferences, dispatched an officer to Rome with instructions to Oudinot's replacement to publish a letter in which Louis proclaimed that France 'did not send an army to Rome to trample on Italian liberty', but General Rostolan declined to publish the document.[95]

Having so dramatically failed to achieve their goals, the French then experienced enormous difficulty in extracting themselves from the occupation. It would not be, with the exception of a brief interlude from December 1866 to October 1867, until the crisis of 1870 that French troops would finally withdraw from Rome. The impact of this prolonged occupation could also be seen in the changing views of outsiders. Initially, in 1851, the British, having disavowed any involvement in the matter, stated that the French 'must be left to judge for themselves as to the period at which the occupation may cease consistently with the objects in view – objects which are disinterested ones as far as France is concerned, for she never professed to have in view any territorial acquisition by that occupation'.[96] Over a decade later, however, the British Foreign Minister Russell noted that intervention and occupation had taken place in Europe in several places, 'but limited to terms of two, three or five years'. He continued, 'It is only in Rome that we are presented with the spectacle of a foreign occupation prolonged for thirteen years and at the same time of a people less reconciled with its government and sovereign than the point at which this period commenced.'⁹⁷ By this point the French were no less exasperated. Agreement had been reached in May 1860 but was derailed by Garibaldi's expedition and the threat to papal authority posed by Italian nationalism. In October, Louis Napoleon wrote that French troops 'occupy Rome militarily but not politically' and that while they should assure tranquillity, they should never be associated with the papal gendarmerie lest they draw on themselves the 'odium of their political repression'. He added that foreign troops in Paris in 1815 had taken care not to be associated with 'Bourbon vengeance'.⁹⁸ In the eyes of some at least of Rome's inhabitants no amount of evasion or caution by the French could conceal the all too political significance of their occupation. Thus when the French departed in 1866 a self-proclaimed Committee of Action declared: 'Thus falls the aegis which for seventeen years has defended a government, as inefficient as it was unmerciful, from the anger of Rome.'⁹⁹As Garibaldi once again threatened Rome in the name of Italian unity the French returned in their 'second expedition', invited the other powers to a conference to finally resolve the Roman Question, to no avail, and continued to occupy Rome. Only the war with Prussia, which would bring humiliation and occupation to France, forced the final withdrawal and the solution of the Roman Question.[100]

The upheavals of 1848 which had led to the French intervention in Rome had led to occupation elsewhere. Faced with revolt in the eastern, Hungarian, half of their empire, the Habsburgs turned to Russia for aid. Russian intervention was substantial but closely regulated by a Convention and comparatively brief, lasting some eight weeks.[101] Predictably there were significant differences in attitude between the Austrians and their allies. In general Russian forces enjoyed a better reputation for discipline though reprisals were swift and brutal.[102] For the Austrians, of course, their opponents were traitors who deserved the severest punishment. The Russians, besides tending to favour a more conciliatory policy as better conducive to the stability of the Austrian Empire, were irate that men who had surrendered to them as prisoners of war, and whom they had handed over to the Austrian authorities, were subsequently executed as traitors.[103] Since the Austrians had no further need of Russian support once the immediate military challenge from the Hungarians was overcome, the Russians had even less leverage over their allies than the French had had over vengeful Spanish monarchists.

Revolt and occupation in Hungary had wider implications. The Hungarians had been supported by Polish exiles hostile to both Austria and Russia. Austria had deliberately exaggerated Polish involvement in order to encourage Russia to intervene while Russia was also concerned that the conflict would spill over into the Danubian Principalities. The Russians had already intervened in the Principalities in 1848 in response to a revolt originating in Wallachia with a marked anti-Russian emphasis. As both Russia, the protecting power, and the Ottoman Empire, the sovereign power, intervened, an Ottoman commission proved far too lenient for Russian taste, giving way under Russian pressure to a commission supervised by General Duhamel which proved more rigorous in arresting and expelling anti-Russian elements, while disavowing any infringement of Ottoman sovereignty.[104] That arrangement was sanctioned by the Treaty of Balt-Liman of 1 May 1849, which agreed 'to prolong the presence of a certain portion of the Russian and Ottoman Troops which at present occupy the country' and provided for the activity of their Extraordinary Commissioners 'pending the duration of the Occupation'.[105] The duration of the occupation turned out to be longer than provided for in the treaty with the Russians not finally withdrawing until 1851.

Two years later the Russians returned, this time in order to press the wider claims made by Russia against the Ottoman Empire. Russian occupation of the Principalities was one of the factors leading to the outbreak of the Crimean War, though Russia withdrew from the Principalities in order to avert the entry of Austria on the side of Britain and France. Its place, however, was promptly taken by Austrian and Ottoman occupation. One of the striking features of this occupation was that Austria, or at least its Foreign Minister Buol, had resisted French attempts to draw Austria into active hostility to Russia with the promise of the annexation of the Principalities.[106] Ironically, given his subsequent comments on the length of the French occupation of Rome, Russell had received a letter from a fellow minister in respect of Austrian occupation of the Principalities suggesting 'that her permanent occupation of them would be an advantage to us all'.[107] That, however, did not represent the dominant British view, either in London or amongst its agents in the region, which remained suspicious of Austrian ambitions. In reality Buol wanted only to prevent the further increase of Russian influence and the Principalities becoming a refuge for Poles and Hungarians, especially those who had fled from Habsburg lands in the wake of the failed revolt.[108] Some such refugees or otherwise discontent members of the empire's minorities had indeed found employment, and even high office, in the service of the sultan and their antipathy to the Austrians would be a significant factor in souring the relationship between the two occupying powers.[109]

There was also marked disagreement within the ranks of the Austrians. Many generals, including the commander of the Austrian forces in the Principalities, General Coronini, had much more far reaching ambitions, seeking the military and economic incorporation of the Principalities into an Austrian system, though most stopped short of arguing for outright annexation.[110] Such schemes, of course, fed British suspicions of Austrian motives, as Buol had occasion to complain.[111] Some Austrian agents and military officers were in league with the Austrian Internuncio in Constantinople, Bruck, who had his own visions of a Germanic Mitteleuropa into which the Principalities would be integrated. Buol's only solution to these tensions, besides remonstrating with Bruck, was to centralise decision making in Vienna, removing political decisions from the hands of both the generals and Bruck.[112] These tensions were present in the administration of the Principalities themselves. Here the Turkish commanders, themselves pursuing a more confrontational policy than desired by Constantinople, sought to curtail the political influence of the Austrian occupying forces, refusing to recognise the Austrian civil commissioner on the grounds that the Austrians had no business meddling in such matters.[113] This was reflected in Turkish opposition to the issuing of the customary proclamation by the Austrian forces, threatening to arrest anyone who read it out. Indeed this was identified as one of the three most important issues of contention by one of the Austrian generals.[114] The second concerned the return of one of the former hospodars despite the fact that the treaty between the Austrians and Ottoman Empire provided that they would seek 'to re-establish in the Principalities the legal state of things', which would include the office of the hospodar, which still had several years to run.[115] It is notable though that the opponents of the hospodar, who included the British ambassador in Constantinople, sought to undermine him by citing his delay in leaving office under the Russian occupation as evidence of his disloyalty to the Porte.[116] The third tension was the inevitable clash over their respective zones of occupation.[117] All of these tension were clearly aggravated by the presence of Poles, Hungarians and Croats in the Ottoman forces, all of whom the Austrians saw as animated by fundamental animosity to the Austrian Empire.[118] That aspect of this occupation of the Principalities was unusual though much else reflected the frequent tensions and suspicions of occupation under the aegis of the Vienna system even at this point of its decay and, according to some, collapse.

Prussia's Wars

The years 1848–9 had also set in motion a series of occupations associated with Prussia's expansion. Here, conquest was firmly on the agenda and annexation of territory would follow a quite brief period of occupation. That was not initially the case though in respect of the Danish province of Schleswig, which was invaded by Prussian troops in 1849, acting in the name of the German Confederation. Here the Preliminary Peace of July 1849 assigned the task of occupation to Swedish forces, though Sweden had not been party to the war. The mutual suspicions of the Prussians and Danes resulted in this occupation by a neutral state, pending a peace treaty, which confirmed Danish possession.[119] In 1863 and 1864 first Holstein, then Schleswig was occupied by German troops, with Prussian and Austrian forces eventually taking over both provinces. Although both had given assurances that Schleswig would be held as a guarantee, not as a conquest, the two powers promptly set aside all sign of Danish sovereignty, agreeing, by the Convention of Gastein of August 1865, to exercise a condominium over the provinces.[120] Their ultimate fate, incorporation into Prussia, was not settled until the war of 1866.[121]

Prussia's main opponent in 1866, Austria, did not have to surrender territory as part of the settlement already set out in the preliminary peace agreement at Nikolsburg of 26 July 1866, just over three weeks after the decisive battle. That preliminary agreement also provided for the evacuation of Austrian territory occupied by Prussian troops in its first article.[122] In what would become a point of considerable concern and dispute in the subsequent codification of a law of occupation, the Prussians had in fact proclaimed their occupation of territory they did not strictly hold, proclaiming occupation of the entirety of Bohemia upon taking Prague.[123] The occupation itself would be remembered more widely, above all for the deleterious effect upon the inhabitants of occupied territory of the flight of Austrian officials.[124] Austrian policy was in fact more discriminating than was subsequently suggested, specifying, for example, that courts could remain in operation in occupied territory so long as they were allowed to apply Austrian law.[125] Nevertheless, the flight of officials was, in this occupation as in many others, significant, requiring the provision in the armistice that Austrian officials be allowed to return to their posts to organise supplies for the occupying forces.[126] The rapid agreement on a preliminary peace and armistice curtailed any development of a less well remembered facet of the occupation, namely attempts to incite civilian resistance to Prussian occupation. In terms of its impact, a mere thirty Prussian soldiers killed, this was of minimal significance, dwarfed by the impact of the outbreak of cholera in occupied Austrian territory.[127] Paper occupations, the proclamation of occupation over territory not under the actual control of an army, the flight of officials and civilian resistance, all evident in the Prussian occupation of Austrian territory, would soon attract attention on a scale that would not be as easily forgotten.

Occupation in the north was marked by the anticipation of conquest in some degree, though its extent was initially uncertain. So too were the attitudes of the inhabitants of occupied territory. The Prussian proclamation to their 'Hessian brothers' announced that 'we come not as enemies and conquerors but to extend to you the German hand of brotherhood'.[128] Although there were pockets of pro-Prussian sentiment, hostility and suspicion were widespread. Amongst the peasants of Hesse a few were still old enough to remember French occupation in 1806 or the Russians in 1813.[129] In Hanover, a Prussian officer recalled the hatred of Prussia exhibited by the aristocracy, who incited the peasantry against his country, and conceded that the prospect of union with Prussia was not exactly popular amongst Hanover's numerous civil servants.[130]

While Bismarck set the scene for unification, the Prussians established a pattern of military governors aided by civil commissioners in occupied territory, coinciding in part with existing state boundaries but also embracing territory which was not in the event annexed.[131] Ironically, Gustav Diest entering Hesse as its civil commissioner felt obliged to object to a proclamation of his General, von Beyer, which promised the inhabitants that he would respect their constitution, something Diest knew Bismarck had no intent of doing.[132] Diest and his fellow commissioners sought to retain the services of the existing administration. That was in accord with the proclamations of the military governors, such as that of General Falckenstein which asserted that the existing administrative authorities would 'provisionally remain in their positions', receiving their orders from Falckenstein.[133] That meant extracting oaths of obedience from the officials. In Hesse, Diest was able to persuade the most reluctant official to do so only after invoking the analogy of Prussian officials who had taken oaths of obedience to Napoleon.[134] In contrast, in Nassau, Diest felt so confident that he was able to dispense with an oath of loyalty entirely. Yet initially these Prussian commissars proceeded cautiously, as occasionally did the generals. In Hanover, Falckenstein warned against the rapid application of Prussian procedures by hordes of occupation officials.[135] The civil commissioners who had the most frequent and direct contact with indigenous officials were dependent of course on their relationship with their generals, which in one case, that of Diest and General Manteuffel, was very bad. Wider political considerations could also intervene. Thus in Hesse, General von Beyer turned to the nationalist politician Max Duncker. Their attempt, however, to co-opt leading Hessian liberals on the standing committee of the prorogued Parliament failed. Though not unsympathetic, these men were too unsure of the final outcome to take an unequivocal stance.[136]

The tensions, the blend of threat and conciliation which dominated in most of the occupied territories intended for annexation took on a distinctly different colouring in the case of Frankfurt. Typical of the climate there was the early arrest of two prominent members of the city's Senate, though they were later released. Pressed to explain their arrest, Falckenstein replied that the only purpose was to deny them the opportunity to express their anti-Prussian sentiments.[137] That in turn may have been linked to the issue of contributions demanded from the City by the occupation authorities.[138] The level of contributions imposed on Frankfurt was severe enough to cause some dissent amongst the highest ranks of Prussian decision making.[139] Yet the Prussians remained implacable, enforcing contributions and requisitions on Frankfurt with a vigour not visited upon any other part of occupied territory. General Manteuffel even threatened to submit the city to pillage if payment were not made, prompting protest by foreign consuls in the city.[140] That threats of that kind in occupied territory, at least in the heart of Europe, were regarded as no longer acceptable was reflected in the fact that even Bismarck experienced some embarrassment at the foreign reaction.[141]

Occupation beyond Europe

The comparative lack of restraint beyond the boundaries of Europe meant that the language and practice of occupation was less frequent. There conquest was the norm where European powers intervened in non-European political systems, though there were a limited number of examples where occupation appeared as a guarantee of the fulfilment of the provisions of a treaty, most notably the treaties of Tsien-Tsin of 1858 and Peking of 1860 between the Chinese on the one hand and the British and French on the other, as well as a treaty of 1862 with Annam.[142] Two other occupations, however, stand out by virtue of the level of engagement and attention they received at the time, and later. Both entailed a French occupation force though they took place on opposite sides of the Atlantic: one in Syria, the other in Mexico.

The intervention in Syria was undertaken ostensibly for humanitarian reasons, in response to a number of massacres and other atrocities that took place in the area of Lebanon and in Damascus in 1860. The crisis also involved the conflicting interests of the French and the British, the former in support of the Maronite Christians, whom France portrayed as the innocent victims, the British more supportive of the Druze, whom they regarded as undoubtedly perpetrators of many atrocities but also as having been provoked by the Maronites. The existence of powerful interests did not mean, however, that the sense of outrage at the atrocities was insincere. Indeed the French seem to have been genuinely indignant at the level of British suspicion of their motives.[143] Similarly the French minister of war complained that unilateral French action was not well appreciated even where it was undertaken in the 'common interest', giving this as a reason for his wish and hope that other powers would participate in the intervention.[144] The French Foreign Minister, Edouard-Antoine de Thouvenal, also felt that a multilateral act would enjoy greater legitimacy.[145] One French senator sought to find a simpler and more direct route to justifying intervention by arguing that 'The Porte has never been sovereign in the Lebanon; he has only ever been the suzerain'.[146] Suzerainty, rather than sovereignty, had already been employed, to the disadvantage of the Porte, though it was, if not capable of any interpretation, certainly elastic enough to justify more than one.[147] In that it resembled the term occupation as well.

At a Convention in London the powers, including the Ottoman Empire, agreed on two protocols on 3 August 1860 that duly sanctioned the intervention. The first provided for 'a body of European troops', not exceeding 12,000 men, half of whom were to be immediately provided by France. Crucially, it specified that the commander of this 'expedition, will, on his arrival, enter into communication with the Commissioner Extraordinary of the Porte, in order to concert all the measures required by circumstances'. They also agreed to 'fix at six months the duration of the occupation of the European troops in Syria'.[148] The second protocol formally renounced not only any territorial ambitions in Syria but also any exclusive economic concessions.[149] The instructions given to the French commander, General Beaufort d'Hautpoul, were vague, leaving him 'free to adopt the measures and to occupy the positions that he deems necessary'.[150] Despite this potentially expansive remit, the limited size of the force and brief extent of the occupation, and requirement to coordinate action with the Syrian authorities all amounted to severe constraints on the scope of the French force. Underlying these constraints were fears that the purpose of the expedition could all too easily escape control. Evaluating the situation in November 1860 Lord Russell argued against any increase in the size of the occupation force, fearing that the occupation 'Would soon degenerate into a transfer of the local Government of Syria to the Five Powers, and thus, instead of giving a useful example, well fitted to terrify the Mahometan fanatics, the European occupation would be a precedent for other occupations in Bulgaria, Bosnia, and other Provinces, and thus lead the way to a partition of the Turkish Empire.'[151]

Russell's expression of concern arose from his conviction that the violence had been contained and that the only further purpose could be the pursuit of those deemed guilty and still free, leading to the undesired expansion of the occupation's purpose. Yet the addition of the pursuit of justice to the task of simply stopping 'the effusion of blood' had occurred partly at Russell's own insistence.[152] Overseeing that justice was in fact administered was a task that had been assigned to Commission of Representatives of the European powers, which met in Beirut from September 1860 onwards. Its remit also included making recommendations for the future administrative organisation of the region, with a view to preventing a recurrence of the violence. This strictly civilian, but multilateral, body, alongside Beaufort d'Hautpoul's French troops, was also supposed to cooperate with the Ottoman authorities and the Commissioner Extraordinary of the Porte. Since no precise arrangements, let alone line of command, between these three bodies was established the scope for disagreement and duplication of effort was considerable. Complete unwillingness to confront this problem was evident in the bland assurance given to the French commissioner in respect of his colleagues, namely that he should 'study to maintain a perfect understanding with them, and you will, I have no doubt, find them, on their part, animated by the same disposition towards you'.[153]

When General Beaufort d'Hautpoul's small force arrived, Fuad Pasha, the Porte's Commissioner Extraordinary, had already contained the violence and set about punishing some of those deemed guilty. He was, moreover, determined to minimise the role of the French troops and to preserve as much as possible of the symbolism and substance of the Porte's authority. That brought him into implicit conflict with General Beaufort d'Hautpoul who, like his men, wished not only to play an active role, but also to distinguish himself in battle. Fuad Pasha could not, of course, directly rebuff the French force, seeking instead to deflect it while avoiding open confrontation.[154] According to the expedition's paymaster, Ernest Louet, Fuad's attempt to assign the French to a peaceful Maronite area while Fuad set out in pursuit of guilty Druze met with an indignant response from Beaufort d'Hautpoul.[155] When the expedition turned out to be largely fruitless, recriminations arose, with the French accusing Fuad of deliberately allowing the Druze to escape.[156] Louet even wrote of 'Turkish treason', while one of Beaufort d'Hautpoul's generals, Ducrot, complained that instead of dominating the situation, Beaufort had been outmanoeuvred by Fuad. Ducrot added that 'our intervention threatens to become harmful to our influence and to the cause that we have come to defend', by which he meant the Christian cause.[157]

A frustrated Beaufort d'Hautpoul increasingly turned to interfering in political matters, both local politics and the grander designs for the future which were the task of the Commission, but he also cooperated in the task of reconstruction. Although the task was accompanied by constant mutual recrimination, his soldiers cooperated with Ottoman authorities in improving sanitation and roads as well as rebuilding houses, all in an attempt, of limited success, to encourage the return of refugees.[158] Beaufort d'Hautpoul's political ambitions, however, increased British pressure for an end to the occupation, pressure the French resisted, negotiating an extension of the occupation at a conference in February 1861, with a view to withdrawal in June. The French withdrew amidst a host of regrets and reservations. Members of the occupying force would complain of their 'betrayal'.[159] Yet, for all its faults, the occupation had been limited and controlled by the powers acting in concert. That would prove impossible to achieve in Mexico.

There was no humanitarian dimension to the occupation of Mexico. The immediate cause for the intervention was Mexican failure to pay their debts amidst a situation of growing lawlessness and internal conflict, sufficient to raise doubt at some points about which claimant to the government could be held responsible.[160] Occupation as a measure to enforce the payment of debts sat alongside occupation to prevent the 'effusion of blood' without any discomfort for most of the nineteenth century. In this case the Convention of London of October 1861 between France, Spain and Britain provided for the seizure and occupation of 'various fortresses and military positions' on the Mexican coast. It also specified that they would not seek to acquire territory or gain any particular advantage but also 'not to exercise any influence in the internal affairs of Mexico of such a nature as to infringe the right of the Mexican nation to choose and freely constitute its form of government'.[161] This self-restraint was of particular significance to Louis Napoleon, who still saw himself as the proponent of the principle of nationalities. Napoleon had also long dreamt of expanding French interests in the region even to the exclusion of the United States, and of various schemes, including a canal across the isthmus. All this was bolstered by wild images of the supposedly untold wealth of Mexico and the encouragement of Mexican conservatives who invited Napoleon to intervene and install a monarch upon a Mexican throne.[162] Mexican émigrés and adventurers of various kinds would exercise a baleful influence upon the entire affair.

From the outset there were signs of divisions between the parties to the Convention, with the instructions to their respective agents varying in their ambitions.[163] The proclamation which they issued from Veracruz in January 1862 already went beyond the Convention in their assertion that they had come to be 'witnesses and if necessary protectors of the regeneration of Mexico', while the admiral in command of French forces, Jurien de La Gravière, privately expressed his dissatisfaction with elements of it.[164] The Allies managed to maintain sufficient unity to agree to the Convention of Soledad the following month. By this Convention, with the 'constitutional government which is actually in power' they secured Mexican agreement to their occupation of inland towns, away from the disease ridden coast that threatened their troops.[165] This created some doubt about the exact status of the European forces, whether they were in some sense allies rather than enemies. At the same time, however, the Mexicans with whom the Europeans negotiated had passed a law providing for the death penalty for anyone who aided the occupying forces.[166] On the French side the Convention of Soledad had the consequence of undermining the position of Admiral Jurien, whom Napoleon blamed for the implicit recognition of the Mexican government, while also inducing Napoleon to endow the French chargé d'affaires, Dubois de Saligny, with 'full political powers'.[167]

Saligny, an adventurer and schemer, fed the illusion promoted by the émigrés of the supposed existence of a powerful conservative party of order merely waiting for French support in order to take control and bring stability. Jurien de La Gravière realised that the French had been misled. The same fact was evident to French officers in Mexico. Echoing, albeit much more strongly and at an earlier phase in the occupation, the disillusion of their colleagues in Spain and Rome, one wrote that 'we support a cause that has and can have no partisans, we have around us such men ... who are an object of horror in the country', while another lamented 'we have come in a word to fight against the liberal principle which we recognise as our own'.[168] Yet Admiral Jurien de La Gravière still favoured a monarchy for Mexico, despite his recognition of its lack of support. Encouraged by Saligny, the French position in Mexico, which was not always quite what Paris thought it should be, diverged more and more from the British and Spanish, though the representatives of those powers did not strictly heed their own instructions either.[169] With the breakdown of the alliance the French moved to formally declare the opening of hostilities with the Mexicans.

After an initial reversal, a reinforced French army under General Forey finally took Mexico City in June 1863. According to one of his officers the general was now confronted with a new task, that of reconstruction rather than conquest, a task for which he was unsuited.[170] Whether that was entirely fair, Forey, still encouraged by Saligny, was unable to organise any nationwide elections in a country much of which was still under the control of followers of Juarez. Instead, he turned to a junta which proclaimed a monarchy, offered the crown to the Austrian Prince Maximilian and formed a three-man Regency. Shortly after, Forey received a letter from France making no reference to a monarchy or to Maximilian but suggesting a far more conciliatory and wide-ranging search for a viable government.[171] By then it was too late. The development was one consequence of running an occupation over great distances in an era of slow communications. This dramatic decision did, however, finally bring about the disgrace and recall of Saligny, much to the delight of the French soldiers, amongst whom he was detested as 'the author of all the mistakes ... the fomenter of the reactionary and clerical policies'.[172]

General Forey's replacement, General Bazaine, who had already had experience of occupation in the Crimea, effectively presided over the remainder of the French occupation, though he was constrained by the decisions already taken by Saligny and Forey. His instructions from Napoleon were:

> Do not become reactionary; do not retract the sale of clerical property; finally try to keep peace in the country while using mostly Mexican troops to do it. I have regretted the decrees of Forey on the confiscation of hostile persons, and I am afraid that the triumvirate named in Mexico may be too reactionary.[173]

That suspicion was shared by Bazaine. By October 1863 he personally confronted the Regency, with 200 Zouaves standing behind him, forcing them to rescind laws intended to secure the return of as much clerical property as possible.[174] The eventual acceptance of the crown by Maximilian and his appearance in Mexico in 1864 led to the transformation of the legal basis of the occupation insofar as the Convention of Miramar of April 1864 then regulated the presence of French troops. It could do nothing for the fundamental unpopularity of the regime. Bazaine could, by the end of 1865, come close to destroying the remnants of the forces of Juarez. By then, however, the occupation had also exhausted any possibility of conciliation.[175] The climate was encapsulated by a decree formally issued by Maximilian, but whose true authorship was disputed. According to this decree of October 1865, in the light of the defeat of Juarist forces, remaining belligerents would be treated as members of bands 'and if found guilty even of the only fact of belonging to the band, they shall be condemned to capital punishment'.[176] Bazaine welcomed the fact that the 'odium' of 'repressive measures' which had hitherto fallen on the French would now be shared by the Mexicans, and implicitly, Maximilian.[177] Confidentially Bazaine wrote that 'it is a war to the death between civilization and barbarity'.[178] Maximilian's regime could not in fact survive without French support and soon after the October decree Napoleon began turning more and more to seeking a way out of the occupation. Indeed the collapse came promptly upon French withdrawal in 1867, leaving the hapless Maximilian to face a Juarist firing squad.[179]

Judging Occupation

While French military courts had played an active role in the occupation of Mexico, as yet the higher courts of the European states played a limited role in reviewing the practices and implications of occupation. The French Court of Cassation did receive appeals against the judgement of military courts in Mexico, and even more so from courts in Rome. It consistently rejected those appeals and was now aided in formulating these dismissals by the recently enacted code of military justice of 1857.[180] The appeals sought to challenge the competence of the military court, on the grounds that it did not have jurisdiction given the nature of the accused, being neither a member of the military nor assimilable to military personnel, or occasionally given the nature of the crime. In respect of those appeals from courts in the Roman states, the Court of Cassation was also concerned with the nature of the occupation, a matter on which there was no guidance in the military code. The court nevertheless confidently asserted, at the beginning of 1865, that the term 'enemy territory', as applied in article 63 of the military code, included 'foreign territory occupied by French troops, even following a war for the protection of public interests'.[181] The court also had to engage in some liberal interpretation in order to cover the silence of the code in respect of specific crimes. Mostly, however, it consistently invoked a limited number of articles, themselves very brief, in order to establish the competence of the military court and hence, following article 80 of the code, to deny the condemned a right of appeal, recognising thereby the autonomy of the military court system. The court did, however, sometimes supplement the specific positive law provisions of the code by reference to 'the higher rules of natural law and public morals' or 'the higher rules of public and international law', deeming these sufficient in their own right.[182] The court also invoked the security of the occupying force as a general argument reinforcing the activities of its courts. As yet the French courts did not have to confront the legal dilemmas resulting from the occupation of French territory.

Nor did British high courts. Indeed the most prominent case did not even concern territory occupied by British forces. The case, relating to the seizure of a vessel as a prize of war off the mouth of the Danube in 1854 and more specifically whether the Russian occupation of Moldavia, from which the vessel had set sail, transformed its owners into enemies of the British. A British Admiralty court had agreed that it did but the Privy Council reversed the decision. It argued that occupation alone and such control as the occupying power 'may think fit to exercise' were not sufficient, amounting to less than the incorporation of occupied territory into its dominions.[183] The Privy Council turned for support to a handful of cases relating to the Napoleonic Wars and repeatedly drew attention to the Russian disavowal of any intent to incorporate these territories. It also, following what it admitted was the 'very anomalous' nature of these territories, suggested that the most that Russia could have acquired was the '*Suzeraineté*' of the Porte which had been suspended by virtue of the occupation.[184] It is notable that while both British and French superior courts showed sufficient confidence to identify a distinct status of military occupation, though, in different ways, both could find limited legal guidance.[185]

The practice of occupation, including the treaties and conventions as well as diplomatic agreements which frequently regulated it with varying degrees of success, also demonstrate that occupation, as something distinct from conquest, was an established part of the international repertoire. Sensitivity to the challenge to sovereignty it posed was frequently marked, yet this did not result in any automatic or principled opposition to the change in the institutions of the occupied territory. Opposition did exist but it arose from the suspicion, a suspicion sometimes if not entirely unfounded at least exaggerated, that the occupant would exploit its position in preparation for conquest or at least to extort specific concessions from the occupied. To that extent the relative stability and constraints of the Vienna Congress system marked the development and nature of occupation in the period. What resounds most loudly from these occupations, though, is the disappointment and frustration that accompanied them. Both propping up governments challenged from below and creating new governments proved difficult, especially when faced with recalcitrant indigenous authorities, who were crucial to providing an exit which would avoid the immediate collapse of the governments in question; something the French most dramatically failed to avoid in the case of Mexico. Those occupations which arguably escaped this recurrent pattern of ambition and disappointment were precisely those which were indeed preparatory to conquest.

Notes

1. On the emergence of the principle of the Great Powers see Genevieve Peterson, 'Political inequality at the Congress of Vienna', *Political Science Quarterly*, 60 (1945), 532–54.
2. Michael Hurst (ed.), *Key Treaties for the Great Powers, vol. 1, 1814–1870* (Newton Abbot: David & Charles, 1972), p. 122.
3. Harold Temperley and Lillian Penson (eds), *Foundations of British Foreign Policy from Pitt (1792) to Salisbury (1902)* (Cambridge: Cambridge University Press, 1938), p. 40.
4. Nehal Bhuta, 'The antinomies of transformative occupation', *European Journal of International Law*, 16 (2005), 731–3.
5. The literature is enormous. See especially Henry Kissinger, *A World Restored* (London: Weidenfeld and Nicolson, 1957); Paul W. Schroeder, *The Transformation of European Politics 1763–1848* (Oxford: Clarendon Press, 1994); Matthias Schulz, *Norm und Praxis: Das europäische Konzert der Großmächte als Sicherheitsrat 1815–1860* (Munich: Oldenbourg, 2009); Jennifer Mitzen, *Power in Concert* (Chicago: University of Chicago Press, 2013).
6. William E. Echard, 'Louis Napoleon and the French decision to intervene at Rome in 1849', *Canadian Journal of History*, 9 (1974), 269.
7. Ian Clark, *Hegemony in International Society* (Oxford: Oxford University Press, 2011), p. 96, in a chapter specifying a chronology of 1815–1914.
8. Martti Koskenniemi, *The Gentle Civilizer of Nations* (Cambridge: Cambridge University Press, 2002), pp. 35–6.
9. See the title of Frederick B. Artz, *Reaction and Revolution 1814–1832* (New York: Harper & Row, 1934).

10. Thus Mervyn Lyons, *Post-Revolutionary Europe 1815–1856* (Basingstoke: Palgrave Macmillan, 2006).
11. Schroeder, *Transformation of European Politics*, p. 673.
12. See the excellent works of Gary J. Bass, *Freedom's Battle: The Origins of Humanitarian Intervention* (New York: Vintage, 2008), and Davide Rodogno, *Against Massacre: Humanitarian Interventions in the Ottoman Empire 1815–1914* (Princeton: Princeton University Press, 2012).
13. P. H. Winfield, 'The history of intervention in international law', *British Yearbook of International Law*, 3 (1922–3), 131.
14. Ibid. p. 134.
15. Robert Phillimore, *Commentaries upon International Law*, vol. 1 (Philadelphia: Johnson, 1854), pp. 314–46 and vol. 3 (Philadelphia: Johnson, 1857), pp. 467–505.
16. As in the reference to 'the occupation of the Morea by French troops' in Henry Wheaton, *Elements of International Law* (Boston: Little, Brown and Co., 1863), p. 128.
17. This dubious claim is asserted with great conviction by Roger Bullen, 'The Great Powers and the Iberian peninsula, 1815–48', in Alan Sked (ed.), *Europe's Balance of Power 1815–1848* (London: Macmillan, 1979), p. 54. See also Rodogno, *Against Massacre*, p. 22.
18. It is the latter case in fact that Bullen invokes as evidence of his wider claim. See Roger Bullen, 'France and the problem of intervention in Spain, 1834–1836', *Historical Journal*, 20 (1977), 375. The rights in question involved those of neutral shipping, which rights were amongst the most formalised and sensitive of the period. Quite how bizarre the equivocations could become was evident much later: John Bassett Moore, *A Digest of International Law*, vol. 7 (Washington DC: Government Printing Office, 1906), pp. 140–1.
19. Thus H. W. Halleck, *International Law* (San Francisco: Bancroft, 1861), p. 335.
20. More widely see Kathryn L. Einspanier, 'Burlamaqui, the constitution and the imperfect war on terror', *Georgetown Law Journal*, 96 (2008), 986–1026.
21. Charles Webster, *The Foreign Policy of Castlereagh 1815–1822* (London: Bell, 1963), p. 295.
22. Edward Hertslet, *The Map of Europe by Treaty*, vol. 1 (London: Butterworths, 1875), p. 666.
23. On the Piedmontese circumstances see Paul Schroeder, *Metternich's Diplomacy at its Zenith 1820–1823* (Austin: University of Texas Press, 1962), pp. 115–18.
24. Ferdinand I of Naples sent formal promises of loyalty to his Parliament in order to gain its consent to his escape to the Conference of

Laibach where he would denounce the Parliament and the constitution. See George Romani, *The Neapolitan Revolution of 1820–1821* (Evanston, IL: Northwestern University Press, 1950), pp. 146–51.

25. Raymond Robin, *Des occupations militaires en dehors des occupations de guerre* (Paris: Larose, 1913), p. 174; Romani, *The Neapolitan Revolution*, p. 165.
26. Louis Viel-Castel, *Histoire de la Restauration*, vol. 9 (Paris: Lévy, 1866), p. 534; Susan Horner, *Naples and Sicily* (Edinburgh: Edmonston and Douglas, 1860), p. 74.
27. Colletta, *Histoire du Royaume de Naples* (Paris: Ladvocat, 1835), p. 342.
28. Viel-Castel, *Histoire de la Restauration*, vol. 9, p. 537.
29. Schroeder, *Metternich's Diplomacy*, pp. 136–7.
30. Ibid. p. 139.
31. Ibid. pp. 148–55.
32. Ibid. p. 157.
33. Viel-Castel, *Histoire de la Restauration*, vol. 9, pp. 532–3.
34. Robin, *Des occupations militaires*, pp. 181–2.
35. The diplomatic moves are succinctly summarised in Schroeder, *The Transformation of European Politics*, pp. 623–8.
36. H. Baumgarten, 'Zur Geschichte der französischen Intervention in Spanien (1823)', *Historische Zeitschrift*, 17 (1867), 49. See also the French proclamation as they entered Spanish territory, ibid. pp. 56–7.
37. Ibid. p. 53.
38. Louis de Viel-Castel, *Histoire de la Restauration*, vol. 12 (Paris: Lévy, 1869), p. 514.
39. See especially their Protocol of 7 June and its impact, Baumgarten, 'Zur Geschichte der französischen Intervention in Spanien', p. 65. The prime minister's letter is in *Mémoires et correspondance du Comte de Villèle*, vol. 4 (Paris: Perrin, 1904), pp. 25–30.
40. Duvergier de Hauranne, *Histoire du gouvernement parlamentaire in France*, vol. 7 (Paris: Lévy, 1865), p. 386.
41. Viel-Castel, *Histoire de la Restauration*, vol. 12, pp. 530–2.
42. Alphonse d'Hautpoul, *Mémoires du général marquis Alphonse d'Hautpoul* (Paris: Perrin, 1906), p. 148.
43. Achille de Vaulabelle, *Histoire des deux restaurations*, vol. 6 (Paris: Perrotin, 1852), p. 152.
44. The text is in Abel Hugo, *Histoire de la campagne d'Espagne en 1823* (Paris: Lefuel, 1825), pp. 45–6.
45. Vaulabelle, *Histoire des deux restaurations* , vol. 6, p. 167.
46. Geoffrey de Grandmaison, *L'expédition française d'Espagne en 1823* (Paris: Plon, 1928), pp. 148–56.

47. François-René Chateaubriand, *Oeuvres complètes de Chateaubriand*, vol. 12 (Paris: Garnier, n.d.), p. 405.
48. Alexander De Clercq (ed.), *Recueil des traités de la France*, vol. 3 (Paris: Pedone-Lauriel, 1880), p. 309.
49. For the complications and final stages see Robin, *Des occupations militaires*, pp. 190–6.
50. Roger Bullen, 'France and the problem of intervention in Spain, 1834–1836', *Historical Journal*, 20 (1977), 381.
51. 'Castlereagh to the Tsar, 16 July 1821', in Charles Vane (ed.), *Correspondence of Castlereagh*, vol. 4 (London: John Murray, 1853), p. 406.
52. With differing emphases see Bass, *Freedom's Battle* and Rodogno, *Against Massacre*. John Bew, with explicit reference to Bass, recommends caution: '"From and umpire to a competitor": Castlereagh, Canning and the issue of international intervention in the wake of the Napoleonic Wars', in Brendan Simms and D. J. B. Trim (eds), *Humanitarian Intervention: A History* (Cambridge: Cambridge University Press, 2011), pp. 117–38.
53. On Russian motives see M. S. Anderson, *The Eastern Question 1774–1923* (London: Macmillan, 1966), pp. 68–9. The purpose of the 'corps of troops' is set out in *Papers Relative to the Affairs of Greece 1826–1830* (London: Harrison, 1831), pp. 99–100.
54. De Clercq (ed.), *Recueil des traités de la France*, vol. 3, p. 496.
55. Jean Pellion, *La Grèce et les Capodistrias pendant l'occupation française de 1828–1834* (Paris: Dumaine, 1855), pp. 95–6.
56. George Finlay, *History of the Greek Revolution*, vol. 2 (Edinburgh: Blackwood, 1861), p. 193. With some further details, Rodogno, *Against Massacre*, p. 87.
57. W. Alison Phillips, *The War of Greek Independence 1821 to 1833* (New York: Scribner, 1897), pp. 303–4.
58. Pellion, *La Grèce et les Capodistrias*, pp. 126–7.
59. Ibid. p. 127.
60. *Papers Relative to the Affairs of Greece 1826–1832* (London: Harrison, 1835), p. 261.
61. Pellion, *La Grèce et les Capodistrias*, p. 227.
62. Anton von Prokesch-Osten, *Geschichte der Abfalls der Griechen vom Türkischen Reiche*, vol. 2 (Vienna: Gerold, 1867), p. 515.
63. Robin, *Des occupations militaires*, p. 236.
64. Raymond Guyot, *La première Entente Cordiale* (Paris: Rieder, 1926), pp. 57, 63, 65–6.
65. Jean-Baptiste Nothomb, *Essai historique et politique sur la revolution belge*, vol. 1 (Brussels: Muquardt, 1876), p. 222; Paul Thureau-Dangin, *Histoire de la monarchie de juillet*, vol. 1 (Paris: Plon, 1888), p. 492.

66. Robert Adair to Palmerston, 19 August 1831, H. T. Colenbrander, *Gedenkstukken der Algemeene Geschiednis van Nederland van 1790 tot 1840*, vol. 10, part 1 ('s-Gravenhage: Martinus Nijhoff, 1918), p. 215.
67. See also the Anglo-French Convention of 22 October 1832 regulating the same: Alexandre De Clercq (ed.), *Recueil des traités de la France*, vol. 3 (Paris: Pedone-Lauriel, 1880), pp. 200–2. The Franco-Belgian Convention is in ibid. pp. 207–8.
68. Robin, *Des occupations militaires*, p. 227.
69. Ibid. p. 215.
70. Leonard Olson, 'P. D. Kiselev and the Rumanian Peasantry: The Influence of the Russian Occupation on Agrarian Relations in the Danubian Principalities, 1828–1934', unpublished PhD thesis, University of Illinois, 1975, p. 106.
71. Alexander Bitis, *Russia and the Eastern Question: Army, Government and Society 1815–1833* (Oxford: Oxford University Press, 2006), p. 442; Jean Filitti, *Les Principautés Roumaines sous l'occupation Russe (1828–1934)* (Bucharest: L'Indépendance, 1904), p. 232.
72. Miroslav Sedivý, 'From hostility to cooperation: Austria, Russia and the Danubian Principalities 1829–1840', *Slavonic and East European Review*, 89 (2011), 633.
73. Olson, 'Kiselev and the Rumanian Peasantry', pp. 69–70.
74. Hurst (ed.), *Key Treaties for the Great Powers*, vol. 1, p. 194.
75. Filitti, *Les Principautés Roumaines*, p. 73.
76. Bitis, *Russia and the Eastern Question*, p. 443, and Olson, 'Kiselev and the Rumanian Peasantry', p. 85. On the later clash, Filitti, *Les Principautés Roumaines*, pp. 70–1.
77. Bitis, *Russia and the Eastern Question*, p. 443.
78. Gabriel Leanca, 'Orientalisme, construction territorial et histoire urbaine: l'example de l'occupation militaire russe des principautés de Moldavie et de Valachie (1828–1836)', *Cahiers de la Méditerranée*, 86 (2013), 179–93.
79. Quoted in Bitis, *Russia and the Eastern Question*, p. 447.
80. Filitti, *Les Principautés Roumaines*, p. 232.
81. For this description of Kiselev see Olson, 'Kiselev and the Rumanian Peasantry', p. 124.
82. Bitis, *Russia and the Eastern Question*, p. 461. On Liprandi see ibid. p. 135.
83. For the republicans' repudiation of the Pope's temporal authority and the bickering and conflicting interest of the various powers see Ivan Scott, *The Roman Question and the Powers 1848–1865* (The Hague: Martinus Nijhoff, 1969), pp. 36–45.
84. Schulz, *Norm und Praxis*, describes it as a 'loosely coordinated multilateral intervention', though this is stretching the point, p. 200.

85. As well summarised by Françoise Melonio, 'Tocqueville et la restauration du pouvoir temporal du pape (juin-octobre 1849)', *Revue historique*, no. 271 (1984), 109. See also David Clinton, 'Tocqueville on democracy, obligation and the international system', *Review of International Studies*, 19 (1993), 236–8.
86. Schulz, *Norm und Praxis*, p. 197.
87. Quoted in Ferdinand de Lesseps, *Recollections of Forty Years*, vol. 1 (London: Chapman, 1887), p. 6.
88. Ibid. pp. 82–90; Scott, *The Roman Question*, pp. 58–9.
89. René des Portes, *L'Expedition française de Rome* (Paris: Douniol, 1904), pp. 406–7; Luigi Farini, *The Roman State from 1815 to 1850*, vol. 4 (London: Murray, 1854), pp. 228–9.
90. Schulz, *Norm und Praxis*, p. 195.
91. Farini, *The Roman State from 1815 to 1850*, vol. 4, pp. 242–3.
92. Ibid. p. 248.
93. G. Mollat, 'Les débuts de l'occupation française à Rome en 1849, d'après une correspondence inédite', *Revue d'histoire ecclésiastique*, 30 (1934), 339.
94. Odilon Barrot, *Mémoires posthumes de Odilon Barrot*, vol. 3 (Paris: Charpentier, 1876), pp. 409–13.
95. Farini, *The Roman State from 1815 to 1850*, vol. 4, pp. 281–3.
96. Thus Plamerston, 9 May 1851, quoted in Scott, *The Roman Question*, p. 83.
97. *Archives diplomatiques 1863*, vol. 2, 241.
98. Jacques Randon, *Mémoires du Maréchal Randon*, vol. 2 (Paris: Lahure, 1877), p. 35.
99. R. De Cesare, *The Last Days of Papal Rome* (London: Archibald, 1909), pp. 372–3. The reality of relations between the French and the papal authorities were often acrimonious, including clashes between French soldiers and those of the Pope; see, for example, A. Kaufmann, *Chroniques de Rome* (Paris: Barba, 1865), pp. 132–4.
100. Robin, *Des occupations militaires*, pp. 264–5.
101. The Convention is in Fedor Martens, *Recueil des traités et conventions* (St Petersburg: Devrient, 1878), pp. 585–601. On earlier Russian incursions prior to the formal request for aid and their justification by reference to 'motives of humanity' see Peter Hidas, 'The first Russian intervention in Transylvania in 1849', in H. C. Schlieper (ed.), *Eastern Europe: Historical Essays* (Toronto: New Review Books, 1969), especially p. 76.
102. *Correspondence Respecting the Affairs of Hungary 1847–1849* (London: Harrison, 1850), pp. 277, 351–2; Peter Hidas, 'The Russian Intervention in Hungary in 1849', unpublished MA thesis, McGill University, 1967, pp. 136–7.

103. I. Roberts, 'The Russian intervention in Hungary in 1849', *Hungarian Studies*, 5 (1989), 59.
104. Robin, *Des occupations militaires*, p. 269; Ernest Lavisse and Alfred Rambaud, *Histoire générale*, vol. 11 (Paris: Colin, 1899), pp. 196–7.
105. Edward Hertslet (ed.), *The Map of Europe by Treaty*, vol. 2 (London: Butterworths, 1875), pp. 1092–3.
106. My account here follows Paul Schroeder, 'Bruck versus Buol', *Journal of Modern History*, 40 (1968), 193–217; 'Austria and the Danubian Principalities, 1853–1856', *Central European History*, 2 (1969), 216–36; and *Austria, Great Britain and the Crimean War* (Ithaca, NY: Cornell University Press, 1972).
107. Quoted in Schroeder 'Austria and the Danubian Principalities', p. 225.
108. Ibid. p. 226.
109. This is a prominent issue in the memoirs of Alfons Wimpffen, *Erinnerungen aus der Wallachei während der Besetzung durch die österreichischen Truppen in den Jahren 1854–1856* (Vienna: Gerold, 1878).
110. Schroeder, 'Austria and the Danubian Principalities', pp. 228–9.
111. Schroeder, *Austria, Great Britain and the Crimean War*, p. 215.
112. Ibid. pp. 213–14; Schroeder, 'Bruck versus Buol', pp. 210–13.
113. Schroeder, *Austria, Great Britain and the Crimean War*, p. 211.
114. Wimpffen, *Erinnerungen aus der Wallachei*, pp. 105–10.
115. Hertslet (ed.), *The Map of Europe by Treaty*, vol. 2, p. 1214.
116. Schroeder, *Austria, Great Britain and the Crimean War*, p. 209.
117. Wimpffen, *Erinnerungen aus der Wallachei*, p. 131.
118. Ibid. pp. 99–101.
119. Robin, *Des occupations militaires*, pp. 286–7.
120. Ibid. pp. 289–90.
121. The unusual position of these provinces is reflected in the exclusion of them from an article on annexations arising from 1866 on the grounds, amongst others, that 'their acquisition had not involved dispossession of an indigenous dynasty, but merely the appropriation of Austrian occupation rights', Hans Schmitt, 'From sovereign states to Prussian provinces', *Journal of Modern History*, 57 (1985), 26. For detailed consideration of the occupation and subsequent annexation see Werner Franz, 'Einführung und erste Jahre der preussischen Verwaltung in Schleswig-Holstein', *Zeitschrift für Schleswig-Holsteinische Geschichte*, 82 (1958), 163–216 and 83 (1959), 117–242.
122. Edward Hertslet (ed.), *The Map of Europe by Treaty*, vol. 3 (London: Buttterworths, 1875), pp. 1698–9.
123. Generalstabs-Bureau für Kriegsgeschichte, *Österreichs Kämpfe im Jahre 1866*, vol. 4 (Vienna: Gerold, 1869), p. 192.
124. See Johann Bluntschli, *Le droit international codifié* (Paris: Guillaumin,

1895), p. 306, quoted, for example, by J. M. Spaight, *War Rights on Land* (London: Macmillan, 1911), p. 363.
125. See the report of the decree of the minister of justice in *Gerichtshalle* (18 July 1866).
126. Generalstabs-Bureau für Kriegsgeschichte, *Österreichs Kämpfe im Jahre 1866*, vol. 4, p. 189.
127. Wolfgang Etschmann, 'Guerillas und Franctireurs, 1866 und 1870/71', in Erwin Schmidl (ed.), *Freund oder Feind?* (Frankfurt am Main: Lang, 1995), pp. 34–7. On the impact of cholera, Frederick Loë, *Erinnerungen aus meinem Berusfsleben 1849 bis 1867* (Stuttgart: DVA, 1906), p. 117.
128. Quoted in Robert Frederici, *1866: Bismarcks Okkupation und Annexion Kurhessens* (Kassel: Wenderoth, 1989), p. 55.
129. Ibid. p. 56.
130. Otto Meisner (ed.), *Denkwürdigkeiten des General-Feldmarschalls Alfred Graf von Waldersee*, vol. 1 (Stuttgart: DVA, 1922), pp. 42–3.
131. For an overview see Hans Schmitt, 'Prussia's last fling: the annexation of Hanover, Hesse, Frankfurt and Nassau, June 15 – October 8, 1866', *Central European History*, 8 (1975), 332.
132. Gustav von Diest, *Aus dem Leben eines Glücklichen* (Berlin: Mittler, 1904), pp. 290–1.
133. Wilhelm Hopf, *Die deutsche Krisis des Jahres 1866* (Melsungen: Hopf, 1896), p. 268.
134. Diest, *Aus dem Leben eines Glücklichen*, p. 292.
135. Schmitt, 'Prussia's last fling', p. 335.
136. Frederici, *1866*, pp. 76–9.
137. *Actenstücke zur neuesten Geschichte von Frankfurt am Main* (Stuttgart: Schweitzerbartsche, 1866), p. 196. The two arrested senators would later write to their colleagues saying they had no wish to be complicit in the 'temporary suspension' of the constitution; Margaret Sterne, 'The end of the Free City of Frankfort', *Journal of Modern History*, 30 (1958), 210.
138. As is suggested in Otto Kanngiesser, *Geschichte der Eroberung der freien Stadt Frankfurt* (Frankfurt am Main: Keller, 1877), pp. 208–9. The bitterness of the occupation still pervades this publication, ten years after the events.
139. Jonathon Steinberg, *Bismarck* (Oxford: Oxford University Press, 2011), p. 277.
140. See their note of 21 July 1866 in Kanngiesser, *Geschichte der Eroberung der freien Stadt Frankfurt*, p. 291. Diest claimed the threat was not serious, but still foolish, *Aus dem Leben eines Glücklichen*, p. 305.
141. Erich Eyck, *Bismarck*, vol. 2 (Erlenbach-Zurich: Rentsch, 1944), pp. 268–70.

142. Robin, *Des occupations militaires*, pp. 310–13.
143. Bass, *Freedom's Battle*, pp. 214–15.
144. Randon, *Mémoires du Maréchal Randon*, vol. 2, p. 30.
145. Rodogno, *Against Massacre*, p. 102.
146. Quoted by Richard Edwards, *La Syrie 1840–1862* (Paris: Amyot, 1862), p. 30. Edwards was not impressed by the argument, quoting article 9 of the Treaty of Paris of 1856 against it, pp. 68–9.
147. Again its use long predates any attempt at formal clarity and definition. See W. H. H. Kelke, 'Feudal suzerains and modern suzerainty', *Law Quarterly Review*, 47 (1896), pp. 213–27. As will become clearer later, the concept of suzerainty could be used to enhance the authority of intervening powers in different ways from that intended by the French senator.
148. *Correspondence Relating to the Affairs of Syria 1860–61* (London: Harrison, 1861), pp. 37–8.
149. Ibid. p. 38.
150. Leila Fawaz, *An Occasion for War: Civil Conflict in Lebanon and Damascus in 1860* (London: Tauris, 1994), p. 114.
151. *Correspondence Relating to the Affairs of Syria 1860–61*, p. 186.
152. Bass, *Freedom's Battle*, pp. 186–7.
153. *Correspondence Relating to the Affairs of Syria 1860–61*, p. 53. On the Commission's work see Rodgono, *Against Massacre*, pp. 109–14.
154. According to the British Commissioner, 'Fuad Pasha is mortally afraid of him [Beaufort d'Hautpoul] and can only get the better of him by cunning and deception', Caesar Farah, *The Politics of Intervention in Ottoman Lebanon 1830–1861* (London: Tauris, 2000), p. 652.
155. Ernest Louet, *Expédition de Syrie* (Paris: Amyot, 1862), p. 91.
156. Interestingly the Austrian Commissioner did not believe this, Farah, *The Politics of Intervention*, p. 669.
157. Louet, *Expédition de Syrie*, p. 112; Auguste Ducrot, *La Vie Militaire du Général Ducrot d'après sa correspondance* (Paris: Plon, 1895), p. 412.
158. Farah, *The Politics of Intervention*, p. 655; Fawaz, *An Occasion for War*, pp. 173–7.
159. Camille de Rochemonteix, *Le Liban et l'expedition française en Syrie* (Paris: Picard, 1921), pp. 207–9, 215.
160. Pierre de la Gorce, *Histoire de Second Empire*, vol. 4 (Paris: Plon-Nourrit, 1904), pp. 5–12.
161. Alexandre De Clercq (ed.), *Recueil des traités de la France*, vol. 8 (Paris: Pedone-Lauriel, 1880), p. 319.
162. Both the fantastic images of Mexico and conservative encouragement are emphasised in Romain Delmon, 'Les acteurs de la politique imperial lors de l'expedition au Mexique', in Gabriel Leanca (ed.),

La politique extérieure de Napoléon III (Paris: Hartmann, 2011), pp. 75–99.
163. Gorce, Histoire de Second Empire, vol. 4, pp. 28–9.
164. Archives diplomatiques 1862, vol. 3, 364–5; Michele Cunningham, Mexico and the Foreign Policy of Napoleon III (Houndmills: Palgrave, 2001), pp. 78–9.
165. Archives diplomatiques 1862, vol. 3, 386–7.
166. Gorce, Histoire de Second Empire, vol. 4, p. 46.
167. Jack Dabbs, The French Army in Mexico 1861–1867 (The Hague: Mouton, 1963), p. 28.
168. Quoted in Delmon, 'Les acteurs de la politique imperial', p. 80.
169. A detailed account is provided under the indicative chapter title 'A life of its own', in Cunningham, Mexico and the Foreign Policy of Napoleon III, pp. 78–107.
170. Charles Blanchot, Mémoires: L'intervention fraçaise au Mexique, vol. 2 (Paris: Nourry, 1911), pp. 1–2.
171. Gorce, Histoire de Second Empire, vol. 4, pp. 109–11.
172. Thus Général Barail, Mes souvenirs, vol. 2 (Paris: Plon, 1898), p. 478.
173. Dabbs, The French Army in Mexico, p. 61.
174. Ibid. p. 80–1.
175. Even earlier, in November 1864, there was nothing left but a policy of coercion, according to Dabbs, ibid. pp. 104–5.
176. Henry Flint, Mexico under Maximilian (Philadelphia: National Publishing, 1867), p. 110.
177. Charles Blanchot, Mémoires: L'intervention française au Mexique, vol. 3 (Paris: Nourry, 1911), p. 14.
178. Alain Guttman, La guerre du Mexique (Paris: Perrin, 2008), p. 371.
179. See Dabbs, The French Army in Mexico, pp. 183–216, for an account of the process.
180. J.-B. Duvergier, Code de justice militaire (Paris: Directeur de l'administration, 1858).
181. Case no. 14 (19 January 1865), Bulletin des arrêts de la Cour de cassation, 70, no. 1 (1865), 23.
182. Case no. 179 (24 August 1865), Bulletin des arrêts de la Cour de cassation, 70 (1865), 302; case no. 89 (31 March 1866), Bulletin des arrêts de la Cour de cassation, 71 (1866), 150.
183. 'The Gerasimo', English Reports, 14 (1857), 630.
184. Ibid. pp. 633–5.
185. In retrospect it seemed that the Privy Council was so concerned to preserve the idea of sovereignty from mere occupation that it was blind to other arguments about the implications of occupation. See Arnold D. McNair, 'Municipal effects of belligerent occupation', Law Quarterly Review, 57 (1941), 42.

Chapter 3
Military Occupation and America: Expansion and Civil War

Occupation, Conquest and the Constitution of the United States of America

Although the American experience of occupation and conquest was similar enough to that of the Europeans for the Americans to invoke European experiences in order to make sense of their own, the peculiarities of the United States of America stand out in any account of those military occupations. One of the most obvious of these, both to the Americans themselves and to contemporary Europeans, was the US constitution. In matters of conquest, occupation and civil war, the 'very peculiar constitution of this Government', as Justice Grier put it in the Prize Cases, played a key role.[1] Justice Grier had in mind the bifurcated allegiance of Americans to both the federal government and the individual state of which they were a member, the respective claims of which were then being tested by civil war. The constitution had also shaped how Americans responded to the possibility and then the increasing reality of territorial expansion. At the outset of the process of expansion, with the Louisiana Purchase of massive tracts from France in 1803, Thomas Jefferson had expressed concern that there was no constitutional provision for the impending ratification of the Louisiana Purchase: the 'general government has no powers but such as the constitution has given it: and it has not given it a power of holding foreign territory, & still less of incorporating it into a Union'.[2] Jefferson was none the less determined to make the purchase and to 'rely on the nation to sanction an act done for its great good, without its previous authority'.[3] Jefferson's determination upon conquest would later receive the principled sanction of the Supreme Court, holding that the 'Constitution confers absolutely on the government of the Union, the powers of making war, and of making treaties: consequently, that government possesses the power of acquiring territory, either by conquest or by treaty'.[4] The court promptly added: 'The usage of the world is, if a nation be not entirely subdued, to consider the holding of conquered territory as a mere military occupation, until its fate shall be determined at the treaty of peace.'[5] Its concern though was not with occupied territory but with the precise status and form of government of ceded territory.

The territory in question was the former Spanish territory of Florida, which had been ceded to the United States by the treaty of February 1819. The territory, though being thenceforth that of the United States, did not constitute a state of the Union and could not do so until it was duly admitted as a state by Congress. Moreover, the only explicit constitutional provision relating to the government of such territory empowered Congress to 'make all needful rules and regulations respecting the territory, or other property belonging to the United States'.[6] Since Congress did not necessarily act with any great alacrity to make such rules some provisional measures were necessary. In the case of the Louisiana Purchase of 1803 Congress specifically authorised the exercise of the necessary governmental powers by 'such person or persons, and ... in such manner as the President of the United States shall direct'.[7] Congress had not reached this decision without some concern over the extent of powers being conceded to the president and the dangers posed by such military government as he might establish under those powers.[8] In both the matter of the acquisition and incorporation of territory it was the impact on the relationship between Congress and the president and fear of excessive executive power that dominated this debate, which was a debate over ceded territory to which the United States had sovereign title.

There was, however, some uncertainty as to the extent of that sovereign title, with the United States laying claim to the western parts of Spanish Florida under the terms of the Louisiana Purchase, though no attempt was made to assert this claim until 1810, at which point President Madison issued a Proclamation giving effect to the American claim.[9] No such claim existed in respect of the eastern parts of Florida, in which the United State was also keenly interested, in part because of fears of British intervention, arising out of the conflicts of the Napoleonic Wars and the deteriorating relations between Britain and the United States. Here, President Madison invoked fear that these territories might 'pass from the hands of Spain' into those of a foreign power to seek Congressional authorisation for taking 'temporary possession' of them. Congress duly empowered the president to 'occupy' them in order to forestall seizure by another foreign power.[10] Occupation distinct from seizure backed by the claim of sovereignty was clearly acknowledged here, though the possibility of territorial acquisition was also kept open. More far reaching provisions, 'to occupy and hold' all Florida territory not yet in American possession, failed in the Senate the following year, though incursions into Spanish territory in 1812 and subsequently in 1814 and 1818 involved the limited assertion of authority to govern, but with clear acquisitive territorial ambition.[11]

Greater clarity about occupation in the War of 1812 with Britain emerged not from the territorial ambitions of the United States but from the American response to the limited British occupations of American territory.[12] This emerged in the 1819 case of *United States v. Rice*, in which the US Supreme Court had to determine the implications of British occupation of the port of Castine between September 1814 and February 1815 when the peace treaty came into effect. The court concluded that

> By the conquest and military occupation of Castine, the enemy acquired that firm possession which enabled him to exercise the fullest right of sovereignty over that place. The sovereignty of the United States was, of course, suspended, and the laws of the United States could no longer be rightfully enforced there, or be obligatory upon the inhabitants who remained and submitted to the conquerors. By the surrender the inhabitants passed under a temporary allegiance to the British government.[13]

The idea of temporary allegiance indicated a conception of occupation distinct from conquest, though the provision that the British had exercised the 'fullest rights of sovereignty over that place' pointed to doctrines of conquest.[14] American ambivalence in these matters, at least in the eyes of the British Prime Minister Lord Liverpool, was more than slightly self-serving, for the Americans, he complained, invoked the 'extravagant doctrine' of Revolutionary France in refusing to acknowledge a right of conquest over their territory, whilst asserting precisely that right in respect of territory they seized.[15]

This early phase of expansion, with its faltering recognition of occupation as a distinct phenomenon, was connected with the convulsions on the other side of the Atlantic, inducing Napoleonic France to sell Louisiana, while Spain's ability to maintain its authority in the New World was further weakened by occupation of Spain itself, and

Military Occupation and America: Expansion and Civil War 149

the war with Britain sprang in part from the impact on the United States of the British naval blockade of French-held territory. In the war of 1846–8 with Mexico the cause and the occasion were much more affairs of the New World, but they forced the United States into much more direct confrontation with the nature of military occupation, albeit in what many saw as a naked war of conquest. Relations between Mexico and the United States had deteriorated as Texas first asserted its independence from Mexico and subsequently was formally annexed by the United States. Though still formally claimed by Mexico, there was no real prospect of its return. From the American perspective, or at least that of President Polk and those who supported him, the real cause of the 1846 war was not Texas, nor even the boundary between Texas and Mexico, which provided the occasion for the outbreak of war, but much more extensive ambitions, above all desire for the acquisition of California. President Polk's precise motives remain disputed. Whether he deliberately provoked the war, or, more charitably, wanted peace but wanted Mexican territory even more, Polk was the driving force behind it.[16] Moreover, once embarked upon it he was committed to territorial acquisition When his Secretary of State, James Buchanan, produced a draft disavowing territorial gains, Polk asserted that 'though we had not gone to war for conquest, yet it was clear that in making peace we would if practicable obtain California and such other portion of the Mexican territory as would be sufficient . . . to defray the expenses of the war'.[17] Even at the time the war divided the nation, more so as peace proved more difficult to attain than anticipated. The war itself began in April 1846 with American armies striking south into the heart of Mexico and westwards towards California. The less populated California was the more quickly subdued though a small American force also seized Mexico City by September 1847. Despite calls for the annexation of the entirety of Mexico, the Americans had even less prospect of subduing the entire country than the French did in the 1860s. Polk did now long for peace, albeit peace on his terms, which the Mexicans proved reluctant to concede, prolonging the occupation. The increasingly unpopular Polk found himself constrained to accept a treaty granting the United States far less than he desired and leaving Polk embittered towards its American negotiator.[18] Even so the Treaty of Guadalupe-Hidalgo of 3 February 1848 still surrendered a third of Mexican territory and provided the basis for the rapid evacuation of Mexico and the end of the occupation of Mexican territory. The peculiar constitution of the United States, however, and the failure of Congress to act, ensured that the institutions of military occupation in California continued until the last military governor handed over power to an elected civilian governor in December 1849. California finally became a state of the Union in September 1850. In retrospect it seemed to Ulysses S. Grant to have been a 'wicked war'. It had certainly been divisive.[19] One factor behind the divisions amongst the victors was slavery. As an institution it had no impact upon the understanding or direct impact upon the conduct of military occupation in connection with the war, but it was seen as a war to increase the number of slaveholding states.[20]

Slavery, the 'peculiar institution' of the South, as even southerners called it, did have an impact on the conduct of military occupation during the American Civil War.[21] Even for many who opposed the idea of a war to free slaves and shared the racist sentiments of most white members of southern society, emancipation came to be seen as a way of striking at the power on which the rebellion was based.[22] By the same token freed slaves could automatically be included in the tally of those loyal to the Union and constitution.[23] Identifying loyalty and disloyalty, often fraught enough in military occupations, took on added sharpness in a civil war in which southern sympathies were often held by residents of northern states, while Unionists could be found in varying degrees in Confederate states. The dynamics of loyalty and disloyalty became themselves key factors in shaping the conduct of occupation, and prolonging the institutions of occupation, military government, well beyond the end of the war into the Reconstruction period. One consequence of this was that elements of military government and tests of loyalty, above all the loyalty oaths, could be found both in what was occupied territory of Confederate states and the territory of northern states. Similarly the lines between civilian policing of loyalty and military policing of loyalty could become blurred.[24] Yet despite these confusions there were attempts to disentangle different forms of authority and law. This was put most succinctly and clearly in the dissenting judgement in *Ex parte Milligan* in the wake of the Civil War.[25] There military law, that is the laws provided for the regulation of the armed forces themselves, was distinguished from martial law, that emergency military jurisdiction exercised within the limits of the country 'or during rebellion within the limits of states maintaining adhesion to the National Government', and military government as exercised over foreign territory or during civil war 'within states or districts occupied by rebels treated as belligerents'.[26] Although not necessarily expressed with the clarity of Supreme Court judges, such distinctions were evident to some officers during the Civil War, as is suggested by the recollections of Joshua Lawrence Chamberlain.[27] Nevertheless, such clarity as existed was episodic and fragmentary. There was more than enough confusion to justify Harold Hyman's description of the occupations as a 'guideless tour' in which, '[l]acking even an agreed vocabulary, most commentators lumped military occupation questions under the catch-all rubric, martial law'; a tendency which not even modern commentators are free from.[28]

Uncertainty of another kind arose from the nature of the war and the military operations. From the initial exchange of fire at Fort Sumter in April 1861 the conflict spread across a vast territorial range but with much of the fighting and operations of the armies in more restricted areas, primarily of Confederate territory. The area between Richmond and Washington, including the much disputed Shenandoah Valley, saw repeated and increasingly bloody but indecisive clashes. Armies moved back and forth, with some towns, such as Winchester in the Shenandoah Valley, changing hands repeatedly. Occupation was primarily Union occupation of Confederate territory, with General Lee's major incursions into Union territory being stopped at Antietam in 1862 and Gettysburg in 1863. Yet, although the Union struggled to subjugate the Confederacy, the Confederates did not have the capacity to subjugate the Union, but did not need to do so. They had only to prevent Union victory and wait for northern weariness and hopefully foreign recognition of the Confederacy to do their work. In this context, occupation policies became themselves weapons in the war, means of pressuring the occupied into accepting defeat, and returning to loyalty.[29] This alone they could not do. It was left to the relentless advance of General Ulysses Grant in 1864 and then the exhaustion of the Confederacy until Grant finally bludgeoned Lee into surrender at Appomattox Court House in 1865. Control of the Mississippi and neighbouring rivers had funnelled armies into another set of battles until Grant secured the last, and vital, Confederate stronghold on the Mississippi, Vicksburg. Prior to these events Union naval power provided the basis for Union incursions, most notably in North Carolina and Louisiana. The outcome was that for most of the war full Union military occupation was confined to a limited number of garrisoned towns, beyond which, as Stephen Ash has argued, lay a no-man's-land, subject to frequent Union incursions but without constant Union presence. Beyond that, in turn, lay a Confederate frontier subject only to sporadic Union incursion, before untouched Confederate territory was reached.[30] Ultimately these incursions turned into the massive raids of which General Sherman's march through Georgia in 1864 was the most dramatic. Although shaped by the peculiarities of the American Civil War, episodic subjection to alien military authority and uncertainty about the persistence or extent of such authority would be recurrent features of military occupation. For those subject to it in the Civil War, the combination of this uncertainty with the competing claims to loyalty, and not just temporary obedience, with the possibility of retribution for those deemed disloyal, produced acute tensions.[31]

It was these dynamics of loyalty and disloyalty as well as the provisions of that peculiar constitution which ensured that, as with the occupations of the Mexican war, military government stretched beyond the end of the war. Not convinced that the governments of southern states were loyal or even in accordance with the constitution, Congress imposed the continuation of military government against the opposition of the president and commander-in-chief of the army. While the war had ended with the surrender of Confederate forces in 1865, military government lasted until 1868 for most states and longer for some.

The War with Mexico

Although occupation of Mexican territory lacked the complications inevitably encountered by deploying the language and practices of military occupation in a civil war, the lack of direction was sufficient to warrant the extension of Hyman's description of a 'guideless tour' to that experience as well. That was close to the experience of General Kearny as he set out for Santa Fe and beyond that, California. The Secretary of War instructed him to 'establish temporary civil government', suggested that it would be 'wise and prudent' to maintain existing officials, at least those known to be friendly to the United States and who would take the oath of allegiance to them, adding though that it was 'foreseen that what related to the civil government will be a difficult and unpleasant part of your duty, and much must necessarily be left to your own discretion'.[32] Kearny was also promised a proclamation in Spanish which he could use, though none was sent to him. When Kearny arrived in Santa Fe he set about instituting a provisional government, as instructed, but also issued his own proclamation in which he promised the inhabitants of New Mexico free government, adding that the United States, 'absolves all persons residing within the boundaries of New Mexico from any further allegiance to the Republic of Mexico, and hereby claims them as citizens of the United States'.[33] Given the distances and means of communication, it was some time before there was any response to these acts, justification in part for the Secretary of War's emphasis on the commanders' discretion. Not only did Kearny claim the allegiance of the entire population, he drafted an Organic Law for the territory, which was in fact a veritable constitution drawn, as he noted, from a mixture of Mexican law and those of several states of the Union.[34] General Scott warned him that annexation, for that was what his proclamation amounted to, was premature. Much stronger protest emerged from Congress, again, though, as much for fear of excessive executive power and ambition, replete with imagery of an American president playing the role of a Roman emperor, as anything else. Kearny found some defenders, including the president, who acknowledged his constitutional error but offered patriotic zeal in mitigation.[35]

Kearny had shown some tact in attending mass and making protection of religion prominent in his proclamation.[36] Confident that he had established control in the territory, he set out for California. Both Kearny and the man he had appointed as Governor, Bent, had underestimated the extent of resentment still felt and Bent was killed in a brief uprising which was quickly suppressed.[37] The following March a few ringleaders were arraigned and condemned on charges of treason, once again raising wider questions about the status of the land and its inhabitants.[38] Doubts about the proceedings, including the doubts of attorney Frank Blair, who had prepared the indictment, led to debate in Washington and more questions about the exercise of judicial authority in the territory. The Secretary of War conveyed the government's view that the inhabitants owed 'obedience' to the 'temporary civil government in a conquered country' but, since they were 'not, to the full extent of the term, citizens of the United States', it was 'not the proper use of legal terms to say that their offence was treason committed against the United States'.[39]

Judicial matters figured prominently in the considerations of General Scott as American forces advanced southwards. According to Scott's own memoirs, 'the 'wild volunteers as soon as beyond the Rio Grande, committed, with impunity, all sorts of atrocities'.[40] The volunteers, comprising a substantial part of the American forces, were indeed especially ill disciplined, and resentful of attempts by their officers to exert authority. In June 1846 alone Americans were responsible for at least twenty murders in the town of Matamoros. So problematic were the volunteers that a deliberate effort was made to garrison them away from towns.[41] The quartermaster's men, including the numerous teamsters needed by the army, were problematic because of their ambiguous status, not being formally part of the army, an ambiguity they exploited to evade any legal responsibility.[42] There was indeed a much wider reason for the impunity about which Scott complained. Beyond the boundaries of the United States there was no legal system or law to hold these men accountable for acts committed against foreign civilians. Courts martial dealt only with offences against the Articles of War which had made no provision for such matters.[43] Scott, being both indignant at the behaviour of some of his soldiers and conscious of the consequences of antagonising the local populations, responded with General Order no. 20 of February 1847 instituting a system of military commissions to try such persons, specifying that this included 'any individual of the United States forces, retainer or follower of the same'; an order largely reiterated in his General Order no. 287, issued in Mexico City on 17 September.[44] Scott recalled that he had shown a draft of the orders to the Secretary of War, and that the Attorney General had also seen a copy, but that neither would offer any comment upon it, apparently unwilling to bear any responsibility for it.[45] Scott himself claimed that the order 'worked like a charm', 'conciliated Mexicans' and 'intimidated the vicious of the several races'.[46] This was an exaggeration, but crimes were punished and the system of justice was vigorous, but not arbitrary, with similar acquittal rates for both Americans and Mexicans brought before Scott's courts.[47] Complaints from volunteers about Scott's system of justice, including complaints of what was seen as his excessive concern for Mexicans, also suggest the system was of some effect.

Scott's concern to discipline his men extended especially to their behaviour towards the institutions and practices of the Catholic Church. Like Kearny in Santa Fe, Scott would attend mass, despite his personal antipathy to Roman Catholicism. His General Order no. 287 provided that the capital's 'churches and religious worship, its convents and monasteries, its inhabitants and property are, moreover, placed under the special safeguard of the faith and honor of the American army.'[48] Scott also prohibited the sale of Church property, contrary to the decision of the Mexican Vice President to confiscate and sell Church assets to fund the war, which induced vigorous resistance from many Mexicans.[49] There was indeed need for such safeguard. As the Mexicans well knew, anti-Catholicism was strong in North American society. Mexican churches were targets of theft and priests of assault.[50] Even those not necessarily disposed towards offences of this kind viewed the Catholic religion as in part responsible for what they regarded as other deplorable features of Mexican society, especially the poverty which struck many in the occupying armies.[51] Whatever their limitations, the efforts of Scott and other commanders proved sufficient to prevent the religiously coloured opposition that Napoleon's forces had faced in Spain and which could have easily proven fatal to Scott's small force.

Relations with existing Mexican authorities, as well as consideration of religious sensitivity, were crucial to Scott and the other commanders to the south who also presided over relatively small forces. In Mexico City, withdrawal of the Mexican army, reluctance to see the city subject to more damage, especially when faced with Scott's threats if sporadic resistance continued, combined to induce the *ayuntamiento*, or city council, to order the cessation of resistance and to embark upon a policy of reluctant cooperation. This brought first *Alcalde* Manuel Reyes y Veramendi reproaches, including the threat of execution, from the retreating General Santa Anna, and a spirited response of the patriotic commitment of the councillors from Veramendi, justifying their 'protection of the sacred treasures of our unfortunate country'.[52] The city councillors found themselves confronted with the effective municipalisation of authority, so far as it remained in indigenous hands, frequent in military occupations. The principled exclusion of the political authority of the central organs of state, accepted as part of international law, was compounded in the case of Mexico by the near disintegration of an already divided and fragile state structure. In some respects the city councillors' authority was enhanced as Scott authorised their assumption of control over federal sources of revenue, if only to pay the $150,000 contribution, imposed 'in consideration' of the protection offered in Scott's General Order no. 287.[53] Elsewhere American commanders also sought to utilise the existing authorities and engaged, as did Scott's force, in miscellaneous activities from sanitation to public order. Much was left to the discretion of individual commanders. Those at Puebla and Tampico even established chambers of commerce amongst their other activities.[54]

Establishing military government in less populated California encountered other problems. Kearny, who had been entrusted with the establishment of military government, did not arrive in San Diego until December 1846. By then several attempts had been made to establish a form of government, though these were frustrated in part by lack of effective control in the face of vigorous resistance from the Californios.[55] Nevertheless, as early as 7 July 1846 Commodore Sloat had proclaimed that 'henceforth California will be a portion of the United States, and its peaceable inhabitants will enjoy the same rights and privileges as the citizens of any other portion of that nation'.[56] Like Kearny's proclamation in Santa Fe, this one almost met with vigorous criticism.[57] It was left to Sloat's successor, Commodore Stockton, to attempt to implement Sloat's proclamation, soon supplemented by Stockton's own proclamation to the same effect.[58] Stockton was heavily influenced by John Frémont, the famous explorer and topographer, who had been involved in a revolt by American settlers even prior to the outbreak of war. It was Frémont to whom Stockton intended to hand control of California, appointing him governor. These schemes faltered upon the arrival of Kearny, though Stockton initially refused to accept his authority. The ensuing disputes finally issued in the arrest of and later court martial of Frémont.[59] Again, great distances, the available means of communication and imprecise instructions contributed to these confusions, though the obduracy and ambition of Stockton and Frémont were more important factors. Once the initial military opposition of the Californios was set aside, it was indeed fellow Americans who would give the American military governors of California the greatest difficulty.

Stockton's replacement, Commodore Shubrick, had no difficulty recognising Kearny's authority, as set out in his orders. The arrival of Colonel Mason, with more recent instructions from Washington also confirmed Kearny's authority. Kearny, however, had not grasped some of the wider limits to that authority, despite his rebuff after his proclamation at Santa Fe; for his proclamation of 1 March 1847 announced that the 'undersigned hereby absolves all the inhabitants of Cal. from any further allegiance to the Republic of Mexico'.⁶⁰ Mason, who succeeded Kearny in May 1847, did have a better appreciation of these limits and soon asserted that '[n]o political rights can be conferred on the inhabitants ... emanating from the Constitution of the United States'.⁶¹ Mason was well aware that this set him in opposition to his fellow countrymen.⁶² This involved setting aside appointees of Stockton, the implementation of which fell on one occasion to Lieutenant William Tecumseh Sherman.⁶³ More broadly it arose from Mason's determination to uphold existing law and to work through existing institutions until the fate of California was settled. The existing institutions included the office of *alcalde*, whose combination of executive, legislative and judicial functions was resented by the American immigrants, as were the restrictions under Mexican land law, which Mason also sought to maintain, with the assistance of Henry Halleck, who served as Mason's secretary of the interior. These clashes accelerated as immigration increased with the discovery of gold in January 1848, becoming a major issue by July. Seeking to respond to the changing environment Mason, while remaining within his understanding of his authority, prepared a new legal code, drawing on a mixture of Spanish and American law.⁶⁴ Mason was close to publishing this code when news arrived in California in August of the Treaty of Guadalupe-Hidalgo.

For Mexico, at least those parts not ceded by the treaty, this meant the reassertion of some form of national authority. In Mexico City it signified the end of the local administration headed by Francisco Suárez Iriarte which had come to power with the aid of the Americans, ousting the Veramendi administration, which in turn thereby recovered its tarnished patriotic credentials. Iriarte's faction had favoured extreme decentralisation and Mexico's negotiators had pressed for an end to American support for Iriarte. On the American side the signing of the treaty was also followed by change as Scott, the victim of Washington partisan conflict, was replaced. The new commander agreed to an armistice in March. Though American forces did not depart fully until September, the Americans now assisted the central Mexican authorities in reasserting control. The armistice agreement obliged both sides to disperse armed bodies opposed to either side. Moreover, from June 1848 the United States sold extensive quantities of arms and munitions, at discounted rates, to their former adversaries.⁶⁵ As the Americans departed, Mexicans turned on those deemed to have been too compliant with the occupier in one form or another. Iriarte faced trial and a brief period of imprisonment.[66] Less well-known Mexicans met with more immediate and often brutal treatment. As Grant noted, 'some barbarities have been committed such as shaving the heads of females'.[67]

While the Treaty of Guadalupe-Hidalgo brought clarity to the situation to the south, in California it brought more confusion as the practical difficulties of maintaining military government increased. Desertion, as the lure of the gold fields grew, depleted the military's resources. In August, soon after the news of Guadalupe-Hidalgo, Captain Folsom reported from San Francisco:

> Government, both civil and military, is abandoned. Offences are committed with impunity, and property, and lives even, are no longer safe ... Tomorrow morning the volunteers will be mustered out of service, and we shall be utterly without resource for the protection of public property.[68]

Equally striking was Governor Mason's uncertainty of the basis of his own authority once the peace treaty had been ratified and the state of war ended, for with the war his powers derived from his understanding of the laws of war ended too. On the same day that Folsom lamented conditions in San Francisco, Mason wrote to the War Department asking

> what right or authority do I have to exercise civil control in time of peace in a Territory of the United States? ... Yet ... I feel compelled to exercise control over the alcaldes appointed and to maintain order if possible ... the calamities and disorders which would surely follow the absolute withdrawal of even a show of authority, impose on me, in my opinion, the imperative duty to pursue the course indicated, until the arrival of dispatches from Washington ... relative to the organization of a regular civil government.[69]

Even though Mason believed he had to continue governing, or appearing to do so, his authority was diminished in comparison with its previous extent. According to Halleck, neither Mason nor his successor 'has claimed authority to make any new laws for California since the war, that power being vested in Congress alone'.[70]

The peculiar constitution insisted that Congress alone could legislate and Congress alone could make regulations for territories and admit new states to the Union. But Congress was paralysed over the issue of whether a Californian state would be a slave state or a free state. In this condition Secretary of State Buchanan concluded that:

> The termination of the war left an existing government, a government de facto ... and this will continue, with the presumed consent of the people ... The consent of the people is irresistibly inferred from the fact that no civilized community could possibly desire to abrogate an existing government when the alternative presented would be to place themselves in a state of anarchy, beyond the protection of all laws, and reduce them to the unhappy necessity of submitting to the dominion of the strongest.[71]

Meanwhile, President Polk called on Congress to organize a territorial government, and Senator Douglas sought to accelerate the entire process by admitting California directly as a state. The latter proposal, however, met with the objection that while Congress had the power to admit new states, the creation of states was an act of popular sovereignty.[72] The idea of popular sovereignty was shared by many inhabitants of California and by Senator Benton, according to whom, given Congress's failure to act, it was the right and duty of the people to form a government for themselves.[73]

With the encouragement of Senator Benton some of the inhabitants held a series of meetings from December 1848 onwards, issuing in a self-proclaimed Legislative Assembly. Mason's successor, General Riley, declared its activities illegal. Riley, however, had recognised the unsatisfactory nature of the current condition but had hoped for Congressional initiative. Upon hearing that Congress had adjourned without acting, Riley himself called a constitutional convention. In the same proclamation he gave his own interpretation of the existing arrangements, claiming that he was a civil governor rather than a military governor. Military government, he argued, had ceased with the termination of the war: 'what remains is the *civil* government', albeit one entrusted to the same person as military affairs in California.[74] It was this authority that Riley surrendered on 20 December 1849, after the ratification of the constitution and due election of Governor Burnett. Of the two prospective senators elected days earlier one was John Frémont.[75]

Both Mason and Riley had had difficulty clarifying or even justifying their authority. Their governments, despite Riley's equivocation, were clearly continuations of those military governments of occupied Mexico, relying on military force to sustain them and fading away to the mere 'show of authority' with the diminution of that force. Called upon for its verdict on the nature of that authority in the case of *Cross v. Harrison*, the Supreme Court set out the dilemma in detail but in substantial accordance with the self-understanding of the military governors and some of their officers. The court concluded that Mason

> may not have comprehended fully the principle applicable to what he might rightly do in such a case, but he felt rightly, and acted accordingly ... The government of which Colonel Mason was the executive, had its origin in the lawful exercise of a belligerent right over a conquered territory ... It was the government when the territory was ceded as a conquest, and it did not cease, as a matter of course, or as a necessary consequence of the restoration of peace. The president might have dissolved it by withdrawing the army and navy officers who administered it, but he did not do so. Congress might have put an end to it, but that was not done. The right inference from the inaction of both is, that it was meant to be continued until it had been legislatively changed.[76]

The court's deduction from the failure of either the president or Congress to act, like Mason's 'imperative duty' and Buchanan's 'presumed consent', was a confession of the difficulty of making sense of the circumstances that arose from the experience of military occupation, especially when combined with the peculiar constitution of the United States.

The Civil War

Understanding the experience of the Civil War in terms of the language and practices of occupation was made possible, and necessary, both by conscious decisions about the legal nature of what was happening and by the practical experiences in the encounters between northern authorities and southern citizenry. It was made possible and necessary in the first place by treating the conflict as a war between belligerents, both endowed with at least some of the customary rights of belligerents, and secondly, by the fact that when Union forces took hold of southern territory it proved necessary to institute military government, and indeed to maintain military government, even beyond the end of the war. While this second condition was a practical necessity, even here there were subsequent arguments to the effect that legally the reestablishment of the full panoply of normal relations should have automatically followed upon northern possession of southern territory. In the case of the first condition, practical necessity prevailed again, but not without at least partial attempt to choose an alternative path and persistent, ultimately irresolvable, equivocation. For, from the perspective of the North, the Union was faced with treasonous rebellion. Indeed, as has been aptly observed: 'Unionists had no vocabulary beyond the word "treason" to describe and respond to the enormity of what was happening'.[77] To this extent its opponents were not legitimate belligerents but traitors who should stand before federal courts to answer for their crimes. This was complicated by the fact that many putative traitors already lay within the grasp of Union authorities, being citizens of northern states, though this too encouraged Union authorities to back away from the full consequences of their official stance.[78] A more decisive test came in relation to Confederate privateers following Lincoln's proclamation of 19 April 1861 denouncing the crews of Confederate naval vessels as pirates.[79] By the summer the crews of two Confederate privateers were awaiting trial on charges of piracy. Responding to the first, *Savannah*, Confederate President Jefferson Davis wrote to Lincoln on 6 July 1861, invoking 'the desire of this Government so to conduct the war now existing as to mitigate its horrors as far as may be possible' and protesting against Union treatment of the captured seamen as 'a practice unknown to the warfare of civilized man' and warning of retaliation.[80] Behind Lincoln's and the northern courts' actions lay the denial of belligerent status to the Confederacy, and hence refusal to acknowledge the letters of marque which endowed privateers sailing in its name with the status of legitimate belligerents. When one of the trials ended in conviction Davis responded by ordering a selection to be made amongst Union prisoners in preparation for retaliation.[81] The embarrassment of the Union's position was evident in the outburst by one of the judges: 'But why make a difference between those taken on land and on water? Why not try all those taken on land and hang them?'[82] Justice Grier promptly concluded that this was unthinkable. Nor could the Union government sustain its position, transferring the seamen to military prisons and treating them as prisoners of war.

That decision was more consistent with the other element of Lincoln's proclamation of 19 April 1861, namely the institution of a blockade of southern ports, for blockade was a legitimate institution in international law governing warfare. Lincoln had opted for a policy of blockade rather than a policy of closing southern ports, which would have been more consistent with putting down an insurrection, because of vehement British opposition and the implicit threat to retaliate in the event of closure by recognising the Confederacy.[83] On the other hand, the legality of blockade rested upon the presumption of legitimate belligerency of the two sides. Maintaining the difference between recognition of the belligerency of the Confederacy and recognition of the Confederacy, though there was a difference, was not easy.

The policy of blockade had other legal ramifications when its consequence, the seizure of vessels caught running the blockade and their condemnation as prizes of war, came before the courts, and finally before the Supreme Court at the beginning of 1863, one of the few war-related cases to appear before that court during the war.[84] Even before they reached the Supreme Court, Judge Peleg Sprague in Boston had concluded that the Union could be both a belligerent power, a party to a war, and a sovereign power, suppressing an insurrection.[85] The Supreme Court, by a majority of a single vote, concluded that war existed, that 'it is not necessary to constitute war, that both parties should be acknowledged as independent nations or sovereign states', and that the blockade was therefore legal.[86] The majority acknowledged, but set aside, the objection, that 'the President himself, in his proclamation, admits that great numbers of the persons residing within the territories in possession of the insurgent government, are loyal in their feeling' and had a right to be treated as such.[87] Though the dissenting Justice Nelson only accepted the existence of a state of territorial belligerency from a later date than the majority, the conclusion he drew was no less dramatic, for it meant the 'conversion of the personal into the a territorial war', the consequence of which was to 'confound all distinction between guilt and innocence'.[88]

The attempt to insist on the treacherous nature of the rebellion but, for certain purposes, to treat the Confederacy, its soldiers and seamen, as if they were legitimate belligerents was the solution adopted by the Lieber Code, that is, the Instructions for the Government of the Armies of the United States in the Field, issued as General Orders no. 100 in April 1863. These instructions had been drafted by Francis Lieber, with the support and authorisation of Henry Halleck, now General-in-Chief of Union Armies.[89] According to the instructions,

[w]hen humanity induces the adoption of the rules of regular war towards rebels . . . it does in no way whatever imply a partial or complete acknowledgement of their Government, if they have set up one, or of them as an independent or sovereign power.[90]

Like later general codes and codified international laws, adherence to them, or knowledge of them, even amongst officers, was often limited. Yet, the Lieber Code reflected broader assumptions about the conduct of war, recollections of experience in Mexico, the orders and regulations of individual commanders, including Halleck's own regulations of 1861 for his forces in Missouri.[91]

Military government became a reality as soon as Union troops entered Confederate territory. Just as legal interpretation construed the southern states as if they were belligerents, and hence their territory as occupied territory, or, as the habit was 'conquered' territory, so too Union soldiers, though by their own understanding operating on territory of the United States and liberating the inhabitants from manipulation by a slaveowning aristocracy, effectively treated the territory of the South as occupied. In this, the great diversity of culture and economic life, genuinely alien to many northern soldiers, contributed to this perception and the associated behaviour.[92] Although not as bad as the volunteers in Mexico, the behaviour of northern soldiers was often poor in the eyes of their officers. General Milroy, for example, expressed his dismay at plundering by Union regiments.[93] All commanders issued instructions on respect for persons and private property and called for the strictest discipline. General Mitchel, not noted for any softness towards secessionists, took the unusual step in military occupations of threatening to hand over errant soldiers 'to the civil authorities of the neighbourhood in which the offense is perpetrated, to be detained and dealt with by them according to their laws'.[94] While Mitchel's order was unusual, the general emphasis on discipline was in accordance with the policy of the Union government, and with the overwhelming initial sentiments of the military commanders that the rebellion was to be explained in terms of the manipulation of the population by a clique, and that underlying loyalty to the Union was widespread. General Burnside's proclamation to the people of North Carolina on seizing Roanoke Island in February 1862 reflected these sentiments, referring to the 'desolating war brought on your State by comparatively a few bad men in your midst', and called on the inhabitants to 'separate yourselves at once from their malign influence'.[95] Even later in the war, when this policy had increasingly given way to the 'hard hand of war', the initial sentiment was still present in orders issued in Florida in February 1864, reminding Union soldiers that 'we are here to bring back the sentiment of the people by kindness and protection, and not to exasperate by improper and barbarous irregularities unbecoming to discipline'.[96]

As part of that policy Lincoln made some early prominent appointments, namely Andrew Johnson as Military Governor of Tennessee on 3 March 1862, when its capital, Nashville, became the first capital of a Confederate state taken by Union forces. Johnson, a politician not a soldier, was, however, given the rank of Brigadier General. Edward Stanley followed in May, though without Union forces seizing the state capital of North Carolina. George Shepley was appointed Military Governor of Louisiana in June 1862. Finally, John S. Phelps, a Missouri congressman, was appointed Governor of Arkansas in July 1862, though his military governorship was formally abolished a year later.[97] Generals customarily appointed military commanders of towns they occupied. General Butler, often assimilated to the military governors though his position was formally different, had appointed Shepley 'military commandant' of New Orleans earlier.[98] The position, as Halleck later had occasion to emphasise to General Rosecrans, endowed these men with 'authority to administer civil government', with the intention to 'mitigate as much as possible the evils resulting from a government purely military, and to restore to the loyal people, and to those who are willing to return to their allegiance, the benefits of civil government'.[99] The appointments raised concerns in Congress. As on earlier occasions, the concern was with the possibility of excessive presidential power and departure from the normal rule that appointments should be made 'with the advice and consent of the Senate'. One senator asked rhetorically 'Is there any law of Congress vesting the power in the President to appoint a military Governor in North Carolina?'; though he conceded that the president 'may detail Andrew Johnson, a brigadier general in the Army of the United States, to keep the peace of Nashville'.[100] Another objected to Butler's appointment of 'a Governor of that city, to control it and govern it' and to Lincoln's appointment of a Governor of the State of North Carolina; though he conceded the president 'might appoint a Governor of that conquered district or territory, or rather of the people, the public enemies who were making war against the Government of the United States'.[101] Behind these distinctions, imprecisions and simple errors, the senators grasped and vainly objected to the blurring of the line between the military and the political inherent in the very idea of military government.

Ironically the appointment of distinct military governors might be said to have been intended to restore that line, or at least to restore it as soon as possible. To the extent that it did, it tended to generate tensions between the military governors and the generals in command of Union armies. It was precisely recurrent conflict between General Rosecrans and Governor Johnson that was the occasion for Halleck's attempt to clarify the two roles. Relations with Generals Rosecrans and Buell were not helped by Johnson's desire to have a military force at his own disposal and his conviction in the superiority of his own strategic insight.[102] Nor were they helped by Rosecrans' establishment of a police force that Johnson thought counterproductive and his support of Colonel Truesdail, whom Johnson detested, to run it.[103] Such conflicts were clearly aggravated by personal differences but were rooted in overlapping authority and lack of clarity about the precise functions of these roles. The indeterminacy of the role of military governor was apparent when Secretary of War Stanton was pressed to reveal the extent of the powers conferred on Edward Stanley and responded by forwarding his letter of appointment granting him

> all and singular the powers, duties and functions pertaining to the office of Military Governor (including the power to establish all necessary offices and tribunals and suspend the writ of habeas corpus) during the pleasure of the President or until the loyal inhabitants of that State shall organize a government in conformity with the Constitution of the United States.[104]

It is notable that while Halleck sought to persuade Rosecrans of the possibility of a clear division of responsibility, he reported to Sherman his opposition to the 'origination of civico-military government, under civilians', while Grant wrote to the secretary of war in 1864 'Please advise the President not to attempt to doctor up a State Government for Georgia by the appointment of citizens in any capacity whatever'.[105] By that point, however, Lincoln had also come to doubt the wisdom of appointing a separate military governor given his experience of the conflict between those governors and the military commanders.[106]

One difficulty experienced by both military governors and military officers exercising military government, as well as soldiers of varying rank in the more normal performance of their duties, was discerning the disloyal from the loyal, and coming to terms with the fact that loyalty was far less extensive than they had expected. Disloyalty could even increase as a reaction to the rigours of occupation, consolidating secessionist sentiment.[107] As with most military occupants, those of America's Civil War hoped for cooperation from the existing local authorities, a hope bolstered in this instance by the expectation of loyalty amongst significant sections of the population. Just as with the post of military governor, so too with the policy of conciliation, as they called it, there was no precise guidance as to its meaning. So much was this the case that in a commission investigating the conduct of General Buell it was noted that his policy of conciliation was that of the government, adding: 'At least he could violate no orders on the subject because there were none'.[108] Nevertheless the policy of conciliation was clearly based on that presumption of underlying loyalty or susceptibility to such. Both expectations, linked as they were, soon proved deceptive.[109] Ben Butler's expectation of cooperation was clear when he announced to the city council of New Orleans, 'I desire only to govern the military forces of the department [and to sustain] the government of the United States against its enemies'.[110]

Butler soon found that a combination of a recalcitrant council, waves of refugees from the fighting, shortage of food, fear of disease in the shape of the yellow fever that was an annual affliction, and against which his northern soldiers had no immunity at all, forced him into a range of governmental functions from organising foodstuffs and labour to sanitation and the provision of emergency hospitals. It is indicative that one of Shepley's first acts as military commandant of New Orleans was setting the price of bread and other basic commodities.[111] Johnson's version of the policy of conciliation involved a rapid return to the election of local officials. Here, the policy met with an abrupt check when the election for a circuit court judge resulted in the choice of a notorious secessionist, obliging Johnson to comply with the formalities of the election by handing the judge his commission only to then have the same man arrested and imprisoned on account of his disloyalty, appointing his defeated opponent in his place.[112] Even General Sherman, less inclined to conciliation, preferring indeed the simplicity of the doctrine that the war made enemies of all of the inhabitants of the South, began his government of Memphis in July 1862 professing to want to strictly limit his involvement. He too soon began to expand the remit, threatening one judge that if he 'uses his court for political purposes so as to nullify the law of Congress . . . he will find himself change places with the criminal at the bar'.[113]

All military governments faced problems with more diffuse opposition from less prominent citizens than judges and councillors. Southern women especially exploited mid-nineteenth century expectations about gender and the indeterminate immunity it gave them to publicly demonstrate their hostility to the occupation forces. It was this that led to the notorious order of Ben Butler, General Orders no. 27 of 13 May 1862. In the light of the 'repeated insults from the women (calling themselves ladies) of New Orleans' to which his officers and soldiers had been subjected, Butler ordered that

> hereafter when any female shall by word, gesture, or movement insult or show contempt for any officer or soldier of the United States she shall be regarded and held liable to be treated as a woman of the town plying her avocation.[114]

With rare exceptions, Butler succeeded in intimidating the women of New Orleans into less obvious displays of their hostility. Butler's order caused outrage in the South and was even invoked unfavourably in the British Parliament. Yet it was not this which gave Butler the greatest difficulty or caused his transfer later in the year. That was his relationship with the foreign consuls, of which New Orleans had an especially large number. Butler had even drawn up a special oath for these troublesome individuals but it was his suspicion that they were concealing assets on behalf of the Confederate government and his pursuit of those assets that aroused their indignation, and their protests to their own governments. Fear of foreign recognition of the Confederacy, especially by Britain and France, whose navies had the power to break the Union blockade, effectively determined aspects of Union occupation policy. Indeed Butler himself blamed Secretary of State Seward for his removal from New Orleans.[115]

Awareness of the strength of secessionist sentiment and hostility to the occupation grew throughout the war and occupation but it impressed itself on some Union soldiers quite early, prompting their recommendation of harsher policies, as well as disagreements with fellow Unionists who continued to believe in a policy of conciliation. Here too the function of oaths changed. The imposition of oaths was sanctioned in the Lieber Code, though only in respect of 'magistrates and civil officers'.[116] In practice administering oaths had become the norm. Everybody, from judges to schoolteachers and prospective voters in Nashville, was compelled to take an oath. On this matter General Rosecrans and Military Governor Johnson could work together.[117] Oaths served, initially it was thought, to distinguish the loyal from the disloyal. Butler, for example, justified the imposition of an oath on the grounds of it 'having become necessary ... to distinguish those who are well-disposed toward the Government of the United States from those who still hold allegiance to the Confederate States'.[118] Yet from the outset there were doubts as to their efficacy. Salmon Chase, though he had enforced oaths within his own Treasury Department, suspected that southerners would too easily take and then break an oath.[119] A Union colonel reporting a pursuit of John Morgan's cavalry near Nashville concluded that 'We have reason to know we are surrounded with treachery ... Many who take the oath of allegiance only do it to betray us'.[120] On the other hand, oaths were often refused as they were by many in Nashville. Southern women were often particularly emphatic in refusing oaths and policing southern men who were tempted to take the oath. One female resident of New Orleans recorded her intent to steadfastly refuse the oath, 'let me lose what I may by refusing'.[121] Elaborate justification for swearing, but not feeling bound by the 'detestable oath' mixed with mockery of the Yankees who 'cling to the oath as a political touchstone' suggests that taking the oath was not easily treated lightly.[122] So too did the argument of the New Orleans newspaper that invoked the linkage of allegiance and protection in Blackstone's *Commentaries on the Laws of England* to reassure its readers that they had been freed from allegiance to the Confederacy.[123]

From being a device for encouraging the willing, a demonstration of return to allegiance, oaths became increasingly a part of a coercive repertoire. One dramatic early instance of that was General Pope's order of 23 July 1862:

> Such as are willing to take the oath of allegiance to the U.S., and will furnish sufficient security for its observation, shall be permitted to remain at their homes and pursue in good faith their accustomed avocations. Those

who refuse shall be conducted south beyond the extreme pickets of this army, and be notified that if found again anywhere within our lines, or at any point in rear, they will be considered spies, and subjected to the extreme rigour of military law.[124]

One alarmed female secessionist of Winchester recorded two days later: 'We cannot believe that this last tyrannical order will be carried out, but the Provost Marshall is coming back into town today, it is said, to apply the test.'[125] Although in practice few were driven south in execution of Pope's order, another order, of 18 July, decreeing that 'the troops of this command will subsist upon the country in which their operations are carried on', was implemented with rigour and became an increasing, and oppressive pattern.[126] It was this order of Pope's that induced Johnson to write to the Secretary of War welcoming the order and proclaiming that '[t]he rebels must be made to feel the weight and ravages of the war they have brought upon the country. Treason must be made odious and traitors impoverished.'[127] Pope had instructed that receipts were to be issued, which the loyal would be able to redeem at the end of the war. Even this discrimination though was often abandoned as southern Unionists saw their property taken without warning or receipt.[128] By the summer of 1862 Union enthusiasm for the policy of conciliation was fading. Along with Pope, General Wright in Florida and General Mitchel in Tennessee and northern Alabama pursued more aggressive policies. Mitchel's officers judged oaths to be unreliable: the 'oath is taken to be broken', wrote one.[129] Mitchel gave a new twist to Pope's logic, ordering the confiscation of food from occupied territory in response to the severing of his supply lines by Confederate cavalry, intending not only to replenish his force's food supplies but also to turn the population against the Confederate raiders. It was, however, censorship, generating prolonged uncertainty about family, especially soldiers in the Confederate armies, which proved most effective, much more so than oaths, in gnawing at southern will to resist.[130]

In what became a war on property in occupied territory, the peculiar form of property of the South was the ultimate weapon. Some Unionists, including a few generals, had thought so from the outset. The Lieber Code proclaimed that 'Slavery, complicating and confounding the idea of property (that is, of a thing), and of personality (that is, of humanity), exists according to municipal or local law only. The law of nature and nations has never acknowledged it.'[131]

From this the Code concluded not only that freedom came automatically with the 'protection of the military forces of the United States', bound as they were by the law of nations but not the municipal laws of the enemy, but that such freedom fell under 'the shield of the law of nations' and could not be extinguished by any right of postliminium.[132] This principled and clear argument came only after the Emancipation Proclamation came into effect on 31 January 1863. Prior to that military commanders lacked clear guidance, as they did on much else. Some were inclined to respect the institution of slavery and to refuse protection to escaped slaves. Others were not. The issue could divide officers and men. In July 1862 General Milroy noted the 'prejudices against fugitive slaves and a strong disposition to abuse and drive them away from camp'.[133] On the other hand, General Jacob Cox recorded that hostility in the army to returning slaves was so widespread that it poisoned the relationships with officers who did return them.[134] It also raised additional complications as when General Mitchel, citing the effects of guerrilla attacks upon his forces and supply lines, wrote to the Secretary of War:

> I have some prisoners (citizens) against whom the negroes will prove charges of unauthorized war. Am I to convict on the testimony of the blacks? . . . May I offer the protection of the Government to the negroes who give valuable information?[135]

While Lincoln hesitated, avoiding any principled stance in favour of emancipation for fear of driving border states into secession and alienating otherwise staunch Unionists who were nevertheless opposed to emancipation, Union generals, as well as lower ranking officers and ordinary soldiers, were faced with escaped slaves seeking protection. Confrontation over the issue was provoked by the ever wilful John Frémont as Commander of the Western Department in Missouri when he issued a proclamation of 30 August 1861 that armed persons within designated occupied territory would be tried and if found guilty shot, that the property of all secessionists in Missouri would be 'confiscated to their public use, and their slaves, if any they have, are hereby declared freemen'.[136] Unwilling to give the impression of having thought his proclamation hasty, when Frémont was faced with Lincoln's reservations about both points in his proclamation, he insisted upon being formally ordered to cancel the proclamation.[137] General Hunter's proclamation of 9 May went much further than Frémont's. Announcing, though failing to elaborate, that '[s]lavery and martial law in a free country are altogether incompatible', Hunter declared that all slaves in Georgia, Florida and South Carolina 'are therefore declared forever free'.[138] Hunter received no suggestion, let alone order, to rescind his proclamation. Lincoln's response was a proclamation disavowing knowledge or authorisation of Hunter's proclamation and stating that such matters were beyond the remit of commanders in the field. Lincoln also added that he reserved judgement for himself on 'whether it be competent for me, as commander-in-chief of the army and navy to declare the slaves of any State or States free'.[139]

These diverse views brought together principled attitudes to slavery, political calculation, personal and otherwise, and understandings of what was and was not appropriate at different levels of command of occupied territory. The latter, of course, has to be set in the context of the constitution of the United States. These issues had, however, already found one kind of solution. Faced with escaped slaves seeking protection and calls from Confederates for their return, Ben Butler, then at Fort Monroe on the coast of Virginia, had not responded with a principled proclamation but had refused to return the slaves on the grounds that they were contraband of war.[140] Arguing that slaves had been used to construct Confederate fortifications, Butler argued that they resembled any other form of contraband, liable to seizure as an act of war. While Butler's designation of these people as contraband legally perpetuated what the Lieber Code identified as the error of confounding the ideas of property and personality, it met with approval from the President and his cabinet.[141] Secretary of War Cameron informed him that while he was not to interfere 'with the relations of persons held to service under the laws of any State', he was not to return such persons who came within his lines.[142] The apparent equivocation reflected the division between what had to be seen as political principle, requiring therefore the consent of Congress, and what could be presented as an act of war within the competence of the president as commander-in-chief. The latter, however, as Lincoln's proclamation in response to Hunter indicates, was itself unsettled.[143]

The principle that property, including slaves, useful to the Confederate war effort could be seized was sanctioned in the first Confiscation Act of 6 August 1861, which left the fate of the 'contrabands' after the war undecided. This Confiscation Act, like the stronger

Confiscation Act of July 1862, provided elaborate legal machinery for the enforcement of confiscation through federal courts. In practice, however, little property was formally confiscated through the machinery of these acts.[144] Confiscation was extensive but implemented by military commanders on their own authority. This does not mean, though, that the confiscation acts were unimportant. As in the case of Butler's designation of escaped slaves as contraband, the Confiscation Act provided moral, political and, if the prescribed machinery were ignored, legal support for military commanders. To some, although a lesser, extent, the same could be said of the Emancipation Proclamation of 31 January 1863.[145] By then Union army incursions into Confederate territory were already shattering slavery as a system. The Emancipation Proclamation gave sanction and support especially to those officers, such as General Milroy in occupied Winchester, who were already opposed to slavery on principled or pragmatic grounds.[146] Yet since it applied only to territory at that point in Confederate hands, it still left uncertainty about the position of slavery in territory already under Union occupation, especially in Tennessee and Louisiana, already setting conservative Unionists against radical Unionists.[147]

Not even the successful conclusion of the war, in the sense of the defeat of Confederate forces, put an end to the uncertainty. Slavery as a system was doomed, destroyed by the war fought to save it. Whether the former slaves would enjoy political equality and what economic relations would replace slavery were not settled. Nor was it clear when military authority over what had been Confederate territory would end or who was to be counted amongst the loyal and who not. The dynamics of loyalty and disloyalty in fact perpetuated military rule. In part the question of loyalty was a question of definition. The definition was supplied by the form of the loyalty oath which was imposed. While loyalty typically took the form of commitments to future behaviour, the ironclad test oath of July 1862 and its variants required an oath as to past behaviour:

> I have voluntarily given no aid, countenance or counsel or encouragement to persons engaged in armed hostilities ... have neither sought nor accepted nor attempted to exercise the functions of any office whatever, under any authority or pretended authority in hostility to the United States.[148]

Military Occupation and America: Expansion and Civil War 173

Carried over, as it was, into the post-war era, this form of oath perpetuated the divisions of loyalty and disloyalty of the war, and was intended to do so. That disloyalty persisted, in the sense of persistent Confederate sentiment and hostility to the policies of the Union, was manifest in numerous ways. It was evident in the report by a Major Stanhope of a riot in Norfolk in April 1866, which noted that the rioters 'were to a man, dressed in rebel gray'.[149] It was evident in the assertion of the man from Georgia who declared that he would 'vote for no man who could take the Congressional oath, because it is the highest evidence of infidelity to the people of the State'.[150] Yet perpetuating the test of loyalty as a condition of public office meant excluding entire swathes of the population. Strict enforcement paralysed the business of government, postponing the opening of the federal court in Charleston until April 1866 for want of a district attorney who could take the oath.[151] Yet the practice of the claims commissions, especially the Southern Claims Commission, established to hear claims for compensation from loyal men, suggested more than pragmatic dissatisfaction with the system of oaths. In one instance the fact that a claimant took the oath when the army occupied the area was judged 'far from conclusive on the subject', with the Commission adding: 'He did not suffer for the Union cause'.[152] They were no closer to being sure of loyalty and disloyalty than they had been at the beginning of the war.

Both President Lincoln and his successor, President Johnson, favoured future-oriented oaths and wanted rapid reintegration of occupied states into the Union. That had been Lincoln's purpose in the appointment of military governors and his subsequent pleas and plans for reconstruction. Although Johnson as Military Governor in Nashville had demanded that 'treason be made odious', as president he too favoured rehabilitation. The peculiar constitution, however, made the admissions of representative and senators the business of Congress. And Congress, the president and the military commanders were divided about the status of the occupied territory they were contemplating, which was linked back to disagreements about the nature of the war.[153] Ironically the southern view now was that it had indeed been an insurrection and all that was required was for duly elected officers to take the oath to the constitution of the United States. Generals Sherman and Joseph Johnston had reached an agreement to this effect in April 1865.[154] At the other extreme, the radical Republican Senator Thaddeus Stevens, accepting that the Confederate

States had left the Union, concluded that they were no longer States at all but mere conquered territory and their inhabitants no citizens of the Union. Since most were unwilling to accept the former view, not believing in the loyalty of the officers elected by the defeated southern states, yet shrank from the consequences of Stevens' view, they readily adopted the option offered by Representative Samuel Shellabarger, according to which the states had continued to exist, the territory and inhabitants had remained within the Union, but, as the Majority Report of the Joint Committee on Reconstruction put it in June 1866: the rebellious states had 'destroyed their State constitutions in respect of the vital principle which connected their respective States with the Union'.[155]

Such interpretations mattered because they affected the extent and distribution of authority between the various elements of the American constitutional field, as was clear to all of them, including military commanders.[156] President Johnson's plan of Amnesty and Reconstruction was announced on 29 May 1865. Amnesty would follow from a simple future-oriented oath, save for a small Confederate elite who would have to apply personally to the president for amnesty. Provisional governors would organise conventions to rescind secession and ratify the Thirteenth Amendment abolishing slavery as well as to organise elections whose representative would be admitted to Congress. Neither Congress nor many army commanders, including Grant, were convinced of the loyalty of these southern governments, which did indeed work to perpetuate as much of the subjugation of the black population as they could.[157] It was Congress that blocked Johnson's scheme by refusing to admit southern representatives in December 1865.

At the same time the army's authority was being challenged through a wave of civil suits claiming damages for actions both during and after the war. Still being deeply involved in the Reconstruction process, especially through the Freedmen's Bureau, established in March 1865 to assist the former slaves, and so deeply entwined in the army that it was not clear whether officers seconded to it were still responsible to their former commanders, military officers often felt especially exposed.[158] Despite the provisions of the 1863 Habeas Corpus Act providing indemnity for military officers, doubt about whether the president or the States would enforce it induced Grant to issue General Order no. 3 requiring the army to 'protect' army personnel and veterans from such legal suits and to make arrests where the civil authorities would not or could not.[159] Though not always unsupportive of the army's conflicts with civil authorities, Johnson's priority was the restoration of southern civil authority. In April 1866 he proclaimed the end of the rebellion throughout the south. This coincided with the preliminary decision of the Supreme Court in the case of *Ex parte Milligan*, denying the jurisdiction of military commissions. Other judgements followed, condemning strict enforcement of the test oath.

As the gap between continuing military authority in the south and the restoration of civil authority widened, Congress struck back with its own reconstruction plan. The Reconstruction Act of 2 March 1867 provided that

> Whereas no legal State governments or adequate protection for life or property now exists in the rebel States of Virginia, North Carolina, South Carolina, Georgia, Mississippi, Alabama, Louisiana, Florida, Texas and Arkansas ... *Be it enacted, &c.*, That said rebel States shall be divided into military districts and made subject to the military authority of the United States.[160]

When Johnson sought to curtail military authority by inviting the attorney general to issue a restrictive opinion on the army's authority, Congress replied with the Reconstruction Act of 19 July 1867 reaffirming military authority and adding the extraordinary provision 'That no district commander ... shall be bound in his action by any opinion of any civil officer of the United States'.[161] Whereas it had been Congressional paralysis that had perpetuated military government in California, here it was Congressional resolution that perpetuated it. By the same token it was only continuing Congressional resolution that could maintain military authority. As southern states were readmitted Congressional resolution faded, as too eventually did that of President Grant when he failed to respond to appeals from Adalbert Ames, Governor of Mississippi, for military support against a wave of intimidation and murder of Republicans and black people.[162] In one sense regime transformation had been built into the military occupations of the American Civil War. The mere presence of Union armies in slaveowning states had ensured that. Yet much more had been needed to prevent southern reassertion of political and economic discrimination, and that was not forthcoming.

The Supreme Court, Secession and Military Occupation

The Supreme Court found it difficult over the following decades to make sense of the military occupation of American territory by Union forces in the name of a Union claiming to be suppressing a war of rebellion. The Court followed Shellabarger in its judgement in *Texas v. White*, arguing that at a time when Texas was still without representation in Congress and subject to military rule, as well as during the war, 'the State did not cease to be a State, nor her citizens to be citizens of the Union'.[163] The apparent irony of the contrast drew comment from both southern and northern papers.[164] Following through the logic of *Texas v. White* the court sometimes succumbed to the temptation to declare that the Confederacy had been a legal nullity, that none of its acts or decisions of its courts had any validity.[165] Yet just as the restored authorities of occupied territory have had to concede at least in some measure the validity of the acts of the occupant, so too did the Supreme Court have to concede some validity to Confederate acts. Sometimes this analogy between the status of the Confederate States and that of a military occupant was explicit in the court's judgements. Invoking the court's own judgements in respect of the British occupation of Custine and the Union's occupation of Tampico during the war with Mexico, the court concluded that 'the people of the insurgent States, under the Confederate government were, in legal contemplation, substantially in the same condition as inhabitants of a country occupied and controlled by an invading belligerent'.[166] This legal device allowed the court to accept the validity of acts of a power it denied any legitimacy to. Yet the analogy, carrying with it the presumption of the hostility of the population to the supposed Confederate occupant, had to be implicitly denied in order to explain other aspects of the experience. Thus, in *Dow v. Johnson*, where the court dealt with events in New Orleans, it judged that this was not territory

> restored to its normal relations to the Union, by the fact that they had been captured by our forces, and were held in subjection. A feeling of intense hostility against the government of the Union prevailed, as before, with the people, which was ready to break out into insurrection upon the appearance of the enemy in force, or upon the withdrawal of our troops. The country was under martial law; and its armed occupation gave no jurisdiction to the civil tribunals over the officers and soldiers of the occupying army.[167]

That was an accurate depiction of the conditions in New Orleans during the Civil War and at the time of the July 1866 riot that undermined the plausibility of Johnson's reconstruction plan.[168] The clear specification of the forces of the Union as occupants is difficult to reconcile, however, with the analogy which made the Confederate governments the occupant. Yet the court believed it had succeeded in resolving the problem of the Union's status, namely, whether it was a belligerent engaged in a war or a sovereign engaged in suppressing an insurrection. In *Lamar v. Brown* the court declared that

> It is quite true that the United States, during the late war, occupied a peculiar position. They were, to borrow the language of the counsel for the plaintiff, both 'belligerent and constitutional sovereign'; but, for the enforcement of their constitutional rights against armed insurrection, they had all the powers of the most favoured belligerent. They could act both as belligerent and sovereign. As belligerent they might enforce their authority by capture; and, as sovereign, they might recall their revolted subjects to allegiance by pardon, and restoration to all rights, civil as well as political. All this they might do when, where, and as they chose. It was a matter entirely within their sovereign discretion.[169]

The court had confronted a central dilemma of the Civil War expedience and simply decided it was not a dilemma at all.

The American experience of occupation had been marked by the peculiarities of the United States: of its constitution, of the peculiar form of property that was slavery, and of the great test of its existence which was the Civil War. Yet for all that was so distinctive about it many aspects of its experience and understanding of occupation were in evidence on the other side of the Atlantic. Doubts about the nature of the occupant's authority, the problems of reconciling justice and occupation, the conflict between civil and military authority, the strains facing the occupant from a hostile population and even the choice between conciliation and the hard hand of war were familiar enough. It was the inherent nature of these problems, compounded indeed by the peculiarities of the United States, which accounted for the American experience of occupation.

Notes

1. 'Prize Cases', *US Reports*, 67 (1862), 673.
2. Paul Ford, *The Works of Thomas Jefferson*, vol. 10 (New York: Putnam, 1905), p. 29.

3. Ibid. p. 29. He soon added that the less said about constitutional difficulty the better: letter of 30 August 1803, in Thomas Randolph (ed.), *Memoir, Correspondence and Miscellaneous from the Papers of Thomas Jefferson*, vol. 4 (Boston: Gray and Bowen, 1830), p. 2. The constitutional position is assessed by Gary Lawson and Guy Seidman, *The Constitution of Empire* (New Haven: Yale University Press, 2004). Jefferson had been sufficiently concerned to consider constitutional amendment. See David Currie, 'The constitution in Congress: Jefferson and the west', *William and Mary Law Review*, 39 (1998), 1460.
4. 'American Insurance Company v. 356 Bales of Cotton', *US Reports*, 26 (1828), 542.
5. Ibid. p. 542.
6. Lawson and Seidman, *The Constitution of Empire*, p. 3.
7. David Yancy Thomas, *A History of Military Government in Newly Acquired Territory of the United States* (Honolulu: University Press of the Pacific, 2002).
8. See, for example, the debate in *Annals of Congress*, 8th Congress, 1st Session, 497–515.
9. For the complex manoeuvring in relation to Florida see especially Isaac Cox, *The West Florida Controversy, 1798–1818* (Baltimore: Johns Hopkins Press, 1918).
10. David Hunter Miller, *Secret Statutes of the United States* (Washington DC: Government Printing Office, 1918), pp. 4–6.
11. See Rembert W. Patrick, *Florida Fiasco* (Athens, GA: University of Georgia Press, 2010).
12. It is notable that even in retrospect the Supreme Court viewed all the Floridas as 'disputed territory'. 'Lessee of Pollard's heirs v. Kibbe', *US Reports*, 39 (1840), 372. Clarity was not helped by the language of the 1819 treaty that allowed both parties to uphold their claims to sovereignty over West Florida, see Lawson and Seidman, *The Constitution of Empire*, p. 90. The same point had been noted by the Supreme Court in 'Foster & Elam v. Neilson', *US Reports*, 27 (1829), 311.
13. *US Reports*, 17 (1819), 254. See also the complex case of 'Shanks et al. v. Dupont et al.', *US Reports*, 28 (1830), 242–50, especially 246.
14. The slightly later case of 'Shanks v. Dupont' was more precise, specifying that the occupation 'did not destroy but only suspend their former allegiance', p. 246.
15. *Supplementary Despatches, Correspondence and Memoranda of Field Marshal Arthur Duke of Wellington*, vol. 9 (London: Murray, 1862), p. 384.
16. Amy S. Greenberg, *A Wicked War* (New York: Vintage, 2013), p. 95; Robert W. Merry *A Country of Vast Designs* (New York: Simon & Schuster, 2009), p. 195.

17. Greenberg, *A Wicked War*, p. 109.
18. Ibid. pp. 238–40.
19. See the title of Seymour V. Connor and Odie B. Faulk, *North America Divided: The Mexican War 1846–1848* (New York: Oxford University Press, 1971), noting that it was divisive for both nations, p. 133.
20. See Adam Smith, *The American Civil War* (Basingstoke: Palgrave Macmillan, 2007), pp. 27–9.
21. Paul Finkelman, 'The centrality of the peculiar institution in American legal development', *Chicago-Kent Law Review*, 68 (1992), 1009–33.
22. This point is not dependent on assumptions about the complex issues of the causes of the Civil War. For a succinct overview of the historiography see Frank Towers, 'Partisans, new history and modernization: the historiography of the Civil War's causes, 1861–2011', *Journal of the Civil War Era*, 1 (2011), 237–64.
23. See the comment of General Gillmore, reporting from Savannah on the general disloyalty of the white population 'while the colored people, with rare unanimity, have been true to the national flag and national authority, and have never, except under armed compulsion, given aid and comfort to the insurgents', War Department, *The War of the Rebellion* (Washington DC: Government Printing Office, 1880–1901) [hereafter: *War of the Rebellion*], series 1, vol. 47, part 3, p. 467.
24. See especially Chapter 4, 'The Provost Marshal confusion', in William A. Blair, *With Malice toward Some: Treason and Loyalty in the Civil War Era* (Chapel Hill, NC: North Carolina Press, 2014). See also the earlier reference by A. H. Carpernter to a special commission to review cases of those imprisoned by provost marshals as itself 'another curious bit of machinery, half military and half civil in character', 'Military government of Southern territory, 1861–1865', *Annual Report of the American Historical Association*, 1 (1900), 473.
25. This was identified as a key turning point by William Birkhimer, *Military Government and Martial Law* (Washington DC: J. J. Chapman, 1892), p. vi.
26. 'Ex parte Milligan', *US Reports*, 71 (1866), 141–2.
27. Joshua Lawrence Chamberlain, *The Passing of the Armies* (New York: Putnam, 1915), p. 291.
28. Harold Hyman, *A More Perfect Union* (New York: Knopf, 1973), p. 157. Clarity was not helped by contemporaries' habit of quoting the Duke of Wellington's well-known but misleading comments. See ibid. pp. 163–4. For the modern confusion in the reference to 'martial law' 'being employed for government of occupied territory' see James Sefton, *The United States Army and Reconstruction, 1865–1877* (Baton Rouge, LA: Louisiana State University Press, 1969), p. 7.
29. Occupation policies were also a means to exert pressure to agree to

peace in Mexico. See especially the idea of restricting the occupation to an area demarcated by an indemnity line: Norman Graebner, 'Lessons of the Mexican war', *Pacific Historical Review*, 47 (1978), 333–5.
30. Stephen Ash, *When the Yankees Came. Conflict and Chaos in the Occupied South, 1861–65* (Chapel Hill, NC: University of North Carolina Press, 1999), p. 77. A tripartitie structure was also suggested, albeit in a different context, by Hubert van Houtte, *Les occupations étrangères en Belgique sous l'Ancien Régime*, vol. 1 (Ghent: Van Rysselberghe and Rambaut, 1930), p. 144.
31. See for example the report of a Colonel Kennett in Tennessee in March 1862: 'We found the Union sentiment subdued on account of our contemplated departure, the people fearing a demonstration against them', *The War of the Rebellion*, series 1, vol. 10, part 1, p. 49.
32. *Occupation of Mexican Territory* (Washington DC: Government Printing Office, 1912), p. 8. Described by Ralph Gabriel as 'one of the first directives in American history relating to military government', 'American experience with military government', *American Political Science Review*, 37 (1943), 419.
33. *Occupation of Mexican Territory*, p. 23.
34. Ibid. pp. 27–76. Kearny gracefully acknowledge his debt to a Colonel Doniphan and Private Hall for these laws, ibid. p. 23. Both Doniphan and Hall were lawyers. Joseph Dawson, 'American civil-military relations and military government: The service of Colonel Alexander Doniphan in the Mexican War', *Armed Forces and Society*, 22 (1996), 558–60.
35. Thomas, *A History of Military Government*.
36. K. Jack Bauer, *The Mexican War 1846–1848* (New York: Macmillan, 1974), p. 134.
37. The appointment of the civilian Bent did not detract from the seniority of military authority as the Secretary of War later made clear, Mary Loyola, 'The American occupation of New Mexico, 1821–1852', *New Mexico Historical Review*, 14 (1939), 231–2.
38. For the indictment see Ralph Twitchell, *The History of the Military Occupation of the Territory of New Mexico* (Denver: Smith-Brooks, 1909), pp. 140–1.
39. Thomas, *A History of Military Government*, pp. 123–4.
40. Winfield Scott, *Memoirs of Lieut.-General Scott*, vol. 2 (New York: Sheldon, 1864), p. 392.
41. Paul Foos, *A Short, Offhand Killing Affair: Soldiers and Social Conflict during the Mexican-American War* (Chapel Hill, NC: University of North Carolina Press, 2002), pp. 98, 120.
42. Ibid. p. 100.

43. David Glazier, 'Kangaroo court or competent tribunal? Judging the 21st century military commission', *Virginia Law Review*, 89 (2005), 2027–8.
44. Birkhimer, *Military Government and Martial Law*, p. 467.
45. Scott, *Memoirs of Lieut.-General Scott*, vol. 2, pp. 393–4.
46. Ibid. p. 396.
47. Glazier, 'Kangaroo court or competent tribunal?', pp. 2031–3.
48. Birkhimer, *Military Government and Martial Law*, p. 468.
49. Irving Levinas, 'A new paradigm for an old conflict: The Mexico-United States war', *Journal of Military History*, 73 (2009), 406–7.
50. For anti-Catholicism and violence see Foos, *A Short, Offhand Killing Affair*, pp. 129–31. For some important limitations see Ted Hinckley, 'American anti-Catholicism during the Mexican War', *Pacific Historical Review*, 31 (1962), 121–37.
51. See, for example, the views of Private Ballentine, in Grady McWhiney and Sue McWhiney (eds), *To Mexico with Taylor and Scott 1845–1847* (Waltham: Blaisdell, 1969), pp. 157–8.
52. Dennis Berge, 'A Mexican dilemma: The Mexico city ayuntamiento and the question of loyalty, 1846–1848', *Hispanic American Historical Review*, 50 (1970), 236–7.
53. Ibid. pp. 239–40.
54. Justin Smith, 'American rule in Mexico', *American Historical Review*, 23 (1918), 298.
55. This is often neglected: see Lisbeth Haas, 'War in California, 1846–1848', *California History*, 76 (1997), 331–55. The term Californios designates inhabitants of Mexican heritage from pre-conquest California.
56. Joseph Ellison, 'The struggle for civil government in California, 1846–1850', *California Historical Quarterly*, 10 (1931), 11.
57. Ibid. p. 11.
58. Thedore Grivas, *Military Governments in California 1846–1850* (Glendale, CA: Clark, 1963), p. 55.
59. Thomas Kearney, 'The Mexican war and the conquest of California: Stockton or Kearny conqueror and first Governor?', *California Historical Society Quarterly*, 8 (1929), 251–61, concluding firmly for Kearny, as indeed do most other studies.
60. Grivas, *Military Governments in California*, p. 102, despite having received a letter from Scott stating 'You will not, however, formally declare the province to be annexed', ibid. p. 104.
61. Ibid. p. 110.
62. Myra Saunders, 'California legal history: the legal system under United States military government, 1846–1849', *Law Library Journal*, 88 (1996), 494.

63. Ellison, 'The struggle for civil government in California', p. 23.
64. Saunders, 'California legal history', pp. 499–502; Lindley Binum, 'Laws for the better government of California, 1848', *Pacific Historical Review*, 2 (1933), 279–91.
65. Levinas, 'A new paradigm for an old conflict', pp. 413–14.
66. Berge, 'A Mexican dilemma', pp. 253–5.
67. James McCaffery, *Army of Manifest Destiny* (New York: New York University Press, 1992), p. 200.
68. Lawson and Seidman, *The Constitution of Empire*, p. 186.
69. Ibid. pp. 155–6.
70. Saunders, 'California legal history', p. 503.
71. 'Cross v. Harrison', *US Reports*, 57 (1853), 184–5.
72. Joseph Ellison, 'The struggle for civil government in California, 1846–1850 (continued)', *California Historical Quarterly*, 10 (1931), 140–1.
73. Grivas, *Military Governments in California*, pp. 204–6.
74. Ellison, 'The struggle for civil government in California, 1846–1850 (continued)', pp. 145–6.
75. Grivas, *Military Governments in California*, p. 148; Ellison, 'The struggle for civil government in California, 1846–1850 (continued)', p. 164.
76. 'Cross v. Harrison', *US Reports*, 57 (1853), 193. For a detailed analysis of the Court's judgement see Lawson and Seidman, *The Constitution of Empire*, pp. 151–79.
77. Blair, *With Malice toward Some*, p. 36.
78. J. G. Randall, *Constitutional Problems under Lincoln* (New York: Appleton, 1926), pp. 87–8, but see also Blair, *With Malice toward Some*, passim.
79. James Richardson (ed.), *A Compilation of the Messages and Papers of the Presidents*, vol. 8 (Washington DC: Bureau of National Literature, 1902), pp. 3215–16.
80. James D. Richardson (ed.), *A Compilation of the Messages and Papers of the Confederacy*, vol 1 (Nashville: United States Publishing, 1906), pp. 115–16.
81. According to Mark A. Weitz they were convicted 'because to do otherwise added weight to the growing fear in the North that the Confederacy might be something other than a rebellion. It might be a nation', *The Confederacy on Trial. The Piracy and Sequestration Cases of 1861* (Lawrence, KS: University of Kansas Press, 2005), p. 162.
82. Randall, *Constitutional Problems under Lincoln*, p. 93.
83. Closure would have exposed British sailors to arrest as common smugglers, Jeffrey Amestoy, 'The Supreme Court argument that saved the Union', *Journal of Supreme Court History*, 35 (2010), 12.

84. On this see Jonathon White, 'The strangely insignificant role of the U.S. Supreme Court in the Civil War', *Journal of the Civil War Era*, 3 (2013), 211–38.
85. Amestoy, 'The Supreme Court argument that saved the Union', p. 15.
86. 'Prize Cases', p. 666. It was significant that the Court treated this as a legal matter whereas previous 'piracy' trials had insisted that recognition of belligerency was a political matter, Stephen Neff, *Justice in Blue and Gray* (Cambridge: Harvard University Press, 2010), pp. 23–6.
87. Prize Cases', p. 672.
88. Ibid. p. 696.
89. Halleck played a larger role in this code than merely authorising Lieber to draft it.
90. Article 152, *War of the Rebellion*, series 3, vol. 3, p. 163.
91. Frank Freidel, 'General Orders 100 and military government', *Mississippi Valley Historical Review*, 32 (1946), 543–4.
92. As noted by Edward Philips, 'The Lower Shenandoah Valley during the Civil War', unpublished PhD thesis, University of North Carolina, 1958, pp. 172–4; for recent elaboration in the context of North Carolina, see Judkin Browning, *Shifting Loyalties: The Union Occupation of Eastern North Carolina* (Chapel Hill, NC: University of North Carolina Press, 2011), pp. 126–35.
93. Jonathon Noyalas, *'My will is absolute law': A Biography of Union General Robert H. Milroy* (Jefferson, NC: McFarland, 2006), pp. 50–1.
94. *War of the Rebellion*, series 1, vol. 10, part 2, p. 293. Something judged to be 'singularly absurd' by the Supreme Court, 'Dow v. Johnson', *US Reports*, 100 (1879), 165.
95. *War of the Rebellion*, series 1, vol. 9, pp. 363–4.
96. *War of the Rebellion*, series 1, vol. 35, part 1, p. 483.
97. Ruth Cowen, 'Reorganization of Federal Arkansas, 1862–1865', *Arkansas Historical Quarterly*, 18 (1959), 35–7.
98. *War of the Rebellion*, series 1, vol. 9, p. 396. On Butler as a *de facto* military governor, see Edwin Hardison, 'In the Toils of War: Andrew Johnson and the Federal Occupation of Tennessee, 1862–1865', unpublished PhD thesis, University of Tennessee, 1981, pp. 369–70.
99. *War of the Rebellion*, series 3, vol. 3, p. 77.
100. *Congressional Globe*, 37th Congress, 2nd session, p. 2973.
101. Ibid. p. 2973.
102. Buell for his part thought a military government inopportune and possibly totally unnecessary, Peter Maslowski, *Treason Must be Made Odious. Military Occupation and Reconstruction in Nashville, Tennessee, 1862–65* (Millwood, NY: KTO Press, 1978), p. 37.

103. The 'principal bone of contention' between them according to Clayton Hall, *Andrew Johnson. Military Governor of Tennessee* (Princeton: Princeton University Press, 1916), p. 78. For an even less charitable view of Truesdail and the vices of this kind of police operation see Walter Durham, *Reluctant Partners: Nashville and the Union July 1, 1863 to June 30, 1865* (Nashville: Tennessee Historical Society, 1987), pp. 33–7.
104. *War of the Rebellion*, series 1, vol. 9, p. 397. There was no more clarity about the duties of a military commander of a city, as noted in respect of Shepley's appointment by Chester Hearn, *When the Devil Came Down to Dixie: Ben Butler in New Orleans* (Baton Rouge, LA: Louisiana University Press, 1997), p. 98.
105. Robert Futtrell, 'Federal military government in the South, 1861–1865', *Military Affairs*, 15 (1951), 184.
106. As he told a delegation from Arkansas, 22 January 1864, in Roy Basler (ed.), *The Collected Works of Abraham Lincoln* (New Brunswick, NJ: Rutgers University Press, 1953), vol. 7, p. 144.
107. Thus the conclusion of Browning, *Shifting Loyalties*, p. 176. Much depended on the precise local circumstances. See the conclusion in Barton Myers of a retreat into 'public neutrality' and then deception, *Executing Daniel Bright: Race, Loyalty and Guerrilla Violence in a Coastal Carolina Community 1861–1865* (Baton Rouge, LA: Louisiana State University Press, 2009), pp. 132–3.
108. *War of the Rebellion*, series 1, vol. 16, part 1, p. 9.
109. Some officers claimed to have had success with the policy of conciliation. See the comments of Colonel Mundy, though this was in defence of General Buell, a firm supporter of conciliation, *War of the Rebellion*, series 1, vol. 16, part 1, pp. 632–4.
110. Christopher Pena, *General Butler: Beast or Patriot* (Bloomington, IN: 1st Book Library, 2003), p. 68.
111. Hearn, *When the Devil Came Down to Dixie*, pp. 98–9.
112. Hall, *Andrew Johnson*, pp. 48–9.
113. Futtrell, 'Federal military government in the South', p. 185. Even Sherman showed questionable optimism in Memphis: Joseph Parks, 'A Confederate trade centre under federal occupation: Memphis, 1862–1865', *Journal of Southern History*, 7 (1941), 294–301. For his preference for simplicity see Maslowski, *Treason Must be Made Odious*, p. 75.
114. *War of the Rebellion*, series 1, vol. 15, p. 426.
115. Gerald Capers, *Occupied City. New Orleans under the Federals 1862–1865* (Lexington, KY: University of Kentucky Press, 1965), p. 103.
116. Article 26, *War of the Rebellion*, series 3, vol. 3, p. 151.

117. Harold Hyman, *Era of the Oath: Northern Loyalty Tests during the Civil War and Reconstruction* (Philadelphia: University of Pennsylvania Press, 1954), p. 39.
118. Benjamin Butler, *Private and Official Correspondence*, vol. 1 (privately issued, 1917), p. 575.
119. Hyman, *Era of the Oath*, pp. 2 and 35.
120. *War of the Rebellion*, series 1, vol. 10, part 1, p. 6.
121. Kate Rowland and Morris Croxall (eds), *The Journal of Julia Le Grand: New Orleans 1862–1863* (Richmond, VA: Everett Waddey, 1911), p. 63.
122. Judkin Browning (ed.), *The Southern Mind under Union Rule: The Diary of James Rumley, Beaufort, North Carolina, 1862–1865* (Gainesville, FL: University Press of Florida, 2009), pp. 63–5.
123. Thomas Dabney, 'The Butler regime in Louisiana', *Louisiana Historical Quarterly*, 27 (1944), 514.
124. *War of the Rebellion*, series 1, vol. 12, part 2, p. 52.
125. Michael Mahon (ed.), *Winchester Divided: The Civil War Diaries of Julia Chase and Laura Lee* (Mechanicsburg, PA: Stackpole, 2002), p. 49.
126. *War of the Rebellion*, series 1, vol. 12, part 2, p. 50. On the implementation of this order but not the one of 23 July see Mark Grimsley, *The Hard Hand of War: Union Military Policy toward Southern Civilians, 1861–1865* (Cambridge: Cambridge University Press, 1995), pp. 90–1. Donald Sutherland, 'Abraham Lincoln, John Pope and the origins of total law', *Journal of Military History*, 56 (1992), 567–86 for an evaluation of the broader significance.
127. *War of the Rebellion*, series 1, vol. 16, part 2, p. 216.
128. For an example of the changing experience of one Unionist see Wayne Durrill, *War of Another Kind: A Southern Community in the Great Rebellion* (Oxford: Oxford University Press, 1990), pp. 134–5.
129. Joseph Danielson, *War's Desolating Scourge: The Union Occupation of North Alabama* (Lawrence, KS: University Press of Kansas, 2012), p. 54.
130. Ibid. pp. 66–7, 54–8.
131. Article 42, *War of the Rebellion*, series 3, vol. 3, p. 153.
132. Article 43, ibid.
133. Noyalas, '*My will is absolute law*', pp. 56–7.
134. Jacob Cox, *Military Reminiscences of the Civil War*, vol. 1 (New York: Scribner, 1900), pp. 157–8.
135. *War of the Rebellion*, series 1, vol. 10, part 2, p. 166.
136. *War of the Rebellion*, series 1, vol. 3, p. 467.
137. For the context see James McPherson, *Battle Cry of Freedom* (London: Penguin, 1990), pp. 352–3.

138. *War of the Rebellion*, series 1, vol. 14, p. 311.
139. John G. Nicolay and John Hay (eds), *The Life and Works of Abraham Lincoln*, vol. 7 (New York: Tandy, 1905), pp. 171–2. Lincoln's curious mode of response may have been influenced by personal factors, Edward Miller, *Lincoln's Abolitionist General* (Columbia, SC: University of South Carolina Press, 1997), pp. 102–3.
140. For Butler's own account see Benjamin Butler, *Butler's Book: Autobiography and Personal Reminiscences* (Boston: Thayer, 1892), pp. 256–8.
141. The confusion and the irony of its consequences in Butler's hands were noted by the abolitionist Horace Greeley: Murray Horowitz, 'Ben Butler and the negro', *Louisiana History*, 17 (1976), 167.
142. *War of the Rebellion*, series 2, vol. 1, p. 755.
143. For some of the interpretations of these issues see Robert Fabrikant, 'Lincoln, emancipation and "military necessity"', *Howard Law Journal*, 52 (2009), 375–405, arguing for Lincoln's expansive view of the latter.
144. Patricia Lucie, 'Confiscation: constitutional crossroads', *Civil War History*, 23 (1977), 307–21.
145. With some exaggeration, Robert Fabrikant, 'Emancipation and the Proclamation', *Howard Law Journal*, 49 (2006), 314–15.
146. Noyalas, '*My will is absolute law*', pp. 81–3.
147. For Louisiana see Ann Berler, 'A Most Unpleasant Part of Your Duties. Military Occupation in Four Southern Cities, 1861–1865', unpublished PhD thesis, University of North Carolina, 2013, pp. 204–5; for Tennessee see Durham, *Reluctant Partners*, pp. 52–3.
148. Hyman, *Era of the Oath*, p. 158. For the passing of this oath, pp. 22–3.
149. John Moore, 'The Norfolk riot', *Virginia Magazine of History and Biography*, 90 (1982), 58.
150. Hyman, *Era of the Oath*, p. 86.
151. Ibid. p. 56.
152. Browning, *Shifting Loyalties*, p. 162.
153. For clear survey of the range of options see William Dunning, *Essays on the Civil War and Reconstruction* (New York: Macmillan, 1898), pp. 99–121: John Harrison, 'The lawfulness of the Reconstruction Acts', *University of Chicago Law Review*, 68 (2001), 390–3.
154. Randall, *Constitutional Problems under Lincoln*, notes that Sherman 'included the whole subject of political reconstruction in his terms of capitulation', p. 149.
155. Harrison, 'The lawfulness of the Reconstruction Acts', p. 402.
156. See, for example, John Schofield, *Forty-Six Years in the Army* (New York: Century, 1897), p. 374. This does not mean, of course, that they agreed on the precise implications of any one interpretation.

157. For early emphasis of the importance of the army's role see Harold Hyman, 'Johnson, Stanton and Grant: a reconsideration of the army's role in the events leading to impeachment', *American Historical Review*, 66 (1960), 85–100.
158. Shortage of manpower, a recurrent problem as the armies of the occupant were disbanded, added to this, inducing General Terry in Virginia to combine the positions of provost marshal and bureau agent, Sefton, *The United States Army and Reconstruction*, p. 47.
159. Hyman, *A More Perfect Union*, pp. 452–3; Sefton, *The United States Army and Reconstruction*, p. 73.
160. Edward McPherson (ed.), *The Political History of the United States of America during the Period of the Reconstruction (from April 15, 1865 to July 15, 1870)* (Washington DC: Philip & Solomons, 1871), p. 191.
161. Ibid. p. 336.
162. Eric Foner, *Reconstruction: America's Unfinished Revolution 1863–1877* (New York: Harper Collins, 2002), pp. 558–63.
163. 'Texas v. White', *US Reports*, 74 (1868), 726.
164. Cynthia Nicoletti, 'The Great Question of the War: The Legal Status of Secession in the Aftermath of the American Civil War', unpublished PhD thesis, University of Virginia, 2010, pp. 462–3.
165. 'Hickman v. Jones', *US Reports*, 76 (1869), 200.
166. 'Thorington v. Smith', *US Reports*, 75 (1868), 12–13.
167. 'Dow v. Johnson', *US Reports*, 166–7.
168. Joseph Dawson, *Army Generals and Reconstruction. Louisiana, 1862–1877* (Baton Rouge, LA: Louisiana State University Press, 1982), pp. 38–40.
169. 'Lamar v. Brown', *US Reports* 92 (1875), 195.

Chapter 4
The Franco-German War and Occupation of France

The Long Short War

The conflict which began with the French declaration of war on 19 July 1870 was the culmination of a progressive deterioration in Franco-German relations since the Austro-Prussian War. French neutrality in that war entitled them, so they believed, to some form of compensation, of which one possibility was the acquisition of Luxembourg. That option was excluded by the Treaty of London of 11 May 1867 which provided for collective guarantee of the neutrality of Luxembourg and also ended the prolonged Prussian right of occupation of Luxembourg.[1] One of the reasons the French had to be dissatisfied was that European governments were finding it increasingly difficult to engage in the territorial transactions by which they had adjusted the shifting balance of power. This difficulty was no longer just a residue of the territorial settlement of Vienna, fading as its significance was, but was also a product of the growth of nationalist sentiment that made such transactions less acceptable.[2]

While the precise causes of the war remain disputed, both sides invoked and manipulated national sentiment: Napoleon in order to prop up his increasingly fragile and unpopular regime; Bismarck in order to promote Prussian hegemony within the context of a unified Germany.[3] It was, moreover, less the cause than the conduct of the war and its outcome that determined the nature of the occupation and so shocked contemporaries. The sheer speed and extent of the French defeat was remarkable. At the end of what would seem from the perspective of the protracted European conflicts of the twentieth century to be a short war, the European balance of power had been turned upside down, so it seemed to Disraeli.[4] Yet the relative brevity of the war belied the difficulty in ending it, which in turn prolonged and exacerbated the occupation in the process.

Initially it seemed that the siege of one of the French armies in the fortress of Metz and the crushing defeat of the other main army at Sedan on 1 September 1870, ending with the surrender of over 100,000 men and the captivity of Emperor Napoleon, signified the end of the war. From the time of this great victory Bismarck was looking for a peace treaty to end the war. The possibility of a sudden and neat end to crown German military victory began to unravel as a republic was proclaimed in Paris under pressure from the street on 4 September. Even by this point it was well known that German war aims now included the cession of Alsace and parts of Lorraine; an aim for which there was widespread enthusiasm in the German states.[5] The newly self-proclaimed Government of National Defence in Paris, in the shape of Jules Favre, responded to this aim with the proclamation on 6 September that 'We will not cede an inch of our territory or a stone of our fortresses' and warned that a shameful peace would lead to a war of 'extermination'.[6] After the new government held initial discussions with Bismarck, the *Journal officiel* reiterated Favre's words and complained that Prussia claimed Alsace and Lorraine by right of conquest, adding that it 'will not even consent to consult the population; wanting to dispose of them like a flock of sheep'.[7] With one of France's main armies defeated and the other besieged in Metz, and with Paris itself encircled, the Minister of the Interior and War Léon Gambetta called for a *levée en masse* and the conduct of a partisan war against the invader.[8]

Despite his rhetoric of a partisan war, Gambetta placed his hopes in a repetition of the *levée en masse* of 1792, believing that patriotic republican armies could overwhelm Prussian forces.[9] There was in reality little prospect that they could. Yet the formation of new French armies drew the Germans south towards Orleans, seeking to destroy them, and extending occupied territory in the process. Not even the humiliating surrender of Marshal Bazaine's army at Metz at the end of October could dissuade Gambetta and many inspired by him from their conviction of the inherent superiority of the citizen in arms.[10] Nor could the *francs-tireurs* who came closest to fulfilling Gambetta's rhetoric of partisan warfare pose any serious challenge to German military superiority. They did tie down considerable numbers of German soldiers and contributed to a bitterness that also led General Voigts-Rhetz to speculate on the emergence of a war of extermination.[11] The American General Phil Sheridan, present as an observer with German forces, doubtless recalling his devastation of the Shenandoah Valley, advised Bismarck there had to be 'more smoke from burning villages' before the French would give in.[12] Yet most Frenchmen did not share the enthusiasm of Gambetta and the *francs-tireurs* and did not need to see more villages burn before wanting only peace. It was in full knowledge of this that Bismarck had offered to assist with the holding of scheduled elections in October: elections which Gambetta and the head of the Government of National Defence, General Trochu, had postponed on 18 October.

Although Bismarck was confident the French people would help him bring the war to an end, he had to find a government with which to negotiate a peace and which could ensure that France would abide by that peace. The Government of National Defence, soon divided between Paris and Tours, represented as yet only a republican faction. It was regarded as no more than a *de facto* government even by the neutral powers. Nor, at least prior to the signature of a peace agreement, did Bismarck have an interest in helping it to achieve international recognition. For that would have deprived Bismarck of his other option, that is, a peace negotiated with a restored imperial family, though how the Bonapartists were to be levered back into power was another matter.[13] Though willing to agree a peace with either the republicans or the Bonapartists, if they would agree to his terms and proved credible negotiating partners, Bismarck also had to guard against the involvement of the neutral powers in any settlement, an involvement which the French ardently desired. Further motivation for rapid conclusion of peace and frustration at its postponement came from divisions within the Germans own ranks. Here the Chief of the General Staff, Helmuth von Moltke, was determined upon extending the war and occupation across all of the country until France's position as a European Great Power was utterly destroyed. Bitter clashes between the two men resulted, with Moltke accusing Bismarck of interfering in military affairs and Bismarck accusing Molke of interfering in political matters. Both were right.

It was Bismarck who gained the backing of the Prussian king amidst negotiations for an armistice with Favre. Faced with the exhaustion of the capital's food supplies Favre was ready to accept key elements of Bismarck's terms. The fragility of the French side was evident even in the signing of the armistice which came into effect on 28 January, when they had some difficulty identifying a credible military representative for the armistice.[14] The armistice changed the nature of the occupation but did not end it. Nor did it ensure that a peace agreement would follow. Gambetta intended to exclude people associated with the previous regime from the planned elections for a National Assembly, in the hope of producing an Assembly that would reject a peace agreement. Under intense pressure from Bismarck, Favre and his colleagues overruled Gambetta, forcing his resignation. The election, organised under German supervision in occupied territory, including the areas of Alsace and Lorraine that Germany intended to retain, produced a majority in favour of peace. It was one of the few occasions on which an occupant allowed inhabitants of occupied territory to participate in a national election.[15]

The new government under Adolphe Thiers quickly negotiated a preliminary peace that was ratified on 2 March 1871. This too changed the nature of the occupation but did not end it. Indeed the French prolonged the Brussels negotiations for a definitive peace, intending to gain significant revisions of the harsher elements of the preliminary peace. At this point, on 18 March, a further complication arose as a revolt in Paris produced the Paris Commune opposed to Thiers' government. This threat to the government with whom Bismarck had negotiated the preliminary peace and threat to French credit, which was vital to payment of the indemnity demanded by the Germans, initially induced Bismarck to support the Thiers government.[16] Though feigning non-interference in French internal affairs, Bismarck increased the permitted number of French troops in the occupied zone around Paris and transported released French soldiers held as prisoners of war to allow for suppression of the Commune. Yet as the French showed no sign of urgency, Bismarck curtailed the transfer of French troops and instructed the German Governor General Fabrice to increase the burden of the occupation as well as showing himself less hostile to the Paris Commune. As French interest in suppressing the Commune increased, Bismarck, affirming the occupant's right to neutrality in internal disputes, now proved uncooperative. Under these pressures Thiers negotiated a definitive peace: on Bismarck's terms. He also won Germany cooperation in allowing the French to suppress the Commune.

Once again though, the political process of terminating the war did not bring an end to the occupation but only changed its nature. The Treaty of Frankfurt, signed on 10 May 1871, provided not only for the territorial gains and the indemnity Germany wanted but also for the staged withdrawal of German troops tied to the payment of the indemnity. Even then the partial evacuation of the Departments and forts around Paris was to 'take place so soon as the German government shall consider the re-establishment of order, both in France and Germany, sufficient to ensure the execution of the engagements contracted by France'.[17] Although a series of Conventions now regulated the conduct of the occupation, it was not until 16 September 1873, a full three years after Bismarck had embarked on his search for peace, that the last portions of French territory were evacuated by German soldiers.

Establishing the Occupation

Although there was as yet still no internationally recognised code governing military occupation, both sides invoked the laws of war as they understood them, showing a strong desire to justify their actions. The Prussian king's much quoted proclamation of 8 August 1870, 'We do not make war on peaceful citizens', was studiously repeated in many German proclamations and they took care to respond to accusations that they had violated this promise.[18] Initially at least, strenuous efforts were made to enforce discipline, sometimes with a brutality that shocked French observers.[19] For their part the French cited the same promise in order to denounce German violation of the laws of war, especially in respect of the treatment of civilians. Given the increasing codification of law in other sectors of life and the growth and specialisation of lawyers, both sides had access to skilled and erudite advocates, ones not always blind to the shortcomings of their own armies and citizens but who nevertheless found the other side's version of the law impractical or perverse. This advocacy took place during the war and occupation itself as well as for decades after.[20] German sensitivity was exposed by one of the innovations of the era, namely the international committee that had promoted the Geneva Conference of 1864 and the resulting convention on the treatment of the wounded which became the basis for the assciated national Red Cross societies. Attempts by a German police official to curtail the activities of the French society at Versailles, the location of German headquarters, brought protest from the president of the French society to Prince Putbus, a member of the German society, about inappropriate searches of such a nature as to be a 'violation of its neutrality'.[21] German embarrassment, especially in the light of the presence of foreign journalists at Versailles, led to a humiliating retraction from the police official. Faced with the indeterminacy of customary law both sides turned to historical precedent for support, most notably their mutual occupations of the Napoleonic era. Indeed this was an especially effective argument with the Prussian king, who had participated in the campaign of 1814 as a young captain.[22] Such analogies were, of course, imprecise guides, as Bismarck's response to Favre's reminder that Germans had espoused partisan warfare in 1813: 'That is quite true, but our trees still bear the marks where your generals hanged our people on them.'[23]

If there was uncertainty about the customary rules of occupation there was also uncertainty about the fact of occupation, about what counted as occupied territory and what did not count. That was compounded by the absence of any clear and consistent distinction between invasion and occupation.[24] The latter distinction, however, was beginning to appear and to find practical application, albeit as a point of considerable dispute.[25] The reality was that the Germans had limited numbers of men crossing the country in pursuit of French armies. The British journalist Henry Sutherland Edwards recalled: 'I once travelled from St. Germain to Louviers, a distance of fifty miles, along a road occupied theoretically by the Prussians, without seeing a Prussian soldier'.[26] A town such as Saint-Dié might have German soldiers present for no more than three months between August 1870 and May 1871, and even then not as a continuous block of time.[27] While in some areas, along the strategically important Strasbourg–Paris railway for example, occupation was relatively dense, elsewhere towns might be occupied on several discrete occasions. Even in Lorraine, some villages scarcely ever saw Germans.[28] According to François Roth it was in the areas of intermittent occupation that the occupation imposed the greatest hardship.[29] In that respect they resembled the no-man's-lands of the American Civil War.

The lack of a clear and enforced distinction between occupied and non-occupied territory did at least have the advantage for the inhabitants that news, even if usually far from reliable, could circulate. Where tighter control was exercised the sense of uncertainty and isolation could become acute. Indeed it was experienced as one of cruellest features of life under occupation alongside the billeting that exposed inhabitants to the often exorbitant demands of individual soldiers.[30] As the chief secretary of the sub-prefecture of d'Epernay later recalled, 'we were left without certain news and isolated within our own country'.[31] Ironically, Bismarck had initially been keen to see the reappearance of the local press and had promised as much freedom as under Napoleon's Empire, though that was not necessarily a lot. As the Germans found that the patriotic French press urged a continuation of the war, that initial liberality gave way to censorship of the press.[32] The Germans also censored the postal service when they reopened it, sometimes inducing the French to boycott the German controlled service.[33] Control of the post, according to an inhabitant of Versailles, was part of a '"psychological" strategy' deployed by the Germans, in parallel with their military strategy, for the demoralisation of the defeated.[34] Under the eyes of the censor such news as was received seemed only to increase the recipients' ignorance.[35] Rumours abounded. The mayor of Bordes lamented that they did not even know what was happening in neighbouring communes.[36] A decade after the occupation the mayor of Reims recalled with evident bitterness the rumours in other parts of France according to which the inhabitants of Reims had welcomed the German invaders.[37]

Responses to the arrival of the invaders did, however, vary. While the Germans sometimes met with resistance, this was not always the case. Indeed the French government in Tours censored and recalled officials who either did not stay at their posts or who exhibited insufficient patriotic zeal.[38] At Reims, the French army having retreated, resistance was not in fact a plausible option, though the town council, seeking to balance recognition of their impotence and patriotic spirit, declined to open the town gates to the insubstantial force of a Prussian patrol that first appeared. The council did hand to the Germans a copy of its own proclamation to the citizens of Reims calling for calm and the acceptance 'with sad resignation' of what they could not prevent.[39] Similarly the municipal council of Beauvais called for a 'calm and dignified attitude' as the only hope of security.[40] Elsewhere municipal officials sought to manage the arrival of the invaders and to provide a framework for the occupation. This they did by trying to negotiate a formal capitulation by the town or by a convention. German commanders often accepted such agreements. In the case of Versailles the mayor even had recourse to the capitulation of the town in 1814 as a model for its imminent surrender.[41] These agreements, serving as substitutes for codified law, sought to regulate such matters as requisitions and even specified the continued operation of courts and commerce. The extent to which they were respected varied. In Péronne, German officers did attempt to prohibit requisitioning in accordance with such an agreement.[42] In the town of Mouy, however, protests to the German intendant about requisitioning beyond the terms specified met with no response.[43] In the case of Versailles, the capitulation was not ratified by higher German authorities on the grounds that capitulations only applied to fortified places, not open towns like Versailles.[44] There was some reservation about such agreements when the Germans approached Tours in January 1871, though while the German general declined to sign a written convention he did come to an informal agreement with the mayor.[45]

It was, of course, not only the French who sought to establish a framework for occupation from the outset. That was in German interests as well, hence their willingness to make such agreements. As the more powerful party they were in a position to issue unilateral proclamations. That did not mean that they were not nervous. Indeed the nature of their proclamations sought to balance reassurance of respect for life and property with intimidation designed to pre-empt resistance. The proclamation issued in the town of Beauvais was relatively brief, noting that the authority of the French government was suspended, but that its employees would continue to exercise their functions. While reassuring the inhabitants that the Germans did not come as enemies of 'peaceful inhabitants', it threatened that houses where arms were discovered or from which attacks came would be burned down.[46] General Werder in Alsace issued four proclamations on 3 September. One provided for the continuation of civil administration but threatened that resistance or disobedience would be met with 'dismissal, arrest and deportation to captivity in Germany'.[47] A second proclamation threatened armed civilians with execution, as well as penalties for both the commune where the offence was committed and the one from which the perpetrators came. The third specified the daily ration for each soldier that would be requisitioned. The fourth provided for penalties against any official violating the prohibition on continued recruitment for the French army.[48] The latter proved to be the occasion for a progressive escalation of threats. The abolition of conscription in occupied territory had been decreed on 13 August, along with the penalties for officials who continued its operation. By 27 October a decree provided for the punishment by fine of the relatives of any individual of military age who had left to join French armies. Another decree of 17 December provided for a penalty of up to twenty years of hard labour for such individuals. Slightly earlier a royal ordinance, though only published in Alsace, provided for confiscation of the individual's assets and banishment for ten years. This proved, however, to be one of the more contentious sets of measures, with even the German lawyer Loening criticising the ordinance of 15 December as excessive and unjustifiable.[49] The German Prefect of Meurthe, however, went further still and threatened that inhabitants of occupied territory who enrolled in the French army would not be treated as prisoners of war but condemned to hard labour or shot.[50] Yet such draconian penalties were either not implemented at all or, in the case of the penalties under the royal ordinance, imposed in only a few cases.[51] The discrepancy between the threat and its limited application reveals that its purpose, having this in common with many such decrees, was intimidation.[52] It was the same logic that lay behind the provision that military jurisdiction extended to the 'entire area of a canton as soon as it is published by proclamation in one locality'.[53] By running ahead of the actual reach of German forces the intent was to induce submission in advance.

Improvising Military Government

Although it has been claimed that the Germans operated from the outset with a 'system of military government' to implement this assertion of military jurisdiction, the reality was one of improvisation.[54] What the Prussian army especially did have was a relatively sophisticated structure, of which the General Staff was the most eminent embodiment. Prussian organisation also extended to the management of supply depots, communications, troop movements and related activities by special rear area commands (*Etappengebieten*). These were often occupied by more elderly officers, some clearly past their prime, and relations with the inhabitants of occupied territory inevitably fell in part within their remit.[55] Initially especially, the rapid movement of German forces effectively limited the administrative activities of this structure.[56] Yet the range of activities, including the administration of the German field police and the detection of covert French postal services, could be extensive.[57]

While these structures remained in place given their specifically military functions, they were soon deemed insufficient for the wider purposes of military government. It was for this reason that the Germans created a limited number of governments general, beginning with those for Alsace and Lorraine on 14 August, followed later by one centred on Reims on 16 September, part of whose territorial remit was taken over by a government general in Versailles on 16 December.[58] It was notable that, as in the American Civil War, there was no centralised administrative structure for military government across the entirety of occupied territory. To the French lawyer Rolin-Jaequemyns, it was precisely the lack of central coordination, rather than renowned Prussian central control, which accounted for much of the arbitrary nature of the German administration.[59] There was, however, a broad specification of the functions of the governors general, issued on 21 August 1870. These instructions endowed the governors with 'all administrative and military power', although they gave them authority only over the troops not forming part of a distinct army.[60] A civil commissioner was to serve as the intermediary between the governor general and the existing civil administrations within his area. These men were typically government officials drawn from German provinces. Only in the absence of existing administrative structures and staff was the governor general to construct his own. The governor general also had a military staff and civil commissars a small number of specialist assistants.[61] By the time of the establishment of the fourth governor generalship, however, there seemed little for the Civil Commissioner, Nostiz-Walwitz, a financial official from Saxony, to do.[62]

The fact that separate governor generalships were established for Alsace and Lorraine also, of course, had a political significance that was clear to everyone, given German intent to annex the two areas. The Governor General of Alsace, Count Bismarck-Bohlen, promised respect for existing laws and 'complete liberty' for the 'the religion of the inhabitants, the institutions and customs of the country'.[63] The reality was the beginning of a process of Germanisation in both Alsace and Lorraine, with the supervision of the French ministry over education being suspended and the German language being promoted.[64] Ironically, German efforts were aided by the widespread refusal of French officials to cooperate, leading not only to their dismissal but also their expulsion. The German jurist Bluntschli explicitly sanctioned 'strong supervision' of hostile Francophile parts of the population, the encouragement of the Germanophile part and even the acceptance of 'suitable immigrants' from Germany.[65] Yet Bluntschli, and more importantly Bismarck, insisted that the status of these areas as occupied territory be maintained until otherwise determined by the peace treaty. In reality, moreover, the exactions of the occupant and the intimidation revealed a widespread antipathy which was all too evident to the Civil Commissioner of Alsace.

In Alsace and Lorraine, as in other parts of occupied territory, with one exception, the French prefects had either fled on the advance of the Germans or followed instructions not to cooperate with the Germans. The exception, the Prefect of Meurthe, was generally seen as having ignominiously failed in his duties.[66] This was quite in accordance with the view that the prefects were representatives of the state and that by virtue of this political status, could not serve the invader. Faced with this administrative vacuum the Germans appointed their own prefects in place of the absent Frenchmen. In case of the Prefect of Versailles, Brauchitsch, this took place on the basis of a sound knowledge of the French administrative system and awareness that it was the prefect who gave direction to the French administrative system and served as the public face of the administration.[67] It was for this reason that Brauchitsch not only styled himself as prefect but continued to use the notepaper of his predecessor as prefect. So far did he take this imitation that he took exception to being addressed by the mayor as 'Prefect for the German armies', seeing this as an attempt to slight his authority as 'Prefect of the Department of Seine-et-Oise'. Nor would he tolerate the mayor's distinction between the Prefect *de jure*, that is the absent Frenchman, and the Prefect *de facto*, that is, Brauchitsch.[68] Such sensitivities could reach the point of caricature, as they did with the German Prefect of Oise, Schwartzkoppen, of whom Bismarck was contemptuous for his needless antagonism of the French officials.[69] The German prefects, though, had to deal not only with French officials but also with their own military, especially the military commandants of the towns, who were sometimes more sympathetic to the French than the prefects, as was General Voigts-Rhetz in his rather demonstrative visit to the mayor of Versailles during his imprisonment on Brauchitsch's instructions. Yet Voigts-Rhetz had his own difficulties given his limited authority as town commandant over other senior offices, especially in the headquarters town of Versailles.[70]

Though sometimes aided by German sub-prefects, the German prefects formed the most important interface between the German authorities and the French administrative system, a system without which they would face the unmanageable task of administering the occupied territories themselves. It was in part for this reason that both sides showed acute sensitivity about questions of status and the wider implications of their actions in conditions of uncertainty. French prefects were clear that as political agents of the state they could not openly take part in the process while the German authorities would not tolerate the covert control of the administration by officially absent prefects. Indeed the Governor General of Lorraine declared that such activity would be treated as equivalent to actively assisting the enemy.[71] Attempts to co-opt other senior officials, within the prefectures and elsewhere, proved uneven. Even the reaction of surveyors of roads was variable with some refusing cooperation outright and others engaging in limited cooperation.[72] Brauchitsch, however, met with the principled response: 'We are moreover employees of the prefect appointed by the French government. Since French departmental administration has been suppressed, our functions have ceased with it'.[73] As agents of the state they feared being held guilty of treason if they cooperated.

Faced with this recalcitrance Brauchitsch decreed that since the sub-prefects had refused fulfil their functions and since 'it is necessary to assure the exercise of diverse public services as well as the prompt and complete execution of official decisions in all the communes of the department' the mayors of the major towns would be delegated to execute the decisions of 'superior authorities'.[74] The absence of higher levels of indigenous authority and the effective expansion of the remit of the mayors, endowing them with some of the function of sub-prefects, entailed the municipalisation of indigenous authority which was to be such a typical by-product of occupation. It inevitably exposed the mayors to a level of public responsibility for which there was little or no guidance save the advice of their councillors.[75] In Versailles the mayor and councillors had already considered resigning en masse in protest at what they regarded as the intolerable burdens imposed upon the open town. They decided, however, to remain in post, seeking to act as intermediaries between their fellow citizens and the occupant. It was a dilemma and decision to which they would return several times.[76] The very appointment of Bauchitsch as prefect automatically caused further concern about their position. It was not clear, given that a military administration already existed, what the purpose of establishing this prefect was, or what his relationship with the military commandant was. In the case of Versailles, these uncertainties were aggravated by incorporating Versailles within the Government General of Reims.[77]

At Montereau the arrival of the German prefect did prompt a resignation of the municipal council. The immediate response of the town commandant was to refuse to accept their resignations and to threaten not only the councillors but all inhabitants of the town with unspecified penalties. The councillors decided to remain in post.[78] At Reims resignation of the mayor was prompted by the fall of the French imperial government and doubts about the constitutionality of his position according to French law; though the councillors did constitute a municipal commission for which they thought there was adequate legal provision. The Germans, acting on instruction from Bismarck, refused to accept this arrangement, arguing that while the mayor was 'under the protection of Prussian weapons' events in Paris could have no impact upon arrangements in Reims, threatening to impose a heavy contribution on the town in the event of refusal.[79]

Whether they sought to resign or not, municipal officials could take some comfort in historical precedent and the argument that they were representatives of their local community rather than the state, or at least could act solely in their capacity as local representatives. It was on the basis of the presumed communal character of school staff, in fact a fiction conjured up by the municipal authorities and accepted by the Germans, that it proved possible to reopen schools in some areas.[80] It is also arguable that most mayors and councils did in fact act in the interests of their communities, even if this set them at odds with the injunctions coming from Paris and especially Tours.[81] This still left them caught between the demands of the German authorities and the protests of their fellow citizens and always exposed to the risk of being held to have too willingly collaborated. It was for this reason that they would often take considerable personal risk to ward off what they considered to be a dishonourable course of conduct. It was a balancing act which many managed well enough to secure re-election and public commemoration after the war.[82]

The difficulty that these French officials faced was in part recognised by the Germans as well. The *Moniteur officiel du Gouvernment Général à Reims* recalled that the Treaty of Paris of 1814 and the Treaty of Prague of 1866 had included specific provisions against the subsequent punishment of officials who had cooperated with the occupant, suggesting that similar clauses would probably be included in the treaty at the end of the war.[83] There were indeed good grounds for fearing retaliation after the war. Officials had been threatened with the loss of their pensions should they cooperate with the Germans. In what would be one of most quoted incidents subsequently, Gambetta even raised the prospect of the death penalty for forestry officials who continued to work for the Germans.[84] Occasionally, German authorities proved more sympathetic to the position of people caught between these two pressures. That was evident when the mayor of Montereau protested against instructions according to which the mayor should prohibit recruitment for the French army on the grounds that this would be dishonourable and that the mayor could hardly disavow the right of his own government to recruit its citizens. The town commandant, who had forced the mayor to remain in post, now conceded that he understood the 'delicacy' of the mayor's position and that he could consider the order as not having been issued.[85] Behind this concession lay also recognition of the limits to which the mayors could be pushed and consideration of German priorities. The demand that mayors supply lists that would readily enable the Germans to identify men of military age who had left, probably to join French forces, met with complete failure to comply, without the imposition of the penalties which the Germans had threatened. Intimidation was not always effective.

Other public officials and employees also found that too overt an insistence on their obedience or too close symbolic cooperation could expose them to a degree that they could not accept. That was the case when the director of the German postal service demanded that postal employees take an oath whereby they promised to 'avoid anything which might harm the interests of the High German Allies and their armies'.[86] This provoked widespread refusal in a service whose directors were already inclined to refuse to cooperate, even penalising postal workers who sought to maintain a covert service in the case of Reims.[87] Members of the French police were also in a prominent position, though the extent to which the French police continued to operate varied, as did the level of cooperation with the German authorities. In Rouen, joint patrols of Prussian field police and French municipal police operated.[88] In Orleans, however, German gendarmes took over the patrolling of the town.[89] In Versailles, the Prefect Brauchitsch and the German Director of Police, Stieber, tried to insist that the French municipal police wear armbands of the Prussian colours. This, however, was seen by the French as an attempt to treat France as a 'conquered' country rather than an occupied one and as an affront to their patriotism. The ensuing compromise was that the municipal police would wear an armband, but of the tricolour.[90]

If the symbols of authority and loyalty provided the occasions for the most pronounced clashes, and often doubts, the requisitions and other exactions, as well as the looting which sometimes broke out, were the focus of a more or less continual confrontation. While the Germans took pride in their logistical proficiency, which Moltke would later boast was responsible for great improvements in the behaviour of invading soldiers, Moltke's rapid deployment put considerable strain on the ability to provide for German armies.[91] Although looting did occur efforts were made to constrain it, often to the surprise of the French. That looting was not a justifiable practice was effectively conceded when, in consequence and acknowledgement of the looting that took place in Orleans, the contribution imposed on the town was reduced in compensation.[92] More isolated dwellings, especially of the wealthy, were more prone to outright pillage. In Beauvais, however, the town commandant initially offered to pay for the provisions he demanded.[93] Even later on General Voigts-Rhetz justified the extent of requisitioning, not on German unwillingness to pay but the reluctance of French farmers to sell to them, having been warned of reprisals by their own government.[94] Sheer insecurity, and fear of having produce seized, as other Germans recognised, also accounted for reluctance of farmers to bring provisions to the Germans. Often, though, the arrival of German forces meant immediate demands for vast quantities of foodstuffs, aggravated where soldiers were billeted on the inhabitants, as well as the seizure of horses and vehicles. The initial chaos added to the burden, with the mayor of Versailles' first letter to General Voigts-Rhetz as town commandant being a complaint about the multiplicity of self-proclaimed intendants all making requisitions.[95] As the Germans established an occupation administration the requisitioning did become less arbitrary, though even where there were promises to curtail the activities of military intendants the latter continued to operate.[96] Less arbitrary requisitioning did not necessarily mean less burdensome requisitioning. Towns had to hand over existing stocks of food and goods but also to manufacture goods, usually under the threat of some penalty if the demand was not met.[97]

Contributions were imposed repeatedly. While French commentators acknowledged an occupant's right to impose contributions and to collect existing taxes, they condemned the extent of German exactions and vehemently denied any right of pillage.[98] The Germans, of course, referred not only to contemporary understanding of the laws of war but also to French levies imposed on Prussia between 1806 and 1813 in justification.[99] Collecting existing taxes, as the Germans openly acknowledged in their proclamations, was impossible given the flight of the senior French taxation officers. Instead the Germans imposed contributions to be collected by the mayors, leaving any equity in the levying of these contributions to the mayors.[100] Considerations of equity were prominent in the minds of some officials, especially given the fact that it was the wealthy inhabitants who were more likely to have fled before the arrival of the Germans. To these contributions in lieu of taxes were added others imposed in retaliation for the expulsion of Germans from France and for the French seizure of German shipping as prizes of war. Contributions also resulted in reprisal for attacks on German soldiers or the disruption of communications. In part the sheer pressure of these exactions was intended and political in nature. German officials openly told the French that the contributions would be increased until the French agreed to peace.[101] German publicists also admitted that even after the armistice and after the French elections it was primarily political motives that drove the Germans to exact contributions in order to drive the French to agree and ratify a peace treaty.[102]

It was clear to the French not only that the size of some of these demands was beyond the resources of the community but that the Germans knew that they were. The tactics of the French officials were to resists payment of the full amount, sometimes even refusing to pay at all, especially where the contribution was by way of a fine for payment of which one of the municipal officials was held in prison. Sometimes, as at La Sarthe, payment of an initial tranche was followed by demands for a reduction in the total amount before any further payments were made, resulting in a significant reduction in that case.[103] At Bordes, the council resolved on refusing to pay but with a fall-back position already agreed amongst themselves.[104] For their part, the Germans deliberately made demands in excess of what they knew towns could pay, in order to then present themselves as gracious in accepting a lesser amount.[105] Nevertheless, the final sums were oppressive enough. Municipalities had to resort to loans to finance the payment of the contributions. Though often raised by public subscription, some loans were contracted abroad. At Versailles, Prefect Brauchitsch issued a decree allowing the council to contract loans secured on municipal revenues and introduced a syndicate of German banks offering to provide such loans to fund contributions to the German government. That was an offer the mayor of Versailles successfully evaded.[106]

While the form and extent of these contributions and requisitions was highly contentious, the requisitioning of labour and other services aroused even greater indignation. Events at Fontenoy in January 1871 were much cited in this respect. In response to a successful attack on the rail line the German Prefect of Meurthe not only imposed a contribution on the department but requisitioned 500 labourers to repair the line. Upon their refusal to cooperate, he decreed that public transportation be suspended, larger industrial establishments closed and owners of closed establishments forbidden to pay workers. Lest that were insufficient, another decree threatened to seize and execute a certain number of labourers. Under these pressures the German obtained the requisite labour force.[107] Compulsion to repair damaged bridges and roads was common. There were accusations as well of compulsion to perform work more directly related to the military capacity of the occupants and to serve as guides.[108] The latter brought with it the threat of the death penalty should the hapless guide mislead German forces.

These latter forms of requisitioning had to be seen as the most contentious for they effectively compelled the inhabitant to act as if he were disloyal even though it was under compulsion. Avoiding compromising actions, whether by mayors or labourers and guides, was one difficulty. Demonstrating one's continuing loyalty and bearing the consequences of more active resistance were even sterner tests. Officials frequently had occasion to assert their loyalty but the wider population also found occasion to demonstrate their loyalty in Rouen when the Germans held a review of troops by the Crown Prince of Prussia by way of celebration. Many inhabitants responded by hanging black flags from their windows and decorating windows as if to mark a funeral. This symbolic challenge led to no more than some altercations with German soldiers and a threat from the German commandant that houses displaying black flags would be singled out for the billeting of German troops.[109]

It was, however, the issues associated with the *francs-tireurs* that became the great symbol of French resistance, German repression and mutual recrimination. The term *francs-tireurs* properly applied to local units formed at their own initiative, which, once duly authorised by the government, were expected by the French to be recognised as legitimate combatants.[110] German commanders, initially at least, and German soldiers used the term more indiscriminately to include the *Garde nationale mobile* and French civilians responsible for fragmentary sniping from hedges and houses. Some distinction, recognising at least the legitimacy of the *Garde nationale mobile*, came quite early, though it did not put an end to the widespread indiscriminate use of the terms by German soldiers and the fact that several decrees were issued in August alone indicates the difficulty the German army had in drawing the line.[111] Even in the case of the *francs-tireurs* General von Werder wrote, in a letter of 9 December 1870 to a *francs-tireurs* commander in Vosges, published in the Belgian press, that there was no order to shoot members of units of *francs-tireurs* taken prisoner. He promptly added, however, that 'peasants not wearing military uniform who shoot at our soldiers will, after summary process, invariably be put to death'.[112] General Wittich, after clashes with ill-organised units in November, had been less discriminating but also expressed an important strand of thought in German attitudes: 'all persons who, not being military personnel, are caught bearing arms against German troops or committing other acts of hostility or treason, will invariably be put to death'.[113] While Wittich restricted this penalty to non-military personnel, it was the nature of the acts, the treacherous character ascribed to them, that helped to blur the lines between the problematic but arguably legitimate irregular, the civilian mobilised in defence against the invader, again arguably legitimately at least under certain conditions, and the civilian who rose in arms in occupied territory. Treacherous behaviour in the sense of disreputable ways of fighting, even fed by rumours of women participating in such attacks, as much as anything else alarmed German soldiers. Those sentiments were clearly expressed even in the diary of the Prussian Crown Prince:

> shots are fired everywhere at patrols, mostly in a treacherous, cowardly manner, so that we have no choice but to resort to the countermeasures of setting fire to the houses whence the shots came or demanding hostages and imposition of contributions. It is ghastly but necessary to prevent worse misfortune.[114]

That soldiers, and even their commanders, did not always discriminate between individuals of different status, sometimes subtly different status, and at other times denied the status of legitimate combatant to an entire class of people regardless of circumstance, is not surprising. What was clear, to both sides, was that the distinction between military personnel and civilians was becoming blurred. Behind this lay a clash of values evident in the judgement of the British journalist and observer of such scenes, Henry Sutherland Edwards:

> If the apparently noble, but really barbarous, principle be recognised, that every man has, without condition, a right to defend his native land, his village, and the house in which he was born, then it follows that an invading army must, for its own safety, imprison or destroy all inhabitants thus claiming an absolute right to resist it.[115]

The attitude of inhabitants to the *francs-tireurs* was in fact more ambivalent than the patriotic advocates of the *francs-tireurs* suggested. Subject to collective German reprisals, stripped of provisions by German requisitioning, inhabitants were often neither inclined to welcome *francs-tireurs* nor able to support them. In an extreme case, one *francs-tireurs* leader even suspected that the shots fired at his men in the night came not from the enemy but from local inhabitants trying to drive the *francs-tireurs* away.[116] Around Épernay, the *francs-tireurs* were said to be neither well-organised nor effective and to be more feared by the local population than by the enemy.[117] Indiscipline appeared to be an important factor to one English war correspondent in explaining what struck him as the lack of patriotism in the hostility of inhabitants to the *francs-tireurs*.[118] Another *francs-tireurs* leader even came to recognise that the harm done to the Germans by his activities was slight compared to the harm suffered as a result of German reprisals, and left the area to join more regular French forces.[119] In general German reprisals grew harsher as the war dragged on into December and January 1871, with an increasing tendency for villages to be subject to pillage and fire as the Germans regained control.[120]

Severe reprisals had, however, been applied in some cases from the early days of the war in cases which the publicists on both sides were to invoke in disputes about whether specific towns counted as occupied as not. In the case of L'Isle-Adam in September 1870 Prussian forces had occupied the town, but then departed, though warning the inhabitants that they would return. The inhabitants, however, fired upon the returning Prussians who, once they had managed finally to reassert control, resorted to pillage and fire in punishment of the inhabitants. From the Prussian stance the town counted as part of occupied territory, despite their temporary absence, and hence the inhabitants were bound to desist from any hostile acts.[121] The same sentiment was expressed in Saint-Quentin, which had successfully repulsed an initial attack. Upon occupying the town and preparing to leave, the commanding officer posted a proclamation in which he declared that in the event of 'new manifestations of disloyalty' or of 'any disorder whatever of a nature to necessitate the return of the troops' he would proceed with great rigour, imposing heavy contributions and that each person 'compromised or suspected' of involvement would be shot.[122]

The seizure of hostages, and especially placing hostages on railway locomotives in order to inhibit attempts to derail them, was similarly contentious, though not as novel as some seemed to believe.[123] It was, however, seen as new and contrary to the laws of war by the councillors of La Ferté-sous-Jouarre who protested to the town commandant in these terms, but complied with the order to provide hostages from their own ranks for the trains.[124] The same pattern emerged in Reims, where the council drew up a formal protest that placing civilians on trains as hostages was 'contrary to all principles of justice and the law of war', that there was no justification for selecting hostages from Reims for derailments which might take place anywhere on the line and that it would in any case be ineffective.[125] Lawyers and publicists pointed to the difference between taking hostages where the penalty was deprivation of liberty and taking hostages where the penalty was the risk of their lives in order to condemn the practice. French lawyers instantly seized on the doubts of their German counterparts, some of whom had expressed quite strong reservations. Yet protests to the German authorities received vigorous responses. They invoked the inevitably random nature of the attacks on trains, symbolised by the presence of wounded French soldiers in the carriages of one much publicised derailment. That the Germans resorted to the practice at all was testament to the fear of the *francs-tireurs*, though derailments were not frequent and none seem to have involved any harm to a hostage. It is also significant that the implementation of this order in the General Government of Reims varied considerably. At Soissons the German sub-prefect suggested that people wishing to travel to Reims on business might be selected so that the journey might not be too onerous. Elsewhere designated notables paid replacements with an openness which the German can hardly have failed to notice.[126] At Senlis the councillors decided that while they would not resist they would wait at their homes until the Germans came to collect them for the journey in order to demonstrate that they were ceding only to force. Within a matter of days, however, the Germans in Senlis had decided that a surety of 10,000 francs was a better guarantee of the safety of the trains.[127] On both sides, placing hostages on trains took on a disproportionate significance to its actual impact because it, or the practices that led the Germans to resort to it, symbolised the violation of their sense of justice and understanding of what was morally and legally permissible in occupied territory.

Both principles of justice and the machinery for the administration of justice were inevitably key areas of contention because of the general problems of the administration of justice in occupied territory, because of the specific nature of elements of German penalties for acts of resistance and because of the impact of the fall of the imperial regime. That law under conditions of occupation had to diverge in important respects from law as normally understood was clearly grasped by the English journalist Henry Sutherland Edwards, for, he argued, the occupant 'has to deal with a population unanimously opposed to him, and bent, not, as in a well-ordered civil state of society, on supporting the government, but on subverting and destroying it'.[128] Consistent with this, military law, that is, the occupant's law, must ignore the proportionality of the punishment to the offence, considering only the deterrent effect. Furthermore, the important principle must be that while it was preferable to punish the guilty it was essential that no offence go unpunished.[129] This was indeed the logic that lay behind the repeated assertion that in the event of attacks on German soldiers or communications not only would the guilty face the death sentence but both the commune in which the offence was committed and the commune from which the perpetrator came would be liable to heavy fines.[130] As French critics took pleasure in noting, even German lawyers held that extending the principle of collective liability to communes from which perpetrators came went too far.[131] One German lawyer, emphasising the same characteristics of law as Edwards, denied that the home communes had in fact been penalised, suggesting that the cumulative threat was intended purely as intimidation.[132]

While principles of law and punishment provided one occasion for dispute, the administration of justice provided another. The

Germans, following the normal practice of occupants, reserved adjudication of offences against themselves or alleged offences of their personnel to their own military courts. A decree issued by the Governor General of Reims on 5 November 1870 added that: 'Save in these cases, there is no change in the competence of the tribunals and of the French judicial officers which function in the forms legally constituted before the war'.[133] By then, however, as Governor General Rosemberg-Gruszcynski well knew, that concession contained a highly contentious element. Immediately following the overthrow of the French Empire the Civil Commissioner of Alsace and Lorraine instructed the court at Nancy to declare justice in the name of the Allied High Powers. At a meeting a few days later the Germans suggested that if this caused any scruples the court could continue to use the formula employed under the Empire. While the president of the court suggested declaring justice in the name of the people or in the name of the French government, formulae which avoided specifying any form of government, the Germans saw in this implicit recognition of the Republic, a recognition Bismarck would not make until sure of a government willing to make peace. Consequently on 8 September the court at Nancy, seeing this constraint as a threat to its dignity and independence, suspended its sittings.[134] By mid October courts were taking into account the decree of the Government of National Defence, of 6 September, that justice be declared in the name of the Republic. For the court at Laon, already occupied at that time, even had the Germans allowed this formula there were still insuperable obstacles to its continued operation, including the very presence of a Prussian civil commissioner. Indeed the court, arguing from the unity of administrative, judicial and legislative power found obstacles in the very existence of a 'foreign administration'.[135] The court at Versailles, occupied on 19 September, had been using the new formula when Prefect Brauchitsch inquired as to its practice in October, avowing that while personally he would have left such matters to the court, in the light of their wider political significance they had to be referred to Bismarck. By the end of the month Brauchitsch reported that the new formula was not acceptable and the court duly suspended its sittings.[136]

Elsewhere, however, practice differed widely. The court of assizes at Colmar and commercial tribunals at Strasbourg and Mulhouse reopened in November 1870, simply recording their judgements without any specific formula identifying a form of regime. The court of assizes at Eure also sat.[137] At Dijon the mayor even secured oral agreement in a convention with the German army at the end of October that justice continue to be rendered in the name of the Republic.[138] At Epernay, where the Germans were anxious for French courts to reopen, they decreed that the pre-war formula should be used, but then did nothing when the reopened courts declared justice 'in the name of the French people'.[139] The embarrassment that the Germans found themselves in, as well as the varied behaviour and sensitivities of French judges, was quite obvious to some inhabitants.[140] While the problem of recognition, central to many aspects of this occupation, meant that some conflict was unavoidable, exactly how, and on the basis of what rationale, both sides negotiated the administration of justice varied. Here too, it is the diversity of practice, even in matters of apparent principle, that is striking.

Occupation after the End of Belligerency

While the later stages of the occupation, those governed by the armistice, the provisional peace and then the definitive peace, increasingly mitigated these tensions, they did so neither immediately nor simultaneously. The armistice, besides putting an end to the fighting, had done nothing to end the exactions of the Germans, though the sense of isolation to which some had been subject began to lift as a more normal postal service reappeared and small numbers of people who obtained the necessary safe conducts could travel and bring back further news.[141] The French press began to reappear and the German prefects allowed public meetings in connection with the February elections. Yet German supervision had not disappeared and some editors were subject to fines for what the Germans deemed provocative articles.[142] The execution of a priest in Reims who had concealed arms in his church, on 12 February, illustrated the possibility of more dramatic reprisals.[143]

The preliminary peace already marked a more significant easing of the occupation insofar as article 4 provided that 'German troops shall abstain from levying contributions in money or kind in the occupied departments'.[144] Moreover, four separate conventions in March began to make more significant changes. The first two conventions, of 9 and 10 March 1871, dealt with the transfer of postal and rail services back to the French. The third convention, 11 March 1871, regulated the subsistence of the German army and the quartering of

German soldiers, intending to end the billeting of soldiers in private houses, though not always doing so as rapidly as the French wished. At the same time French officials obstructed the provision of the very facilities which were intended to relieve their fellow citizens of the burden.[145] It was, however, the Rouen Convention of 16 March that was the most important. This Convention for the Restoration of French Administrative Authority over Departments Occupied by German Troops provided in its first article for the re-establishment of French departmental and communal administration and for French authority over 'public safety and the maintenance of public order in the departments occupied by German troops'.[146] Article 2 allowed the French government to re-establish its prefects and noted the appointment of German civil commissioners attached to the occupying forces, whose direction the French had to abide by in matters relating to German interests. Article 3 provided for the reopening of French courts but again added a qualification: 'Nevertheless the state of siege, with all its consequences, will be maintained by the German authorities in the occupied departments'.[147] A letter from General de Fabrice, the new German governor, amplified these arrangements in relation to public order, offering German support, at the request of the French, but reserving the right to act on his own authority to assure the security of his troops where the French 'could not or did not wish to maintain public order'.[148] This was a complex balancing act, seeking to restore French authority but with the reservation of the authority of the occupant to act in certain circumstances. The ambiguity of the situation is reflected in the fact that it has been suggested that the state of emergency was understood as being governed by the French law of 9 August 1849.[149] Yet it is far from clear that all German officers shared this understanding. It was clearly not the understanding of the Rear Area Commander in Stenay, well after the exchange of ratifications of the Treaty of Frankfurt on 21 May, when he reminded the inhabitants on 9 August 1871 that 'the state of siege is still not lifted in the Department of the Meuse. Everyone is still subject to military jurisdiction and each offense against German soldiers will be punished with the severity of the laws of war.'[150]

The Treaty of Frankfurt did not make any substantial alteration to the operation of the occupation as opposed to settling the condition under which German troops would be evacuated from specified departments. Neither this, the preliminary treaty, nor the various conventions had managed to make provision for suitable locations for

Protestant religious services despite the fact that this had caused difficulty throughout the occupation where the Germans appropriated Catholic churches for the purpose. Other grey areas were aggravated by another omission, namely the failure to place any constraints on French rearmament and the subsequent immediate measures by the French to enhance their military capacity, and consequent German alarm about a war of revenge. That, in turn, led to disputes about the proposed armament of French customs and forestry officials, despite the fact that they could be of no conceivable military significance.[151] Even where the fulfilment of the treaties and conventions was clear difficulties arose. French prefects and sub-prefects, keen to assert their patriotic credentials, clashed with Germans repeatedly.[152]

Many of these issues had to be resolved by General Manteuffel, who had replaced General Fabrice as head of the occupation forces in June 1871, and Charles de Saint-Vallier, appointed as Plenipotentiary of the French Government to the Commanding General of the Army of Occupation, who reported directly to Thiers. The peculiarity of Saint-Vallier's title was indicative of the ambiguity of the situation.[153] The fact that they were often able to resolve the conflicts and problems was a product of the good will of both men and especially Manteuffel's sympathetic disposition towards France. As Saint-Vallier was well aware, Manteuffel's willingness to cooperate brought him considerable criticism from the German press and from Bismarck's entourage, all of whom thought him too pro-French. Indeed Saint-Vallier recalled to Thiers the extent to which Berlin journalists had 'accused him of sacrificing the interests of his own army to the French'.[154] In the same letter, as well as complaining about the hostility and duplicity of members of Manteuffel's staff, but not of the general himself, he lamented the tendency of the French military intendant to needlessly antagonise the Germans.[155]

One issue of particular sensitivity concerned attacks on German soldiers. In fact these were relatively few given the level of animosity, estimated at a total of only twenty-one, of which seven involved the death of the soldier.[156] Although the Germans retained the authority to try such cases themselves, they had relinquished any policing powers to the French, weakening the effectiveness of their residual authority, short of invoking the state of siege, and effectively meaning that the Germans could only exercise their rights concurrently with the French.[157] In November 1871 the Germans demanded that the French hand over two murderers, which they duly did. The two were shot by the Germans. On other occasions Manteuffel went further than strictly required, allowing French courts to try the accused. When French courts acquitted two men despite the strength of evidence against them, an incensed Bismarck threatened reprisals. Even towards the end of the occupation in 1873 it required the intervention of Saint-Vallier to avert coercive measures against Saint-Dié, where the Germans had found French justice deficient.[158] Despite these tensions, the wider diplomatic settlement and the crucial payments of the French indemnity moved towards the end of the occupation. Ambassadors were exchanged in January 1872 and Saint-Vallier became Commissioner Extraordinary to the Commander in Chief of the Army of Occupation, though the connection with Manteuffel via Saint-Vallier remained Thiers' preferred channel for managing the final phases of the occupation.[159]

The French Courts and the Integrity of the Commnuity

Even during the occupation the reopened French courts began to work through their own assessment of the experience of occupation. They held that the Court of Assizes in Colmar had rendered justice 'in the name of sovereignty' during the occupation, and noted German respect for the validity of its judgements in allowing an appeal to the French Court of Cassation, even though Colmar had been ceded to France by the Treaty of Frankfurt and the appellant was now in German custody.[160] Considerations of sovereignty figured prominently in the case of a forestry official who had availed himself of the support of the occupation authorities, in the shape of two Prussian gendarmes, to conduct a search for illegal logging. While noting that the official had a right to appeal to 'public force' in support of his duties, the court concluded that his appeal to a foreign military authority had stripped his act of 'all legal character': he was the delegate of a 'portion of authority in virtue of the principle of national sovereignty; that such delegation did not allow the immixture in any degree of elements borrowed from a foreign sovereignty' and that his act therefore was 'vitiated in its essence'.[161]

While a small number of cases dealt with principles of jurisdiction and sovereignty, reflecting the heightened sensitivity evident amongst elements of the French judiciary during the earlier phases of the occupation, most dealt with more prosaic matters and showed more pragmatic consideration of the problems of communal authority and communal obligations under the pressures of occupation. Thus the Court of Cassation was not deterred by the fact that an extraordinary tax imposed in Rouen was implemented 'neither by ordinary authority nor in ordinary legal forms' but by authorities replacing those 'disrupted and destroyed' by the invasion.[162] Similarly it held that a mayor had a right to impose the burden of lodging the occupant's soldiers and to impose the costs thereof, where, for whatever reason, the individual could not fulfil the obligation and a hotelier had to fulfil it for them.[163] By the same token, where the property of individuals was manifestly sacrificed to the occupant to avoid retribution that would have fallen on the entire community, those individuals had a right to some measure of compensation.[164] In fact both principled defence of French sovereignty, implausible though it may have been, and the pragmatic assertion of communal authority and assertion of communal liability were different aspects of the same attempt to preserve national and communal integrity against the disruption caused by military occupation.

The broader memories of the occupation, though exhibiting considerable diversity of experience and judgement, are nevertheless characterised by a general atmosphere of bitterness even amongst those less disposed towards such sentiments. That was evident in recording the experience of Versailles and the hopes of General Voigts-Rhetz for a 'kind of parting without hatred' when the chronicler, though far from ill-disposed toward Voigts-Rhetz, promptly added that 'it was a chimerical desire', and that after the burning villages and 'odious brutalities' the victor could count only on 'unalloyed hatred'.[165] For many Germans it was the experience and even more so the myth of the *francs-tireurs* that would haunt memories and contribute to the brutalities of a later occupation.[166] The German occupation of France had been shaped by modern conceptions of national patriotism, and their limitations, and modern sensitivities to national sovereignty. It pointed towards new obstacles to ending occupations once begun, despite the deceptive reputation of the brevity of the Franco-German War. It also had a profound impact upon the wave of codification then just beginning and which would issue in the first internationally binding law of occupation.

Notes

1. The Prussian occupation which dated back to 1815 was little more than a 'simple right of garrison', Raymond Robin, *Des occupations militaires en dehors des occupations de guerre* (Paris: Larose, 1913), p. 293.
2. For the impact on the Luxembourg question and the wider significance see Mark Ohnezeit, 'Der Deutsch-Französische Krieg 1870/1871: Vorgeschichte, Ursachen and Kriegsausbruch', in Jan Ganschow et al. (eds), *Der Deutsch-Französische Krieg 1870–71* (Graz: Ares, 2009), pp. 35–9.
3. This does not mean that the war was deliberately engineered by either side. It is quite compatible with the concluding judgement of David Wetzel: 'In truth, the French rulers blundered into a war that was not unwelcome to them, and Bismarck, though taken by surprise, turned their blunder to his advantage', *A Duel of Giants* (Madison, WI: University of Wisconsin Press, 2001), p. 180.
4. George Buckle and W. Monypenny, *The Life of Benjamin Disraeli*, vol. 5 (New York: Macmillan, 1920), pp. 133–4.
5. Lothar Gall, 'Das Problem Elsass-Lothringen', in Theodor Schieder and Ernst Deuerlien, *Reichsgründung 1870/71* (Stuttgart: Seewald, 1970), pp. 373–7.
6. Comte D'Angeberg (ed.), *Recueil des traités, conventions et pieces diplomatiques*, vol. 2 (Paris: Amyot, 1873), pp. 512–13.
7. Ibid. p. 603.
8. Joseph Reinach (ed.), *Dépêches et discours de Léon Gambetta*, vol. 1 (Paris: Charpentier, 1886), pp. 44–5.
9. The invocation of 1792 was no mere rhetorical flourish but genuine conviction. See J. P. T. Bury, *Gambetta and the National Defence: A Republican Dictatorship in France* (Westport, CT: Greenwood, 1971), p. 125. For the idea that Gambetta had not fully grasped or committed himself to a guerrilla war see Heidi Mehrkens, *Statuswechsel: Kriegserfahrung und nationale Wahrnehmung im Deutsch-Französischen Krieg 1870/71* (Essen: Klartext, 2008), pp. 130–1.
10. See, for example, François Roth, *La guerre de 1870* (Paris: Fayard, 1990), p. 417.
11. This on 17 November 1870, A. Von Voigts-Rhetz (ed.), *Briefe von Voigts-Rhetz aus den Kriegsjahren 1866 und 1870/71* (Berlin: Rittler, 1906), p. 197 For an assessment of their military significance see Mehrkens, *Statuswechsel*, p. 131, and Geoffrey Wawro, *The Franco-Prussian War: The German Conquest of France in 1870–1871* (Cambridge: Cambridge University Press, 2003), p. 309.
12. Heinrich Meisner (ed.), *Denkwürdigkeiten des General-Feldmarschalls Alfred Grafen von Waldersee* (Stuttgart: DVA, 1922), pp. 100–1.

13. For strong emphasis on Bismarck's pragmatism as well as important general reflections upon the process of ending wars see Eberhard Kolb, 'Der schwierige Weg zum Frieden. Das Problem der Kriegsbeendigung 1870/71', *Historische Zeitschrift*, 241 (1985), 51–79.
14. Michael Howard, *The Franco-Prussian War: The German Invasion of France, 1870–1871* (London: Hart-Davis, 1962), p. 441; Wetzel, *Duel of Giants*, pp. 187–8.
15. Gerhard von Glahn, *The Occupation of Enemy Territory* (Minneapolis: University of Minnesota Press, 1957), p. 141.
16. For this aspect see Eberhard Kolb, 'Der Pariser Commune-Aufstand und die Beendigung des Deutsch-Französischen Krieges', *Historische Zeitschrift*, 215 (1972), 265–98.
17. Article 7, Treaty of Frankfurt, in Robert Giesberg, *The Treaty of Frankfort* (Philadelphia: University of Philadelphia Press, 1966), p. 288.
18. As noted by Joseph Bray, *De l'occupation militaire en temps de guerre* (Paris, Larose, 1894), pp. 179–80.
19. Émile Deleriot, *Versailles pendant l'occupation (1870–1871)* (Versailles: Bernard, 1900), p. 25.
20. For contemporary instances see J. C. Bluntschli, *Der modern Völkerrecht in dem französisch-deutschen Kriege von 1870, Eine Rectoratsrede am 22. November 1870* (Heidelberg: Bassermann, 1871); G. Rolin-Jaecquemyns, 'La guerre actuelle', *Revue de droit international et de législation comparée*, 2 (1870), 643–718, dated December 1870, 718, and 'Essai complémentaire sur la guerre Franco-Allemande dans ses rapports avec la droit internationale', *Revue de droit international et de législation comparée*, 3 (1871), 288–384.
21. Deleriot, *Versailles pendant l'occupation*, pp. 351–3.
22. Jan Ganschow, 'Kriegsvölkerrecht im Deutsch-Französischen Krieg 1870/71', in Ganschow et al. (eds), *Der Deutsch-Französische Krieg*, p. 375.
23. David Wetzel, *A Duel of Nations* (Madison, WI: University of Wisconsin Press, 2012), p. 146.
24. According to Bray, *De L'occupation militaire en temps de guerre*, the disinction first appeared in Platon de Wexel's *L'armée d'invasion* of 1874 but even he did not make much of it, pp. 148–9. The lack of consistency was also evident in the way the distinct terminology was employed in V. Diancourt, *Les Allemands à Reims* (Reims: Michaud, 1883), referring to the termination of the Government General of Reims: 'But if the Germans were no longer our masters, we remained their hostages; occupation replaced invasion', p. 131.
25. A principled distinction was drawn by Felix Dahn, 'Der Deutsch-Französische Krieg und das Völkerrecht', *Jahbücher für die deutsche*

Armee und Marine, 3 (1872), 64. See also the judgement of the Court of Cassation: 'L'Aigle c. Faveau', *Recueil des lois et des arrêts* (1973), part 1, 71. Neither quite make the distinction that would soon become a key part of the definition of occupation.

26. Henry Sutherland Edwards, *The Germans in France* (London: Stanford, 1874), p. 254.
27. Noëlle Sauvée-Dauphin, 'L'occupation prussienne à Versailles', in Philippe Levillain and Rainer Riemschneider (eds), *La guerre de 1870/71 et ses consequences* (Paris: Bouvier, 199), p. 314.
28. François Roth, *Lorraine dans la guerre de 1870* (Nancy: Presses Universitaires de Nancy, 1984), p. 64.
29. Roth, *La guerre de 1870*, p. 397.
30. Emile Chantriot, *L'administration des départements envahis* (Paris: Berger-Levrault, 1916), p. 20; Deleriot, *Versailles pendant l'occupation*, p. 103.
31. L.-M. Petit, *Histoire d'Épernay et de l'invasion 1870–1871* (Éperney: Villers, 1898), p. 264.
32. Claude Farenc, 'Guerre, information et propaganda en 1870–1971: Le cas de la Champagne', *Revue d'histoire moderne et contemporaine*, 31 (1984), 30–1.
33. Émile Dessolins, *Les Prussiens en Normandie* (Paris: Sagnier, 1873), pp. 77–8.
34. Deleriot, *Versailles pendant l'occupation*, p. 47.
35. Amédée Fauche, *Montereau-Faut-Yonne. Journal de l'occupation prussienne* (Montereau: Zanote, 1871), pp. 85, 92.
36. D. Laizeau, *Récits de l'invasion 1870–1871* (Orleans: Puget, 1871), p. 21.
37. Diancourt, *Les Allemands à Reims*, pp. 61–3.
38. F. F. Steenackers and F. Le Goff, *Histoire du Gouvernement de la Défense Nationale en Provence*, vol. 2 (Paris: Charpentier, 1884), pp. 111–15.
39. Ibid. p. 14.
40. A. Bellou, *Les Prussiens à Beauvais* (Beauvais: Baltzard-Roussel, 1879), p. 7.
41. Deleriot, *Versailles pendant l'occupation*, pp. 20–3. For the terms of the capitulation see J.-E. Dieuleveut, *Versailles. Quartier Général Prussien* (Paris: Lachaud, 1872), pp. 19–20.
42. Bray, *De L'occupation militaire en temps de guerre*, pp. 159–60. On these agreements in general see pp. 155–68.
43. Th. Lemas, *Un département pendant l'invasion 1870–1871* (Paris: Fischbacher, 1884), pp. 117–18.
44. Deleriot, *Versailles pendant l'occupation*, p. 29.
45. Ingo Fellrath and Francine Fellrath-Bacart, *La guerre de 1870–1871*

en Touraine (Paris: L'Harmattan, 2011), p. 90. In Dijon on 31 October the mayor reported oral agreements supplementary to a written convention, Anon. (ed.), *Les murailles dijonnaises pendant la guerre 1870–1871* (Dijon: Darantiere, n.d.), pp. 147–50.
46. Bellou, *Les Prussiens à Beauvais*, pp. 11–12.
47. Georg Hirth and Julius V. Gosen (eds), *Tagebuch des Deutsch-Französischen Krieges 1870–1871*, vol. 2 (Leipzig: Hirth, 1872), p. 1869.
48. Ibid. Not all proclamations were so threatening. See, for example, that of the Governor General in Alsace of 30 August, in Amédée Brenet, *La France et l'Allemagne devant le droit international* (Paris: Rousseau, 1902), p. 148.
49. It still stood out for special criticism in a French text 30 years later as amounting to a proclamation of sovereignty: Arthur Lorriot, *De la nature de l'occupation de guerre* (Paris: Charles-Vavauzelle, 1903), pp. 172–4. For Edgar Loening's concession, 'L'administration du Gouvernement-Général de l'Alsace durant la guerre de 1870–1871', *Revue de droit international et de législation comparée*, 5 (1873), 85–6.
50. Alfred Rambaud, 'La Lorraine sous le regime prussien', *Revue des deux mondes*, 93 (1871), 161–2.
51. Bray, *De L'occupation militaire en temps de guerre*, pp. 282–7.
52. Although force was used and severe penalties imposed, the system as a whole 'functioned more by intimidation than execution'. Thus Guillaume Parisot, 'De la négociation comme instrument d'occupation pacifiée et d'exploitation économique efficace pendant la guerre de 1870–1871', in Jean-François Chanet, Annie Crépin and Christian Windler (eds), *Le temps des hommes doubles* (Rennes: Presses Universitaires de Rennes, 2013), p. 296.
53. Comte D'Angeberg (ed.), *Recueil des traités, conventions et pieces diplomatiques*, vol. 1 (Paris: Amyot, 1873), p. 358.
54. The claim of a 'system of military government' is made by Wetzel, *Duel of Nations*, p. 5. The lack of planning is noted by Farenc, 'Guerre, information et propaganda en 1870–1971', p. 27.
55. Georg Cardinal von Widdern, *Der Krieg an den rückwärtigen Verbindungen der deutschen Heere und der Etappendienst*, part 3, vol. 1 (Berlin: Eisenschmidt, 1895), pp. 240–1.
56. See the report of General Inspector of the Third Army described by Rudolf Thierfelder, 'Die Verwaltung der besetzten französischen Gebiete 1870–1873', *Reich-Volksordnung-Lebensraum*, 4 (1943), 372–3.
57. Widdern, *Der Krieg an den rückwärtigen Verbindungen der deutschen Heere*, pp. 269–76.
58. Thierfelder, 'Die Verwaltung der besetzten französischen Gebiete 1870–1873', 374–5.

59. Rolin-Jaequemyns, 'Essai complémentaire sur la guerre Franco-Allemande', p. 313.
60. The instructions are in Bray, *De L'occupation militaire en temps de guerre*, pp. 276–8; here pp. 276–7.
61. These staff structures are outlined in Thierfelder, 'Die Verwaltung der besetzten französischen Gebiete 1870–1873', 375–7.
62. He did not take up his appointment until 16 January 1871. Deleriot, *Versailles pendant l'occupation*, p. 411.
63. Roth, *La guerre de 1870*, p. 378.
64. Brenet, *La France et l'Allemagne devant le droit international*, pp. 153–4.
65. J. C. Bluntschli, 'Völkerrechtliche Betrachtungen über den französisch-deutsch Krieg 1870/71', *Jahrbuch für Gesetzgebung, Verwaltung und Rechtspflege des Deutschen Reiches*, 2 (1872), 309.
66. See, for example, Alf. Mézières, *Récits de l'invasion. Alsace et Lorraine* (Paris: Didier, 1871), pp. 8–10.
67. Gustave Desjardins, *Tableau de la guerre des Allemandes dans le Département de Seine-et-Oise 1870–1871* (Versailles: Cerfe, 1873), p. 37.
68. Deleriot, *Versailles pendant l'occupation*, pp. 252–3.
69. For a French view of Schwartzkoppen see Lemas, *Un département pendant l'invasion*, pp. 131–3: for Bismarck's view see Moritz Busch, *Bismarck: Some Secret Pages of his History* (London: Macmillan, 1898), vol. 1, p. 561.
70. Deleriot, *Versailles pendant l'occupation*, pp. 389 and 424.
71. Chantriot, *L'administration des départements envahis*, p. 9.
72. Desjardins, *Tableau de la guerre*, pp. 37–9.
73. Deleriot, *Versailles pendant l'occupation*, p. 97.
74. Dieuleveut, *Versailles*, pp. 58–9.
75. Olivier Berger, 'L'administration prussienne dans le département de l'Essonne pendant l'occupation de 1870–1871', in Yann Delbrel, Pierre Allorant and Philippe Tanchoux (eds), *France occupée, France occupant* (Orleans: Presses universitaires d'Orléans, 2008), pp. 135–6.
76. Deleriot, *Versailles pendant l'occupation*, p. 54.
77. Ibid. pp. 89–90.
78. Fauche, *Montereau-Faut-Yonne*, p. 102.
79. Hirth and Gosen (eds), *Tagebuch des Deutsch-Französischen Krieges 1870–1871*, vol. 2, p. 2016, and Diancourt, *Les Allemands à Reims*, pp. 33–4.
80. Chantriot, *L'administration des départements envahis*, p. 29.
81. Parisot, 'De la négociation comme instrument d'occupation pacifiée', p. 281.
82. Roth, *La guerre de 1870*, pp. 391–2.

83. Parisot, 'De la négociation comme instrument d'occuption pacifiée', p. 281.
84. See the observations of William Edward Hall, *A Treatise on International Law*, 2nd edn (Oxford: Clarendon, 1884), p. 440.
85. Fauche, *Montereau-Faut-Yonne*, pp. 94–5.
86. Bray, *De L'occupation militaire en temps de guerre*, p. 246.
87. Diancourt, *Les Allemands à Reims*, pp. 68–70. Some irritation with the postal authorities is also evident in Petit, *Histoire d'Épernay et de l'invasion 1870–1871*, pp. 265–6.
88. J. M. Spaight, *War Rights on Land* (London: Macmillan, 1911), p. 362.
89. Th. Cochard, *L'invasion prussienne de 1870: Les Prussiens à Orléans* (Orleans: Sejourné, 1871), pp. 178–9.
90. Deleriot, *Versailles pendant l'occupation*, p. 150.
91. For Moltke's boast see Percy Bordwell, *The Law of War between Belligerents* (Chicago: Callaghan, 1908), p. 114.
92. Armand Surmont, 'Les allemands dans la Sarthe', *Bulletin de la société d'agriculture, sciences et arts de la Sarthe*, 2 (1873), 229.
93. Bellou, *Les Prussiens à Beauvais*, p. 10.
94. Voigts-Rhetz (ed.), *Briefe von Voigts-Rhetz*, p. 272.
95. Deleriot, *Versailles pendant l'occupation*, pp. 35–6.
96. Fauche, *Montereau-Faut-Yonne*, p. 79; Desjardins, *Tableau de la guerre des Allemandes*, pp. 48–50.
97. As in the demand for 3000 pairs of boots demanded from the mayor of Sens in Janaury 1871, V. Dauphiné and Louis Humbert, *L'invasion allemande dans l'arrondissement de Sens* (Sens: Duchemin, 1904), pp. 118–19.
98. On the precise form the exactions took and its significance see especially Surmont, 'Les allemands dans la Sarthe', passim.
99. Deleriot, *Versailles pendant l'occupation*, p. 223.
100. See Brachitsch's decree of 10 October 1870, Dieuleveut, *Versailles*, pp. 59–61.
101. Berger, 'L'administration prussienne dans le département de l'Essone', p. 140.
102. Thus Edgar Loening, 'L'administration du Gouvernement-Général de l'Alsace', 105–6.
103. Surmont, 'Les allemands dans la Sarthe', pp. 221–2.
104. Laizeau, *Récits de l'invasion 1870–1871*, p. 27.
105. Parisot, 'De la négociation comme instrument d'occuption pacifiée', p. 294.
106. Deleriot, *Versailles pendant l'occupation*, pp. 231–4.
107. Bray, *De L'occupation militaire en temps de guerre*, pp. 213–15.
108. For an example of a mayor acknowledging that he had been forced to

instruct an inhabitant to act as a guide see Laizeau, *Récits de l'invasion 1870–1871*, p. 29.
109. Dessolins, *Les Prussiens en Normandie*, pp. 82–3.
110. Rolin-Jaecquemyns, 'La guerre actuelle', pp. 660–1.
111. Brenet, *La France et l'Allemagne devant le droit international*, pp. 23–4; Mehrkens, *Statuswechsel*, pp. 129–30, 133.
112. Dahn, 'Der Deutsch-Französische Krieg und das Völkerrecht', 58.
113. Brenet, *La France et l'Allemagne devant le droit international*, p. 24.
114. Mark Stoneman, 'The Bavarian army and French civilians in the war of 1870–1871', *War in History*, 8 (2001), 274.
115. Edwards, *The Germans in France*, p. 153.
116. Armel Dirou, *La guérilla en 1870* (Paris: Bernard Giovanangeli, 2014), pp. 228–9.
117. Petit, *Histoire d'Épernay*, p. 272.
118. *The War Correspondence of the Daily News* (London: Macmillan, 1871), pp. 301–2.
119. Desjardins, *Tableau de la guerre*, p. 57.
120. Roth, *La guerre de 1870*, pp. 397–401.
121. The events are presented in Albert Leroy, *Le Havre et la Seine-Inférieure pendant la guerre de 1870–1871* (Le Havre: Roquencourt, 1877), pp. 89–90; describing the defenders as national guards and *francs-tireurs*. Bray discusses this in the context of the distinction between invasion and occupation, *De l'occupation militaire en temps de guerre*, pp. 170–1. Lorriot sets it in the context of the criterion of effective occupation, *De la nature de l'occupation de guerre*, pp. 72–3.
122. Ernest Lavisse, 'L'invasion dan les départements du nord', *Revue des deux mondes* (1871), 59.
123. Mehrkens argues that Moltke thought it new, *Statuswechsel*, pp. 188–9. The practice had been employed in the American Civil War.
124. Ibid. pp. 190–1.
125. Diancourt, *Les Allemands à Reims*, pp. 160–1. The events are described at pp. 79–82.
126. Parisot, 'De la négociation comme instrument d'occuption pacifiée', pp. 290–1.
127. Lemas, *Un département pendant l'invasion*, p. 121.
128. Edwards, *The Germans in France*, p. 286.
129. Ibid. pp. 284–5.
130. As in the proclamation of General Tann, Auguste Boucher, *Récits de l'invasion. Journal d'un bourgeois d'Orléans* (Orleans: Herluson, 1871), pp. 436–7.
131. P. Deloynes, 'Droit penal de la guerre. De la responsabilité des communes', *Revue de droit international et de législation comparée*, 6 (1874), 155–6. It is significant that this was a reply to Edgar Loening,

addressed to Gustave Rolibn-Jaequemyns in the leading journal of its nature at the time.
132. Dahn, 'Der Deutsch-Französische Krieg und das Völkerrecht', 61.
133. Dieuleveut, *Versailles*, p. 234.
134. *Recueil générale des lois et des arrêts* (1872), part 2, 34. Loening implies that the court was offered the neutral formula, 'in the name of the law', Loening, 'L'administration du Gouvernement-Général de l'Alsace', 95. It is not clear that this was the case.
135. *Recueil générale des lois et des arrêts* (1872), part 2, 33.
136. Deleriot, *Versailles pendant l'occupation*, pp. 241–2.
137. Loening, 'L'administration du Gouvernement-Général de l'Alsace', 96; Bray, *De L'occupation militaire en temps de guerre*, p. 317.
138. Anon. (ed.), *Les murailles dijonnaises pendant la guerre*, p. 149.
139. Petit, *Histoire d'Épernay*, p. 290.
140. See the comments of A. De la Rue, *Sous Paris pendant l'invasion 1870–1871* (Paris: Furen and Jouvet, 1871), pp. 135–8.
141. Deleriot, *Versailles pendant l'occupation*, p. 440.
142. Chantriot, *L'adminstration des départements envahis*, pp. 38–9.
143. Diancourt, *Les Allemands à Reims*, p. 131.
144. Giesberg, *The Treaty of Frankfort*, p. 280.
145. George Kyte, 'Louis Adolphe Thiers and the liberation of French territory, 1871–1873', *The Historian*, 6 (1944), 136.
146. A. Villefort, *Recueil des traités, conventions, lois, décrets et autres actes relatives à la paix avec l'Allemagne*, vol. 1 (Paris: Imprimerie nationale, 1872), p. 57.
147. Ibid. p. 57.
148. A. Villefort, *Recueil des traités, conventions, lois, décrets et autres actes relatives à la paix avec l'Allemagne*, vol. 2 (Paris: Imprimerie nationale, 1872), p. 261.
149. Robin, *Des occupations militaires en dehors des occupations de guerre*, p. 334.
150. J. J. Laguerre, *Les Allemands à Bar-le-Duc et dans la Meuse 1870–1873* (Bar-le-Duc: Comte-Jacquet, 1874), p. 222.
151. Gaston May, *Le traité de Francfort* (Paris: Berger-Levrault, 1909), pp. 207, 209–10.
152. Roth, *La guerre de 1870*, pp. 532–3.
153. According to Robin a 'novelty in international annals', *Des occupations militaires en dehors des occupations de guerre*, p. 348.
154. Louis Thiers, *Occupation et libération du territoire 1871–1875*, vol. 1 (Paris: Calman-Lévy, 1903), p. 227.
155. Ibid. pp. 228, 232.
156. Roth, *La guerre de 1870*, p. 537.
157. L. Cavaré, 'Quelques notions générals sur l'occupation pacifique',

Revue de droit international public, 31 (1924), 351, noting that the same arrangements for policing had been made in 1815.
158. Robin, *Des occupations militaires en dehors des occupations de guerre*, p. 360; May, *Le traité de Francfort*, pp. 218–20.
159. Robin, *Des occupations militaires en dehors des occupations de guerre*, pp. 349–50.
160. 'Loubert' (21 September 1871), *Recueil générale des lois et des arrêts* (1871), part 1, 108–9.
161. 'C. c. Admin. forest' (29 June 1872), *Recueil générale des lois et des arrêts* (1873), part 1, 191.
162. 'Lepillier c. Prévost-Hommet' (22 January 1873), ibid. p. 335.
163. 'Comm. De Vitry-le-Français c. Adenet et de Morlaincourt' (12 August 1874), *Recueil générale des lois et des arrêts* (1874) part 1, 489–90.
164. 'Ville de Chartres c. Michard' (25 March 1874), ibid. pp. 265–6.
165. Deleriot, *Versailles pendant l'occupation*, p. 484.
166. On this see John Horne and Alan Kramer, *German Atrocities, 1914* (New Haven: Yale University Press, 2001), pp. 89–113.

Chapter 5
Codification of a Law of Occupation

The Laws of War in the Era of Codification

The codification of the law of military occupation was a minor part of a wider process of the codification of international law that accelerated towards the latter parts of the nineteenth century.[1] It amounted to a veritable 'cult of codification'.[2] It was fuelled by the same sentiments that lay behind the codification of continental European domestic legal systems, occasionally inducing some of the reservations encountered in that process, namely that codification would inhibit the natural evolution and progress of customary law.[3] Codification of international law, the idea of which went back at least to the beginning of the nineteenth century, clearly presented problems that codification of domestic law did not.[4] Lack of any central international agency to legislate meant that international law had to be understood either in terms of natural law, as a matter of custom and usage, or treaty based law, with the latter being especially difficult to achieve in the highly sensitive area of the laws of war. Only treaty based law brought with it the promise, but not the reality, of the coherence and comprehensiveness that were seen as some of the virtues of domestic codification.

In the case of international law the process was complicated by other factors, some of which facilitated the difficult process of reaching agreement and some of which did not. The process was not helped by the fact that international law as a distinct body of law with dedicated textbooks, institutionalised in European universities, barely existed in the first half of the nineteenth century.[5] Furthermore while in contrast to the general stage of development some elements of international law and the laws of war were relatively well developed, most notably maritime law and the law of prizes in warfare, the very concept of military occupation was recent, inchoate and still frequently entangled in the language of conquest. Ironically, it was helped by some of the very limitations of international law. This law was restricted in scope in the sense that it was seen as regulating a limited number of states, primarily European states. Entire tracts of the globe were seen as populated by peoples lacking the requisite sovereignty and attainment of the standard of civilisation to engage as subjects of international law.[6] By the same token, European military incursions into these areas were not typically understood in terms of military occupation. The European quality of international law can be seen in the titles of some of the emergent textbooks, in, for example, August Wilhelm Heffter's *Das europäische Völkerrecht der Gegenwart* of 1844, which had also entered an early plea for consistent distinction between occupation and conquest.[7] That European characteristic had to be sure diminished towards the end of the century, because of the increasing importance in conferences and debates on international law of the American states and because of the emergence of Japan as a significant naval and military power and one seen as worthy of admission to the charmed circle of international law, in part at least because of its conduct in military occupations.[8]

The men who promoted the codification of international law and a law of military occupation were quite conscious of the additional difficulties that might have arisen from a wider circle of participants.[9] Yet many of them shared a confidence in what they saw as the progress of international law. Though sometimes seen as symbolic of the triumph of positivist conceptions of law over a defunct natural law tradition, their confidence had different roots. Positivism was in any event far from triumphant. Their confidence was derived rather from evolutionary models and from belief in the existence of a European society of states and an associated 'collective (European) *conscience*'.[10] Several gathered around the *Association internationale pour le progrès des sciences sociales*, formed in 1862. A small group went on to found the first international law journal, the *Revue de droit international et de législation comparée* in 1868 and five years later, prompted by the Franco-German War, the Institute of International Law dedicated to becoming the 'legal conscience of the civilized world'.[11] The confidence contained in that proclamation was not unlimited. As one of the Institute's members, Gustave Moynier put it at the end of the decade, it would not suffice to instruct jurists in the laws of war or to preach moderation in times of war to men 'excited by the smell of powder'. The laws of war had to be set down in military regulations, inculcated in times of peace and enforced by severe penalties.[12] They already had a model for this in the existence of the Union's General Orders no. 100 of 1863, whose author, Francis Lieber, had encouraged the German lawyer and member of the Institute, Johann Caspar Bluntschli.[13] Bluntschli had explicitly taken Lieber's code as his model in his 1866 *Das moderne Kriegsrecht der civilisirten Staaten*, following very closely its first five articles.[14] The Lieber Code, of course, owed its renown not only to its qualities as a model but precisely to the fact that it was a set of military orders and in principle could be enforced by the severe penalties of military justice.

Prospects that a similar backing might be found for an international code improved with an initiative not from the west but from the east, from Russia. It would, indeed, be Russian initiatives that provided the diplomatic impetus for all of the conferences that finally resulted in a codified and enforceable law of war. That these initiatives for the promotion of the rule of law internationally should come from a state that overtly proclaimed its autocratic nature is striking. Principles of humanity and international law were, however, recurrent themes in Imperial Russian rhetoric and diplomacy.[15] They were embodied in the St Petersburg declaration of 1868 prohibiting small explosive projectiles on the grounds that 'the necessities of war ought to yield to the requirements of humanity'.[16] Nor was this purely a matter of rhetoric. Russian lawyers, precisely because of the autocratic domestic system, promoted international law both to enhance the external reputation of Russia and to promote the cause of the rule of law, if only indirectly.[17] One of those lawyers, Fedor Martens, then a junior official, succeeded in persuading the Foreign Ministry and the war minister to propose a conference on a code for land warfare. Martens, as well as embodying those general sentiments of humanity, had also been influenced by the Franco-German War, which he witnessed at close quarters, and took the Lieber Code as the basis for his own draft code which fed into the official Russian proposal to the conference.[18]

The Conferences and Military Manuals

Despite the influence of the American code, the United States was not initially invited to the conference and declined to attend when a belated and indirect invitation was issued.[19] The European states, with one notable exception, had responded positively to the Russian proposal. Britain attended reluctantly and only after receiving assurances that the conference would confine itself strictly to the remit set out in the Russian proposal and would not stray into matters of maritime operations.[20] The conference, which lasted from 27 July to 27 August 1874, issued in a code, though not one the conference's participants had the authority to sign on behalf of their states. The difficulty of reaching agreement on anything had resulted both in agreement on what was at least claimed to be widely accepted principles in any event and a substantial record of divergence on much else and even more equivocation. One unimpressed critic observed that 'one knows for sure many of the points they could not agree on, but is not sure that they agree on the others'.[21] A Russian circular of 26 September soliciting views on the best way to advance the project met with some initial equivocation even from the Germans and French.[22] The British response was clear and negative. In a dispatch from the Earl of Derby, shown to Prince Gorchakov, the Russian chancellor, the British foreign minister complained of 'numerous innovations' and objected to the violation of the 'rule that only unanimity of opinions should be recorded' and selected disagreement as to 'the meaning of "occupation"' as indicative of the 'striking differences of opinion' found in the record.[23] Britain, he concluded, 'cannot consent to pursue the matter or to take part in any further negotiations or Conferences upon it'.[24] While sections of the Russian and German press cast aspersions on British motives in blocking further progress, the British press responded by presenting the entire project as designed to further subordinate the weak to the strong. The *Pall Mall Gazette* sarcastically suggested that to

> restrict the area of combatancy as narrowly as possible, to make war as completely as possible an affair of professional fighting men – this is, unquestionably to humanize war; and if it happens at the same time to give an overwhelming advantage in warfare to the nation which can muster the greatest number of professional fighting men, that Prince Gortschakoff may say is merely an accident, fortunate or unfortunate as the case may be.[25]

Nor were such sentiments restricted to a defensive British press. It was a French journal that suggested, in the section headed 'Of military authority on the territory of the enemy state', that the authors of the project had sought to 'inculcate a spirit of resignation by the defeated'.[26] Given recent French experience and the acrimonious dispute over the *francs-tireurs* that was not surprising.

When Gustave Moynier, on behalf of the Institute for International Law, reviewed the state of progress towards the end of the decade he could record limited progress. There was a Russian decree and regulations relating to prisoners of war of 1877 and there were signs of consideration being given to the modernisation of the laws of war in England, Switzerland and Denmark.[27] There was also the French *Manuel de droit international à l'usage des officiers de l'armée de terre* published in 1877, which, while not constituting military regulations, was authorised for use in military schools.[28] It was also clearly influenced by the Brussels code.[29] The Institute went on to provide its own code, known as the Oxford code of 1880 in the light of the Institute's agreement on the code at its meeting there. The code itself was not innovative, by the Institute's own account. It was not intended to serve as the basis for a treaty, an enterprise the Institute held to be premature or at least very difficult. It was hoped that it might serve as the basis for national regulations and was expressed in what the Institute took to be simplified form to facilitate its impact upon the troops.[30]

Between the Franco-German War and the Brussels Conference and the end of the century there would be further development. Moynier was able to report that Serbia had adopted the French manual. Britain produced a *Manual of Military Law* in 1884 which was in its fourth edition before the turn of the century. The United States made no innovation, still issuing the Lieber Code as it embarked on war with Spain in 1898. They did see the publication of two substantial volumes by military lawyers: William Winthrop's *Military Law and Precedents*, with a section on 'The Status of Military Government', appeared in 1886, while William E. Birkhimer's *Military Government and Martial Law* appeared in 1892.[31] Both naturally relied heavily on specifically American material with prominence given to the Civil War in which both had served. In the European literature there was an increasing number of volumes, especially by French authors, on the laws of war and some specifically on military occupation, such as Joseph Bray's *De l'occupation militaire en temps de guerre* of 1894.[32] Equally important, the advance of the codification of law and growth and professionalisation of interest in international law encouraged the publication of texts on international law across Europe, most having smaller or greater reference to military occupation. They typically drew on a common stock of material and authors. William Edward Hall's *A Treatise on International Law* invoked the work of Heffter, Rolin-Jaequemyns, the Argentinian Carlos Calvo and Bluntschli as well as the Brussels and Lieber codes and the French manual as examples of 'recent doctrine'.[33] While not fulfilling the hopes of the Institute or most members of the Brussels Conference, the density and dissemination of ideas about the law of military occupation accelerated dramatically in the last quarter of the nineteenth century.

It was again a Russian initiative which led to the consolidation of these efforts by the Hague Conference, soon popularly designated the Hague Peace Conference. The initiative went back to the response of the Russian war minister to the development of new field artillery by the central powers and to his desire for an agreement between Russia and Austria for a moratorium on such development. The War Minister Aleksei Kuropatkin, however, appealed to wider issues of peace and prospects of at least halting the arms race in order to win over Tsar Nicholas II. Although it took months before the hesitant Nicholas, pulled in diverse directions by differing ministers and advisers, decided to launch an appeal for a conference, it was those broader sentiments that prevailed in the Rescript handed to a surprised diplomatic staff in Saint Petersburg on 24 August 1898.[34] This time it was the Germans who were hesitant, but they too agreed to attend, as did the United States, though Brazil was the only representative from South America. Japan was invited, as were China, Persia and Siam. When the Conference met in May 1899 there was considerable press attention although only the American delegation felt obliged to see the representatives of various American movements and organisations.[35] The Conference itself made little progress with the idea of a reduction of armaments but it did agree on a Convention Respecting the Laws and Customs of War on Land, article 1 of which specified that they would 'issue instructions to their armed land forces, which shall be in conformity with the "Regulations respecting the laws and customs of war on land" annexed to the present Convention'.[36] These regulations were in fact heavily shaped by the initial Brussels Conference of 1874, though some modifications were of importance.

Having specified no time limit for the implementation of that provision it was not surprising that progress was slow. By 1907, the French, Russians and English had implemented the commitment. The

English even embodied the fact in the title: *The Laws and Customs of War on Land as Defined by the Hague Convention of 1899*.[37] The Swiss, though not even a party to the Convention, had made the Regulations obligatory for its army.[38] The Germans, whose *Kriegsbrauch im Landkriege* appeared in 1902, made explicit reference to the Brussels and Oxford codes as well as the Hague Regulations.[39] It was against this background that the second Hague Peace Conference assembled in 1907 having been provided for by the first Conference but delayed because of the intervention of the Russo-Japanese War of 1904–5. Here the rules of land warfare played an even more subordinate role, with the hopes for a Permanent Court of Arbitral Justice dominating debate and forming the focus of the disputes amongst the enlarged membership of the Conference.[40] Even less amendment was made to the actual Regulations, though article 3 to the 1907 Convention specified that 'A belligerent party which violates the provisions of the said regulations shall, if the case demands, be liable to pay compensation'.[41] There had, however, been a price to pay for such agreement as they had reached. As he opened the Second Commission of the 1907 Conference, Auguste Beernaert looked back over the preceding decades and congratulated the delegates on the fact that they had been able to agree on a body of rules at the earlier conferences, adding, 'gentlemen, we have succeeded, thanks to a broad conciliatory spirit, and also, because we have contented ourselves when necessary with formulas, rather vague and thereby susceptible of satisfying different tendencies'.[42]

The Brussels Conference of 1874

The disagreements that the Earl of Derby had lamented and formulas in which Beernaert took satisfaction had marked the proceedings at the Brussels Conference in 1874. It was soon recognised that the initial Russian draft, resembling as it did the permissive character of the Lieber Code was problematic.[43] The Russian draft, after enunciating some general principles, had begun its proposal on 'military authority on the territory of the enemy state' by specifying that occupation automatically suspends the authority of the legal power, substituting that of the occupying state, while the second article gave the occupant scope to modify or suspend entirely existing legislation and the third set out the occupant's power to constrain public officials to continue in their functions.[44] The redrafted version presented on 5 August began instead by changing the emphasis from the powers of the occupant to the very definition of occupation. As the conference turned from matters such as prisoners of war and the treatment of spies to this mater of definition the major fault line promptly appeared. It was aptly summarised by Major General Alfred Horsford, the British representative, as he reported to the Earl of Derby:

> The two really important and practical questions discussed were-
>
> 1. The definition and nature of occupation;
> 2. The rights of defence possessed by the inhabitants of an invaded country.
>
> On these points two views, diametrically opposite were taken.
>
> The first, supported by the Delegates of Belgium, the Netherlands, Spain and Portugal, Switzerland, and others, was to the effect that an invaded country cannot be in any way restricted as to the sources whence it may draw its means of defence, and that it may have recourse to every aid that patriotism may proffer or suggest.
>
> The Delegates who supported this view not only ignore but deny the theory that an invader has any authority in an occupied country, save what he acquires by force. They recognize no such authority *de jure*, and will not allow that the inhabitants have any duties towards the invader. They, moreover, declare that for the occupation to carry with it even such authority as is derived from 'might', such occupation must be actual and practical, and in no case constructive.[45]

The second position was 'explicitly stated and ably advocated by the German Delegate, General Voigts-Rhetz'. At the heart of this division lay the opposition of the smaller states, especially Belgium and the Netherlands, to the very idea of the occupant having a recognised legal status and to the associated idea that the occupant exercised a form of authority, distinct from that of the legal power, insofar as it was not sovereign authority, but nevertheless some form of authority. Even as occupants had come to avoid the language of conquest and claims to exercise sovereign power, a temptation to which some still succumbed, they nevertheless insisted upon their authority and the correlative obligations of those subject to that authority to obey it, without which, indeed, the very idea of authority makes no sense. It was precisely because of these connotations that the Dutch delegate de Lansberge suggested that the word 'authority' in the draft be replaced by the word 'power'.[46] It was the representatives of the weaker states who had picked up one side of the Janus face of law, namely that the law is a form of power. While it was often left to the representatives of the stronger to insist on the other side of the Janus face of the law, namely, that it was a limitation on power from which the weak could benefit, Lansberge quite explicitly, if implausibly, demanded that he have the one side of the law without the other. Every clause, he proclaimed, 'which, instead of limiting the power of the enemy would establish as a right facts brought about solely by the employment of force' had to be rejected.[47]

That this was intimately bound up with the conditions under which citizens might resist either an invader or an occupant was made clear by Lansberge as he read into the record a declaration of principle summarising his view of the law and the crucial issue of the right of defence: 'Every clause, therefore, which has a tendency in any manner whatsoever to detach citizens from the sacred duty of defending their country by every means in their power . . . would be condemned by public opinion.'[48] This stance was supported by the other smaller powers, liable, as they feared, to be the victims of occupation. By the same token Voigts-Rhetz insisted that anything which encouraged futile resistance and was likely to provoke harsh reprisals by the occupant would hardly serve the interest of humanity. All accepted the idea embodied in article 10 of the final code that civilians who rose in arms upon the approach of an invader were acting not only honourably but also legitimately and would enjoy belligerent status provided only that they respected 'the laws and custom of war'. They did not even insist that these citizens comply with the other criteria for militias and volunteer corps set out in article 9, namely that they 'have at their head a person responsible for his subordinates', wear 'some settled distinctive badge recognizable at a distance' and bear arms openly.[49] Citizens who rose in arms against an established occupation were quite a different matter. Here the Russian draft had provided that such people 'may be referred to justice and are not considered as prisoners of war', that is, they would be regarded as having committed an illegal act and placed before a military court.[50] This came under criticism from the smaller powers and even Voigts-Rhetz showed limited enthusiasm for it. It was the Belgian delegate Lambermont who formulated the difficulty of agreeing to a law applicable to occupied territory in this matter:

> the defence of a country is not only the right , but also the duty of a population. Events take place during war which will continue to take place, and which must be accepted. But the question before them is that of converting them into laws, into positive and international laws. If citizens are to be sacrificed for having attempted to defend their country at the peril of their lives, they need not find inscribed on the post at the foot of which they are about to be shot the Article of a Treaty signed by their own government which had in advance condemned them to death ... the Belgian delegate would prefer that the question should be left in the province of the law of nations ... and that the proposed text should be abandoned.[51]

On this Voigts-Rhetz agreed. The outcome, as they all knew, was that armies would continue to treat risings in occupied territory as illegal acts punishable by their military courts.

It was this distinction between the treatment that would be accorded to those who rose on the approach of the enemy and those who rose in occupied territory that made the definition of occupied territory so crucial. There was in this respect no established law or clear guidance despite the now substantial record of military occupations. The revised draft stated that territory is 'occupied when it is actually placed under the authority of the hostile army. The occupation extends to those territories where this authority is established, and only can be exercised'.[52] The precise significance and implications of this were not, however, clear to the delegates. Lacking established precedent they cast about for analogies, finding that of a naval blockade which was also said to have legal status only to the extent that it was effective. Recognising a blockade as effective entailed in the first place that it was visible.[53] It was precisely this that worried Voigts-Rhetz and attracted the Swiss delegate Colonel Hammer. Both certainly had in mind recent experience in France, where General Voigts-Rhetz had served. For Hammer it was a matter of excluding paper occupations, of claiming territory was occupied even where the presence of the supposed occupant was nominal. Voigts-Rhetz, almost certainly recalling the case of L'Isle-Adam in September 1870, insisted that he was not only viewing the position of the occupier; that of the occupied must also be taken into consideration ... If the words in question be retained, as soon as the authority of the occupier is no longer visible, insurrections will break out, followed by cruel repression and the war will become barbarous.[54]

All delegates in practice recognised the problems that Hammer and Voigts-Rhetz had raised. Circling around other formulations they eventually settled on a slightly modified version of the article, recording though that not all agreed that it was entirely satisfactory.[55] It was this dispute upon which the Earl of Derby pounced in justifying British refusal to continue the Brussels project. He noted that 'an effort was made to reconcile conflicting views by the use of carefully balanced expressions' and expressed British fears that the 'inhabitants of the invaded territory would find in such colourless phrases very inadequate protection' from putative occupants intent on maximising the extent of territory deemed to be occupied.[56]

Consideration of the authority of the occupant in relation to existing laws again raised the question of the nature of the authority possessed by the occupant. There was no objection to the formulation of the occupant's obligation to 'take all the measure in his power to re-establish and secure as far as possible order and public life'.[57] Lambermont did seek clarification about the meaning of 'order and public life', suggesting his own understanding of the former as 'security and general safety only' and of the latter as 'social functions, ordinary transactions, which make up an everyday life'.[58] The other delegates simply agreed. This had some bearing, though not one explicitly set out by the delegates, upon the extent of the legislative activity of the occupant. Here, in relation to the provision that the occupant would 'maintain the laws which were in force in the country in time of peace, and will only modify, suspend or replace them by others if obliged to do so', the Italian Count Lanza suggested that 'the principle should be established that civil and penal laws, not having a political character remain in force ... the modification of the legal system, exceptionally admitted, should be confined to laws of a political, administrative and financial order'.[59] Although his compatriot Baron Blanc returned to this distinction, recommending the desirability of explicitly incorporating it, he added that the potential legislative activity of the occupant should not be construed as indicating any 'right' exercised by the occupant over the inhabitants of occupied territory but that reference to it 'merely anticipates a fact ... and prejudges no question of national Sovereignty'. Neither his attempt to strip away the authority they accorded the occupant nor the distinction between political and civil laws received any recognition in the code, though the president of the conference, Baron Jomini, assured him his reservations would be recorded.[60] The same fate befell a related proposal, insofar as it also touched upon the legal status of the occupant, though confirming rather than denying it. Here it was Voigts-Rhetz who wanted to make provision for the continuing validity of civil contracts, including those between the occupant and private individuals, after the cessation of the occupation. Though meeting with no explicit opposition, concern about the unspecified difficulties this might create led to the preference to simply record Voigts-Rhetz's proposal.[61]

Although the problem of the nature of the occupant's authority created some of their greatest difficulties, restricting the obligations of the occupied also gave them difficulty. It did prove easier to agree on strengthening the initial Russian restrictions on oaths, prohibiting any 'oath of allegiance' rather than merely an 'oath of perpetual subjection'.[62] Dealing with the fate of officials was more problematic, though more because of the nature of their position and the need to retain their services in what were already complex societies with high levels of state and municipal activity than any irresolvable conflict between the negotiators.[63] Baude for France promptly drew the distinction between the government's officials and municipal officials, though Lambermont and Lansberge pointed out that the institutional arrangements in their countries did not necessarily fit in with this simple distinction. The main issue, however, was the extent to which officials could be compelled to continue as the initial Russian draft had proposed and whether they should be subject to any punishment should they not adequately carry out their functions. Though showing some concern for the awkward position in which officials would find themselves, the negotiators still retained punitive elements of the Russian draft, agreeing that:

> The public services and functionaries and officials of every class who, at the instance of the occupier, consent to continue to perform their duties, shall be under his protection. They shall not be dismissed, unless they fail in fulfilling the obligations they have undertaken, and shall not be handed over to justice unless they violate those obligations by unfaithfulness.[64]

Again Blanc of Italy entered a reservation, expressing concern that the article seemed to make their continuing in office, something he presumed they would feel themselves morally obliged to do, contingent upon an invitation from the occupant which would call into question their patriotism.[65]

Some of the most protracted discussion concerned the interlinked issues of requisitions, both for goods and services, contributions and fines. All recognised that armies would make such demands and that these demands clashed with 'respect for private property' which they also accepted. The difficulty, as Lambermont put it, 'arises when there is a question of laying down between these two interests an exact limit'.[66] Amongst the numerous formulations they explored was the idea that the occupant should be governed by regulations governing levies which could be imposed by an army in its own country. This, however, led to the practical concern that all armies might not have such regulations, while the Danish delegate Vedel saw a concern of principle, since the proposal 'tends to nothing less than recognizing the right of the occupier to introduce his own legislation into a country provisionally occupied'.[67] Lansberge opined that excluding contributions, that is, payments in cash, might lead to more moderation, only for Voigts-Rhetz to point out that this would lead to social injustice as the livestock of poor farmers was entirely appropriated while rich urban inhabitants would escape from any burden.[68] By that point, Voigts-Rhetz had already suggested that

> in order to come without difficulty to an understanding, they must not go beyond generalities. If they attempt to regulate special cases, it will always be discovered that there are some which have not been provided for, and this omission might, in practice, give rise to difficulties, if not to abuses.[69]

Their plight was, in fact, worse than he suggested, for even the generalities raised conflicts of principle which they could not remove. Yet once again they struggled through to some general formulations which at least tried to set down a principle of proportionality and some regulation of the formality with which contributions and requisitions should be levied. That was not always the case. Following on from the protracted discussion of requisitions and contributions, they dealt with the section of the Russian draft on reprisals by agreeing to suppress it entirely.[70] The matter of hostages which had played such a prominent role in the polemics at the time of the Franco-Prussian War, and continued to play a prominent role in the burgeoning literature, was not discussed at all, possibly precisely because of its sensitivity.[71]

The Oxford Code, Sovereignty and Allegiance

While there were some who shared the Earl of Derby's criticism of elastic formulations, which had indeed often been the only means of securing agreement, or suggested that the code would give rise to 'a new science, military casuistry', most recognised the significance of providing some common basis for the phenomenon of military occupation.[72] Those who expressed more serious reservations did so on the basis not of fundamental objection to the formulation of the code as on the basis of doubts about the desirability of any code at all. That reservation was also found within the ranks of the Institute for International Law as it turned to evaluate the Brussels code. Rolin-Jaecquemyns insisted, however, that uncertainty of the law was much more likely to benefit the stronger than the weaker.[73] The objections of Helmuth von Moltke were of a different kind. Moltke had responded to receipt of a copy of the Oxford code and expressed his reservations about the need for a code. His praise of the virtues of warfare as part of the divine order of things tended to distract attention from his claims that other factors contributed more to moderating the conduct of war, notably compulsory military service, widening the social bases of the army and 'rigorous discipline maintained in time of peace and of which the soldier has gotten the habit, and the vigilance of administration which provides for the subsistence of the troops in the field'.[74] That was an understandable reproach to those who saw codification as a panacea, though the members of Institute seemed well aware of the limits of codes and exhortations.

The specific provisions of the Brussels code, though the formulation of them might find criticism, did not find widespread objection. Consistent with this reception the Oxford code largely followed the Brussels code, though it offered a somewhat different definition of occupied territory, providing that 'Territory is considered as occupied when, following its invasion by enemy forces, the state to which it belongs, has ceased in fact to exercise regular authority and the invading state is the only one to maintain order there'.[75] While the

Brussels code had also identified the suspension of the authority of the invaded state, it had done so in article 2, dealing with the obligations of the occupant, which began by noting the fact of the 'authority of the legal power being suspended'.[76] The Oxford code not only explicitly made this suspension of authority central to the definition of occupation but also brought out more clearly the idea that occupation was a two-step process, involving first the suspension of the legal authority and secondly the assumption of authority by the invader. That was even more clearly set out in the French military manual, which was heavily influenced by the Brussels code. According to this manual,

> A territory is considered occupied: 1. When the legal government is, by the existence of the invader, put in a position where it cannot publicly exercise its authority; 2. And when the invader finds itself in a position to substitute the exercise of its own authority.[77]

This opened up the possibility of a gap brought about by the existence of the first condition but not of the second.[78] It also brought into focus the position of the ousted sovereign and the nature of the sovereignty still retained. The latter problem led to a variety of formulations. Some interpretations more or less explicitly accorded the occupant temporary sovereignty, reverting to the position of the US Supreme Court in *United States v. Rice* of 1819. According to Doris Graber's later summary, 'Following in Bluntschli's footsteps ... Martens ... justifies the assumption of sovereign rights by the occupant on the theory that two sovereign powers cannot remain within the same territory.'[79] By contrast the French author Frantz Despagnet allowed for the coexistence of two sovereignties but of a different nature, distinguishing between a sovereignty *en droit* and a sovereignty *en fait*, while admitting that the only criterion for distinguishing between them was 'the necessities of war'.[80] Joseph Bray picked up both elements of the Oxford definition in a series of formulations. Having accepted the suspension of legal authority as 'the primordial element' of occupation, he linked this suspension to the withdrawal of the political functionaries of the state.[81] Yet he also considered the possibility of continuing covert communication with the legal government, conceding that this was insufficient for 'the maintenance of true and complete sovereignty'.[82] He also suggested that the withdrawal of political officials did not entail the immediate existence of a state of occupation, since local officials could continue to maintain order and must be understood to be acting in the name of the legal sovereign rather than on their own account, implying the continuation of some measure of legal sovereignty.[83] Carlos Calvo insisted more consistently on the suspension of the 'power of the sovereign state', the idea that occupation entailed a completely different kind of relationship between government, that of the occupant, and governed, while justifying the idea that sovereignty was only suspended on the basis that territory is not yet separated from the state and the inhabitants remained citizens of that state.[84] These various formulations all reflected the difficulty of acknowledging precisely the issue that had worried the Belgian and Dutch delegates at Brussels, namely that the occupant was being accorded a legal status and understood to possess authority, while at the same time preserving the distinction between conquest and occupation, which was understood to require in some sense the persistence of the sovereignty of the occupied state. They also reflected, imperfectly to be sure, the recent national experiences of the authors' countries.

Nor was there full clarity about key issues such as the extent of the occupant's legislative authority and the position of officials. While the Brussels code prescribed retaining existing laws, a practice that was seen as embodying respect for the sovereignty of the occupied state and being in the practical interests of both occupied and occupants, this restraint was always qualified by the exemption allowed by necessity. The restraint was also qualified by the distinction between political functions and laws and civil functions and laws which had been raised during the discussions at Brussels, but not taken up in the code. It did, however, frequently reappear in commentaries. Indeed 'political, administrative and financial laws' were often accepted as being inconsistent with the interests of the occupant and subject to suspension or modification.[85] The most quoted such law was the French conscription law that had been suspended by the Germans during the occupation of France in 1870–1. These were specific laws characterised by the clash of interest arising from the fact of occupation. Sometimes, however, a wider legislative activity was ascribed to the occupant, on the grounds of the suspension of the legal government's capacity to legislate, with this general capacity then being restrained by the exigencies of war.[86] At its most extreme precisely where an occupant was intent upon retaining occupied territory, fundamental constitutional changes were accepted. That both Bluntschli and Martens sanctioned such far reaching innovation reflected the actual polices of their respective states.[87]

Similar sensitivity revolved around the position of officials. The Brussels code had issued a general prohibition against oaths of allegiance and mitigated the punitive dimensions of the Russian draft, as well as stipulating that the occupant had a duty to protect them, but oaths other than those of allegiance had not been excluded. Hall, for example, explicitly allowed for an oath of faithful service.[88] The French *Manuel* of 1878, clearly reflecting the pressures to which French officials had been subjected, as well as being consistent with the reservation of Blanc at Brussels, recommended greater consideration of their position. It suggested that occupants should not 'personally invite' officials to continue or demand from them 'formal consent or an oath' and generally avoid anything that might give them cause to fear they would be seen as acting 'by virtue of delegation by the enemy'.[89] The clear implication was such invitations and oaths could expose the unfortunate officials to charges of treason.

The Hague Conference of 1899

None of these uncertainties or dilemmas had found any resolution by the time the Hague Conference of 1899 opened, basing itself on the Brussels code and the arguments that lay behind it. Indeed immediately the sub-commission dealing with the laws and customs of land warfare turned to these matters the Belgian delegate Auguste Beernaert asked leave to deliver an address in which he called into question the entire attempt to regulate fundamental aspects of occupation in the Brussels code:

> In my opinion there are certain points which cannot be the subject of a convention and which it would be better to leave, as at present, under the government of that tacit and common law which arises from the principles of the law of nations ... Under the Brussels draft the conquered or invaded country recognizes the invader in advance as having rights on its territory ... The officials of the invaded country are authorized to place themselves in the service of the conqueror ... The invader is authorized to collect existing taxes.
>
> Not that I wish to criticize the fact ... But although it is natural for the conqueror to derive the power to act thus from victory, I cannot understand a convention giving him the right ... Is it conceivable that

the State that is beaten would grant rights to its conqueror in its own territory, in advance and in case of war, and that it would organize a régime of defeat? Could it be by anticipated and written consent of the conquered party that the conqueror would levy taxes and impose fines or engage in his service officials whose first duty is to be faithful to their own country?[90]

Although these were arguments which had earlier been advanced against having a law of occupation at all, Beernaert's conclusions were less drastic but substantial enough, calling for removal of the words 'being suspended' in relation to the authority of the legal power in article 2 and the complete removal of several other articles including those relating to existing laws and the position of public officials.[91] The significance of the challenge was not lost on Martens, who responded with his own lengthy address in which he recalled

> It was said in 1874, and it has been said to-day, that it is preferable to leave these question in 'a vague state and in the exclusive domain of the law of nations'. But is this opinion quite just? Do the weak become stronger because the *duties* of the strong are not determined? Do the strong become weaker because their *rights* are specifically defined and consequently limited? . . . To leave uncertainty hovering over these questions would necessarily be to allow the interest of force to triumph over those of humanity.[92]

They agreed that both statements should be printed but Martens effectively won the principled argument.

As they turned to consider the specific articles, the problem of definition resurfaced. Eduard Rolin proposed a version incorporating the dual elements of the Oxford code. Whereas, however, the French *Manuel* had seen both of the elements as necessary to define occupation, Beernaert feared that the first alone might be taken as sufficient and occupation declared on the withdrawal of the legal authorities without the invader having established his authority. Implicitly picking up options raised by Bray, Colonel Gilinsky of the Russian delegation wondered what the relevant authorities were, asking: 'Could it be said that the legal authorities have withdrawn when only the mayors continue to exercise authority?'[93] Faced with these complications they retreated to the wording of 1874, with Beernaert's agreement.

Beernaert was more successful with his call for removal of any reference to the authority of the legal power being suspended, to which the others agreed without any objection.[94] His proposal to drop articles 3, 4 and 5 proved more complicated. On provisional votes they agreed only the removal of article 4, relating to officials. They continued though to alternately worry over the wider principles, as expounded by Beernaert and Martens, and the implications of specific formulations. When, for example, an amendment was suggested which would have removed any possibility of suspending or amending existing laws, Colonel Gross von Schwarzhoff of Germany protested that the consequence would be that the occupant would not be able to declare martial law and would have to respect existing laws on recruitment.[95] As they returned to article 4 the dilemma that certain officials had a duty to remain at their posts, but in doing so under article 4 might thereby be judged guilty of treason, seemed irresolvable. At that point, Voislave Veljkovitch of Serbia suggested that the reworded article 2, including reference to maintaining existing laws, 'implies the retention of the functionaries appointed by those laws'.[96] The desperate president pounced on this 'judicious interpretation', which allowed them to drop article 4 without apparent significance. In fact the obligation of the occupant to protect officials who remained in post fell by the wayside without notice.

The desire to escape uncomfortable consequences and distinctions surfaced again in the drafting committee where a suggestion was made that the words 'of invasion or occupation' be inserted into one of the articles. Colonel Gross von Schwarzhoff, though uncertain of the implications, expressed his concern that this

> might place in doubt the whole system of the articles of the third Section ... The first article of this section, that is Article 42, gives a quasi-juridical definition of the term 'occupation', but in the majority of the following articles the words 'occupied, occupant and occupation' are used in a broader and so to speak military sense, which comprises at once invasion and occupation.[97]

Opening up the distinction might, he feared, permit the invader to claim that restrictions upon the occupant did not apply to the invader. By way of illustration he suggested that this might be taken to 'warrant the *invader* for instance in forcing the population to take part in the operations against its country'.[98] Faced with that consequence the proposer of the amendment promptly withdrew,

Codification of a Law of Occupation 243

though no mention was made of the potential significance of this more expansive understanding of occupation compared with the definition they had laboriously agreed at Brussels.

The most intractable of the Brussels debates, concerning the conditions of legitimate defence, inevitably resurfaced as they turned to articles 9 and 10 of the Brussels code dealing with that issue. Here the British General John Ardagh had suggested a new article stating that nothing in that section 'shall be considered as tending to lessen or abolish the right belonging to the population of an invaded country to fulfil its duty of offering by all lawful means, the most energetic patriotic resistance against the invaders'.[99] The German delegate Colonel Gross von Schwarzhoff conceded that at first Ardagh's proposal seemed 'harmless, almost anodyne' but asserted that the eloquence with which its advocates spoke in its favour revealed that it was intended to widen the scope of the existing articles, adding that 'soldiers are also men' and should not be expected to be faced with 'peaceable inhabitants' who 'change suddenly into furious enemies'.[100] As they searched for a way out of the dilemma a suggestion was made that they have recourse to a general declaration which Martens had asked be recorded in the minutes. According to this, while the Conference had striven to regulate and define the usages of war, agreement on all issues had not been possible. Therefore,

> Until a perfectly complete code of the laws of war is issued, the Conference thinks it right to declare that in cases not included in the present arrangement, population and belligerents remain under the protection and empire of the principles of international law, as they result from the usages established between civilized nations, from the laws of humanity, and the requirements of the public conscience.[101]

This they agreed should not only be recorded in the minutes but be turned into *'an official act of the Conference'*.[102] With that, the Martens Clause, as it would be known, covered over their inability to agree. It was an option that some preferred to having any agreement at all.

The Hague Conference of 1907 and Military Manuals

There was very little left to disagree over at the Hague Conference of 1907, or rather little that they chose to raise for agreement beyond what they had already settled or abandoned hope of settling. An ill-phrased German proposal sought again to tighten the limits of volunteer corps but without success. One significant innovation was the provision that occupants could not abolish or suspend in principle the rights of citizens of the enemy states to seek redress in courts.[103] There was more substantive debate focused around article 44 of the 1899 text: 'It is forbidden to force the population of occupied territory to take part in military operations against its own country'.[104] The dispute centred on what should properly count as taking part in operations against one's country. Germany and Austria, with Russian support, favoured a narrow interpretation, allowing them to compel inhabitants to undertake a wide range of activities, including acting as guides. The smaller countries favoured a wider interpretation, specifically excluding compelling inhabitants to act as guides. General Jonkheer den Beer Poortugael summarised the fate of the hapless guide: 'if he betrays his country he will be guillotined, hung or imprisoned for life: on the other hand if he refuses he will be shot'.[105] Although the prohibition they settled on was not as clearly formulated as it might have been, leaving scope for some dispute, those who defended the coercion of guides had lost the argument.[106]

With the ratification of the Hague Regulations there was now an internationally agreed and enforceable law of occupation. Discussion of the law of occupation, its meaning, virtues, opacities and omissions had a common reference point for the first time. Guides and manuals could take the form essentially of commentaries upon the Hague Regulations.[107] That they should have this impact was evident in the fact that the fifth edition of the British *Manual of Military Law*, published in 1907, simply omitted Chapter 14, 'The laws and customs of war on land', pending the results of the Hague Conference.[108] Even before the 1907 conference the German *Kriegsbrauch in Landkriege*, published in 1902, was castigated for insufficient attention to the 1899 Hague Regulations. Yet the Hague Regulations had succeeded as much by the elasticity of their formulation, by setting aside issues they could not agree on, and by hoping to cover the gaps by means of the Martens declaration. The Regulations were also a reflection of wider trends including the more systematic development and dissemination of international law and legal approaches to warfare, which sometimes threatened to lose touch with the understanding and practices of military establishments or simply failed to pay much attention to issues prominent in military manuals.

Ironically, one of the issues prominent in military manuals but finding no reflection in the codes from Brussels through to the Hague conferences, was that of judicial administration.[109] Indeed in the relatively brief consideration given to military occupation in the British *Manual of Military Law* of 1894, it was civil tribunals and the 'special tribunals created by an invader for carrying into effect the rule of military occupation' which were the only intuitions specially identified and the power of punishment was picked out as the 'most important power' exercised by the occupant.[110] Matters of judicial administration remained prominent in the *Manual* of 1914, while taking account of the Hague Regulations, including the right of inhabitants to seek redress through courts.[111] The silence of the Hague Regulations could also be taken as licence to continue practices not expressly forbidden. That was the view of the British *Manual* in respect of inhabitants who relayed information to the enemy:

> The Hague Rules do not refer to cases in which inhabitants of invaded or occupied territory . . . furnish, or attempt to furnish, information to the enemy . . . Such persons should be charged with war treason, for although treason as such is not mentioned in the Hague Rules, belligerents are by customary international law empowered to punish treason by death.[112]

Both the British and the American manuals provided for the administration of oaths to officials, even though the British *Manual* suggested that it would be 'advisable not to require an oath but merely to ask for assurance that they will loyally fulfil the service confided to them'.[113] Again there was no prohibition of this practice in the Hague Regulations though it was increasingly disapproved in legal commentaries. In that respect the changed tone was reflected in the objection raised by Spaight to the imposition of oaths:

> Any attempt to make the moral sanction of an oath supply the material deficiencies of an occupant's material power – to substitute, as it were, the restrictive force of the inhabitant's conscience for that of an effective garrison is as much to be deprecated as the abandoned German system of occupying districts 'theoretically'.[114]

In other respects, however, the military manuals were more in tune with other formulations of the law of occupation and with the equivocations often found there. The British *Manual* showed some sign of the equivocation of the negotiators in The Hague in terms of the distinction between invasion and occupation, noting that invasion 'is not necessarily occupation, although as a rule occupation will be coincident with it'.[115] The American manual, albeit under the heading '*Distinguished from invasion*', similarly claimed that 'invasion is not necessarily occupation, although it precedes and may frequently coincide with it'.[116] Both also agreed on a solution to the problem of determining when territory was occupied given that the physical presence of the force of the occupant in all places was not a plausible option. In the British formulation which was effectively adopted by the American manual:

> It is sufficient that the national forces should not be in possession, that the inhabitants have been disarmed, that measures have been taken to protect life and property and to secure the prevalence of order, and that, should it be necessary, troops can within reasonable time be sent to make the authority of the occupying army felt.[117]

There was also clarity that occupation was not conquest though here there was some difference in the formulation, with the British *Manual* insisting that the sovereignty of the legitimate power 'is only temporarily latent and in no way passes to the occupant' while the American manual suggested that occupation 'does not transfer the sovereignty to the occupant, but solely the authority or power to exercise some of the rights of sovereignty'.[118] In this they reflected the continuing difficulty, whether in military manuals or survey of international law, to clearly specify the nature of the authority of the occupant and the fate of the sovereignty of the legitimate power during the occupation.[119]

The British and American manuals differed more significantly in that the American manual, though also noting article 43 of the Hague Regulations and, beyond that, drawing the now established distinction between political and civil laws, showed much more interest in justifying and illustrating the 'new laws and regulations' that an occupant might promulgate. That was a reflection of the American reluctance to abandon the idea of the occupant as an albeit temporary sovereign. Although Charles Magoon's view, still expressed in 1902, that in occupation military government 'takes the place of a deposed sovereignty' was rare, it reflected the legacy of the American experience of occupation and the ways in which it differed from the European.¹²⁰ The interaction between the two sets of experience was to be sure strong. Where Bluntschli had looked to Lieber, the Americans looked to the experience of the Franco-German War and the Brussels code. Both Americans and Europeans had still been tempted to transform occupation into conquest, both overtly, by sleight of hand, and equivocally, and both had taken a broad view of the extent to which as occupants they could legislate. To that extent the conservationist principle embodied in the respect for existing law in article 43 of the Hague Regulations had been treated as a preliminary cautionary principle, not as an absolute one, as a barrier to the immediate presumption of conquest, and above all, as a point on which the interests of the occupant and occupied might coincide at least for a while. That too reflected a common experience.

Notes

1. Doris Graber, *The Development of the Law of Belligerent Occupation 1863–1914* (New York: AMS Press, 1949), remains indispensable.
2. Thus Casper Sylvest, 'International law in nineteenth-century Britain', *British Yearbook of International Law*, 76 (2005), 66.
3. By Travers Twiss. See G. Rolin-Jaequemyns, 'Rapport de M Rolin-Jaequemyns', *Revue de droit international et de législation comparée*, 7 (1875), 467.
4. On the publication of Bentham's idea of a plan for a *Plan du code international* see Ernest Nys, 'The codification of international law', *American Journal of International Law*, 5 (1911), 878–9.
5. See Martti Koskenniemi, *The Gentle Civilizer of Nations: The Rise and Fall of International Law 1870–1960* (Cambridge: Cambridge University Press, 2002), pp. 28–35.
6. On these issues see Antony Anghie, *Imperialism, Sovereignty and the Making of International Law* (Cambridge University Press, 2005), pp. 32–114, and Gerrit Gong, *The Standard of 'Civilization' in International Society* (Oxford: Clarendon Press, 1984).
7. August Wilhelm Heffter in his *Das europäische Völkerrecht der Gegenwart* (Berlin: Schneider, 1844).
8. Douglas Howland, 'Sovereignty and the laws of war: international consequences of Japan's 1905 victory over Russia', *Law and History Review*, 29 (2011), 53–6.
9. See Institut de droit international, 'Cinquième commission d'etude – réglementation des lois et coutumes de la guerre', *Annuaire de l'Institut de droit international*, 3 & 4 (1879 & 1880), part 1, 320.

10. Koskenniemi, *The Gentle Civilizer of Nations*, p. 51. On the importance of evolutionary models see Sylvest, 'International law in nineteenth-century Britain', p. 41.
11. Koskenniemi, *The Gentle Civilizer of Nations*, pp. 12–14, 39–41.
12. Institut de droit international, 'Cinqième commission d'étude – réglementation des lois et coutumes de la guerre', 316.
13. See Bluntschli's letter to Lieber, reproduced as the Foreword to his *Das moderne Völkerrecht der civilisirten Staten* (Nördlingen: Beck, 1868), pp. v–viii.
14. J. C. Bluntschli, *Das moderne Kriegsrecht der civilisirten Staaten* (Nördlingen: Beck, 1866), pp. 7–8. Refrence to others followed, ibid. pp. 9–10.
15. Peter Holquist, 'The Russian Empire as a "Civilized State": International Law as Principle and Practice in Imperial Russia, 1874–1878' (Washington DC: NCEER, 2006), and Eric Myles, '"Humanity", "civilization" and the "international community" in the late imperial Russian mirror', *Journal of the History of International Law*, 4 (2002), 310–34.
16. Ibid. p. 318.
17. Holquist, 'The Russian Empire as a "Civilized State"', pp. 7–8.
18. Ibid. pp. 11–12.
19. G. Rolin-Jaequemyns, 'Chronique du droit international 1871–1874', *Revue de droit international et de législation comparée*, 7 (1875), 88–9.
20. Fedor de Martens, *La paix et la guerre* (Paris: Rousseau, 1901), pp. 106 9.
21. Anon., 'Les conference de Bruxelles et de Saint-Pétersbourg', *Revue des deux mondes*, series 3, 8 (1875), 464.
22. So it seemed to the American legation in Saint-Peterbourg, *Foreign Relations of the United States 1875–6*, vol. 2, 1021–24.
23. Earl of Derby to Lord Loftus, 20 January 1875, *British and Foreign State Papers*, 66 (1874–1875), 446–7.
24. Ibid. p. 451.
25. *Foreign Relations of the United States 1875–6*, vol. 2, 1032.
26. Anon., 'Les conference de Bruxelles et de Saint-Pétersbourg', p. 469.
27. Institut de droit international, 'Cinqième commission d'étude', 316–17.
28. *Manuel de droit international à l'usage des officiers de l'armée de terre* (Paris: Dumaine, 1877).
29. Frantz Despagnet, *La diplomatie de la troisième republique at le droit des gens* (Paris: Larose, 1904), p. 116.
30. See the record of the Institute's meeting in Oxford, in *Annuaire de l'Institut de droit international*, 5 (1882), 158.

31. William Winthrop, *Military Law and Precedents* (Washington DC: Government Printing Office, 1920). This is the reissued second edition of 1895. William E. Birkhhimer, *Military Government and Martial Law* (Washington DC: J. J. Chapman, 1892). On Winthrop see George Pugh, 'Colonel William Winthrop. The tradition of military lawyer', *American Bar Association Journal*, 42 (1956), 126–9 and 188–91.
32. Joseph Bray, *Droit international de l'occupation militaire en temps de guerre* (Paris: Larose, 1894).
33. William Edward Hall's *A Treatise on International Law*, 2nd edn (Oxford: Clarendon, 1884), p. 429.
34. On the motives see Dan Morrill, 'Nicholas II and the call for the First Hague Conference', *Journal of Modern History*, 46 (1974), 296–313.
35. Geoffrey Best, 'Peace conferences and the century of total war: the 1899 Hague Conference and what came after', *International Affairs* 75 (1999), 623. Best suggested that the greater press and public access at the 1907 Conference was not necessarily beneficial, 633.
36. James Brown Scott (ed.), *The Proceedings of the Hague Peace Conferences: The Conference of 1899* (New York: Oxford University Press, 1920), p. 251.
37. Holland recorded that 'many thousand copies ... were issued by authority to the British army in 1904', *The Laws of War on Land* (Oxford: Clarendon, 1908), p. 73.
38. Mérignhac inaccurately complained that in respect of the criteria applicable to irregular troops the Germans ignored the Hague Regulations, 'Les theories du Grand État-Major allemande sur les "lois de la guerre continentale"', *Revue générale du droit international public*, 14 (1907), 202.
39. Ibid. p. 207.
40. See Gerry Simpson, *Great Powers and Outlaw States* (Cambridge: Cambridge University Press, 2004), pp. 132–47.
41. James Brown Scott (ed.), *The Proceedings of the Hague Peace Conferences. The Conference of 1907*, vol. 1 (New York: Oxford University Press, 1920), p. 621.
42. James Brown Scott (ed.), *The Proceedings of the Hague Peace Conferences: The Conference of 1907*, vol. 3 (New York: Oxford University Press, 1921), pp. 97–8.
43. The Russian draft was seen as endowing the occupant with almost all the rights of the occupied state by G. Valbert, 'Le nouveau droit des gens et le mission du Prince Tcherkassky', *Revue des deux mondes*, series 3, 22 (1877), 600–700.
44. *Actes de la Conférence de Bruxelles de 1874* (Paris: Libraire des publications legislatives, 1874), p. 4.

45. *Correspondence Respecting the Brussels Conference on the Rules of Military Warfare* (London: HMSO, 1875), p. 61.
46. Ibid. p. 236.
47. Ibid. p. 235.
48. Ibid. p. 235.
49. Ibid. p. 320.
50. Article 46, *Actes de la Conférence de Bruxelles de 1874*, p. 6.
51. *Correspondence Respecting the Brussels Conference*, p. 264.
52. Ibid. p. 228.
53. For a court ruling that a supposed blockade failed to meet this criterion see 'The Gerasimo', *English Reports*, 14 (1857), 628–40.
54. *Correspondence Respecting the Brussels Conference*, p. 237.
55. Ibid. p. 259.
56. Earl of Derby to Lord Loftus, 20 January 1875, *British and Foreign State Papers*, 66 (1874–1875), 447–8.
57. *Correspondence Respecting the Brussels Conference*, p. 53. The translation in the correspondence giving 'public safety and social order'(p. 228) for 'order and public life' (*'ordre et la vie publique'*) is not entirely accurate, though less problematic than the English translation of the final Hague Regulations of 1907 where the same words were translated as 'public order and safety'. The error is now regularly noted in legal commentaries. See Edmund Schwenk, 'Legislative power of the military occupant under article 43, Hague Regulations', *Yale Law Journal*, 54 (1945), 393.
58. *Correspondence Respecting the Brussels Conference*, p. 239.
59. Ibid. pp. 228 and 239.
60. Ibid. p. 306.
61. Ibid. p. 250.
62. See article 49 of the Russian draft, *Actes de la Conférence de Bruxelles de 1874*, p. 6; article 38 of the Brussels code, *Correspondence Respecting the Brussels Conference*, p. 323.
63. The claim that the negotiators at Brussels and The Hague assumed the existence of essentially self-regulating, 'private' economies and societies is misguided. See Peter Stirk, *The Politics of Military Occupation* (Edinburgh: Edinburgh University Press, 2009), pp. 16–17.
64. *Correspondence Respecting the Brussels Conference*, p. 240.
65. Ibid. p. 306.
66. Ibid., 275.
67. Ibid. p. 269.
68. Ibid. p. 277.
69. Ibid. p. 271.
70. Ibid. p. 281.

71. Graber, *The Development of the Law of Belligerent Occupation*, pp. 209–10.
72. Anon., 'Les conference de Bruxelles et de Saint-Pétersbourg', 471.
73. Rolin-Jaequemyns, 'Rapport de M Rolin-Jaequemyns', 472.
74. Percy Bordwell, *The Law of War between Belligerents* (Chicago: Callahan, 1908), p. 114. For an early critical response see Ch. Lucas, 'Observation sur les lois de la guerre at l'arbitrage international', *Revue critique de législation et de jurisprudence*, 10 (1881), 201–8.
75. 'Les lois de la guerre sur terre', *Annuaire de l'Institut de droit international*, 5 (1882), 166.
76. *Correspondence Respecting the Brussels Conference*, p. 320.
77. *Manuel de droit international à l'usage des officiers de l'armée de terre*, 2nd edn (Paris: Dumaine, 1878), p. 87.
78. This would be a continuing problem in the understanding of occupation. See especially, in the context of the later Geneva Conventions of 1949, the comments of Jean Pictet, *Commentary Fourth Geneva Convention* (Geneva: ICRC, 1958), p. 60.
79. Graber, *The Development of the Law of Belligerent Occupation*, pp. 58–9.
80. Frantz Despagnet, *Cours de droit international public* (Paris: Larose, 1894), pp. 580–1.
81. Bray, *Droit international de l'occupation militaire en temps de guerre*, p. 152.
82. Ibid. p. 152.
83. Ibid. p. 153.
84. Charles [Carlos] Calvo, *Le droit international théorique et pratique*, 5th edn, vol. 4 (Paris: Rousseau, 1896), p. 212.
85. See, for example, Jules Guelle, *Droit international: La guerre continentale et les personnes* (Paris: Dumaine, 1881), p. 162.
86. Pasquale Fiore, *Nouveau droit international public*, 2nd edn, vol. 3 (Paris: Durand and Pedone-Lauriel, 1886), p. 325. In this respect Eyal Benvenisti's presentation of Fiore as the promoter of the 'conservationist principle', stripping out his qualifications, is not entirely convincing, 'The origins of belligerent occupation', *Law and History Review*, 26 (2008), 632–4.
87. See Fedor de Martens, *Traité de droit international*, vol. 3 (Paris: Maresq, 1887), p. 257, citing German policy in Alsace-Lorraine and Russian policy in Bulgaria, 1877–8. Even before the Franco-German War Bluntschli cited the wars of liberation of Revolutionary France and the American Civil War as exceptions, *Das moderne Völkerrecht der civilisirten Staten*, p. 306. See also Fiore's reservation in condemning as an abuse occupants 'transforming civil legislation without reason', *Nouveau droit international public*, vol. 3, p. 325.

88. Graber, *The Development of the Law of Belligerent Occupation*, p. 139.
89. *Manuel de droit international à l'usage des officiers de l'armée de terre*, 2nd edn, p. 98.
90. Scott (ed.), *The Proceedings of the Hague Peace Conferences. The Conference of 1899*, pp. 502–3.
91. Ibid. p. 505.
92. Ibid. pp. 506–7.
93. Ibid. p. 511.
94. It is not clear why, as Graber points out, *The Development of the Law of Belligerent Occupation*, p. 61. It is possible it was a consequence of the debate about the definition of occupation and the Oxford code's version.
95. Scott (ed.), *The Proceedings of the Hague Peace Conferences: The Conference of 1899*, p. 520.
96. Ibid. p. 522.
97. Ibid. p. 558.
98. Ibid. p. 558.
99. Ibid. p. 550.
100. Ibid. pp. 552–3.
101. Ibid. p. 548.
102. Ibid. p. 554.
103. Scott (ed.), *The Proceedings of the Hague Peace Conferences: The Conference of 1907*, vol. 1, p. 627.
104. Scott (ed.), *The Proceedings of the Hague Peace Conferences: The Conference of 1899*, p. 260.
105. James Brown Scott (ed.), *The Proceedings of the Hague Peace Conferences. The Conference of 1907*, vol. 3 (New York: Oxford University Press, 1921), p. 120.
106. See the assessment of J. M. Spaight, *War Rights on Land* (London: Macmillan, 1911), pp. 368–71.
107. See the American *Rules of Land Warfare* (Washington DC: Government Printing Office, 1917) and Holland, *The Laws of War on Land*.
108. War Office, *Manual of Military Law* (London: HMSO, 1907).
109. As pointed out by Graber, *The Development of the Law of Belligerent Occupation*, p. 131, noting also the relative paucity of reference in the legal commentaries, pp. 131–2.
110. War Office, *Manual of Military Law* (London: HMSO, 1894), pp. 314–15.
111. War Office, *Manual of Military Law* (London: HMSO, 1914), pp. 289–90.
112. Ibid. p. 259.
113. Ibid. p. 294.

114. Spaight, *War Rights on Land*, p. 373.
115. War Office, *Manual of Military Law* (1914), p. 314. One of the authors of this section of the *Manual* was more unequivocal elsewhere: Lassa Oppenheim, *International Law*, vol. 2 (London: Longmans, 1906), p. 170: 'Now it is certain that mere invasion is not yet occupation'.
116. War Department, *Rules of Land Warfare*, p. 106.
117. War Office, *Manual of Military Law* (1914), p. 86. The similarity arises from the avowed indebtedness of the American *Rules on Land Warfare* (see p. 7) to J. E. Edmonds and L. Oppenheimer, *Land Warfare: An Exposition of the Laws and Usages of War on Land for the Guidance of Officers of His Majesty's Army* (London: HMSO, 1912), much of which was reproduced in the British *Manual*.
118. War Office, *Manual of Military Law* (1914), p. 288; War Department, *Rules of Land Warfare*, p. 105.
119. A striking example of that is provided by Arthur Lorriot, *De la nature de l'occupation de guerre* (Paris: Lavauzelle, 1903), pp. 81–92, especially p. 86.
120. Charles Magoon, *Reports on the Law of Civil Government in Territory Subject to Military Occupation by the Military Forces of the United States* (Washington DC: War Department, 1902), p. 13. The rarity is noted by Graber, who, however, somewhat misinterprets Magoon's position, *The Development of the Law of Belligerent Occupation*, p. 67.

Chapter 6
Occupations to the Eve of the First World War

Occupation in the Age of Empire

In the decades between the end of the Franco-German War and the outbreak of the First World War there was no occupation by one European Great Power of the territory of another. The territorial simplification of the European map by the unifications of Italy and Germany may have been destabilising for the European international system in the long run, but they removed zones of instability or weakness which had sucked great powers into occupation in the earlier decades of the century.[1] Occupation now took place on the European periphery, with the decaying Ottoman Empire continuing to provide the occasion for resort to occupation as well as risk of war between the Great Powers. The great Eastern Crisis of 1875–8 drew three powers, Britain, Austria-Hungary and Russia, into strategies of occupation but also saw avoidance of war between them as Bismarck orchestrated a settlement at the conference of Berlin in 1878. Although sometimes compared to the Congress of Vienna, the Conference of Berlin symbolised the intricate network overseen by Bismarck which 'tided Europe over a period of several critical years without a rupture'.[2] The Concert of Europe, if the name was still warranted, managed to resolve successive crises on Europe's periphery, containing in the process the occupations, but with increasing difficulty.[3]

The wider pressures to which the European system was subjected were bound up with the pursuit of empire and the belief that the world was beginning to consolidate into continental or imperial blocs.[4] Calculations of surface area and population, contrasts of land based and maritime power all fed into such speculations and anxieties. Insofar as empire involved the language of occupation, it mostly did so in a quite different sense from the understanding of occupation embodied in the laws of war codified in this period. Claims to exercise effective authority here did not signify the extent of occupied territory but amounted to a claim to sovereignty, though that was a criterion with which European states felt uncomfortable, preferring to base their claims on less stringent criteria, as became apparent at the Berlin Conference of 1884–5, called to discuss the European powers' respective claims in Africa.[5] Construing occupation as title to sovereignty worked best in this period where the land over which the claim was made could be construed as *terra nullius*.[6] Where the inhabitants were recognised as being themselves sovereign, even if in some imperfect sense, mere possession alone could not be construed as justifying sovereignty. It was for this reason that Ottoman and Chinese territory became subject to occupation on the explicit understanding that this did not amount to sovereign title, at least initially. This was an assumption adopted by the new entrant to the club of the Great Powers and the charmed circle of fully fledged subjects of international law, namely Japan. Reacting to the consolidation of the Russian Empire in the east, by the construction of the trans-Siberian railway, and fearing European power more widely, Japan sought to acquire the attributes of great power status, including colonies, at the same time as it demonstrated its ability to meet the standard of civilisation by, amongst other means, abiding by the laws of war, including those relating to military occupation in both the Sino-Japanese War of 1895 and the Russo-Japanese War of 1904–5.[7] Chinese resistance to increasing European pressure in the shape of the so-called Boxer Rising, whose antipathy to foreigners was shared by many Chinese officials, was less successful, provoking the occupation of Peking in 1900 by a multilateral force in which both the Japanese and the Americans joined the European powers. Here mutual suspicion helped to restrain the temptation to turn occupation into something else as the powers moved towards the open door policy towards China.[8]

While mutual rivalry contributed to ensuring that the British occupation of Egypt in 1882 was, nominally at least, nothing more than occupation, there was no other power with sufficient reach to restrain Britain in the south of Africa. Here though, Britain was confronted with the Boer Republics of the Orange Free State and the South African Republic. As descendants of Europeans their claims could not so easily be set aside as those of the indigenous peoples of sub-Saharan Africa. Here, however, British ambition was aided by the conceptual ambivalence of much of the imperial world which also had a bearing upon the extent to which instances of occupation could be clearly and unequivocally identified. Even the very term empire had no fixed and obvious meaning within British discourse, leading one recent commentator to suggest that 'the very term was in some sense delusive'.[9] British discourse included the words 'possession' and 'colony' without these having any greater clarity or defined relationship to the other elements of imperial discourse.[10] The imperial world allowed in fact for gradations and types of sovereignty, for ideas of paramountcy, where the sovereignty of others had to be conceded some recognition but more than *de facto* power was claimed.[11] Protectorates were another legal institution which left elements of sovereignty with the protected state, or at least gave the appearance of doing so, though a protectorate might look very similar to a colony or possession.[12] Even more elusive was the idea of suzerainty, a term which had already been employed in the Treaty of London in 1827 in order to define the residual sovereignty of the Porte over Greece. Quite what it meant was not in the least clear. According to some, suzerainty signified control of foreign affairs while leaving internal affairs in the hands of the state over which suzerain authority was exercised. The Marquess of Salisbury, however, asserted that suzerainty in no way excluded interference by the suzerain in internal affairs.[13] It was precisely this elasticity that recommended it to Gladstone in seeking to define the relationship between the British Empire and the Boer Republics. In the Pretoria Convention of 1881 it served in effect as a veil for British disengagement, glossing over what amounted to a retreat.[14] It could equally well serve to claim rights before the advance had been completed, turning occupation into conquest before the occupation was even effective, as soon became clear.

The Occupations of the Eastern Crisis

Although both Russia and Austria-Hungary had ambitions to extend their territory or influence in the Ottoman Empire neither favoured the armed uprisings that began in Herzegovina in 1875 and spread to Rumelia in 1876.[15] Atrocities on both sides provoked indignation in Russia, fed by pan-Slavic sympathies for Serbs and Bulgarians, and Britain, fed by the press and Gladstone's *Bulgarian Horrors and the Question of the East.*[16] Attempts at a settlement, including considerations of occupation of Ottoman territory, failed while the Serb attempt to exploit the crisis by declaring war on the Ottoman Empire led to defeat, inducing in turn Russian intervention. The Peace of San Stefano imposed by Russia would have created a greater Bulgaria, in the shape of 'an autonomous tributary Principality with a Christian Government and a national militia', subject to Russian occupation for two years while an imperial Russian commissioner oversaw the formation of a 'new system' in the territory.[17] So great an extension of Russian influence was intolerable to Britain and Austria-Hungary. War was averted by the Berlin Conference, which generated a settlement more acceptable to those in Britain and Austria-Hungary.

By then Russia was already in occupation of much of the disputed territory. The Russians had demonstratively committed themselves to abiding by the laws of war, whose development they had only recently promoted at the Brussels Conference.[18] In one respect at least the Russian occupation notably failed to abide by one element of the Brussels code, namely the commitment to respect existing laws. It was testimony to the influence of the code, however, that the discrepancy was seen as requiring justification at the time and in retrospect. One argument was that they could not respect existing laws and institutions, for there was no viable civic order which they could respect.[19] It was an argument that was repeated, even more bluntly and less plausibly, by the British commentator Spaight, according to whom the Russians 'were quite unable to comply with the Brussels rule which enjoined respect for local laws and institutions, for local laws and institutions there were none'.[20] Fedor Martens invoked the avowed aim of the occupation, namely the liberation of the Bulgarians from an oppressive Ottoman system. He also argued that the intent of the Brussels restriction was to prevent premature annexation and since Russia had no intention of annexing the territory, the restraint did not apply.[21] It was not a very convincing argument but it was an early indication of how difficult occupants would find it to comply with that element of the Brussels code.

Another discrepancy became apparent during the invasion. The Russians did indeed see themselves as liberators of people who had been depicted by the pan-Slavists as both culturally similar to the Russians and as impoverished. Yet the Bulgarians they encountered seemed relatively prosperous, as even the army chief of staff noted. Moreover, as recalled by Dostoevsky, there was some bitterness on the part of Russian soldiers at what they perceived to be the indifference of the Bulgarians towards their liberators. Relations were not helped by another recurrent problem as the Russian supply system faltered and they turned to plundering.[22] The head of civil affairs, Vladimir Cherkasskii, whose remit in this respect extended only to the intended Bulgarian territory, not Armenian areas occupied by Russia but with the intent to returning them to Ottoman rule, also encountered a recurrent problem as his role provoked resentment by the military commanders jealous of their prerogatives.[23] Ironically, given later arguments about the transformative impact of the Russian occupation, Cherkasskii professed to find the Ottoman system of administration quite adequate, finding fault only with the failure of Ottoman officials to manage it adequately.[24] Cherkasskii, however, who had warned against direct military rule, characterised, he complained, by arbitrariness and brutality, soon acquired the name the 'Pasha of steel' as relations between the Bulgarians and the Russian deteriorated.[25] Martens, who recalled that the praise heaped upon Cherkasskii had soon turned to criticism, argued that a combination of insufficient personnel and sheer ignorance of conditions in Bulgaria underlay the deterioration.[26]

By the time the Treaty of Berlin altered the terms of the Russian occupation Cherkasskii had died. Under the new arrangement, limiting Russian occupation under the terms of the treaty to nine months, the greater Bulgaria so opposed by Britain and Austria-Hungary was broken up into a Bulgaria 'constituted as an autonomous and tributary principality under the suzerainty of His Imperial Majesty the Sultan' and Eastern Rumelia, which was to remain under Ottoman authority, albeit 'under conditions of administrative autonomy' and with a Christian governor general.[27] This division was resented by the Bulgarian people who would inhabit these separate entities and who were not in the least placated by the designation of the southern area as Eastern Rumelia rather than Meridional Bulgaria and lobbied feverishly but vainly for a united state.[28]

The Treaty of Berlin had provided for 'provisional administration' of Bulgaria by an imperial Russian commissary who was to be assisted by an Ottoman commissary and consuls designated by the other signatories. Under this arrangement Bulgarian notables were to draw up an Organic Law. For Eastern Roumelia, however, 'a European Commission shall be formed to arrange, in concert with the Ottoman Porte, the organization of Eastern Roumelia'.[29] Russia inevitably exercised an even greater influence than these provisions suggested, given its presence as the sole occupying power. The Imperial Commissary Aleksander Dondukov-Korsakov, supported by Generals Stolypin and Skobelev, did everything he could to promote the Russian cause and to prepare the ground for a future greater Bulgarian state, tending to be more aggressive in these matters than the tsar, as indeed were some of their predecessors as Russian occupants in the Balkans.[30] Indeed Dondukov-Korsakov boasted to Roumelian notables that he had created 'an order of things identical to that which exists in the Bulgaria to the north'.[31] According to the British representative on the European Commission, Henry Drummond Wolff, Dondukov-Korsakov openly ridiculed the Treaty of Berlin and

> stated his determination not to surrender any part, however small, of the control of the finances of the province, and remarked at the same time, in a sarcastic tone, that he did not understand how the administration was to be carried on by the Commission unless it had control of the finances.[32]

The identical order of things to which he referred probably related to military provisions and the Eastern Roumelian 'gymnastic societies' the Russians promoted, whose true purpose was evident from the fact that Generals Stolypin and Skobelev distributed some 80,000 rifles to them.[33]

The biggest barrier to Russian ambitions turned out to be the Bulgarians themselves. Desirous of a genuinely popular and effective Bulgarian government, if only to prevent any resurgence of Ottoman control in Bulgaria that might be occasioned by disorder, the Russians exercised some restraint in the deliberations of the constituent assembly in Bulgaria. The Bulgarians opted for a liberal constitution, the outcome favoured by the Russian minister of war. The European Commission for Eastern Rumelia, so derided by Dondukov-Korsakov, produced a more problematic outcome. With each of the powers taking responsibility for different sections of the Organic Law, their respective national traditions were reflected in the parts they were responsible for. Taken as a whole it was an unworkable constitution for a principality whose inhabitants had no commitment to its existence. The Russians, however, believing that they could effectively determine the conduct of the two polities, alienated the Bulgarians who proved recalcitrant, turning Russia against the union of the two entities which it had done so much to promote during its occupation. In another reversal of position, faced with the proclamation of their union by the Bulgarians in 1885, Britain, the original opponent of a united Bulgaria, now supported the union of the anti-Russian Bulgarians.[34]

Part of the price Russia paid for their ultimately frustrating attempt to promote Bulgarian independence and unity was the occupation of Bosnia and Herzegovina by Austria. At the Conference of Berlin the Austrian Chancellor Andrássy invoked the impact of refugees upon his country and the Ottoman inability to restore order. He had already agreed with the British that Austria should occupy Bosnia-Herzegovina as a counterweight to the growth of Russian influence through the Bulgarians, though the British presented the occupation as a mandate exercised by Austria in the common interest of Europe.[35] Article 25 of the Treaty of Berlin duly specified that the two provinces 'shall be occupied and administered by Austria-Hungary'.[36] There was no specification that the occupation would be of limited duration analogous to the provisions for continued Russian occupation of Ottoman territory. That Austria had no intention of relinquishing the provinces was a common assumption of contemporaries, some of whom traced the device of occupation rather than outright annexation to Austro-Hungarian domestic opposition about the impact upon the delicate balance within Austria-Hungary of the incorporation of another substantial Slavic population.[37] Indeed Stephan Burián would recall that in accepting the 'mandate' for the occupation Andrássy 'had the public opinion of practically the whole monarchy against him'.[38] Whatever the predominant judgement about Austria's intentions, the fact that it was formally an occupation still provided critics of the Austrian regime with a useful standard with which to berate Austria-Hungary.

The occupation was preceded by a proclamation that laws and institutions would not be 'arbitrarily overturned', that existing laws would remain in force until new ones were issued, that customs and usages would be respected and any income from the territory would be used purely to meet its needs.[39] The commander of the Austro-Hungarian force, General Philippovitch, even had family roots in the provinces.[40] Neither his provenance nor his proclamation or the belated Ottoman instruction that there should be no resistance had the desired effect. Popular risings, sometimes killing Ottoman officials in the process, especially amongst the Muslim inhabitants, reflecting a long tradition of autonomy and resistance to imperial authority, made the invasion phases a painful process.[41] Nevertheless effective resistance was overcome by the end of October 1878.[42]

In the initial phases of the occupation General Philippovitch, lacking dedicated personnel for the task of administration, appointed his troop commanders as military governors, uniting military and civil authority in the same hands. Although those local committees which had supported the resistance were dispersed a pattern soon emerged of working with established local authorities.[43] More problematic was Philippovitch's deployment of Croat officials to relieve his overburdened officers. While this was understandable in that they spoke the same language as the inhabitants of the occupied provinces, their predominance encouraged the Croatian Parliament to voice its Croat ambitions in the area, drawing the predictably hostile response from Magyar and Serb constituencies in the empire.[44] The mutual suspicions and antipathies of Austria-Hungary's various ethnic and religious groups would in fact play a recurrent role in attitudes to the occupation.[45] Such was the outcry about Philippovitch's deployment of Croat officials that it led to his recall and replacement.

The Treaty of Berlin had stated that 'Austria-Hungary reserve to themselves to come to an understanding on the details' of Austro-Hungarian occupation.[46] No such agreement had been reached prior to the invasion though one was subsequently concluded in April 1879. This Convention specified that the occupation did not impair the sovereign rights of the sultan in the provinces and more specifically provided that existing officials were to be retained in office, with preference given to native inhabitants where replacements were necessary, that religious freedom was guaranteed, including 'complete freedom of Muslims in relation to their spiritual superiors', that the sultan would continue to be referred to in Muslim prayers, that the Ottoman flag would be flown from minarets and that Turkish coinage would continue to circulate freely.[47] In these respects that Convention provided explicit and detailed assertion of the symbols of the continuing sovereignty of the Ottoman Empire, and hence the characterisation of the Austro-Hungarian administration as an occupation. In several respects, however, Austro-Hungarian policies called into question the extent to which the limits of occupation were being respected. A decree making Austro-Hungarian currency legal tender, notwithstanding the continued free circulation of Turkish coinage and even more so a series of subsequent regulations clearly intended to exclude the circulation of Ottoman currency called into question the extent to which Austria-Hungary was abiding by the provisions of the Convention, in a matter taken to be of great symbolic importance insofar as the issuing of currency was taken to be a significant right of sovereignty.[48] In some areas, notably the issuing of visas and consular protection, again taken as symbolic of sovereignty, the position was more confused for some time, with both the Austro-Hungarians and the Ottomans acting as if they were exercising sovereign rights in this area in common.[49] What was unequivocally incompatible with the status of Austria-Hungary as an occupant and continuing Ottoman sovereignty was the military service law of November 1881, obliging those called up to take an oath of loyalty to the Habsburg Emperor.[50] This decree and the implementation of conscription in the following year were the immediate occasion for an uprising in parts of the occupied provinces, though the causes of this, the last such event of any significance in the occupation, were complex extending far beyond the fact of conscription.[51]

Contemporary observers, including jurists, were in fact divided on the characterisation of the Austro-Hungarian administration. As early as March 1879 Leopold Neumann asserted that the effect of the Treaty of Berlin was to transfer the provinces to Austria-Hungary. Even after the April Convention with its more explicit assertion of the persistence of Ottoman sovereignty, Neumann was not deterred, mocking Reuters for no longer referring to the sovereignty of the sultan but only to the suzerainty of the sultan.[52] Most Austrian jurists, however, including the most eminent of the day, continued to insist on the persistence of Ottoman sovereignty and the quality of Austria-Hungary as an occupant.[53] Nor was this purely a matter of the interpretation of jurists. In the initial days of the occupation there had even been a petition from Muslim inhabitants of the provinces requesting annexation, though that may well have been a pragmatic response, seeking protection from the new overlords. As the occupation became established both the Muslim community in the provinces and the Ottoman authorities sought to maintain as much of the symbolism of Ottoman sovereignty as possible. Muslims sent petitions to Istanbul, as well as Vienna, asking for the intervention of the sultan. The dual status of the sultan as both a political and religious figure provided some additional scope for maintaining such links.[54] Ottoman authorities also showed sensitivity to the nuances of such matters when they declined the suggestion in a petition that they seek to appoint an official as a consul in Bosnia, analogous to the consuls of the European powers, for fear that this could be interpreted as a renunciation of the claim to sovereignty.[55] The plausibility of that claim, however, inevitably grew weaker as the occupation persisted.

The persistence of the occupation was symbolised by the prolonged oversight of Benjamin Kállay in his capacity as joint minister of finance from 1882 to his death in 1903. Subordinating the occupation to joint ministers was a one of the devices for managing the occupation while trying to avoid favouring either the Austrian or Hungarian halves of the monarchy. In practice Kállay ran the occupation through a civil adlatus, from 1886 onwards Hugo von Kutschera, who operated as a co-governor alongside the military governor of occupied territory and presided over a three section administration.[56] Kállay followed an established approach of not directly challenging the existing economic relations of the provinces, not least because this avoided antagonising the Muslim landowning elite whom Kálley sought to co-opt, with some success. Though consequently placing more political weight on the dominant Muslim sector of the population Kállay also declared that the prime obligation of his government was to treat all the religious confessions equally.[57] That was consistent with his expressed view that: 'Administration is our only politics'.[58] This supposedly depoliticised administration was also consistent with a strategy of promoting a Bosnian identity while trying to isolate all three communities from their co-religionists either in other parts of Austria-Hungary or across the border in Serbia and the Ottoman Empire.[59] Kállay's strategy, however, was beginning to run into the sand at the time of his death. His successor Burián had concluded by 1907 that the limits of 'the cold glitter of a well-led military-administrative enterprise' had been reached and only concessions of autonomy could keep the provinces' Serbs out of the hands of their co-nationals.[60] The limits of the occupation had also been reached in a wider sense, for in 1908, following the seizure of power in the Ottoman Empire by the Young Turks, who threatened to endow the crumbling Empire with more strength and purpose, Austria-Hungary annexed Bosnia and Herzegovina. It was annexation and the international crisis it provoked that finally put an end to what many saw as the fiction of the occupation but also demonstrated the lingering significance of the occupation.[61]

The third occupation to result from the Eastern Crisis had been provided for in a defensive alliance of 4 June 1878 between Britain and the Ottoman Empire, agreed in secret prior to the opening of the Berlin Conference. This stated that should Russia retain specified territory and if it should seek further gains of Ottoman territory Britain would come to the aid of the Ottoman Empire and that 'in order to enable England to make all necessary provision for executing her engagement', the sultan 'consents to assign the Island of Cyprus to be occupied and administered by England'.[62] A further agreement, of 14 August 1878, added that the empire assigned Britain 'full powers for making Laws and Conventions'.[63] This widespread authority was, however, unlike the indeterminate Austro-Hungarian occupation, tied to specific conditions. Indeed an annex to the original Convention stated that in the event of Russia restoring Kars and other territory seized in Armenia, Britain would evacuate the island.[64] British occupation of Cyprus also differed in encountering no resistance. One sceptical observer, noting that a mere 600 men were deemed sufficient to occupy the island, suggested that it amounted 'more to a police force than a military force'.[65] There was some similarity with Bosnia insofar as the initial military administration left Ottoman laws in place if only because, as one British official put it, the British officers were 'to a man ignorant of the laws, languages and customs of the people'.[66]

The British moved quickly, however, to establish a more effective administration and one that showed considerably more activism. By December 1880 the island was transferred to the supervision of the Colonial Office,

> so that with a view to the development of the resources of the island and its future government, it should be under the Department which possess the widest experience in dealing with the questions of administration and local improvement which will arise as the island becomes more settled under British occupation.[67]

This assimilation to colonial possession, despite the continued reference to occupation, was not lost on contemporary observers. Nor was the readiness with which Britain, by simple decree, set aside the right of other foreign powers in respect of the Capitulations consented to by the Ottoman Empire. Equally striking was the promulgation of a Legislative Ordnance of some 252 articles extending much of British civil and commercial law and establishing a High Court adjudicating by British law.[68] Yet the island turned out not to have the strategic value once hoped for it or to benefit from the development promised to it. The outcome was that by the year in which Austria-Hungary annexed Bosnia and Herzegovina, the British Foreign Secretary Edward Grey could proclaim that 'I believe Cyprus is of no use to us and the Convention respecting it an anachronism and an encumbrance, I would therefore give the island away in return for any better arrangements we could obtain'.[69] Legally it was not a British possession to dispose of in this way. Yet occupation turned into annexation here too, as an Order in Council of 5 November 1914, the day on which the Foreign Office noted that a state of war existed with Turkey, asserted that Cyprus 'shall be annexed to and form part of His Majesty's Dominions'.[70]

Egypt and Permanent Occupation

European interest in Egypt was long-standing, as was French and British competition for influence. They had already become heavily involved through the system of Dual Control established in 1876 by which two controllers, one French and one British, oversaw the management of Egypt's finances with a view to its payments through the *Caisse de Dette Publique* to European bondholders. Financial interests and increased instability in Egypt, as discontented army officers with some nationalist appeal clashed with the ruling khedive, were not, however, the only factors that lay behind increased intervention in 1882.[71] As the tension escalated the European powers had signed a Self-Denying Protocol by which they promised not to seek 'any territorial advantage, nor any concession of any exclusive privilege, nor any commercial advantage for their subjects' as a result of future action in respect of Egypt.[72] That was but the first constraint upon Britain as it alone moved to occupy Egypt. Having defeated the Egyptian nationalist forces with relative ease, Britain then had to define its position and to decide what it intended to do in Egypt. Neither proved easy. On 3 January 1883 the British Foreign Minister, Lord Granville, assured the other powers that the British force in Egypt was there purely to secure public order and that the British government's intention was to withdraw as soon as the khedive's authority had been re-established.[73] This, however, was the recurrent problem of the British occupation of Egypt. The British had been reluctant to intervene, often felt eager to get out, but insisted that Egyptian financial and governmental systems be self-sufficient and this they found it difficult to accept was ever the case. Critics, especially the numerous French critics, of the British occupation had no difficultly in drawing up lengthy lists of British reiterations of the desire, and even promise, of withdrawal followed by a list of reasons why this could not yet take place.[74] Nor was this something the British themselves were blind to. Evelyn Baring, who became consul general in Egypt in 1883 and played an even more important role in the British occupation than Benjamin Kállay did in Bosnia and Herzegovina, observed that

> Two alternative policies were open to the British Government. These were, first, the policy of speedy evacuation; and secondly, the policy of reform. It was not sufficiently understood that the adoption of one of these policies was wholly destructive of the other.[75]

Probably the closest the British came to their avowed aim was with the Drummond Wolff mission of 1885. This led to an initial agreement that a senior Ottoman officer, Gazi Mukhtar Pasha, would join Drummond Wolff in Cairo to work on a plan for British withdrawal. This did indeed issue in a Convention duly signed in May 1887, providing for British withdrawal in 1887, so long as there was 'no appearance of danger', but also assigning Britain a right of reoccupation. Britain was desirous of the agreement of the other powers, in accordance with a widespread preference for multilateral sanction for intervention in the affairs of the Ottoman Empire.[76] Now, however, France decided that Britain's undefined and questionable position in Egypt was actually preferable for the defence of its own financial interests in Egypt to an agreement that gave Britain's position international sanction. Hence, together with Russia, it exerted great pressure on the sultan to call for renegotiation of the agreement, leading to its effective collapse.[77]

Legally the position of Consul General Baring, who remained an agent of the Foreign Office rather than the Colonial Office throughout his tenure, was the same as any other consul of the European powers. He had no formal position of authority, not even that authority which could have been claimed by the military commander of an occupation force. Baring was sometimes tempted by some such authority. He had expressed a preference for open assumption of government at the beginning of his office, but this position had been rejected as 'too drastic' by London.[78] Later, in 1893, confronted with a new, young, khedive, seeking to assert his own authority, Baring suggested seizure of key ministries by the army of occupation. William Harcourt, Chancellor of the Exchequer in Gladstone's cabinet, protested that what Baring proposed 'is a military coup d'état ... that amounts to the annexation of Egypt ... and is a breach of the European understanding on which our occupation rests'.[79] Harcourt erred, both in presuming that it would have amounted to annexation and in the claim that Britain's position rested on any European understanding at all. Yet Baring's proposed action would nevertheless have amounted to a radical break with the established mechanism for the indirect exercise of power by Britain in Egypt. Quite how that should be described was never entirely clear. In what would become a popular summary of the position, Alfred Milner, sometime under-secretary of finance in Egypt, concluded that 'we did after all establish a Protectorate in Egypt, but not a complete or legitimate one ... it was a Protectorate which we would not avow ourselves, and therefore could not call upon others to recognize. It was a veiled Protectorate'.[80]

Harcourt's and Milner's references to the other powers pointed to another constraint. Not only did Britain find it difficult to gain anything more than the reluctant acquiescence of the other powers to its position in Egypt, it had to cope with their institutionalised presence through the mechanism of the *Caisse de la Dette* and the Mixed Tribunals. The latter were international courts that fused the jurisdictions of the consular courts operating under the capitulations conceded by the sultan.[81] This second institutionalised presence was indeed invoked when the Egyptian government, on British advice, failed to make the required repayments through the *Caisse*, which sued the government successfully through the tribunal in 1884.[82] The following year Britain won international agreement to financial reforms and a new loan in the London Convention but only at the expense of the addition of German and Russian representatives to the *Caisse*, which led Baring to lament what he saw as 'excessively cumbersome' methods for apportioning Egyptian revenue.[83] Britain could not even shrug off the imprint of other powers in more indirect ways. That was evident in relation to the courts, civil law and legal culture. Here the British sought to draw on their experience in India in order to establish a more familiar legal culture. French legal culture, however, was simply too deeply entrenched prior to the British occupation for this to be fully effective. Indeed French legal culture remained dominant.[84] At the same time the sultan, whom the British still formally recognised as sovereign or suzerain, had less effective authority than the other European powers but nevertheless used whatever opportunity he could, including the continued presence of Gazi Mukhtar Pasha, as a physical symbol of Ottoman claims in Egypt, to promote the symbolic significance of his sovereignty.[85] It was not until the agreement with France of 8 April 1904, which opened with a British declaration of having 'no intention of altering the political status of Egypt' but then contained a French commitment that 'they will not obstruct the action of Great Britain in the country by asking that a limit of time be fixed for the British occupation or in any other manner', that Britain finally gained substantial freedom from the views of its partner under the system of Dual Control.[86] As with Cyprus, it was not until the First World War that Britain finally shook off the 'suzerainty of Turkey', though it did so by establishing a protectorate over Egypt, thus finally claiming legally what Milner insisted had long existed anyway.[87]

Within Egypt the British had exercised power indirectly, through offering advice, either from the consul general or from deputy ministers and other officials notionally in the service of the Egyptian government. At the beginning Baring had insisted that while a European presence was necessary, the tendency to duplicate key personnel with equal power within the Egyptian system of government would not work. He insisted that this 'system of dualism in the Administration, and, generally, the extreme extension of development which internationalism has attained in Egypt, is highly detrimental to the best interests of the country'.[88] That was a sentiment with which many Egyptian ministers agreed as they sought to exclude British interference as much as possible, sometimes grasping that the British need for the facade of Egyptian rule could be exploited to restrict their activities.[89] The British, however, albeit in the interest, as they saw it, of enhanced efficiency and improvement, continually pressed into new areas, from irrigation to the Ministry of the Interior.[90] Under Eldon Gorst, Baring's successor, it had now reached the point where enhancing Egyptian self-government could be proclaimed to be either the precondition of Britain redeeming its 'promise of ultimate Evacuation' or of the British remaining in Egypt 'for ever'.[91] The transformation of occupation into what looked like disguised annexation was indeed even more dramatic in the Sudan, into whose occupation and administration Britain had been drawn, formally in the shape of a condominium with Egypt, as a consequence of its involvement in Egypt. Whereas Egypt was proclaimed to be a protectorate, the Governor of the Sudan was informed at the beginning of the First World War that he was simply 'to regard Anglo-Egyptian Sudan as a British Colony'.[92]

Multilateral Occupation

There was more cooperation between the powers in relation to Crete. Unrest had broken out in 1889, in part involving accusation that the sultan had violated an Organic Law sanctioned by article 23 of the Treaty of Berlin. Diplomatic intervention by the European powers, and concessions by Ottoman authorities, failed to prevent the recurrence of violence when in February a Greek force established itself in the interior of the island and proclaimed its occupation in the name of the Greek king. Though keenly competitive, the French admiral having been told not to allow any other power, that is Britain, to play a more prominent role, the European powers coordinated their response.[93] Their naval forces seized the coast, preventing either Greek or Ottoman reinforcement. Isolating the Ottoman forces in their garrisons and compelling their withdrawal under threat of allowing union of the island with Greece, the European powers found that their responsibilities had increased. As the French ambassador to London observed, they found themselves 'charged with a new and original role for themselves, that of being protectors of the Muslim population', who were now defenceless.[94] On the island itself the admirals justified their creation of a 'military commission of international police' on similar grounds of the evaporation of Ottoman authority and the idea that having accepted 'the trust' placed in their hands by the sultan they had become 'subrogate to all the rights flowing from imperial sovereignty, the exercise of which is indispensable to the accomplishment of their mandate'.[95] That was clearly a more expansive understanding of the authority of an occupant than being formulated in the contemporary codification of the laws of occupation. It did not suffice, however, to provide any great protection for the Muslim population. Unwilling to either allow the Ottoman authorities to return or allow union with Greece, the European powers agreed on an expedient that allowed them to step into the background, even though they did not entirely withdraw until 1908, namely the appointment of a high commissioner with a 'temporary mandate' to establish order and regular administration. In what was now a well-established formula the commissioner recognised the 'high suzerainty of the Sultan'.[96] The appointment of a member of the Greek royal family as high commissioner inevitably favoured long-term Greek ambitions, even though the international arrangement kept the island out of Greek hands for the time being. Greek ambition had also been frustrated when, having resorted to war against the Ottoman Empire amidst the Cretan crisis, they were defeated. This issued in Ottoman occupation of Thessaly as guarantee for payment of an indemnity. That was a unilateral occupation.[97] Nevertheless, the intervention of the European powers was significant. The preliminary peace treaty was agreed between the six European powers and the Ottoman government and it was the European powers who determined when there was sufficient guarantee of the payment of the indemnity and consequent withdrawal of the occupation forces.[98]

Occupation and Conquest in South Africa

The occupation of the Orange Free State and the South African Republic was entirely unilateral. The British had determined upon the war to consolidate their hold on South Africa and conveniently bring the gold-rich Transvaal within their grip. They were also confident of easy victory. Yet these were occupations which turned out to be far more difficult than ever imagined and to bring the British a wave of criticism for violating the newly agreed Hague Regulations of 1899, especially from French and German authors. Although there were claims by British political leaders that the Hague Regulations did not apply because the Boer Republics were not signatories, and even that the laws of war more widely did not apply because of Boer tactics, this argument was not even accepted by the British intelligence division, while Major General John Ardagh, a British representative at the Hague Conference, concurred that for 'practical purposes ... the Hague Convention may properly be applied to by both sides'.[99] There was some confusion following from the fact that the unexpectedly successful Boers invaded the British colony of Natal, provoking the institution of martial law, a law itself undefined in the British tradition.[100] The indeterminacy of the martial law tradition was so acute that the influential *Times History of the War in South Africa* concluded that it was desirable 'to codify a set of Martial Law

Regulations, much in the same manner as the first Hague Conference codified the laws and customs of war applicable to the Military Administration of Occupied Territory'.[101] As the British recovered from the initial humiliating reverses they began to advance, reaching the capital of the Orange Free State, Bloemfontein, on 13 March 1900 and entering Pretoria on 5 June. Between these two dates, in a proclamation dated 24 May 1900, the British commander, Lord Roberts, announced the annexation of the Orange Free State which would 'henceforth form part of His Majesty's dominions' and his own appointment as administrator of the said territories with power to take all such measures and to make and enforce such laws as I may deem necessary'.[102] Annexation of the South African Republic followed in September, being announced with the same formulae. The annexations had been issued at the insistence of the British commander though with the approval of London. Roberts's argument, in part, was that the inhabitants of the Free State were 'afraid to show themselves willing to accept our rule from a feeling of uncertainty as to the future', while Joseph Chamberlain, Secretary for the colonies, simply declared that the 'the Commander of victorious forces can do what he likes practically with the property, the people, the country invaded'.[103] Such considerations swept aside the legal advice that the annexation was premature while Boer forces still controlled large parts of the Orange Free State. At this point, according to the Hague Regulations, the British did not even have the level of effective control over the territory to warrant proclaiming the occupation of the state, let alone the more demanding qualifications sufficient to warrant annexation by reference to *debellatio*, that is the complete subjugation of the state and the acquiescence of the population.[104] In both the Orange Free State and later the South African Republic their respective presidents were indeed quick to point to these considerations in refutation of the annexations.[105]

Amongst the objections raised in London, one consequence of the supposed annexations was that those Boers who continued to oppose the British would effectively be defined as engaged in acts of rebellion and would be criminally liable therefore. Roberts did in fact issue another proclamation on 31 May 1900, warning the inhabitants that any 'found in arms against Her Majesty' within fourteen days 'will be liable to be dealt with as rebels, and to suffer in person and property accordingly'.[106] This caused indignation even amongst critics in the British Parliament.[107] It is notable though that there was no such equivalent proclamation following the annexation of the South African Republic. Moreover the British did not in fact treat captured Boers as rebels, or at least those who were inhabitants and citizens of the two republics.[108] There were, however, punishments, sometimes severe, for the violation of oaths taken by the inhabitants. Yet even here there was some equivocation. Prior to the proclaimed annexation of the Orange Free State, Roberts had issued a proclamation according to which those who had not taken a prominent part in the war and who laid down their arms and were willing to 'bind themselves by an oath to abstain from any further participation in the war' would not even be held as prisoners of war but would be allowed to return home.[109] This 'Oath of Neutrality' was somewhat less than the oath of allegiance condemned by the Hague Regulations, but nevertheless it was still an oath to desist from opposing the British conduct of the war.[110]

The administration of oaths was one of the tasks assigned to the military administration created when the British invaded the Orange Free State. Major General Pretyman, who was appointed military governor of what the British had renamed the Orange River Colony, found that controlling the entire area from Bloemfontein was impractical and for this reason appointed a series of commissioners, who were initially army officers, to the outlying districts. In addition to administering oaths and generally supporting the military formations, administration of justice, sometimes supervising existing magistrates, and collecting taxation figured prominently in their functions. Pretyman, however, was hampered by a lack of clarity about his role. As the editor of the papers of the Governor of the Cape Colony, Milner, later lamented: 'Unfortunately there were no British regulations defining the powers and duties of a Military Governor'.[111] Lack of clarity was especially problematic in Pretyman's relationship with the commander of military forces that remained in the area as the main army advanced. Pretyman and General Kelly-Kenny both maintained their own intelligence officers and provost marshals and showed a pronounced reluctance to cooperate, reflecting personal clashes as well as a lack of clarity about roles.[112] Pretyman's task was further complicated, as he reported in November, by the fact that there was a resurgence of Boer incursions into some of the areas the British had claimed to control, with the consequence that 'every evacuation, to say nothing of surrender, has a most disastrous effect both from a Political and Military standpoint'.[113] In reality the British were sure of control only over major towns and railways which were subject to attack until the very end of the war.

With the Boers refusing to concede defeat despite the loss of their towns and unable to field major armies but quite capable of maintaining smaller formations, their commandos, the British, especially under Roberts's successor Kitchener, resorted to increasingly punitive policies in order to both capture the elusive Boer commandos and to sap their will to continue the fight. Here the British resorted to burning farms presumed to have been used to fire on them or prepare attacks on trains, to compelling inhabitants to travel on trains and to punishing those who had violated their oath of neutrality. None of this was new. Not even the notorious development of concentration camps was new.[114] Their development, more systematically, by the Spanish General Weyler in Cuba was well-known even to ordinary soldiers.[115] The camps themselves had been developed haphazardly for a variety of purposes, to provide protection from Boer commandos, for refugees, as places of confinement to deprive Boer commandos of access to those who might aid them. Lack of clarity about the relationship between military authority and civil authority, a blurred boundary for much of the war, aggravated the conditions which led to extensive deaths from disease.[116]

Managing the return to civil authority was one of the prime tasks of Milner, who had been appointed administrator of the new colonies in February 1901, long before the end of the war with the Peace of Vereeniging in May 1902. Suspicious of military authority, he had despatched his personal secretary to aid, and to watch, the military commanders. Milner himself, however, hoped to exploit the period of military authority as he openly declared to Roberts: 'The great advantage of conquest is that it gives us a clean slate. The great advantage of the period of military government – which is in its nature an *interregnum* – is that it gives us time to lay the foundation of that government which is to succeed it, carefully.'[117] In this respect Milner was over-optimistic. By March 1901 Lionel Curtis, whom Milner had brought in to prepare the transition to civilian rule, was writing about 'a dirty canvas to clean and mend', rather than Milner's new slate.[118] The British had underestimated both the nature of the war and the management of the occupation, neither of which they had been prepared for.

Occupations in the Far East

The Sino-Japanese War of 1894–5 had arisen amidst the occupation of Korean territory by Chinese and Japanese forces, both claiming to be aiding the Korean king against indigenous insurgents, although both had ambitions to dominate Korea in some form or another. It was the Japanese who rapidly prevailed in the race to dominate, effectively holding the Korean king hostage while devising a reform plan. A high profile resident minister, Tetsujiro Inoue, was despatched to Korea, to ensure cooperation between the Japanese military and civil authorities. Inoue explicitly took what he understood to be the British position and experience in Egypt as a model for Japan's relationship with Korea.[119] The relationship between the Japanese and the Koreans, however, was even more problematic than that between the British and the Egyptians. The inevitable tension involved in the suppression of an insurgency was aggravated by the exploitative and aggressive behaviour of Japanese merchants in Korea. Underlying these tensions was the basic failure of the Japanese to decide whether they saw Koreans as allies or enemies.[120]

By contrast the relationship between the Japanese occupying force and Chinese civilians was relatively good, possibly aided by Japanese understanding of the war as the Japan-Ch'ing war, that is, the war between Japan and the Chinese ruling dynasty rather than the war between the two nations.[121] The Japanese constrained inhabitants to serve as guides and relied on requisitioning, though they sought to enforce payment by their soldiers, where possible in the local currency. This was both a matter of conformity to international law, an integral part of wider Japanese claims concerning their conduct of the war and standing in international society, and a pragmatic desire to gain the cooperation of the Chinese, on whom they relied for both food and transport.[122] Faced with the flight of local officials they turned to indigenous deliberative commissions, that is, associations of Chinese merchants who normally acted as purveyors to the Chinese authorities.[123] The establishment of adequate administrative Japanese structures was more difficult. It was not helped by a chronic shortage of interpreters.[124] It was also complicated by the strict separation of the civilian and military structures, though the more fluid lines evident in the British occupations in South Africa also had its problems.[125] Japanese reliance on the structures of their Rear Area Commands soon provided inadequate, however, forcing them to turn to the creation of civil commissions, initially headed by diplomats. That reliance on diplomats, who had no authority whatsoever over military personnel, gave way to the replacement of the civilians by military personnel, re-establishing the separation of the two spheres.[126] At Port Arthur, Marshal Oyama had even instructed his legal adviser, Nagao Ariga, that there was no need to designate special officials for administrative purposes at all, though even he accepted the need for some administrative differentiation with the framework of the Rear Area Command. The rigidity of the separation was threatened as the army prepared to advance towards Peking, necessitating ascribing responsibility for the defence of territory to the provincial governors they had created and assigning them the authority of marshals or corps commanders.[127] The end of the war meant that those structures were not tested.

Within five years the Japanese returned to Chinese territory as occupants, but this time as part of the multinational force despatched by Japan and the European powers to relieve the besieged legations in Peking, and to impose penalties on China for the treatment of foreign nationals. As was common in such multilateral enterprises the powers kept a jealous watch on each other as they pursued their common purpose. The Americans, most committed of all of the powers to an open door policy towards China and opposed to territorial aggrandisement at its expense, took alarm at the introduction of the language of conquest, albeit only in relation to a small tract of land in the international port of Tientsin, by the Russian Consul General, N. Poppé. The Russian minister at Peking promptly disavowed any such intent: 'there is no question whatever of acquiring territory by conquest on the part of Russia . . . if the communication of Mr. Poppé . . . contains any expressions which could be so construed they have certainly been erroneously used by him'.[128] The competitive tensions in the multinational force were even evident in the tendency of the different national contingents to proclaim individual protectorates over towns and to raise their respective national flags. This, Field Marshal Waldersee proclaimed, was inconsistent with the 'international and common character' of the enterprise and clearly betrayed their lack of unity to the Chinese population.[129] The reality of a lack of unity could be seen in the fact that Waldersee, the nominal overall commander, had been appointed late in the day, not even arriving until after the various contingents had reached Peking. Once there, they had divided up the city, each contingent taking responsibility for a sector, where differences between the occupation regimes in the sectors were strong enough to drive the population to flee from the more predatory to the better administered sectors.[130] In terms of security and general administration it was notable that the Japanese sector was the most highly regarded by all sides.

This occupation was distinguished both by its punitive character and by the extent of the looting which accompanied it, the two being in part related. It was punitive in the sense of being used to force the Chinese government to come to the agreement acceptable to the powers and to bring about the punishment of Boxers and of Chinese officials deemed to have been complicit in the activities of the Boxers, especially the murder of the nationals of the powers. In the latter respect it was often as arbitrary as it was brutal. The punitive dimension extended to the deliberate and systematic destruction of many religious structures and cultural symbols.[131] That this was manifestly in violation of the recently agreed Hague Regulations was noted at the time. Yet these practices too divided the occupiers. The American General Wilson, nominally in command of a joint Anglo-American expedition, dissociated himself from the commitment of the British to destroy a temple on the grounds that this would demonstrate the superiority of the Christian god over the Chinese gods to whom the temple was dedicated.[132] The looting blended these punitive intentions with simple personal enrichment, amounting in some case to systematic and organised looting, though again divergent national attitudes led to greater or lesser attempt to impose some restraint upon the practices. Although this was hardly conducive to cooperation between the occupied and the occupants, some measure of cooperation was seen as desirable by both sides in the interest of restoring elementary forms of public order and encouraging a revival of commercial life. This, though, was easier to manage in Peking itself than in the surrounding area, which was subject to periodic expeditions by the various contingents rather than any continuous and effective occupation.[133] As in all occupations those officials who did cooperate ran the risk of being seen as collaborators and being subjected to the retaliation of their compatriots, either at the time or subsequently as national authority was restored.[134]

As the Japanese returned to Chinese territory as occupants for a third time in a decade they were more conscious of the need to establish some form of cooperation with Chinese officials, not least because Chinese territory was being occupied as consequence of a war between Japan and Russia. This time the Japanese already had in place military administration commissions, staffed with people some of whom spoke Chinese and had experience of the country.[135] From the Japanese perspective, the function of these commissions was not to administer territory in the sense of article 43 of the Hague Regulations, since the authority of the legitimate power had not passed into the hands of the occupant but remained with the Chinese. By the same token they reasoned that although cooperation by Chinese officials arguably came into conflict with their obligation to remain neutral, since cooperation did not come into conflict with their patriotic obligations it was in fact eased. This view was strained in the case of a provincial governor deemed to have passed information to the Russians and thus to be guilty of treason against the Japanese. The case divided the Japanese but, on the basis that it involved relations of one state to another, neither of whom were enemies, and hence that it was a political matter, the case was passed to the Emperor as head of state, as well as head of the army. The outcome was the expulsion rather than the execution of the delinquent governor.[136]

Occupation of the Eve of the First World War

That the Japanese occupation of Chinese territory in both the Sino-Japanese and Russo-Japanese wars did not prove more problematic, and so readily served by way of illustration in British and American military manuals, was helped by the tight focus of the Japanese on the central aim of winning the wars and in the latter case by the lack of territorial ambitions against China. The same could not be said of the Italian occupations of Turkish territory in North Africa. Following the British example in South Africa, the Italians proclaimed the annexation of Tripoli on 5 November 1911 although they were at that point only in occupation of five coastal towns. Followed through consistently, as was noted at the time, such practices threatened to do away with the very conceptual distinction by which military occupation, as opposed to conquest was identified at all.[137] As in the case of the British premature annexations, the Italians too failed to follow through the logic of their declarations, continuing to treat local resistance as legitimate. Indeed an Italian military tribunal, though subsequently overruled, treated them as legitimate even after the treaty ratifying the annexation.[138] On the Aegean islands, which the Italians did not intend to hold but where the Greek inhabitants favoured union with Greece, the Italian generals presented themselves as liberators, assuring the inhabitants that Turkish rule would never return to the islands. As wider considerations made themselves felt they stepped back from these commitments, and the inhabitants who had initially welcomed the Italians now denounced them as tyrants.[139] The Greeks, frustrated in the Aegean, were more successful on the mainland where their occupation of Salonica prepared the way for its annexation. The liberationist rhetoric was prevalent here too, in, for example, the justification of the removal of Turkish judges during the occupation on the grounds that they had never enjoyed legitimacy in the eyes of the inhabitants.[140]

In the final decades between the Franco-German War and the end of the long nineteenth century the idea of military occupation had crystallised in the codified form of international law. That meant that where the powers were so inclined they could adopt this law as a guide to their conduct for it allowed them considerable room for manoeuvre anyway, as it did the Japanese in occupation of Chinese territory. It also meant that now there were public standards by which some practices of occupants could be clearly condemned as violations of those laws. In other respects this greater clarity, which was only a relative clarity, had not resolved any of the dilemmas, including the recurrent clash between the rhetoric of liberation and the reality of occupation. Moreover, the temptation to equate invasion with conquest and just title to sovereignty, especially if bolstered by some justification in terms of liberation or pre-existing suzerainty, was as evident as when the concept of occupation first emerged. That was true though in respect of Europe's periphery and the weakened structures of the Ottoman and Chinese empires. The test of the new standards in the context of the occupation of one of the powers by another was still outstanding.

Notes

1. On the detrimental impact of the removal of the intermediate powers in Germany see Paul Schroeder, 'The 19th-century international system: changes in the structure', *World Politics*, 39 (1986), 17–25.
2. William Langer, *European Alliances and Alignments 1871–1890* (New York: Knopf, 1962), p. 459. For positive comparison of Vienna and Berlin see R. B. Mowat, *The Concert of Europe* (London: Macmillan, 1930), p. 43.

3. Hence the title of an account of the last success of the concert of Europe: R. J. Crampton, 'The decline of the concert of Europe in the Balkans, 1913–1914', *Slavonic and East European Review*, 52 (1974), 393–419.
4. Being especially influential in Britain amongst the European powers: Sönke Neitzel, *Weltmacht oder Untergang. Die Weltreichslehre im Zeitalter des Imperialismus* (Paderborn: Schöningh, 2000), p. 255.
5. The criterion had been put forward by Bismarck at the Congress of Berlin of 1884–5 in part to embarrass the British, whose empire rested on more indirect methods of control. See S. E. Crowe, *The Berlin West Africa Conference 1884–1885* (London: Longman, 1942) and Stig Förster, Wolfgang J. Mommsen and Ronald Robinson (eds), *Bismarck, Africa and Europe* (Oxford: Oxford University Press, 1988).
6. This could still be referred to as the 'ordinary' usage of the term at the end of the century: M.-J. Spalaïkovitch, *La Bosnie et l'Herzégovine* (Paris: Rousseau, 1899), p. 164.
7. Although the Japanese went to war with China, that country was not the real enemy. For an important interpretation of the combination of socialisation into the civilised world and external aggression see Shogo Suzuki, 'Japan's socialization into Janus-faced European international society', *European Journal of International Relations*, 11 (2005), 137–64. On the campaign for civilised status see Douglas Howland, 'Japan's civilized war: international law as diplomacy in the Sino-Japanese war (1894–1895)', *Journal of the History of International Law*, 9 (2007), 179–201.
8. The open door policy, disavowing the extension of concession and discriminatory economic provisions by the European powers, was favoured by the United States. See George Kennan, *American Diplomacy* (Chicago: University of Chicago Press, 1984), pp. 21–37.
9. Andrew S. Thompson, 'The language of imperialism and the meanings of empire: imperial discourse in British politics, 1895–1914', *Journal of British Studies*, 36 (1997), 150. See also Duncan S. Bell, 'Empire and international relations in Victorian political thought', *Historical Journal*, 49 (2006), 282.
10. See Finley, 'Colonies – an attempt at a typology', *Transactions of the Royal Historical Society*, 5th series, 26 (1976), 167–88.
11. See especially Lauren Benton, *A Search for Sovereignty* (Cambridge: Cambridge University Press, 2010), pp. 222–78, and 'From international law to imperial constitutions: the problem of quasi-sovereignty, 1870–1900', *Law and History Review*, 26 (2008), 595–619.
12. According to Thomas Baty a 'stipulation placing all its foreign affairs in the hands of its protector is regarded by most authorities as depriving the protected State of its international character, and as reducing

it to a mere possession of the protecting Power', 'Protectorates and mandates', *British Yearbook of International Law*, 2 (1921–2), 110.
13. Charles Stubbs, 'Suzerainty mediaeval and modern', *Law Magazine*, 5th series, 7 (1881–2), 280. See also the conclusion of W. H. H. Kelke that while the term entailed some restriction of sovereignty, 'the scope and extent of the restriction on sovereign rights will be found in, and only in, the treaty, convention, or other public document whereby the suzerainty is constituted', 'Feudal suzerains and modern suzerainty', *Law Quarterly Review* 12 (1896), 226. In fact even the relevant document could confuse as much as clarify. See also Anon., 'International law and South African affairs', *Cape Law Journal*, 13 (1896), 118–20.
14. According to D. M. Schreuder, 'a method of leaving the Transvaal without trailing the imperial cloak too obviously', *Gladstone and Kruger* (London: Routledge, 1969), p. 222. See also Casper Sylvest, '"Our passion for legality": international law and imperialism in late nineteenth-century Britain', *Review of International Studies*, 34 (2008), 418–21.
15. Davide Rodogno, *Against Massacre: Humanitarian Interventions in the Ottoman Empire 1815–1914* (Princeton: Princeton University Press, 2012), pp. 142–6.
16. Gary Bass, *Freedom's Battle: The Origins of Humanitarian Intervention* (New York: Vintage, 2008).
17. Michael Hurst (ed.), *Key Treaties for the Great Powers*, vol. 2, *1871–1914* (Newton Abbot: David & Charles, 1972), pp. 532 and 534.
18. Peter Holquist, 'The Russian Empire as a "Civilized State": International Law as Principle and Practice in Imperial Russia, 1874–1878' (Washington DC: NCEER, 2006), p. 17.
19. Ibid. p. 21.
20. J. M. Spaight, *War Rights on Land* (London: Macmillan, 1911), p. 357.
21. F. De Martens, *La paix et la guerre* (Paris: Rousseau, 1901), pp. 269 and 276–7. Martens found that some initial restraint by the Russians amounted to 'an excess of respect for the Turkish regime', p. 292.
22. Karen Durman, *Lost Illusions. Russian Policies towards Bulgaria in 1877–1887* (Stockholm: Almqvist and Wiksell, 1988), pp. 52–3.
23. Ibid. p. 57. According to Hilquist, in the case of one senior officer this was aggravated by his resentment at Cherkasskii's role in reforms in the officer's native Poland, 'The Russian Empire as a "Civilized State"', p. 21.
24. C. E. Black, *The Establishment of Constitutional Government in Bulgaria* (Princeton: Princeton University Press, 1943), p. 53.
25. Durman, *Lost Illusions*, pp. 54–5.

26. Martens, *La paix et la guerre*, p. 281.
27. Hurst (ed.), *Key Treaties for the Great Powers*, vol. 2, pp. 553 and 559.
28. Charles Serkis, *La Roumélie Orientale et la Bulgarie actuelle* (Paris: Rousseau, 1898), pp. 49–50, 65–7.
29. Hurst (ed.), *Key Treaties for the Great Powers*, vol. 2, pp. 555–6 and 561.
30. Durman, *Lost Illusions*, pp. 62–4. For the predecessors see Chapter 2 of this book.
31. Serkis, *La Roumélie Orientale et la Bulgarie actuelle*, p. 74.
32. Henry Drummond Wolff, *Rambling Recollections* (London: Macmillan, 1908), p. 206.
33. Serkis, *La Roumélie Orientale et la Bulgarie actuelle*, pp. 75–6.
34. Charles Jelavich and Barbara Jelavich, *The Establishment of the Balkan National States, 1804–1920* (Seattle: University of Washington Press, 1977), pp. 159–65.
35. Hans Schmeller, *Die staatsrechtliche Stellung von Bosnien und der Herzogowina* (Leipzig: Wallmann, 1892), pp. 19–35.
36. Hurst (ed.), *Key Treaties for the Great Powers*, vol. 2, p. 563.
37. See Adolf Beer's pointed formulation of this point, *Die orientalische Politik Oesterreichs seit 1774* (Prague: Tempsky, 1883), p. 743.
38. Stephan Burián, *Austria in Dissolution* (New York: Doran, 1925), p. 291.
39. Schmeller, *Die staatsrechtliche Stellung*, p. 42.
40. Spalaïkovitch, *La Bosnie et l'Herzégovine*, p. 159.
41. Leyla Amzi-Erdogdular, 'Afterlife of Empire: Muslim-Ottoman Relations in Habsburg Bosnia-Herzegovina', unpublished PhD thesis, Columbia University, 2013, pp. 27–31.
42. On the military dimension see László Becze, *The Occupation of Bosnia and Herzegovina in 1878* (New York: Columbia University Press, 2005).
43. Etienne Knell, *La Bosnie et l'Herzégovine* (Paris: Rousseau, 1900), pp. 139–40.
44. Karl Gabriel, *Bosnien-Herzegowina 1878* (Frankfurt am Main: Lang, 2003), p. 39.
45. See the complaint of the pro-Serb André Barre about the predominance of Croats possessed of a religious and chauvinistic hostility to Serbs and Poles, described as historic enemies of orthodoxy, in the administration: *La Bosnie-Herzégovine: administration autrichienne de 1878 à 1903* (Paris: Michaud, 1906), pp. 218–20.
46. Hurst (ed.), *Key Treaties for the Great Powers*, vol. 2, p. 564.
47. Schmeller, *Die staatsrechtliche Stellung*, pp. 48–51.
48. Spalaïkovitch, *La Bosnie et l'Herzégovine*, pp. 223–8.

49. A position that Schmeller held to be legally and practically untenable, *Die staatsrechtliche Stellung*, p. 126.
50. Ibid. pp. 210–11.
51. As noted by the Austrians' own account: Abteilung für Kriegsgeschichte, *Der Aufstand in der Hercegovina, Süd-Bosnien und Süd-Dalmatien 1881–1882* (Vienna: Seidel, 1883), pp. 3–12.
52. Leopold Neumann, 'L'Empire Austro-Hungrois, la Bosnie at l'Herzégovine', *Revue de droit international et de législation comparée*, 11 (1879), 38–44.
53. See the detailed account by Schmeller, *Die staatsrechtliche Stellung*, pp. 157–92.
54. Robert Donia, *Islam under the Double Eagle* (New York: Columbia University Press, 1981), pp. 19–20.
55. Amzi-Erdogdular, 'Afterlife of Empire', pp. 124–5.
56. This structure was finalised only in 1882: Eduard Eichler, *Das Justizwesen Bosniens und Hercegovina* (Vienna: Hof- und Staatsdruckerei, 1889), pp. 218–19.
57. Knell, *La Bosnie et l'Herzégovine*, p. 146.
58. Donia, *Islam under the Double Eagle*, p. 14.
59. On Kállay's strategy see Robin Okey, *Taming Balkan Nationalism: The Habsburg 'Civilizing Mission' in Bosnia, 1878–1914* (Oxford: Oxford University Press, 2007).
60. Ibid. p. 147.
61. Especially amongst Serbs. See Christopher Clark, *The Sleepwalkers* (London: Penguin, 2012), pp. 33–5.
62. Hurst (ed.), *Key Treaties for the Great Powers*, vol. 2, p. 547.
63. Ibid. p. 578.
64. Ibid. p. 549.
65. Louis Gérard, *Des cessions déguisées de territoiries en droit international public* (Paris: Larose, 1904), p. 144.
66. G. S. Georghallides, *A Political and Administrative History of Cyprus 1918–1926* (Nicosia: Alfonetis, 2004), p. 38.
67. *Correspondence Respecting the Affairs of Cyprus*, c. 2930 (London: HMSO, 1881), p. 59.
68. Raymond Robin, *Des occupations militaires en dehors des occupations de guerre* (Paris: Larose, 1913), pp. 450–1.
69. Andrekos Varnava, *British Imperialism in Cyprus 1878–1915: The Inconsequential Possession* (Manchester: Manchester University Press, 2009), p. 249.
70. 'Annexation of Cyprus by Great Britain', *American Journal of International Law*, 9 (1915), 204.
71. The reasons for the eventual British occupation are much disputed. For a very helpful assessment see John S. Galbraith and Afaf Lufti

al-Sayyid-Marsot, 'The British occupation of Egypt: another view', *International Journal of Middle East Studies*, 9 (1978), 471–88, especially the observation that the question about the 'true' reasons for intervention 'assumes a degree of coherence in the Gladstone cabinet which has little relation to reality', p. 473.
72. Theodore Rothstein, *Egypt's Ruin* (London: Field, 1910), p. xviii.
73. Jules Cocheris, *Situation international de l'Egypte et du Soudan* (Paris: Plon-Nourrit, 1903), p. 534.
74. The classic example is ibid. pp. 531–41.
75. David Edelstein, *Occupational Hazards* (Ithaca, NY: Cornell University Press, 2008), p. 111.
76. See the argument of Cocheris that there was a right of intervention in the affairs of the Empire, but a strictly collective one, of which Britain's unilateral action was in violation, *Situation international de l'Egypte et du Soudan*, p. 544.
77. Roger Owen, *Lord Cromer: Victorian Imperialist, Edwardian Proconsul* (Oxford: Oxford University Press, 2004), pp. 217, 224–5.
78. Afaf Lufti al-Sayyid, *Egypt and Cromer* (London: Murray, 1968), p. 56.
79. Ibid. p. 111.
80. Alfred Milner, *England in Egypt* (London: Arnold, 1892), p. 34.
81. On the mixed tribunals see Frantz Despagnet, *Cours de droit international public*, 4th edn (Paris: Larose, 1910), pp. 502–5.
82. Owen, *Lord Cromer*, 208.
83. Ibid. pp. 209–10.
84. Robert Tignor, 'The "Indianization" of the Egyptian administration under British rule', *American Historical Review*, 68 (1963), 639–45.
85. See Oded Peri, 'Ottoman symbolism in British-Occupied Egypt, 1882–1909', *Middle Eastern Studies*, 41 (2005), 103–20, and L. Hirszowicz, 'The Sultan and the Khedive, 1892–1908', *Middle Eastern Studies* (1972), 287–311.
86. Hurst (ed.), *Key Treaties for the Great Powers*, vol. 2, p. 760. For an evaluation see Gabriel-Louis Jaray, 'La situation international de l'Egypte depuis l'accord Franco-Anglais du 8 Avril 1904', *Revue de droit international et de législation comparée*, 2nd series, 6 (1904), 407–38.
87. Malcolm McIlwraith, 'The declaration of a protectorate in Egypt and its legal effect', *Journal of the Society of Comparative Legislation*, 17 (1917), 238–59.
88. *Reports on the State of Egypt and the Progress of Administrative Reforms*, C. 4421 (London: HMSO, 1885), p. 42.
89. Robert Tignor, *Modernization and British Colonial Policy in Egypt 1882–1914* (Princeton: Princeton University Press, 1966), p. 65.

90. On the latter see Harold Tollefson, 'The 1894 British takeover of the Egyptian Ministry of the Interior', *Middle Eastern Studies*, 26 (1990), 547–60.
91. Thus Ronald Storrs, one of Gorst's secretaries; Peter Mellini, *Sir Eldon Gorst: The Overshadowed Proconsul* (Stanford, CA: Hoover Institution Press, 1977), pp. 150–1.
92. Gabriel Warburg, 'The Sudan, Egypt and Britain, 1899–1916', *Middle Eastern Studies*, 6 (1970), 178.
93. Rodogno, *Against Massacre*, p. 216.
94. *Documents diplomatiques français*, 14 (1898), 649.
95. Georges Streit, 'La question crétoise', *Revue générale de droit international public*, 10 (1903), 228.
96. *Documents diplomatiques français* 14 (1898), 897.
97. The European consuls did intervene in the port of Volos as did marines from the ships of the powers. See Nicolas Politics, 'Chronique des faits internationaux: Grèce et Turquie', *Revue générale de droit international public*, 4 (1897), 703–4.
98. Robin, *Des occupations militaires en dehors des occupations de guerre*, pp. 478–9.
99. S. B. Spies, *Methods of Barbarism? Roberts and Kitchener and Civilians in the Boer Republics January 1900–May 1902* (Cape Town: Human & Rousseau, 1977), p. 12.
100. See Charles Townsend, 'Martial law: legal and administrative problems of civil emergency in Britain and the Empire, 1800–1940', *Historical Journal*, 25(182), 167–95, with discussion of South Africa on pp. 177–83.
101. L. S. Amery (ed.), *The Times History of the War in South Africa 1899–1902*, vol. 6 (London: Sampson Low, Marston, 1909), p. 571.
102. *Army Proclamations Issued by Field-Marshal Lord Roberts in South Africa*, Cd. 426 (London: HMSO, 1900), p. 6.
103. Spies, *Methods of Barbarism?*, p. 59.
104. As Arthur Lorriot argued that the mere seizure of the capitals was not sufficient to constitute *debellatio* for by that logic Napoleon would have automatically been entitled to annex Prussia in 1806 and Austria in 1808 by occupying their capitals, *De la nature de l'occupation de guerre* (Paris: Lavauzelle, 1903), p. 49.
105. Frantz Despagnet, *La guerre sud-africaine au point de vue du droit international* (Paris: Pedone, 1902), p. 270.
106. *Army Proclamations Issued by Field-Marshal Lord Roberts*, p. 8.
107. See Spaight, *War Rights on Land*, p. 331.
108. See Denis Judd and Keith Surridge on the case of Johannes Lötter, *The Boer War* (London: Tauris, 2013), pp. 234–5, and the interesting case reported in *American Journal of International Law*, 2 (1908), 217–20.

109. *Army Proclamations Issued by Field-Marshal Lord Roberts*, p. 3.
110. Ibid. p. 23. See the nuanced rejection of such oaths by Spaight, *War Rights on Land*, p. 373.
111. Cecil Headlam (ed.), *The Milner Papers. South Africa 1899–1905* (London: Cassell, 1933), pp. 132–3.
112. Amery (ed.), *The Times History of the War in South Africa 1899–1902*, vol. 6, pp. 576–8, and Keith Surridge, *Managing the South African War 1899–1902* (Woodbridge: Boydell, 1998), p. 85.
113. *Further Correspondence Relating to Affairs in South Africa*, Cd. 547 (London: HMSO, 1901), p. 39.
114. For a good evaluation see Spies, *Methods of Barbarism?*, pp. 296–8.
115. See the observation by one soldier in a letter home: 'We did not come out here to play Spaniards and Cubans', Elizabeth van Heyningen, *The Concentration Camps of the Anglo-Boer War* (Johannesburg: Jacan, 2013), p. 323.
116. On the whole issue of camps see Heyningen, *The Concentration Camps*, passim.
117. Headlam (ed.), *The Milner Papers*, p. 138.
118. Diana Cammack, *The Rand at War 1899–1902* (London: Currey, 1990), p. 192.
119. Stewart Lone, *Japan's First Modern War. Army and Society in the Conflict with China, 1894–95* (Basingstoke: Macmillan, 1994), p. 129.
120. Iibid. pp. 131–2 and 135.
121. Ibid. p. 137. The notorious massacre at Port Arthur is an obvious exception. See S. Paine, *The Sino-Japanese War of 1894–1895* (Cambridge: Cambridge University Press, 2003), especially his account of the reaction of Nagao Ariga, pp. 211–12.
122. Nagao Ariga, *La guerre sino-japonaise au point de vue du droit international* (Paris: Pedone, 1896), pp. 161–4.
123. Ibid. p. 165.
124. Lone, *Japan's First Modern War*, p. 137.
125. The impact of this separation is emphasised by Ariga, *La guerre sino-japonaise*, p. 174.
126. Lone, *Japan's First Modern War*, p. 138.
127. Ariga, *La guerre sino-japonaise*, pp. 186–9, 193–5.
128. *Foreign Relations of the United States*, 1901, 45.
129. Fedor von Rauch, *Mit Graf Waldersee in China* (Berlin: Fontane, 1907), pp. 155–6.
130. For an impressionistic tour see George Lynch, *The War of the Civilisations* (London: Longmans, 1901), pp. 134–8.
131. James Hevia, *English Lessons: The Pedagogy of Imperialism in Nineteenth Century China* (Durham: Duke University Press, 2003), pp. 203–5.

132. James Wilson, *Under the Old Flag*, vol. 2 (New York: Appleton, 1912), pp. 530–1.
133. Michael Hunt, 'The forgotten occupation: Peking 1900–1901', *Pacific Historical Review*, 48 (1979), 526.
134. Ibid. pp. 501–29: see especially the observation that 'Patriotism may thus have motivated both the collaborator and the enemy of collaboration', p. 523.
135. Nagao Ariga, *La guerre russo-japonaise au point de vue continental et le droit international* (Paris: Pedone, 1908), pp. 423–4.
136. Ibid. pp. 401–5.
137. Etienne Coquet, 'Chronique des faits internationaux: Italie et Turquie', *Revue générale de droit international public*, 20 (1913), 613.
138. Andrea Rapisardi-Mirabelli, 'La guerre italo-turque et le droit', *Revue de droit international et de législation comparée* (1913), 540.
139. Michel Kebedgy, 'Les iles de la Mer Égee', *Revue générale de droit international public*, 20 (1913), 91–6.
140. Léon Maccas, 'Salonique occupée et administrée par les Grecs', *Revue générale de droit international public*, 20 (1913), 239.

Chapter 7
Occupations by the United States of America and the Spanish-American War

The United States between Empire and Occupation

American experience of occupation was marked by some of the same factors shaping European experience. From an American point of view the trend, and consequences, was forcefully expressed in 1895 by Henry Cabot Lodge:

> The modern movement is all toward the concentration of people and territory into great nations and large dominions. The great nations are rapidly absorbing for their future expansion and their present defense all the waste places of the earth. It is a movement which makes for civilization and advancement of the race. As one of the great nations of the world, the United States must not fall out of the line of march.[1]

The United States contributed one of the most influential theorists and advocates of this trend in the shape of Alfred Thayer Mahan, whose influential text *The Influence of Sea Power upon History* had been published in 1890.[2] More important still, the United States now had the material resources commensurate with these kinds of ambitions. Indeed, in terms of its share of world manufacturing capacity the United States outranked Britain by the turn of the century and stood as the pre-eminent industrial nation in the world.[3] It is true that the United States was still far from having the military capacity these economic resources could support, though the need to develop them was the point of advocacy by men like Mahan.

The events which demonstrated to contemporaries, both American and European, the new status of the United States was the war with Spain of 1898–9, with its striking victory over the Spanish navy in Manila Bay in May 1898. Although this triumph took place in the

Philippines, the initial focus of the dispute between Spain and the United States lay in the Caribbean, specifically Cuba.[4] Cuba had long been of strategic concern to the United States, as well as increasing business interest and the object of intermittent annexationist desires. Prior to the war, however, the United States' position had been to support Spanish colonial authority, if only as an alternative to possible control by more powerful European powers. That position became increasingly problematic as Spain struggled to suppress a Cuban revolt, and the prospect of an independent Cuba under an unstable revolutionary government emerged as another unwelcome alternative for the United States.[5] As early as December 1896 President Grover Cleveland had warned that should Spain prove unable to enforce its sovereignty 'our obligations to the sovereignty of Spain will be superseded by higher obligations'.[6] A year later new President McKinley's annual message set out the possible options as yet untried:

> Recognition of the insurgents as belligerents; recognition of the independence of Cuba; neutral intervention to end the war by imposing a rational compromise between the contestants, and intervention in favour of one or the other party. I speak not of forcible annexation for that can not be thought of.[7]

McKinley focused heavily on ruling out recognition of Cuban belligerency, but otherwise kept American options open. Even annexation had only been excluded if it were 'forcible'. Congress, however, sought a more restrictive framework in the shape of the Turpie and Teller Amendments. The former specified that the United States 'recognizes the Republic of Cuba as the true and lawful government of that Island'.[8] This McKinley was determined to avoid and he successfully opposed the amendment. A version of the Teller Amendment did have to be accepted. According to this amendment, 'the United States hereby disclaims any disposition or intention to exercise sovereignty, jurisdiction or control over said island except for the pacification thereof, and asserts its determination to leave the government and control of the island to its people.'[9] That this constituted inadequate clarity of purpose was clear to senators who asked whether the government that thus emerged would 'be the act of the people or the act of the United states?', or who asked that given the refusal to recognise the Cuban insurgents and the intent to set aside the Spanish: 'Who are we to pacify?'[10]

Occupations by the USA and the Spanish-American War   289

It was on this basis, following an unexplained explosion on an American naval vessel in Havana Bay and amidst mounting public and Congressional agitation, that McKinley led his nation into the war with Spain.[11] Although Spanish forces put up significant resistance in Cuba, with the American forces benefitting from the military action of Cuban insurgents, defeat of the Spaniards in Cuba, the Philippines, where they were also weakened by an insurgency, and their other remaining Caribbean possession, Puerto Rico, where Spanish resistance was minimal, led to an armistice. The preliminary peace protocol prescribed the evacuation of Spanish forces from all three possessions. In respect of Cuba it provided simply that Spain 'will relinquish all claim of sovereignty over or title to Cuba'.[12] In respect of the Philippines it specified, without any reference to Spanish sovereignty, that the 'United States will occupy and hold the city, bay, and harbour of Manila pending the conclusion of a treaty of peace which shall determine the control, disposition and government of the Philippines'.[13] Only in the case of Puerto Rico was there apparent clarity: 'Spain will cede to the United States the island of Porto Rico.'[14]

In reality there was no certainty about the ultimate fate of any of these islands. It was clear they were not amongst the 'waste places of the earth', that is *terra nullius*, that could be simply absorbed without any other consideration. At the time of the Peace Protocol not even Manila had been taken in the Philippines, though occupation of it, and it alone, was provided for in the Protocol, while military occupation was an established fact in Cuba and Puerto Rico. The nature, purpose and manner of ending military occupation were all heavily shaped by those wider considerations about the ultimate fate of the islands. At the time and after, the debate has been heavily shaped by the interpretation of the war and America's subsequent relationship with these islands as signifying the emergence of American imperialism.[15] Indeed the entire debate about the military occupations of these islands stands under the shadow of this wider debate about the American imperial project and especially the extent to which this could be construed as a betrayal of American values.[16] As in earlier decades the prospect of American expansionism raised objections about the constitutional propriety of expansion. Amidst the Senate debate on the ratification of the definitive peace treaty, Senator George Vest's unsuccessful resolution declared that 'under the Constitution of the United States no power is given to the Federal Government to acquire territory to be held or governed permanently as colonies. The colonial system of European nations cannot be established under our present Constitution'.[17] Vest's resolution demonstrated that the debate was now complicated by the prospect that some or all of these islands might be taken not as territories whose inhabitants might in time warrant statehood and admission to the Union, but as possessions to be held on the same basis as European imperial powers held their possessions. That Americans might deny to others the demand that government be by the consent of the governed was a prospect that critics of empire could readily evoke, and advocates of empire could not avoid.[18]

In finding their diverse answers to these issues the Americans looked to European practices, prejudices and claims for models as to how they should proceed. Yet, important though these analogies often were, it was also distinctively American ideas and practices that informed what they did. Elihu Root, formulating instructions in 1900, had begun by examining British colonial administration for guidance but soon concluded that it was American experience and ideals that were the more important.[19] To some extent that was inevitable given the peculiar constitution of the United States. Yet wider dimensions of the American experience were also at work. In differing degrees the progressivism of the late nineteenth century, critical of aspects of big business, favourable to a more activist role for government within the United States, found its way into the policies of some military governors, especially those of Leonard Wood as Military Governor of Cuba.[20] That was a linkage facilitated by the fact that American progressives were often to be found amongst the ranks of the self-avowed imperialists.[21] American exceptionalism may not have been sufficient to deter the United States from embarking in some measure at least on the imperial project favoured by the Europeans, but the distinctiveness of American society impressed itself upon the practice and interpretation of military occupation.

The Military Occupations of Cuba

Some attempt to provide guidance to the military commanders in Cuba came the day after the Spanish surrender at Santiago de Cuba. On 17 July 1898 President McKinley issued instructions for the conduct of the ensuing military occupation. In language owing more to the Lieber Code than to the Brussels Conference of 1874 he began by proclaiming that the 'first effect of the military occupation of the enemy's territory is the severance of the former political relations of the inhabitants and the establishment of a new political power'.[22] The inhabitants were, however, to be assured of respect for persons, property and religion. Although the 'powers of the military occupant are absolute and supreme' existing laws, 'such as affect private rights of person and property and provide for the punishment of crime' were to continue in force, though, McKinley added, 'so far as they are compatible with the new order of things, until they are suspended or superseded by the occupying belligerent'.[23] He emphasised the importance of the collection and administration of taxes. In general the guidance was consistent with the now established understanding in the United States of military occupation. It gave little hint of the attempted transformation of Cuban society upon which the Americans would embark nor did it provide any guidance on the crucial matter of the relationship between the Americans and the Cuban insurgents.

Though refusing to recognise the Cuban insurgents as belligerents the American forces had actively sought their aid. Friction, however, emerged from the outset as the Americans sought to consign the Cubans to menial roles, disparaged the assistance that the insurgents did provide and, especially following the Spanish surrender, found more in common with the defeated foe than their effective allies. In Santiago de Cuba General Shafter even denied the Cuban insurgents entry into the town, not trusting then to refrain from massacring the surrendered Spaniards and their supporters.[24] This often open distrust and disparagement aggravated the inherent difficulty of establishing order in a country wracked by a civil war in which the insurgents had deliberately attacked the colonial economy rather than confronting Spanish troops in open battle. In part, despite his contempt for the Cubans, General Shafter showed some understanding of this and of the problem of the relationship between the occupying American forces and the Cuban army in a report to Washington in August:

> The whole trouble here is that there is nothing for men to do in the country. It has absolutely returned to its wild state and has got to be settled and made anew. The attitude of the pronounced Cubans is hostile. They so far show no disposition to disband and go to work, and until they do there will be trouble, for they have to live, and they will have to live by robbery – there is no other way. A dual government can't exist here; we have got to have full sway of the Cubans.[25]

The Cuban insurgents were in fact refusing to disband until they were paid while the opportunities for employment in the devastated economy were limited. It would take several months until this problem was resolved under Shafter's successor, General Brooke. Brooke had been appointed Governor General of Cuba at the beginning of 1899 but had been given little guidance beyond his formal orders and McKinley's instructions of the preceding August. Indeed one of his subordinates, General Wilson, later recalled that it

> is worthy of note that when I asked Brooke, as I did frequently during that year, what our Government's policy and ultimate purpose were in all it was doing, in short, what was the state of the law under which we were acting, he frankly confessed that he did not know "except by induction".[26]

Given this lack of guidance Brooke confined himself to a relatively minimal role, focusing on public order, sanitation and the honest and efficient collection of revenues. He did, however, preside over the disbanding of the Cuban army. Although this was complicated by tensions amongst the Cubans, who lacked any authoritative decision making body amongst themselves, agreement was finally reached between all the relevant parties in April 1899 on the disbandment of the army and American funded payment of the soldiers. In return the Americans insisted that each man hand in his rifle on receipt of the payment.[27] The outbreak of conflict between American occupying forces and Philippine insurgents in February 1899 had given added urgency to the American desire to see the disbandment of the army. Yet, as was recorded by McKinley's secretary, they were aware that even without arms, leaving large numbers of unemployed men to roam the devastated countryside was not conducive to public order.[28] Efforts were made to find employment for as many as possible. This applied to senior members of the Cuban army as well, with five out of the six provincial governors being former generals of the army.[29] Both officers and rank and file found employment in the Rural Guard established under American authority. This had the advantage of helping to reintroduce some sense of order in the countryside, without overstretching the American forces or exposing them to the likelihood of conflict with Cubans over mundane matters of law and order.[30]

The full development of the Rural Guard took place only after

General Leonard Wood became military governor in place of Brooke in December 1899. It was a post for which he had competed with General Wilson. Both Wood and Wilson conspired against Brooke, though they were his subordinates, and lobbied in Washington for their promotion and their vision of Cuba's future. Their ability to get away with such rank insubordination was due not only to their political friends in Washington but also to the continued lack of a clear policy. The Treaty of Paris that formally ended the war had provided only that Spain relinquish any claim to sovereignty over Cuba and that Cuba was to be occupied by the United States, which would, 'so long as such occupation shall last, assume and discharge the obligations that may under international law result from the fact of its occupation, for the protection of life and property'.[31] There was no specification of the duration of the occupation or of its purpose. Despite the Teller Amendment annexation, especially if this could be construed as voluntary, was still on the agenda. One senator requesting clarification of policy from McKinley, even claimed that he had been told that the amendment 'did not mean any more than the oft made statements of British diplomatists they would give up Egypt whenever a stable government could be formed, which nobody believes now'.[32] The notion of voluntary annexation, that is, annexation requested by Cubans, was far from implausible though the war had strengthened the hand of those who believed in independence. Nevertheless, sections of Cuba's elite continued to favour annexation by the United States.[33] Both General Wood and General Wilson favoured annexation, though Wilson preferred a period of Cuban independence, confident that the Cubans would then turn to the United States, while Wood systematically disparaged Cuban capacity for self-government. In this he resembled Evelyn Baring in Egypt, who in turn recognised a kindred spirit in Wood, praising his administration of Cuba as 'the greatest piece of colonial administration in all history'.[34]

Ironically the man who decided to appoint Wood, not Wilson, to succeed General Brooke was the new Secretary of War, Elihu Root. Prospects of annexation declined sharply after Root's appointment in August 1899, for Root opposed the imposition of reform from outside that Wood was committed to and had no belief in the long term compatibility of Cuban and American culture. It was not, however, until December that he formally set out the intent of the 'temporary occupation', namely that the 'control we are exercising in trust for the people of Cuba should not be, and of course will not be, continued any longer than is necessary to enable the people to establish a suitable government'.[35] Though not setting out a timetable for the end of the occupation, Root meant what he had said and overruled Wood when the latter sought to procrastinate.

In the time that he was allowed Wood embarked upon a frenzied programme of reform which came to be seen as an embodiment of American progressivist zeal. It was a programme closely directed by Wood and a small number of select aids and allies. Wood's own claim, made partly on the basis of the small number of Americans involved, that the 'government of Cuba while called "military" was so in name only' was quite implausible.[36] It was a military government that made as much use as it could of indigenous personnel. While professing that 'the general law was excellent', Wood recalled that the island 'was in need of a general revision of the law of public works, beneficence, education, municipal administration, prison administration, etc; that it needed an electoral law; and in fact, that the whole machinery of government needed overhauling and readjustment'.[37] Even before becoming military governor of the whole island, Wood had insisted that the necessary changes had to be made during the occupation; just as Milner had wanted to use the window of opportunity that was military government to create a new order of things.[38] The achievements of Wood's military administration were indeed impressive in terms of the infrastructure, improvements in sanitation and educational provision and roads. Wood circumvented prohibition of the granting of franchises contained in the Foraker Amendment in order to attract American capital to build railways.[39] The wider and longer term impact on the economy was more questionable. Here Wood had clashed with Wilson over the latter's promotion of agricultural credits for Cuban farmers. Wood's progressivism, while allowing for active government, embodied a late nineteenth century American conviction in capitalism whose impact on a devastated colonial economy did not augur well for many ordinary Cubans.[40]

Although Root was keen to find an exit from Cuba he, along with many others in Washington and the American military, was far from convinced of the stability of their Cuban creation. That was evident in the Platt Amendment which Root insisted had to form part of the Cuban constitution. The central ideas in it, albeit not its attachment to the constitution, had first been provided by General Wilson.[41] In their final shape the Platt Amendment's article 3 specified that the government of Cuba consents that the United States may exercise the right to intervene for the preservation of Cuban independence, the maintenance of a government adequate for the protection of life, property, and individual liberty, and for the discharging of the obligations with respect to Cuba imposed by the Treaty of Paris on the United States, now to be assumed by the government of Cuba.[42]

The Platt Amendment, and especially article 3, met with considerable opposition from the Cubans. A Cuban commission despatched to Washington received assurances from Senator Platt that his amendment would not 'result in the establishment of a protectorate or suzerainty or in any way interfere with the independence or sovereignty of Cuba'.[43] Still suspicious, a Cuban majority finally gave way for fear that the alternative was a continuation of the occupation. On that basis, with the Platt Amendment appended to the Cuban constitution, the occupation ended in 1902. The Americans in Cuba had secured what the British had failed to secure in Egypt, a right to return, and withdrew, whilst the British had remained.

During the debate on the Platt Amendment, Senator Foraker had warned that article 3 of the amendment might have unwelcome consequences. The losing party to an election, he speculated, might decide to create disturbances 'that would lead to an intervention of the United States to put the successful party out'.[44] While not entirely following Foraker's scenario, the events that unfolded in 1905 and 1906 bore substantial resemblance to his fears. The Cuban President Tomás Estrada Palma, a man who had openly expressed sympathy for the idea of American annexation of Cuba, had resorted to the manipulation of elections, including the misuse of the Rural Guard for the purpose. The outcome was a revolt by disaffected elements and indirect appeals to the Americans to intervene.[45] President Theodore Roosevelt was reluctant to invoke the Platt Amendment but the Peace Mission, consisting of Secretary of War William Taft and Assistant Secretary of State Robert Bacon, whom he despatched to avoid intervention, and the marines, whom he sent in case of threat to American lives and commercial interests, were increasingly sucked into the dispute. According to Taft both sides in the Cuban dispute favoured intervention but were unwilling to say so openly. Of course, both hoped it would be intervention in their favour.[46] The outcome was the resignation of Estrada Palma and the failure of the Cuban Congress to agree on a replacement, leaving the Americans to step into his place. There was, however, a notable reluctance to admit the full nature of the occupation. Indeed Taft's proclamation of 29 September 1906 assured Cubans that 'so far as is consistent with the nature of a provisional government established under the authority of the United States, this will be a Cuban government conforming as far as may be, to the Constitution of Cuba'.[47] The *American Journal of International Law*, arguing from the idea that this provisional government was entirely in conformity with article 3 of the Platt Amendment, concluded that it 'is therefore the government of Cuba; it is not the government in any sense of the United States. It follows, therefore, that Cuba is in possession of its own government and is not occupied by the United States'.[48] Utterly implausible though this claim was, it was indicative of an embarrassment about the fact of occupation that would become widespread only much later.[49]

In order to run this provisional government Roosevelt selected Charles Magoon, a civilian rather than a military officer. Magoon's task was to bring about sufficient reform and agreement amongst the feuding Cuban factions to allow the Americans to withdraw as soon as possible. At the same time, however, Taft, having made Cuban chief clerks of departments acting secretaries, in place of the secretaries who had resigned, appointed military officers with experience either of the previous occupation of Cuba or of the Philippines as advisors to the Cubans.[50] The potential tensions inherent in the division between civilian and military authority were aggravated by the different backgrounds, with many of the military officers having been loyal subordinates of General Wood, and by quite different agendas. Magoon's agenda involved compromise with the Cuban factions, especially in relation to the distribution of government appointments and political offices in order to secure early elections that would facilitate American withdrawal. The military officers, hostile in any event to both compromise and patronage, were committed to a technocratic promotion of reform, honest and efficient administration.[51] The differences appeared in the report of Colonel Crowder, whose experience lay in the Philippines rather than under Wood in Cuba, and whom Magoon singled out for praise for his work on the Advisory Law Commission, a mixed but American controlled body acting as a substitute legislature.[52] Writing in November 1907, Crowder noted that the legislative action required in Cuba was analogous to that in Puerto Rico and the Philippines, where work had begun in 1900 and was still not complete. Not surprisingly he concluded that in Cuba, where 'the beginning has hardly been made', the work would 'protract itself over a a period of several years'.[53]

One of the compromises Magoon made in order to secure a rapid American withdrawal concerned the security forces, whose political misuse had in part brought on the crisis. Here Magoon's military advisors favoured a reformed Rural Guard which could be kept out of the hands of the Cuban politicians and would confine itself to the constabulary role originally envisioned for it under the first occupation. That would have made it an ideal instrument for the conservative and often foreign economic elite which showed little interest in Cuban politics. Cuban politicians, however, favoured the creation of a permanent army alongside the Rural Guard, despite the fact that there was no obvious military function for it to perform. Behind this, so the American military advisors suspected, lay the desire to create a new opportunity for patronage as well as an instrument to serve the political interests of the Cuban political factions.[54] Magoon, however, with Taft's approval, agreed on a permanent army, helping to pave the way for elections in 1907 and the end of the occupation in 1909.[55]

Military Occupation and the Disembodied Shade of Puerto Rico

The invasion of Puerto Rico presented little military challenge and no complication in terms of an indigenous force of insurgents. There was some irony though in the fact the American occupation put an end to the recently decreed measures for greater local autonomy from Spain which had exercised centralised control over Puerto Rico, as over all its colonies. General Miles issued a proclamation on 28 July announcing that 'the first effect of this occupation will be the immediate release from your former political relations, and it is hoped a cheerful acceptance of the Government of the United States'.[56] Miles effusively promised to 'bestow upon you the immunities and blessings of the liberal institutions of our Government'.[57] General Wilson was more specific about the meaning of these blessings, recalling that he had told the inhabitants that

> The President would probably appoint a military governor, the length and character of which would depend largely upon their own behaviour; that in the natural course of events it would be replaced by a territorial

government . . . and would be followed by an autonomous state, which would doubtless be finally admitted into the Union.[58]

In the light of such indications, the evident intention of the United States not to return the island to Spain but to retain it, and the weakness of aspirations for independence in Puerto Rico, it is not surprising that many inhabitants, including Muñoz Rivera, prime minister under the Spanish Charter of Autonomy, and the more radical exile José Henna, welcomed the apparent commitments of the Americans.[59]

The generals in command of the occupation had in reality been given no specific guidance. Miles had simply taken McKinley's proclamation intended for Cuba as the basis for his conduct of the occupation. In retrospect the 1902 Report of the Military Governor recalled that there had been some suggestion that these instructions were intended to apply 'only during a state of war', though it promptly added that 'if such limitation were intended, the intention was not communicated, so far as is known'.[60] The status of the military after the formal termination of the war, which came into effect with the ratifications of the Treaty of Paris, in April 1899, was, however, seen as problematic. Given the formal cessation of the war the Report concluded that 'there could no longer be a hostile occupation and control'. 'What then', it continued, 'was the status of the army in the island after the peace treaty was signed?'[61] A further complication was created by the fact that the Treaty of Paris, confirming the cession of the island to the United States already set out in the preliminary peace, had provided that 'The civil rights and political status of the native inhabitants of the territories ceded to the United States shall be determined by Congress'.[62] Yet Congress, as the military governor's report noted, had adjourned without taking any action relating to Puerto Rico, leaving the military governor without any instructions, but also though without any indication that the 'treaty of peace in any way altered, changed, or limited his responsibility or power'.[63] General Brooke, who took over from General Miles after the August armistice, had in fact been told in November that he would remain 'at least until Congress provides for a form of government', though he was to be replaced by General Henry in December 1898, who in turn was replaced by General Davis, the last of the military governors, in May 1899.[64]

General Brooke exercised some restraint, as he would subsequently when he was transferred to Cuba, maintaining the Council of Secretaries established under the Charter of Autonomy, although he did abolish the Provincial Assembly on 29 November 1889 on the grounds it was incompatible with the 'present administration'. He made some changes he thought unavoidable, including establishing a supreme court.[65] General Henry proved to be much more assertive and active. His legislative activity was consistent with his view of his task as being 'to encourage native talent in adopting our ideas or morals, government and institutions'.[66] This was now based on the assumption of the cession of the island to the United States, though Henry's legislative activity was no greater than Wood's in Cuba, based on the assumption of temporary military occupation. Henry had already faced the resignation of the Puerto Rican secretaries, which he had refused to accept, but the tension led to his dissolution of the Council in February 1899 and the resignation of the secretaries.[67] This left Muñoz Rivera protesting at 'the wiping out of the shadow of *self-government* that still existed', though his own removal from office was not unwelcome to all Puerto Ricans.[68] General Davis was more tactful than Henry. Although deeply distrustful of the Puerto Rican capacity for self-government he also began the process of introducing some measure of autonomy in the shape of elections for municipal governments in November 1899.[69] In the same spirit he introduced trial by jury, though this measure, like Henry's introduction of an eight hour working day, met with criticism from Muñoz Rivera and the Puerto Rican liberals.[70]

General Davis also paved the way for the termination of military administration and the advent of a civil governor on 1 May 1900, in accordance with the Foraker Act of 12 April 1900. Congress had finally enacted legislation to determine the institutions and status of the inhabitants of Puerto Rico. The first of the Organic Acts regulating the government of Puerto Rico, referred to by the name of its sponsor Senator Foraker, provided for a civil governor, an appointed Executive Council, which also functioned as the upper chamber of the legislature, and an elected lower body. While it provided institutions of government it also created a new and anomalous constitutional condition under the peculiar constitution of the United States. For as Senator Foraker pointed out in a speech shortly after the Foraker Act was passed, when the United States had acquired Louisiana, Florida and New Mexico there had been explicit provision that the 'the inhabitants should be incorporated into the Union of the United States and be admitted to all the rights, advantages and immunities of citizens of the United States'.[71] No such provision, he added, had been made in the case of Puerto Rico.[72] Military occupation had given way to a new form of conquest: one that left Puerto Rico, as a Supreme Court judge put it, 'like a disembodied shade, in an indeterminate state of ambiguous existence'.[73]

Occupation and Annexation of the Philippines

Military occupation in the Philippines was shaped from the outset by the relationship between the Americans and a significant force of insurgents led by the determined and able Emilio Aguinaldo. Aguinaldo had even been transported back to the Philippines on board the *USS McCulloch* for the purpose of leading the rebellion.[74] As the Americans prepared to seize Manila from the Spanish, Aguinaldo pressed them for recognition of his movement, for reassurance that the Americans did not intend that the Philippines should become a dependency and for joint occupation of the city of Manila.[75] As the American commander General Merritt sought instruction from Washington as to how he should respond to Aguinaldo he was told:

> The President directs that there must be no joint occupation with the insurgents. The United States, in the possession of Manila City, Manila Bay and Harbour, must preserve the peace and protect persons and property within the territory occupied by their military and naval forces. The insurgents and all others must recognize the military occupation and authority of the United States and the cessation of hostilities proclaimed by the President. Use whatever means in your judgement are necessary to this end.[76]

This was quite in accordance with the Preliminary Peace Protocol of 12 August 1898.[77] The Protocol, however, dealing only with the state parties to the war, took no account of the existence of the insurgents who became so central to the reality of the American occupation. In September, though, the Protocol was used by General Otis, Merritt's successor, to claim that joint occupation of the city was incompatible with the responsibilities assumed by the United States as the occupying authority.[78]

The uncertainty was inevitable given that McKinley had not had any clear policy towards the Philippines at the beginning of the war and even as the Americans occupied Manila he was uncertain whether he wished to retain only the port and harbour of Manila or the island of Luzon, or the entire archipelago. This is consistent with the possibility that the occupation may have been initially intended as a means of forcing Spain to conclude an early peace, rather than being conceived as a prelude to annexation.[79] The possibility that the United States might negotiate a return of the islands to Spain was certainly a worry to Aguinaldo and the insurgents.[80] It would also seem to some Americans that failure to make firm and clear their intentions compounded the difficulties that the occupation encountered, though early manifestation of British intentions in South Africa had not obviously lessened their difficulties.[81] Even when McKinley did decide to retain the entire Philippines and had negotiated that outcome in the Treaty of Paris he was still reluctant to see the development of conflict with Aguinaldo's forces, despite the fact that the Americans were even being denied permission to land at Iloilo on Panay Island, that is on territory which according to the treaty was now American.

Amidst these uncertainties McKinley drafted a proclamation in which he announced that since the islands had been ceded to the United States,

> In the fulfilment of the rights of sovereignty thus acquired, and the responsible obligations of government thus assumed, the actual occupation and administration of the entire group of the Philippine islands becomes immediately necessary, and the military government . . . is to be extended with all possible dispatch to the whole of the ceded territory.[82]

McKinley further promised 'support and protection' to those who cooperated with the Americans 'either by active aid or by honest submission' and declared that the 'mission of the United States is one of benevolent assimilation, substituting the mild sway of justice and right for arbitrary rule'.[83] The American commander in the Philippines, General Otis, believing that these references to sovereignty and protection were too provocative, took it upon himself to produce a more anodyne proclamation. General Miller, sitting off Iloilo, to whom Otis had forwarded the president's original proclamation, unwittingly passed it to the insurgents, undermining Otis's strategy and providing yet more evidence to Aguinaldo of American duplicity.[84] In the succeeding days the dispute over the symbols of authority and mutual and incompatible claims to authority by the Americans and Aguinaldo continued to escalate. Aguinaldo responded to Otis's proclamation with a declaration refuting American claims to sovereignty and taking great exception to Otis styling himself 'military governor of the Philippine Islands'.[85] Otis, for his part, refused to recognize in any way the authority claimed by Aguinaldo, claiming that any such recognition was beyond his remit.[86]

The following month the conflict that Otis was now more or less actively seeking with Aguinaldo's forces broke out. Although delayed by the weather and the need to wait for reinforcements, the American pushed out of Manila, chasing but failing to capture Aguinaldo, who in November dispersed his forces, ordering them to resort to guerrilla warfare. The Americans lacked the manpower to effectively garrison even the towns of Luzon Island, with the insurgents reasserting control as the Americans moved on, and then exacting revenge on those Filipinos deemed guilty of collaborating. The outcome, as one American junior officer complained, was that 'We are governing just the spots we sit upon'.[87] From the outset Otis had issued optimistic reports about the imminent suppression of the insurgents. Indeed these were so at odds with the reality and the experience of his own field commanders that as early as July 1899 American newspaper correspondents issued a protest about 'an ultra-optimistic view that is not shared by the general officers in the field', to which Otis responded by threatening to have them court martialed for 'conspiracy against the government'.[88] As more accurate news, including the journalist's protest, reached the United States, opponents to both the very possession of the Philippines as well as the conduct of the war were strengthened. With the approach of a presidential election, scheduled for 1900, that in turn fed back to strengthen the insurgents who held out the prospect that a defeat for McKinley would lead to the desired independence.[89] That Aguinaldo enjoyed genuine and widespread support was something American commanders were forced to concede. The point was openly acknowledged by General MacArthur: 'I have been reluctantly compelled to believe that the Filipino masses are loyal to Aguinaldo'.[90] It was MacArthur who replaced Otis as military governor of the Philippines at the beginning of May 1900.

MacArthur seemed to offer a fresh start in terms of the military campaign and in terms of the relationship between the military and the civilian dimension of the American administration of the Philippines. McKinley had introduced a civilian element in the shape of a Commission headed by Jacob Schurman, who was sympathetic to independence for the Philippines, as early as January 1899. That relations between the civilian element and the military element would be problematic was clear from the beginning when Otis, although himself nominally a member of the Commission, refused to sign its reports. A suggestion by members of the Commission that civilian administration of Manila would relieve him of the burden was interpreted by Otis as a challenge to his authority.[91] Secretary of War Root, however, believed that it was precisely the combination of powers, executive, legislative and judicial in the hands of one person that 'constitutes the chief objection to any unnecessary continuance of military government'.[92] It was in this spirit that a second commission, the Taft Commission, was despatched to the Philippines, arriving in June 1900. McKinley's instructions to the Commission, which was to act as a board under the chairmanship of William Taft, was that it was to promote 'governments essentially popular in their form as fast as territory is held and controlled by our troops'.[93] Given that the transfer of authority from military to civil officers would be gradual it was a task, he conceded, which 'will require the most perfect cooperation between the civil and military authorities'.[94] That was not forthcoming. After what seemed a promising start Taft and his fellow commissioners were dogged by repeated jurisdictional conflicts with MacArthur, who jealously guarded his prerogatives and resented any interference, as he saw it, in the military hierarchy.[95] Eventually MacArthur spelt out his objections to McKinley's decision to assign legislative functions to the Commission on the bizarre grounds that, as Taft reported, this amounted to 'unconstitutional interference with his prerogative as Military Commander in these islands'.[96]

The process also ran into trouble in so far as a Bill sponsored by Senator John Spooner intended to expand the president's powers, albeit only pending more permanent Congressional action, in order to create civilian institutions of government in the Philippines met with opposition in Congress. Despite lack of explicit authorisation McKinley went ahead with the intended transfer of legislative functions to the Taft Commission in September of 1900. Although certain executive powers, including the authority to appoint civil officers, were also transferred, the military governor, MacArthur, continued to be the executive head of government, as well as exercising his more strictly military functions.[97] Yet according to Charles Magoon this already amounted to a transition from military to civil government in that under military government the

President authorizes the military commander, acting as the head of government, to exercise the powers of the three branches of government – legislative, executive and judicial – while under the 'civil' government the President provides that the powers of these three braches shall be exercised by different officials or bodies, although they continue to be united in the president.[98]

It was precisely that union of powers, whether divided amongst different officials and bodies or not, that so alarmed Congressional critics of the president's actions in the Philippines. They also feared that granting the president authority to act in this way, rather than simply allowing him to administer the islands in his capacity as commander-in-chief, would amount to sanctioning the retention of the islands to which they were still opposed, notwithstanding the formal transfer of sovereignty already brought about by ratification of the Treaty of Paris.[99]

McKinley's successful re-election in 1900 was, however, taken as electoral endorsement of his policies relating to the outcome of the Spanish-American War and especially the policies in the Philippines. Yet, only in the following year, in March did a successful amendment, sponsored again by Senator Spooner, grant the President the desired authority to vest in such persons as he thought appropriate all 'military, civil and judicial powers necessary to govern the Philippine Islands'.[100] The president now exercised power by virtue of Congressional authorisation rather than under his war powers. It was this step in the process that MacArthur accepted as entailing the subordination of military power to civilian power in the islands, though it was also the occasion for his outburst denouncing the supposedly unconstitutional character of the previous arrangement.[101] Others saw in this the transition from a 'quasi-civil agency resting on military authority to a pure civil government'.[102] It was, indeed, under this Congressional grant of authority that William Taft was inaugurated as the first civil governor of the Philippines on 4 July 1901. Interestingly, Taft would later refer to this period as still being one of 'quasi civil government'.[103]

The reality of government in the Philippines was more complicated than implied by the suggestion of 'pure civil government'. It is notable that the same month in which Taft took up his new position as head of the civilian executive authority saw the army resume authority in Batangas, Cebu and Bohol provinces in the light of continuing insurgency which made civilian administration untenable.[104] At the beginning of the process of transferring authority to civilian rule the reality of American administration in some provinces remained transient. In 1900 the insurgents still conducted some 350 assassinations of people they deemed to be collaborators.[105] It was against this background that, after the successful re-election of McKinley, General MacArthur announced the introduction of harsher measures in December 1900, although still within the framework of General Orders 100 of 1863. His provost marshal in Manila, General Bell, interpreted MacArthur's order more graphically for his men: 'Create a reign of fear and anxiety among the disaffected which will become unbearable, in hope that they will thereby be brought to their senses.'[106] Even before MacArthur's new orders his officers had been looking to British experience for guidance and finding not the indirect influence of Evelyn Baring in Egypt but General Kitchener's practices in South Africa, an analogy that was taken up by sections of the American press with enthusiasm.[107] It was a version of those methods, but more brutal still, that General James Bell adopted in Batangas province when General Adna Chaffee, MacArthur's successor, gave Bell command of that province in November 1901. Bell established zones of 'concentration' within which food was scarce but outside of which his forces destroyed anything and everything, starving the remaining insurgents into submission.[108] Just prior to Bell's assignment to Batangas, General Chaffee had ordered General Jake Smith to the troublesome island of Samar. Smith arrived shortly after a successful surprise attack on an American outpost. His response was to instruct his men to 'kill and burn', specifying that all males capable of bearing arms, in which he counted anyone over the age of ten, were to be targeted. Most infamously he ordered that Samar was to be turned into a 'howling wilderness'.[109] That was a phrase that would be cited in General Smith's court martial and would find its way onto the pages of the American press, providing confirmation for the anti-imperialists of the folly of the entire enterprise.[110]

The brutality of the American repression eventually began to wear down the resistance of what had always been a divided society. In the same month in which MacArthur had announced the implementation of harsher methods, a Federal Party had been formed in Manila on the basis of acceptance of American sovereignty. Its leaders had been carefully cultivated by Taft and, with an effective monopoly over the appointment of Filipinos to public posts, the party had material rewards to offer as well as the promise of peace.[111] The capture of Aguinaldo in March 1901 also marked a significant turning point. Although parts of the American press clamoured for him to be punished, one editorial, reflecting the ambiguity of American involvement in the Philippines, asked: 'Of course he should be punished for his crime, but what was his crime? Was it his refusal to accept Spain's right to sell him for $2.50 on the hoof?'[112] Aguinaldo was not punished or treated as a rebel, despite American claims to sovereignty. In return he took an oath of allegiance to the United States and called for an end to the war, encouraging other insurgent leaders to abandon resistance. Given the ethnic and social diversity of the Philippines and the uneven impact of the American forces the decline of resistance varied. Roosevelt, however, proclaimed the end of the war in July 1902. It was hardly the end of the violence, which included a bloody and largely pointless incursion by General Leonard Wood in the south where the American presence had hardly been felt when Roosevelt declared peace.[113] In the same year Congress passed an Organic Act providing for what would be in effect a constitution. The implementation of a census and then a further two years of peace, set as a requirement by Congress, finally led to an election in 1907.

Ending military occupation in the Philippines had been arguably as difficult as establishing it in the first place. The formal transfer of sovereignty before anything resembling occupation, let alone effective occupation, had been established, the introduction of some form of 'civilian' government while 'military' government continued, and the recurrence of conflict after the apparent, and claimed, subjugation of the islands in 1902, all contributed to making any clear and comprehensive termination elusive. Moreover, despite the end of the war and the transition to civilian control uncertainty about both the status of the Philippines and the strength of American commitment to the islands persisted. As one participant in the administration, perpetuating the language of occupation, observed, 'the United States has never yet declared whether the American occupation of the Philippines is to be temporary, like our occupation of Cuba was, or permanent like the British occupation of Egypt is'.[114]

The ambiguity had been there from the outset. Days after ratifying the Treaty of Paris the United States Senate resolved that it should be the policy not 'to permanently annex' the islands while rejecting a resolution committing the United States to granting independence to the Philippines.¹¹⁵ When, in 1916, the institutions set out in the 1902 Organic Act were revived, the Jones Act declared that 'it is, as it always has been, the purpose of the people of the United States to withdraw their sovereignty over the Philippine Islands and to recognize their independence as soon as a stable government can be established therein'.¹¹⁶ Just prior to the Jones Act an American constitutional expert concluded yet another assessment of the status of the islands in the wake of the Spanish-American War by noting that the 'Government of the Philippine Islands is a Government foreign to the United States for domestic purposes but domestic for foreign purposes – a position midway between that of being foreign territory absolutely and domestic territory absolutely'.¹¹⁷

Judging Occupation and Annexation

Given the perceived need to resort to such distinction it is not surprising that the occupations of Puerto Rico, Cuba and the Philippines generated significant judicial dispute. Although never reaching the level of litigation induced by the American Civil War this judicial activity and associated legal argument confirmed and clarified some elements of the existing understanding of occupation but also arguably generated new problems. Amongst the latter was the doctrine of unincorporated territory. This concerned territory within the sovereign possession of the United States rather than occupied territory and the wider legal and intellectual context was debated in the language of empire, colonies and possessions rather than occupation. It involved and is remembered for arguments about whether the constitution was regarded as extending automatically to all sovereign territory of the United States and whether territory could only be acquired with the intent that in due course it would be admitted to the Union as a State, the doctrine holding that this did apply to incorporated territory but not to unincorporated territory which was nevertheless within the sovereign possession of the United States. Puerto Rico and the Philippines, so the Supreme Court came to argue, following here Senator Foraker's arguments in relation to Puerto Rico, were instances of such unincorporated territory.¹¹⁸ Yet it has a bearing upon the understanding of occupation by Americans at the time in so far as territory held by virtue of military occupation can be understood as standing at one end of a spectrum with statehood at the other end, but with the possibility of transitional positions in between, some of which might contain elements derived from military occupation, as military governors had noted of their military administration over fifty years before in California and noted again in relation to Puerto Rico. The language of occupation also proved flexible even for trained lawyers such as Secretary of War Elihu Root, who distinguished between the condition of Puerto Rico and that of the Philippines on the basis that Puerto Rico 'was at the time of the cession in full peaceable possession, while state of war has continued in the Philippines'.[119] In this context he then referred to the 'question of the President's power to impose duties in the Philippine Islands under existing conditions of military occupation'.[120] In their formal judgements courts distinguished between what was done by belligerent right, with military occupation being an exercise of such right, and what was done after the state of belligerency, especially where this entailed continued military administration of territory ceded to the United States. Here the Supreme Court decided in *Dooley v. United States*, relating to Puerto Rico, that while military administration continued 'the conclusion of the treaty of peace and the cession of the island to the United States were not without their significance'. More specifically Puerto Rico ceased thereby to be foreign territory and while the military commander's 'power to administer would be absolute . . . his power to legislate would not be without certain restrictions – in other words, they would not extend beyond the necessities of the case'.[121] Justification by necessity, as the court's own analogies and citation of cases illustrated, is so often the justification invoked in military occupation.

The elasticity of occupation, the difficulty of determining the precise point at which all its features, or even the most important features, ceased, emerged in a different way in the key case, *Downes v. Bidwell*, relating to the doctrine of incorporated and unincorporated territory. Here the concurring judgements of Justice White and others found distinct reasoning. In the course of this, they expressed great concern that the United States might be seen as permanently committed to retaining territory which it possessed. They had in mind the territory, which they designated unincorporated, of Puerto Rico and the Philippines, that is, territory ceded to the United States. In their reasoning, however, precisely that kind of territory came close to being elided with occupied territory in their anxiety to separate it out from incorporated territory of the United States. 'Suppose', Justice White argued by way of illustration, at the termination of a war the hostile government had been overthrown and the entire territory or a portion thereof was occupied by the United States, and there was no government to treat with or none willing to cede by treaty, and thus it became necessary for the United States to hold the conquered country for an indefinite period, or at least until such time as Congress deemed that it should be either released or retained because it was apt for incorporation into the United States. If holding was to have the effect which is now claimed for it, would not the exercise of judgement respecting the retention be so fraught with danger to the American people that it could not be safely exercised?

The justice's convoluted reasoning was facilitated by his supposition that the occupation of Cuba had involved the extension of the 'benign sovereignty of the United States' over Cuba.[122] It embodied, however, a longstanding concern, namely the linkage between occupation and conquest. It was unusual in that most legal argument sought to build barriers that would prevent the occupant seeking to transform occupation into conquest; as General Wood had wished to do in Cuba. The presumption was that such acquisitive inclinations were the main threat. Justice White also feared the linkage but out of fear that the occupant, the United States, might be obliged to retain what it held. White, fearing that mere occupation could commit the United States to sovereign possession, effectively treated some at least of what lay within the sovereign possession of the United States as if it were mere occupied territory.

That Justice White's concerns were not imaginary was in fact well illustrated by the occupation of Cuba. Here Carman Randolph cast doubt on the significance of the renunciation of any intent to exercise sovereignty over Cuba. It was true, he conceded, that there were systems of government and judicial administration on that island, 'all officered by Cubans, but these agencies do not emanate from a local sovereignty ... whatever sovereignty there is in Cuba to-day is vested in the representatives of the United States who administer the Government of Cuba'.[123] Similarly, while accepting that Cuba remained 'to some extent a political entity', he did not accept that Cuba was still a foreign state for indeed it was not, it seems, a state at all.[124] Not surprisingly the Supreme Court came to a different conclusion. Its judgement was that notwithstanding the Spanish relinquishment of sovereignty and the fact of occupation, Cuba remained in some respects foreign territory. According to the court in *Neely v. Henkel*:

> It is true that as between Spain and the United States – indeed, as between the United States and all foreign nations – Cuba, upon the cessation of hostilities with Spain and after the Treaty of Paris was to be treated as if it were conquered territory. But as between the United States and Cuba that Island is territory held in trust for the inhabitants of Cuba to whom it rightfully belongs and to whose exclusive control it will be surrendered when a stable government shall have been established by their voluntary action.[125]

The court erred in the assumption that the island would be put in the 'exclusive control' of the Cubans but it had found an answer to what would be a recurrent problem, namely the absence of an obvious 'sovereign' to whom an occupant might return territory when it wished to depart.[126]

A different kind of challenge was presented by those inhabitants of occupied territory who had legally purchased public offices which, by the prevailing law of the Spanish regime, were held to be inheritable. Upon being deprived of those offices by the American military authorities, the dispossessed owners protested against this violation, as they saw it, of their property rights as being inconsistent with both the law of occupation and the Treaty of Paris ceding territory to the United States. Here the court held that it was

> Inconceivable that the United States, when it agreed in the Treaty not to impair the property rights of private individuals, intended to recognize, or to feel itself bound to recognize, the saleability of such positions in perpetuity, or to so restrict its sovereign authority that it could not, consistently with the Treaty, abolish a system that was entirely foreign to the conceptions of the American people, and inconsistent with the spirit of our institutions.[127]

This went further than the Lieber Code's prescription that American military government was not bound to respect the institutions of slavery because such institutions were unknown to natural law and recognised only in municipal law. Here it was the avowedly distinctive spirit of American institutions which was upheld as justification for overriding what others took to be their property rights.

The occupations of the Spanish-American War like the earlier occupations by the forces of the United States were marked in many ways by the distinctive features of that society, most notably its peculiar constitution but much else as well. The tendency to ascribe in various degrees sovereignty to the United States as occupant remained a more prominent feature of American discourse, both legal and non-legal. Yet the United States shared towards the end of the long nineteenth the tendency evident in European occupations to slide from occupation to conquest, to blur the boundaries of military occupation in myriad ways. Its practices and the ideas of its soldiers and lawyers threatened to sweep away the very distinctions which had made military occupation a distinct form. They also shared the difficulty of extracting themselves from occupations they had enthusiastically, and sometimes reluctantly, engaged in and they shared the tensions which emerged when they sought to mitigate the harshness of military government by some admixture of civil government. They shared, most pointedly in the Philippines, uncertainty about exactly when military occupation, or at least military government born amidst military occupation, ended. They shared above all the sheer frustration and uncertainty of military occupation.

Notes

1. E. Berkeley Tompkins, *Anti-Imperialism in the United States: The Great Debate 1890–1920* (Philadelphia: University of Pennsylvania Press, 1970), pp. 4–5.
2. On the complexities see Peter Karsten, 'The nature of "influence": Roosevelt, Mahan and the concept of sea power', *American Quarterly*, 23 ((1971), 585–600.
3. Paul Kennedy, *The Rise and Fall of the Great Powers* (London: Fontana, 1989), pp. 259, 312–21.
4. The reason for the spread of the conflict and the significance of the naval battle are succinctly set out in Joseph Smith, *The Spanish-American War: Conflict in the Caribbean and the Pacific 1895–1902* (London: Longman, 1994), pp. 77–86.
5. Emphasis on American opposition to an independent and revolutionary Cuba is prominent in the work of Louis Pérez. See his *Cuba between Empires 1878–1902* (Pittsburgh: University of Pittsburgh Press, 1983), p. xviii.
6. Ibid. p. 170.
7. *Foreign Relations of the United States 1897*, xv.
8. Paul Holbo, 'Presidential leadership in foreign affairs: William McKinley and the Turpie-Foraker amendment', *American Historical Review*, 72 (1967), 1327–8.
9. David Healy, *The United States in Cuba 1898–1902* (Madison, WI: University of Wisconsin Press, 1963), p. 24.
10. Ibid. pp. 27–8.

11. McKinley has been presented as a weak president swept into the war by popular agitation. That this was an underestimation of him is argued by Joseph Fry, 'William McKinley and the coming of the Spanish-American war: a study of the besmirching and redemption of an historical image', *Diplomatic History*, 3 (1979), 77–97.
12. *Foreign Relations of the United States 1898*, 828.
13. Ibid. p. 829.
14. Ibid. p. 828.
15. This is evident even in many titles. See, for example, Philip Foner, *The Spanish-Cuban War and the Birth of American Imperialism*, 2 vols (New York: Monthly Review Press, 1972). For a survey see Edward Crapol, 'Coming to terms with empire: the historiography of late-nineteenth-century American foreign relations', *Diplomatic History*, 16 (1992), 573–97.
16. For an interesting variant see Myles Beaupre, '"What are the Philippines going to do to us?". E. L. Godkin on democracy, empire and anti-imperialism', *Journal of American Studies*, 46 (2012), 711–27.
17. William Pomeroy, *American Neo-Colonialism: Its Emergence in the Philippines and Asia* (New York: International, 1970), p. 58.
18. See the responses of Elihu Root, Secretary of War, and Woodrow Wilson: Robert Hannigan, *The New World Power: American Foreign Policy, 1898–1917* (Philadelphia: University of Pennsylvania Press, 2002), pp. 10–11.
19. Paul Hutchcroft, 'Colonial masters, national politicos, and provincial lords: central authority and local autonomy in the Philippines, 1900–1913', *Journal of Asian Studies*, 59 (2000), 285.
20. See the judgement of James Pruitt II: 'The military occupation and governance of Cuba and the Philippines provided a showcase for the progressive experiment', 'Leonard Wood and the American Empire', unpublished PhD thesis, Texas A&M University, 2011, p. 3. See also Jack Lane, *Armed Progressive: General Leonard Wood* (Lincoln, NB: University of Nebraska Press, 2009) and Howard Gillette, 'The military occupation of Cuba 1899–1902: workshop for American progressivism', *American Quarterly*, 25 (1973), 410–25.
21. William Leuchtenburg, 'Progressivism and imperialism', *Mississippi Valley Historical Review*, 39 (1952), 483–504.
22. *Correspondence Relating to the War with Spain*, vol. 1 (Washington DC: Government Printing Office, 1902), p. 160.
23. Ibid. p. 160.
24. Pérez, *Cuba between Empires*, p. 209.
25. *Correspondence Relating to the War with Spain*, vol. 1, p. 282.
26. James Wilson, *Under the Old Flag*, vol. 2 (New York: Appleton, 1912), pp. 479–80.

27. On the protracted negotiations and the importance of the Cuban General Gómez see Healy, *The United States in Cuba*, pp. 67–80.
28. Louis Pérez, 'Supervision of a protectorate: the United States and the Cuban army, 1898–1908', *Hispanic American Historical Review*, 52 (1972), 255.
29. Healy, *The United States in Cuba*, p. 59.
30. For fears such incidents could spark a guerrilla war of the kind raging in the Philippines see Louis Pérez, 'The pursuit of pacification: banditry and the United States' occupation of Cuba, 1889–1902', *Journal of Latin American Studies*, 18 (1986), 324.
31. *Foreign Relations of the United States 1989*, 832.
32. Healy, *The United States in Cuba*, p. 87.
33. See Pérez's rather pointed formulation: 'Businessmen, merchants, landowners, and local officials flocked around the occupation in search of salvation from Cuban independence', 'Cuba between empires, 1898–1899', *Pacific Historical Review*, 48 (1979), 486.
34. Foner, *The Spanish-Cuban War and the Birth of American Imperialism*, vol. 2, p. 461.
35. Alan Millett, *The Politics of Intervention: The Military Occupation of Cuba, 1906–1909* (Columbus, OH: Ohio State University Press, 1968), p. 36.
36. Leonard Wood, 'The military government of Cuba', *Annals of the American Academy of Political and Social Science*, 21 (1903), 182.
37. Ibid. p. 156.
38. Leonard Wood, 'The existing conditions and needs in Cuba', *North American Review*, 168 (1899), 601.
39. Resort to a 'revocable permit' rather than a franchise was the device conjured up by Secretary of War Root, a lawyer by profession: Lane, *Armed Progressive*, p. 108.
40. See especially Louis Pérez, 'Insurrection, intervention and the transformation of land tenure systems in Cuba, 1895–1902', *Hispanic American Historical Review*, 65 (1985), 229–54.
41. See Joseph Foraker, *Notes of a Busy Life*, vol. 2 (Cincinnati: Stewart & Kidd, 1916), pp. 60–6.
42. Carmen Randolph, 'The Joint Resolution of Congress respecting relations between the United States and Cuba', *Columbia Law Review*, 1 (1901), 352–3.
43. Pérez, *Cuba between Empires*, p. 326.
44. Foraker, *Notes of a Busy Life*, vol. 2.
45. On his sympathy for annexation see Pérez, *Cuba between Empires*, p. 372; for the events leading to intervention see Millett, *The Politics of Intervention*, pp. 44–82.
46. Ibid. p. 101.

47. Charles Magoon, *Report of Provisional Administration from October 13th, 1906 to December 1st, 1907* (Havana: Rambla and Bouza, 1908), p. 5. Taft privately thought the Cubans to be incapable of self-government and that annexation was the only answer to their problems: Ralph Minger, 'William H. Taft and the United States intervention in Cuba in 1906', *Hispanic American Historical Review*, 41 (1961), 86.
48. 'Editorial comment', *American Journal of International Law*, 1 (1907), 150.
49. It became endemic in the wake of the Second World War. See Eyal Benvenisti, *The International Law of Occupation* (Oxford: Oxford University Press, 2012), pp. 167–9.
50. Millett, *The Politics of Intervention*, pp. 151–2.
51. These tensions are fully brought out by Millett, ibid. pp. 150–7.
52. Magoon, *Report of Provisional Administration*, p. 22.
53. Ibid. p. 139.
54. Allan Millett, 'The rise and fall of the Cuban Rural Guard, 1898–1912', *The Americas*, 29 (1972), 200.
55. Millett, *The Politics of Intervention*, pp. 236–8, 254–8.
56. *Report of the Military Governor of Porto Rico on Civil Affairs* (Washington DC: Government Printing Office, 1902), pp. 19–20.
57. Ibid. p. 20.
58. Wilson, *Under the Old Flag*, vol. 2, p. 455.
59. Raymond Carr, *Puerto Rico: A Colonial Experiment* (New York: Vintage, 1984), pp. 30–3.
60. *Report of the Military Governor of Porto Rico*, p. 21.
61. Ibid. p. 24.
62. *Foreign Relations of the United States 1898*, p. 837.
63. *Report of the Military Governor of Porto Rico*, p. 26. It was assumed that the military commissions introduced in December 1898 were no longer authorised, ibid. pp. 23 and 50.
64. Edward Berbusse, *The United States in Puerto Rico, 1898–1900* (Chapel Hill, NC: University of North Carolina Press, 1966), pp. 78 and 82.
65. Ibid. pp. 81–5.
66. Pedro Cabàn, 'Puerto Rico: state formation in a colonial context', *Caribbean Studies*, 30 (2002), 174.
67. Berbusse, *The United States in Puerto Rico*, pp. 88, 91–2.
68. Ibid. pp. 92–3.
69. L. S. Rowe, 'Political parties in Porto Rico', *Annals of the American Academy of Political and Social Science*, 19 (1902), 355–7.
70. Luis Martinez-Fernández, 'Puerto Rico in the whirlwind of the 1898', *OAH Magazine of History*, 12, no. 3 (1998), 27–8. Jury trials were

not established on the same basis as in the United States; a fact leading to the important case of 'Balzac v. the People of Porto Rico', *US Reports*, 258 (1921), 298–314.
71. Foraker, *Notes of a Busy Life*, vol. 2, pp. 75–6.
72. Ibid. p. 76.
73. 'Downes v. Bidwell', *US Reports*, 182 (1900), 372. The indeterminacy has persisted: see Carr, *Puerto Rico*, passim.
74. For this see Stuart Creighton Miller, *"Benevolent Assimilation". The American Conquest of the Philippines, 1899–1903* (New Haven: Yale University Press, 1982), pp. 35–7.
75. Ibid. pp. 41–4.
76. *Correspondence Relating to the War with Spain*, vol. 2 (Washington DC: Government Printing Office, 1902), p. 754.
77. For a little noted equivocation see Raymond Robin, *Des occupations militaires en dehors des occupations de guerre* (Paris: Larose, 1913), p. 508.
78. *Report of Major-General E. S. Otis on Military Operations and Civil Affairs in the Philippine Islands 1899* (Washington DC: Government Printing Office, 1899), p. 7.
79. Ephraim Smith, '"A question from which we could not escape": William McKinley and the decision to acquire the Philippine islands', *Diplomatic History*, 9 (1985), 371.
80. *Report of Major-General E. S. Otis*, p. 18.
81. James Blount, *The American Occupation of the Philippines 1898–1912* (New York: Putnam, 1912), pp. 155–6.
82. *Correspondence Relating to the War with Spain*, vol. 2, p. 858. According to Stanley Karnow, McKinley enlisted the aid of a University of Michigan zoologist whose only qualification in the matter was to have visited parts of the Philippines, *In Our Image. America's Empire in the Philippines* (New York: Ballantine, 1989), p. 134.
83. *Correspondence Relating to the War with Spain*, vol. 2, pp. 858–9.
84. *Report of Major-General E. S. Otis*, pp. 66–9.
85. Ibid. p. 78.
86. Ibid. p. 81.
87. Gregg Jones, *Honor in the Dust: Theodore Roosevelt, War in the Philippines and the Rise and Fall of America's Imperial Dream* (New York: NAL, 2013), p. 145.
88. Amy Blitz, *Contested State* (Lanham: Rowman & Littlefield, 2000), p. 34.
89. Daniel Williams, *The Odyssey of the Philippine Commission* (Chicago: McClurg, 1913), pp. 87–9.
90. Miller, *"Benevolent Assimilation"*, p. 94.
91. Ibid. p. 132.

92. Charles Elliott, *The Philippines to the End of the Military Regime* (Indianapolis: Bobbs-Merrill, 1916), p. 490.
93. Charles Elliott, *The Philippines to the End of the Commission Government* (Indianapolis: Bobbs-Merrill, 1917), pp. 485–6.
94. Ibid. p. 486.
95. See Ralph Minger, 'Taft, MacArthur and the establishment of civil government in the Philippines', *Ohio Historical Quarterly*, 70 (1961), 308–31, and Rowland Berthoff, 'Taft and MacArthur: a study in civil military relations', *World Politics*, 5 (1953), 196–213.
96. Ibid. p. 207.
97. Charles Magoon, *Reports on the Law of Civil Government in Territory subject to Military Occupation by the Military Forces of the United States* (Washington DC: Government Printing Office, 1902), p. 230.
98. Ibid. p. 232.
99. Senator George Hoar was a vehement critic on both counts. See especially his condemnation of this 'pure, simple, undiluted, unchecked despotism', Miller, *"Benevolent Assimilation"*, p. 160.
100. Magoon, *Reports on the Law of Civil Government*, p. 233.
101. Minger, 'Taft, Mac Arthur and the establishment of civil government in the Philippines', 326.
102. Elliott, *The Philippines to the End of the Commission Government*, p. 62.
103. *Special Reports on the Philippines* (Washington DC: Government Printing Office, 1919), p. 9. This statement is from Taft's Report of 23 January 1908.
104. Elliott, *The Philippines to the End of the Commission Government*, pp. 25–6.
105. Jones, *Honor in the Dust*, p. 205.
106. Ibid. p. 207.
107. Miller, *"Benevolent Assimilation"*, pp. 162–3.
108. Gllenn May, 'Filipino resistance to American occupation: Batangas 1899–1902', *Pacific Historical Review*, 48 (1979), 548–51.
109. Jones, *Honor in the Dust*, pp. 241–4.
110. Miller, *"Benevolent Assimilation"*, pp. 230–8; Jones, *Honor in the Dust*, pp. 312–16.
111. Blitz, *Contested State*, pp. 40–1.
112. Miller, *"Benevolent Assimilation*, p. 170.
113. This conflict with the so-called Moros is presented succinctly by Charles Byler, 'Pacifying the Moros', *Military Review* (May–June 2005), 41–5.
114. Blount, *The American Occupation of the Philippines*.
115. Harold Bradley, 'Observation upon American policy in the Philippines', *Pacific Historical Review*, 11 (1942), 50.

116. Ibid. p. 50
117. George Malcolm, 'The status of the Philippines', *Michigan Law Review*, 14 (1916), 550.
118. 'Neely v. Henkel', *US Reports*, 180 (1900), 120.
119. Carman Randolph, 'The insular cases', *Columbia Law Review*, 1 (1901), 443.
120. Ibid. p. 443.
121. 'Dooley v. United States', *US Reports*, 182 (1900), 234. On these cases see especially Christina Burnett, '*Untied* states: American expansion and territorial deannexation', *University of Chicago Law Review*, 72 (2005), 797–879.
122. 'Downes v. Bidwell', 308, 343.
123. Carman Randolph, 'Some observations on the status of Cuba', *Yale Law Journal*, 9 (1900), 354.
124. Ibid. pp. 359 and 361.
125. *Neely v. Henkel*, US Reports, 180 (1900), 120.
126. This would later be termed the 'missing reversioner' problem. See Peter Stirk, *The Politics of Military Occupation* (Edinburgh: Edinburgh University Press, 2009), pp. 157–8, 160–2. See also the solution that Magoon found to the question about sovereignty in Cuba: that military government 'continues to be a substitute for sovereignty, as though the question of sovereignty were still pending the outcome of a war', *Reports on the Law of Civil Government*, p. 31.
127. 'Sanchez v. United States', *US Reports*, 216 (1909), 175. The military order abolishing the office was issued prior to the cession of the island. The Court repeatedly blurred the line between the conditions of occupation and sovereign possession.

Conclusion

Understanding the nature of military occupation, both from the perspective of an observer and from the perspective of a participant, is difficult because military occupation as a political phenomenon displays in acute form a tension that is at the heart of many concepts in political life. It is a phenomenon that is shaped both by the normative features that define it at one level, above all by the idea that the occupant enjoys authority but is not sovereign, and the factual features that establish it, above all by the military force that stands behind government by the occupant. It is a phenomenon that cannot be reduced to one or the other of these two sets of features, as if one were the essence of the phenomenon and the other were contingent.[1] Shorn of the defining qualification of the exercise of authority without the right of sovereignty, government backed by force could as well be an instance of conquest, or even in at least some measure the ordinary condition of government. Without the factual exercise of authority the claim to military occupation too readily looks at best like an entirely spurious claim and at worst like a sinister strategy to deprive opponents of the status of legitimate belligerency, though occupants have often stepped back from that conclusion, as had the British and the Italians towards the end of the long nineteenth century.

The necessity of the relationship between the two in order for the phenomenon of military occupation to be meaningful was implicit, and sometimes fairly explicit, in the arguments of contemporaries, especially when occupation seemed to be slipping, usually by intention, into conquest and the assertion of sovereignty. Bosnia-Herzegovina, Cyprus and Egypt all seemed to be cases where the retention of the claim to sovereignty by the ousted sovereign seemed less and less plausible as the occupant showed no sign of imminent departure, as the occupant's claims took on increasingly normative form and the factual power became more pervasive. That was the inevitable inverse of the dependency of the claim to sovereignty of the legitimate power upon some factual condition, albeit one which is put in danger by the very fact of occupation.[2] It was a version of this logic, of the tendency of the factual condition to draw to itself, as it were, the normative title, which had worried Justice White as he contemplated the possibility that the United States would be obliged to exercise sovereignty over territory within its factual possession. The converse was also possible. Mere occupants could wilfully assert sovereignty on the basis of nothing more than occupancy, or even more strikingly, they could assert sovereignty before they had even established effective occupation, as the Americans did in the Philippines and the British did in relation to the Orange Free State and the Transvaal. In another twist to the relationship between the normative claim and the factual condition, the institutions and practices of military government could outlast the successful assertion of a new normative claim, a claim to sovereignty, thereby putting a formal end to the phenomenon of military occupation while the institutions and practices of occupation continued. That was markedly true in some occupations by the United States.

This uneasy synthesis of a normative claim and a factual condition induced a wide variety of responses. For the Dutch and Belgian negotiators at Brussels and The Hague, de Lansberge, Lambermont and Beernaert, the idea that the establishment of the factual condition might bring with it the normative claim to authority was so distasteful that they sought to limit the connection of the two elements, the factual and the normative, even preferring to acknowledge the brute reality of the occupant's power rather than risk endowing the occupant with legal authority in the interest of limiting the exercise of power. Yet occupants have frequently been averse to accepting that their exercise of government rested on no more than force. Again it was the United States that provided the most striking examples of that concern. It was prominent though in the occupation of France in the Franco-Prussian War as both sides deployed their understanding of the laws of war and what they believed was permitted, or not, in the case of occupation, in order to undermine the perceived legality of the actions of the other. That they carried these arguments and accusations over into the pages of the foreign press was testament to their importance in the eyes of both sides.

The daily reality of occupation might be said to be dominated by concerns about the factual conditions, whether this be the occupant's concerns about security, supplies for the occupant's own troops, the prevention of the spread of disease or the concerns of the occupied about their food supplies, the real or potential threat of violence, the lack of news about friends and relatives and a myriad other things. Yet it was the normative claim that defined the distinctiveness of the phenomenon of military occupation in the long nineteenth century and simultaneously exposed the fragility of the status it defined to an extent which it has not since the end of the Second World War, and especially not in the twenty-first century. As can be seen from many of the occupations described above, it was the shadow of conquest that hung over the practice of occupation. Yet, though the distinction of occupation from conquest is always noted in more recent accounts, it does not have the prominence it once did. Excursions into the history of military occupation more often focus upon the so-called conservationist principle of article 43 of the Hague Regulations of 1907. It is the apparent prohibition on regime transformation that has come to dominate the legal and moral discourse around military occupation. That concern is neatly encapsulated in a subtitle of one account of the historical development of the law of occupation: 'Historical evolution of the law of occupation with special regard to the "conservationist principle"'.[3] The point is not that the long nineteenth century was indifferent to regime transformation. Concern about it could be prominent, long before the supposed triumph of the 'conservationist principle'.[4] The French Revolution and its heritage, with which the history of the emergence of military occupation as a distinctive concept is so intimately bound up, ensured that this would be so. Once established as a principle at the Brussels Conference of 1874, without great debate or dispute, manifest violation of respect for existing laws was seen as requiring justification, as was provided by Fedor Martens and Johann Bluntschli in respect of occupations by their nations. The point is that conquest, which did not automatically presume the displacement of existing laws in most respects, was the imminent threat in most, but not all cases. Even where the government of the occupying state was not in fact intent upon conquest, as was the case in Russian occupation of the Danubian Principalities in 1828, other powers suspected that it did have such ambitions. Nor were those suspicions entirely groundless in so far as Russian generals did have such ambitions in much the same way as Generals

Wood and Wilson had annexationist ambitions despite the official stance of Washington in respect of Cuba.

It is this proximity of conquest, a proximity rooted in the fact that conquest in the long nineteenth century did not automatically carry the opprobrium which now attaches to it, alongside the disrepute which surrounds the very practice of military occupation in the wake of the Second World War, which marks the greatest distance between the history of military occupation before 1914 and the current day. In most other respects, however, the tendency is for the difference between the history of occupation before 1914 and its development after 1914, or sometimes after 1945, to be exaggerated. One sense in which this is so has affected the very terminology of military occupation. Thus, having noted usage of the term 'belligerent occupation', Eyal Benvenisti adds that

> the history of the twentieth century has shown that occupation is not necessarily the outcome of actual fighting: it could be the result of a threat to use force that prompted the threatened government to concede effective control over its territory to a foreign power; occupation could be established through an armistice agreement between enemies; and it could also be the by-product of a peace agreement.[5]

Yet such instances of occupation can be found from 1795 onwards and were sufficiently numerous for Raymond Robin to have devoted an entire book to them.[6] Importantly they were often referred to as occupations by contemporaries.[7] Moreover, by virtue of the explicit formulation of the powers of the occupant in the agreements regulating them, even where the occupant violated such regulation, these instances played a significant role in stabilising expectations about the nature of military occupation.

A tendency to more explicit statement of some guiding principles was also more probable, as the record shows, in instances of multilateral occupation. Multilateral occupations are also often presumed to be a relatively recent phenomenon.[8] Yet, as has been shown above, multilateral occupation, from its full-blown form where several states participate in the conduct of the occupation to forms in which the forces of one state act as the agent or representative of several states and those in which a state acts under the oversight of several states, are not in the least new. Stein's central administration was indeed unusually clear in its purposes and its status as the agency of a multilateral occupation. That in the case of Stein's central administration or at the end of the century in the multilateral occupation of Peking different elements of the occupation pulled in different directions hardly distinguishes them from the multilateral occupations of the late twentieth or early twenty-first centuries.[9] The occupants of the long nineteenth century chafed under international supervision whether this was the informal supervision of the ambassadors over the duc d'Angoulême in the French occupation of Spain or the more formal supervision of the powers over the remit of General Beaufort d'Hautpoul.

Despite the tendency to emphasise the conservationist principle of article 43 of the Hague Regulations, occupants in the long nineteenth century are often believed to have presumed the existence of a self-regulating society and economy with which they did not need to greatly concern themselves. Claims that indifference is no longer tenable then lead to arguments about the supposed obsolescence of the Hague Regulations and the need for some alternative set of regulations or for an alternative framework from that of military occupation.[10] Here though it is helpful to distinguish two separate groups of societies. Occupants, which largely meant European and North American occupants, sometimes found themselves in occupation of societies recognisably similar to their own. They did not, however, see societies that could be left to their own devices; at least not for long. The presumption that they could take a view of more or less benign indifference underestimates the extent to which well-developed societies of the long nineteenth century were in fact dependent upon the existence of extensive governing structures. Where occupants, like Ben Butler in New Orleans, believed they could avoid extensive interference it was because they expected that the existing municipal structures and officials would continue to operate the administrative machine. The debates about ill effects of the flight of officials, of the extent to which an occupant might coerce officials to continue to carry out their functions, of strategies for avoiding provoking officials into resigning, all point to keen awareness of the problems which would confront the occupant if these administrative structures collapsed.

In a second group of societies the occupants of the long nineteenth century found themselves confronted by societies that they deemed to be dysfunctional or to embody principles which the occupants viewed as intolerable, either in the light of universal principles or because they were incompatible with the specific values of the occupant. The institution of slavery in the American South, the feudal societies that the French revolutionaries did not even want to accord the status of political communities, the purchase and inheritance of public office in Puerto Rico and Cuba all fell into the category of such intolerable principles. Occupants found societies dysfunctional and hence in need of reform on at least as frequent a basis as societies with basically sound institutions. So much was this the case that autocratic Russia sought to impose reform as an occupant that was intended to issue in a more liberal society than Russia itself. From Napoleon's intendants through to the progressive General Wood in Cuba, what is now called regime transformation was a task to which they devoted considerable energy. Often reform became a justification and the success of reform became a precondition for ending the occupation, as it did for the Americans in Cuba who departed in this era and the British in Egypt who remained. Not only was regime transformation part of the dynamics of the occupation, it was usually accompanied by a marked confidence and lack of inhibition about imposing the values of the occupant. Where inhibitions existed they were typically either pragmatic, based on the assumption that the occupied would be more pliant if allowed to retain as much of their laws and customs as possible, or, where principled, motivated by a desire to avoid being seen as preparing for annexation, or at least prematurely so.

There are two other striking features of many of these occupations, features which they share with many subsequent occupations. The first is the frequent sense of frustration experienced by the occupants. The frustration was bound up with the extent and often diffuseness of the occupant's ambitions. Those occupants who experienced the least frustration were those, such as the Prussian occupants of German states in 1866 or Japanese occupants of Chinese territory, especially in the Russo-Japanese War, whose purpose was clearly defined and limited, amounting, respectively, to conquest and military defeat of the enemy. Even with such limited goals, however, occupants could encounter unexpected complications. That was the German experience as they struggled to bring the war with France to an end and to negotiate an end to their occupation of France, an occupation which in turn had become an instrument to enforce a peace settlement on German terms. It is notable though, that for all their frustration and the genuine harshness of the occupation, Bismarck and Moltke did not take up the advice of General Philip Sheridan. There was no equivalent of the devastation of the Shenandoah Valley or of Sherman's march through Georgia in the German occupation of France.[11]

Most occupations, even where incorporating the goals of defeat of an opponent and territorial acquisition, were more complex because of the ambitions of the occupant, often compounded by the need to take account of allies or suspicious competitors. As has been repeatedly emphasised above, most notably in the case of occupations by the United States, the constraints of the occupant's own polity also complicated the task of the occupant. It was, however, most often the ambitions of the occupant to in some measure transform the society of the occupied that were the source of the frustration. All cases of military occupation involve some element of reliance upon elements of the occupied population. That reliance is inevitably more crucial where the purpose of the occupation is in part at least to bring about a change in the political or social condition of the occupied society. Here, even those occupations which were undertaken with the purpose of aiding an embattled government reveal that the aided party could be strikingly recalcitrant from the perspective of the occupant, as the French and the Austrians found in the wake of the Vienna settlement. Aiding opponents of established authorities did not necessarily prove any less frustrating. Indeed if anything it was likely to lead to greater frustration as the occupants wanted to see themselves as liberators rather than occupants. That was an illusion which was present from the beginning with Custine in Mainz and Dumouriez in Belgium.[12] Even where there were real common ambitions, if only in the shared desire to see the Austrians ousted from Belgium or the Spanish ousted from Cuba and the Philippines, differences of interest soon emerged.

Frustration was also rooted in the difficulty encountered by soldiers in undertaking the unaccustomed task of government. When Secretary of War Marcy warned Kearny that the business of government would be a 'difficult and unpleasant part of your duty', adding 'and much must necessarily be left to your own discretion', he was referring to precisely that fact and to the lack of guidance available to the soldier.[13] That there was some need for guidance had been recognised early in the day by the French revolutionaries but the experience of General Brooke in Cuba and the British in South Africa towards the end of the long nineteenth century indicate that despite the intervening codification of a law of occupation soldiers at the end of the period were little better placed in this regard than Kearny or the generals of the French revolutionary armies. Some, it is true, proved more skilful and politically adept than others, as did General Suchet in Spain. Others simply exhibited more enthusiasm for the task of government, as did General Wood in Cuba.

The attempt to remove some of these problems by incorporating civilians within the occupation regime is also a recurring theme in these occupations. It has brought with it a good measure of frustration in its own right as the soldiers have clashed with civilians over their respective prerogatives as well sometimes, as over matters of occupation policy. That can be seen from the days of the Representatives on Mission with the armies of the French Revolution through to the tensions between the prickly General MacArthur and Senator Taft in the Philippines. Personality clashes are not difficult to discern in many of these cases but neither are systematic problems created by a failure to provide adequate mechanism for coordination or to clarify lines of command. It is clear from the British experience in South Africa or Russian experience in the Danubian Principalities in the first half of the century that allocating different roles amongst military officers can generate much the same problems.

These problems of coordination are linked with the second striking feature in the record of military occupation, that is, the weakness of the occupant. The point must not be exaggerated. The occupant, even one as harassed as some Union occupants by Confederate guerrillas or as the British by Boer commandos, enjoys a position of some strength by definition of being an occupant. Occupants can also lash out in more or less unbridled fury as General Jake Smith did on the island of Samar. Yet in relation to the task of military government, occupants are typically deficient in number and expertise. Even basic functions of securing order in societies unable to mount any serious challenge to the occupant can prove problematic. Sometimes that has clearly been linked to the very limited size of the military force of the occupant, as in the case of the French in Greece, but a very large French revolutionary army in Belgium had also encountered difficulty in putting an end to brigandage. At the same time occupants all too conscious of the hostility of the occupied have unwittingly exaggerated their own weakness, as in the case of German fear of the supposedly ubiquitous *francs-tireurs*. The underlying cause of the weakness which emerges from the record of these occupations is, however, simply that as occupants they cannot rely on those elements of common interest and common sympathy that are present in some measure in all but the most dysfunctional societies. Such accord as has been created has had to be consciously and carefully cultivated and almost always only exists because of a mixture of partial common interest and coercion.

One of the main obstacles to such cooperation is, of course, the conflicts between the inhabitants of occupied territory. From the city of Mainz, through Mexico City in 1847 to the Philippines, cooperation with the occupants has often been seen as treason and either at the time or with the departure of the occupant been punished with retribution. It is equally clear that what some have seen as legitimate, even patriotic, defence of one's community has been regarded with suspicion by fellow citizens, even where such activity has not been distorted beyond all recognition by the rumour which typically substitutes for news in occupied societies. The figure of the collaborator and the ensuing *épuration sauvage*, including the barbarities reported by the young Ulysses Grant in Mexico, long predate their better known embodiment in the Second World War and its aftermath.[14] Occupants have recognised these dilemmas in the protection they have sometimes offered to those who have cooperated with them. Ironically, though, formal recognition of their obligation to do so fell by the wayside in the process of codification.

The record of military occupation in the long nineteenth century is also notable for that codification and for the increasing involvement of courts, both those of the occupant and those of the occupied, during and after the occupation. Neither the process of codification nor the wider judicial activity can be described as comprehensive, systematic or even innovative. Codification and judicial activity of the period is better characterised as a fragmentary and often inadequate attempt to make sense of the uncertainty and confusion of the experience of military occupation. Legal judgements and the law of occupation, appropriate to the nature of law as both a form of power and an attempt to restrain power, have served both to define and enhance the authority of the occupant and offer some protection or redress to individuals, and sometimes to protect the integrity of the community which inevitably comes under threat by virtue of military occupation.

It is also part of the record of military occupation in this period that much of the experience of occupation has been forgotten, only for occupants and occupied to have rediscovered the dilemmas and possible solutions anew. Elements of the experience, usually the more dramatic, have been recalled but institutionalised memory of military occupation then, as now, has been weak. That is a good reason for recalling the history of military occupation.

Notes

1. For another illustration of this problem see Jan Grzybowski and Martti Koskenniemi, 'International law and statehood: a performative view', in Robert Schuett and Peter Stirk (eds), *The Concept of the State in International Relations* (Edinburgh: Edinburgh University Press, 2015), pp. 23–47.
2. For the wider theoretical consequences and considerations here see Peter Stirk, *The Politics of Military Occupation* (Edinburgh: Edinburgh University Press, 2009).
3. Yutaka Arai-Takahashi, 'Preoccupied with occupation: critical examination of the historical development of the law of occupation', *International Review of the Red Cross*, 94, no. 885 (2012), 53.
4. For an account in terms of the triumph of this principle see Eyal Benvenisti, 'The origins of the concept of belligerent occupation', *Law and History Review*, 26 (2008), especially 646–7.
5. Eyal Benvenisti, *The International Law of Occupation* (Oxford: Oxford University Press, 2012), pp. 2–3. This is typically taken as entirely accurate. See, for example, Ralph Wilde, 'From trusteeship to self-determination and back again', *Loyola L. A. International and Comparative Law Review*, 31 (2009), 92–3, quoting an earlier edition of Benvenisti's book.
6. Raymond Robin, *Des occupations militaires en dehors des occupations de guerre* (Paris: Larose, 1913).
7. Interestingly Eldridge Colby, to whom Benvenisti refers in connection with usage of the term belligerent occupation, sets aside these other forms of occupation under the heading of '"garrisoning"' citing Joseph Bray, *De l'occupation militaire en temps de guerre* (Paris: Larose, 1894), p. 127, who in turn cited Pasquale Fiore, 'Occupation under the laws of war', *Columbia Law Review*, 25 (1925), 905. It is noteworthy that Colby, however, conceded that Fiore 'seems to be alone among writers on the subject in so holding', ibid. Fiore moreover cites occupation under the Treaty of Frankfurt at the end of the Franco-Prussian War as an illustration of such garrisoning; *Nouveau droit international public*, vol. 3 (Paris: Pedone-Lauriel, 1886), p. 314. As is clear from the account given in Chapter 4 of this work, Fiore's preference is inconsistent with both the usage of the time and the powers of the occupant under that treaty.

8. See, for example, Grant Harris, 'The era of multilateral occupation', *Berkeley Journal of International Law*, 24 (2006), 1–78.
9. Almost any account of the occupations of Bosnia-Herzegovina and Kosovo will serve to illustrate this. A good example is Ian King and Whit Mason, *Peace at any Price* (Ithaca, NY: Cornell University Press, 2006).
10. More recent commitment to regime transformation has been associated with either the view that the law of occupation needs to be changed to accommodate this regime transformation or that these more recent instances cannot count as instances of occupations at all. For an assessment of the former set of issues see Leslie Green, 'Is there a "new" law of intervention and occupation', *Israel Yearbook on Human Rights*, 35 (2005), 33–69. For an example of the latter logic see Richard Caplan, *International Governance of War-Torn Territories* (Oxford: Oxford University Press, 2005).
11. This needs to be recalled in the context of works such as John Horne and Alan Kramer, *German Atrocities, 1914* (New Haven: Yale University Press, 2001).
12. It has become more pronounced as the opprobrium attached to occupation has increased and could be said to culminate in the proclamation by General Tommy Franks at the time of the 2003 invasion of Iraq: 'this has been about liberation not occupation'. Jordan Paust, 'The US as occupying power over portions of Iraq and relevant responsibilities under the laws of war', *ASIL Insights* (April 2003).
13. *Occupation of Mexican Territory* (Washington DC: Government Printing Office, 1912), p. 8.
14. See Pascal Ory, *Les collaborateurs 1940–1945* (Paris: du Seuil, 1976), and Philippe Bourdel, *L'épuration sauvage* (Paris: Perrin, 2002).

Select Bibliography

Actes de la Conférence de Bruxelles de 1874 (Paris: Libraire des publications legislatives, 1874).

Actenstücke zur neuesten Geschichte von Frankfurt am Main (Stuttgart: Schweitzerbartsche, 1866).

Amery, L. S. (ed.), *The Times History of the War in South Africa 1899–1902*, vol. 6 (London: Sampson Low, Marston, 1909).

André, Roger, *L'occupation de la France par les alliés en 1815* (Paris: Boccard, 1924).

Ariga, Nagao, *La guerre sino-japonaise au point de vue du droit international* (Paris: Pedone, 1896).

Ariga, Nagao, *La guerre russo-japonaise au point de vue continental et le droit international* (Paris: Pedone, 1908).

Army Proclamations Issued by Field-Marshal Lord Roberts in South Africa, Cd. 426 (London: HMSO, 1900).

Ash, Stephen, *When the Yankees Came. Conflict and Chaos in the Occupied South, 1861-65* (Chapel Hill, NC: University of North Carolina Press, 1999).

Aulard, F.-A., (ed.) *Recueil des actes du Comité de Salut Public*, 27 vols (Paris: Imprimerie nationale, 1889–1923).

Barre, André, *La Bosnie-Herzégovine: administration autrichienne de 1878 à 1903* (Paris: Michaud, 1906).

Bass, Gary J., *Freedom's Battle: The Origins of Humanitarian Intervention* (New York: Vintage, 2008).

Basdevant, Jules, *La revolution française et la droit de la guerre continentale* (Paris: Larose and Forcel, 1901).

Baty, Thomas, 'The relations of invaders to insurgents', *Yale Law Journal*, 36 (1927), 966–84.

Bauer, Frank, *Napoleon in Berlin* (Berlin: Berlin Story Verlag, 2006).

Berbusse, Myles Edward, *The United States in Puerto Rico, 1898–1900* (Chapel Hill, NC: University of North Carolina Press, 1966).

Belissa, Marc, 'Garran de Coulon, la conquête de la Belgique et l'elaboration d'un nouveau droit public', *Revue du Nord*, 81 (1999), 549–59.
Bellou, A., *Les Prussiens à Beauvais* (Beauvais: Baltzard-Roussel, 1879).
Benvenisti, Eyal, 'The origins of the concept of belligerent occupation', *Law and History Review*, 26 (2008), 621–48.
Benvenisti, Eyal, *The International Law of Occupation* (Princeton: Princeton University Press, 2012).
Berge, Dennis, 'A Mexican dilemma: The Mexico city ayuntamiento and the question of loyalty, 1846–1848', *Hispanic American Historical Review*, 50 (1970), 229–56.
Berger, Olivier, 'L'administration prussienne dans le department de l'Essone pendant l'occupation de 1870–1871', in Yann Delbrel, Pierre Allorant and Philippe Tanchoux (eds), *France occupée, France occupant* (Orleans: Presses universitaires d'Orléans, 2008), 131–45.
Berthoff, Rowland, 'Taft and MacArthur: a study in civil military relations', *World Politics*, 5 (1953), 196–213.
Birkhimer, William E., *Military Government and Martial Law* (Washington DC: J. J. Chapman, 1892).
Bitis, Alexander, *Russia and the Eastern Question: Army, Government and Society 1815–1833* (Oxford: Oxford University Press, 2006).
Blair, William, *With Malice toward Some: Treason and Loyalty in the Civil War Era* (Chapel Hill, NC: North Carolina Press, 2014).
Blanchot, Charles, *Mémoires: L'intervention fraçaise au Mexique*, 3 vols (Paris: Nourry, 1911).
Blanning, T. C. W., *Reform and Revolution in Mainz 1743–1803* (Cambridge: Cambridge University Press, 1974).
Blanning, T. C. W., *The French Revolution in Germany: Occupation and Resistance in the Rhineland 1792–1802* (Oxford: Clarendon Press, 1983).
Blanning, T. C. W., *The French Revolutionary Wars 1787–1802* (London: Arnold, 1996).
Blount, James, *The American Occupation of the Philippines 1898–1912* (New York: Putnam, 1912).
Bluntschli, J. C., *Das moderne Kriegsrecht der civilisirten Staaten* (Nördlingen: Beck, 1866).
Bluntschli, J. C., *Das moderne Völkerrecht der civilisirten Staten* (Nördlingen: Beck, 1868).
Bluntschli, J. C., *Das moderne Völkerrecht in dem französisch-deutschen Kriege von 1870, Eine Rectoratsrede am 22. November 1870* (Heidelberg: Bassermann, 1871).
Bluntschli, J. C., 'Völkerrechtliche Betrachtungen über den französisch-deutsch Krieg 1870/71', *Jahrbuch für Gesetzgebung, Verwaltung und Rechtspflege des Deutschen Reiches*, 2 (1872), 270–342.
Bluntschli, J. C., *Le droit international codifié* (Paris: Guillaumin, 1895).

Bordwell, Percy, *The Law of War Between Belligerents* (Chicago: Callaghan, 1908).
Bray, Joseph, *De l'occupation militaire en temps de guerre* (Paris: Larose, 1894).
Brenet, Amédée, *La France et l'Allemagne devant le droit international* (Paris: Rousseau, 1902).
Browning, Judkin (ed.), *The Southern Mind under Union Rule: The Diary of James Rumley, Beaufort, North Carolina, 1862–1865* (Gainesville, FL: University Press of Florida, 2009).
Browning, Judkin, *Shifting Loyalties: The Union Occupation of Eastern North Carolina* (Chapel Hill, NC: University of North Carolina Press, 2011).
Burián, Stephan, *Austria in Dissolution* (New York: Doran, 1925).
Burnett, Christina, 'Untied states: American expansion and territorial deannexation', *University of Chicago Law Review*, 72 (2005), 797–879.
Burrin, Philippe, 'Writing the history of military occupations', in Sarah Fishman, Laura L. Downs, Ioannis Sinanoglou et al. (eds), *France at War: Vichy and the Historians* (Oxford: Berg, 2000).
Bury, J. P. T., *Gambetta and the National Defence: A Republican Dictatorship in France* (Westport, CT: Greenwood, 1971).
Butler, Benjamin, *Butler's Book: Autobiography and Personal Reminiscences* (Boston: Thayer, 1892).
Calvo, Charles, *Le droit international théorique et pratique*, 5th edn, vol. 4 (Paris: Rousseau, 1896).
Cammack, Diana, *The Rand at War 1899–1902* (London: Currey, 1990).
Capers, Gerald, *Occupied City: New Orleans under the Federals 1862–1865* (Lexington: University of Kentucky Press, 1965).
Carl, Horst, *Okkupation und Regionalismus: Die preussischen Westprovinzen im Siebenjährigen Krieg* (Mainz: von Zabern, 1993).
Carl, Horst, 'Französisches Besatzungsherrschaft im Alten Reich', *Francia*, 23, no. 2 (1996), 33–64.
Carpernter, A. H., 'Military government of Southern territory, 1861–1865', *Annual Report of the American Historical Association*, 1 (1900), 467–89.
Chantriot, Émile, *L'administration des départements envahis* (Paris: Berger-Levrault, 1916).
Chevalley, E., *Essai sur la droit des gens napoléonien* (Paris: Delagrave, 1912).
Chuquet, Arthur, *Jemappes et la conquête de la Belgique 1792–1793* (Paris: Chailley, 1890).
Chuquet, Arthur, *L'expedition de Custine* (Paris: Plon, 1892).
Chuquet, Arthur, *Mayence (1792–1793)* (Paris: Plon, 1892).
Clercq, Alexandre De (ed.), *Recueil des traités de la France*, vols. 1–15 (Paris: Pedone-Lauriel, 1880–8).

Cocheris, Jules, *Situation international de l'Egypte et du Soudan* (Paris: Plon-Nourrit, 1903).
Colby, Eldridge, 'Occupation under the laws of war', *Columbia Law Review*, 25 (1925), 904–22.
Connor, Jacon Elen, *The Development of Belligerent Occupation* (Iowa: Iowa University Press, 1912).
Conrad, Pierre, *Napoléon et la Catalogne 1808–1814* (Paris: Alcan, 1910).
*Correspondance de Napoléon I*er, 32 vols (Paris: Plon, 1858–70).
Correspondence Respecting the Brussels Conference on the Rules of Military Warfare (London: HMSO, 1875).
Cunningham, Michele, *Mexico and the Foreign Policy of Napoleon III* (Houndmills: Palgrave, 2001).
Dabbs, Jack, *The French Army in Mexico 1861–1867* (The Hague: Mouton, 1963).
Daniels, A. V. (ed.), *Handbuch der für die Königl. Preuss. Rheinprovinzen verküngikten Gestetze, Verordnungnen und Regierungsbechlüsse aus der Zeit der Fremdherrschaft*, 8 vols (Cologne: Bachem, 1833–45).
Danielson, Joseph, *War's Desolating Scourge: The Union Occupation of North Alabama* (Lawrence, KS: University Press of Kansas, 2012).
Dauphiné, V. and Louis Humbert, *L'invasion allemande dans l'arrondissement de Sens* (Sens: Duchemin, 1904).
Dawson, Joseph, *Army Generals and Reconstruction. Louisiana, 1862–1877* (Baton Rouge, LA: Louisiana State University Press, 1982).
Deleriot, Émile, *Versailles pendant l'occupation (1870–1871)* (Versailles: Bernard, 1900).
Delmon, Romain, 'Les acteurs de la politique imperial lors de l'expedition au Mexique', in Leanca, Gabriel (ed.), *La politique extérieure de Napoléon III* (Paris: Hartmann, 2011), pp. 75–99.
Desjardins, Gustave, *Tableau de la guerre des Allemandes dans le département de Seine-et-Oise 1870–1871* (Versailles: Cerfe, 1873).
Dessolins, Émile, *Les Prussiens en Normandie* (Paris: Sagnier, 1873).
Diancourt, V., *Les Allemands à Reims* (Reims: Michaud, 1883).
Diest, Gustav von, *Aus dem Leben eines Glücklichen* (Berlin: Mittler, 1904).
Despagnet, Frantz, *Cours de droit international public* (Paris: Larose, 1894).
Despagnet, Frantz, *La guerre sud-africaine au point de vue du droit international* (Paris: Pedone, 1902).
Despréaux, Frignet, *Le Maréchal Mortier*, vol. 3 (Paris: Berger-Levrault, 1920)
Dieuleveut, J.-E., *Versailles: Quartier Général Prussien* (Paris: Lachaud, 1872).
Dinstein, Yoram, *The International Law of Belligerent Occupation* (Cambridge: Cambridge University Press, 2009).
Dirou, Armel, *La guerrilla en 1870* (Paris: Bernard Giovanangeli, 2014).

Donia, Robert, *Islam under the Double Eagle* (New York: Columbia University Press, 1981).
Donnison, F. S. V., *Civil Affairs and Military Government. Central Organization and Planning* (London: HMSO, 1966).
Driault, J.-E., *Napoléon en Italie (1800–1812)* (Paris: Alcan, 1906).
Dufourcq, Albert, *Le régime Jacobin en Italie: Étude sur la République Romaine 1798–1799* (Paris: Perrin, 1900).
Dumont, Franz, *Die Mainzer Republik von 1792/93* (Alzey: RDW, 1982).
Dunant, Emile, *Les relations diplomatiques de la France et de la République Helvétique 1798–1803* (Basel: Basler Buch- und Antiquariatshandlung, 1901).
Dunning, William, *Essays on the Civil War and Reconstruction* (New York: Macmillan, 1898).
Duntze, Johann Hermann, *Geschichte der freien Stadt Bremen* (Bremen: Heyse, 1851).
Durham, Walter, *Reluctant Partners: Nashville and the Union July 1, 1863 to June 30, 1865* (Nashville: Tennessee Historical Society, 1987).
Durman, Karen, *Lost Illusions: Russian Policies towards Bulgaria in 1877–1887* (Stockholm: Almqvist and Wiksell, 1988).
Duvergier, J.-B., *Code de justice militaire* (Paris: Directeur de l'administration, 1858).
Edelstein, David, *Occupational Hazards: Success and Failure in Military Occupation* (Ithaca, NY: Cornell University Press, 2008).
Edmonds, J. E. and L. Oppenheimer, *Land Warfare: An Exposition of the Laws and Usages of War on Land for the Guidance of Officers of His Majesty's Army* (London: HMSO, 1912).
Edwards, Henry Sutherland, *The Germans in France* (London: Stanford, 1874).
Edwards, Richard, *La Syrie 1840–1862* (Paris: Amyot, 1862).
Eichler, Eduard, *Das Justizwesen Bosniens und Hercegovina* (Vienna: Hof- und Staatsdruckerei, 1889).
Elliott, Charles, *The Philippines to the End of the Military Regime* (Indianapolis: Bobbs-Merrill, 1916).
Elliott, Charles, *The Philippines to the End of the Commission Government* (Indianapolis: Bobbs-Merrill, 1917).
Ellison, Joseph, 'The struggle for civil government in California, 1846–1850', *California Historical Quarterly*, 10 (1931), 2–26, 129–64, 220–44.
Etschmann, Wolfgang, 'Guerillas und Franctireurs, 1866 und 1870/71', in Erwin Schmidl (ed.), *Freund oder Feind?* (Frankfurt am Main: Lang, 1995), 3–43.
Farah, Caesar, *The Politics of Intervention in Ottoman Lebanon 1830–1861* (London: Tauris, 2000).
Farenc, Claude, 'Guerre, information et propaganda en 1870–1971: Le

cas de la Champagne', *Revue d'histoire moderne et contemporaine*, 31 (1984), 27–53.

Fauche, Amédée, *Montereau-Faut-Yonne: Journal de l'occupation prussienne* (Montereau: Zanote, 1871).

Fauchille, Paul, *Traité de droit international public*, vol. 1, part 2 (Paris: Rousseau, 1925).

Fawaz, Leila, *An Occasion for War. Civil Conflict in Lebanon and Damascus in 1860* (London: Tauris, 1994).

Feilchenfeld, Ernst H., *The International Economic Law of Belligerent Occupation* (Washington DC: Carnegie, 1942).

Fellrath, Ingo and Francine Fellrath-Bacart, *La guerre de 1870–1871 en Touraine* (Paris: L'Harmattan, 2011).

Filitti, Jean, *Les Principautés Roumaines sous l'occupation Russe (1828–1934)* (Bucharest: L'Indépendance, 1904).

Fiore, Pasquale, *Nouveau droit international public*, 2nd edn, vol. 3 (Paris: Durand and Pedone-Lauriel, 1886).

Fiore, Pasquale, *Le droit international codifié* (Paris: Pedone, 1911).

Flint, Henry, *Mexico under Maximilian* (Philadelphia: National Publishing, 1867).

Foner, Eric, *Reconstruction: America's Unfinished Revolution 1863–1877* (New York: Harper Collins, 2002).

Foos, Paul, *A Short, Offhand Killing Affair: Soldiers and Social Conflict during the Mexican-American War* (Chapel Hill, NC: University of North Carolina Press, 2002).

Fraenkel, Ernst, *Military Occupation and the Rule of Law: Occupation Government in the Rhineland, 1918–1923* (Oxford: Oxford University Press, 1944).

Frederici, Robert, *1866: Bismarcks Okkupation und Annexion Kurhessens* (Kassel: Wenderoth, 1989).

Freidel, Frank, 'General Orders 100 and military government', *Mississippi Valley Historical Review*, 32 (1946), 541–56.

Futtrell, Robert, 'Federal military government in the South, 1861–1865', *Military Affairs* (1951), 181–91.

Gabriel, Karl, *Bosnien-Herzegowina 1878* (Frankfurt am Main: Lang, 2003).

Gabriel, Ralph, 'American experience with military government', *American Political Science Review*, 37 (1943), 417–38.

Gaffarel, Paul, *Bonaparte et les républiques italiennes (1796–1799)* (Paris: Alcan, 1895).

Ganschow, Jan, Olaf Haselhorst and Maik Ohnezeit (eds), *Der Deutsch-Französische Krieg: Vorgeschichte, Verlauf, Folgen* (Graz: Ares, 2009).

Gérard, Louis, *Des cessions déguisées de territoiries en droit international public* (Paris: Larose, 1904).

Giesberg, Robert, *The Treaty of Frankfort* (Philadelphia: University of Philadelphia Press, 1966).
Glahn, Gerhard von, *The Occupation of Enemy Territory* (Minneapolis: University of Minnesota Press, 1957).
Godechot, Jacques, *Les commissaires aux armées sous le Directoire*, 2 vols (Paris: Presses Universitaires de France, 1941).
Godechot, Jacques, *La Grande Nation: L'expansion révolutionnaire de la France dans le monde de 1789 à 1799*, 2nd edn (Paris: Montaigne, 1983).
Graber, Doris A., *The Development of the Law of Belligerent Occupation 1863–1914: A Historical Survey* (New York: AMS, 1949).
Grimsley, Mark, *The Hard Hand of War: Union Military Policy toward Southern Civilians, 1861–1865* (Cambridge: Cambridge University Press, 1995).
Grivas, Theodore, *Military Governments in California 1846–1850* (Glendale: Clark, 1963).
Grotius, Hugo, *The Rights of War and Peace*, vol. 3 (Indianapolis: Liberty Fund, 2005).
Guelle, Jules, *Droit international: La guerre continentale et les personnes* (Paris: Dumaine, 1881).
Guttman, Alain, *La guerre du Mexique* (Paris: Perrin, 2008).
Guyot, Raymond, *Le Directoire et la paix de l'Europe* (Paris: Alcan, 1911).
Guyot, Raymond, *La première Entente Cordiale* (Paris: Rieder, 1926).
Haggenmacher, Peter, 'L'occupation militaire en droit international: genèse et profil d'une institution juridique', *Relations internationales*, no. 79 (1994), 285–301.
Hall, Clayton, *Andrew Johnson: Military Governor of Tennessee* (Princeton: Princeton University Press, 1916).
Hall, William Edward, *A Treatise on International Law*, 2nd edn (Oxford: Clarendon Press, 1884).
Halleck, H. W., *International Law* (San Francisco: Bancroft, 1861).
Handelsman, Marcel, *Napoléon et la Pologne 1806–1807* (Paris: Alcan, 1909).
Handelsman, Marcel (ed.), *Instructions et dépêches des Résidents de France à Varsovie 1807–1813*, vol. 1 (Cracow: L'Academie des Sciences de Cracovie, 1914).
Hansen, Joseph (ed.), *Quellen zur Geschichte des Rheinlandes im Zeitalter der Französischen Revolution 1780–1801*, 4 vols (Bonn: Hanstein, 1931–8).
Hantraye, Jacques, *Les cosaques aux Champs-Élysées* (Paris: Belin, 2005).
Headlam, Cecil (ed.), *The Milner Papers: South Africa 1899–1905* (London: Cassell, 1933).
Healy, David, *The United States in Cuba 1898–1902* (Madison, WI: University of Wisconsin Press, 1963).

Hearn, Chester, *When the Devil Came Down to Dixie: Ben Butler in New Orleans* (Baton Rouge, LA: Louisiana University Press, 1997).

Heffter, Wilhelm Auguste, *Das europäische Völkerrecht der Gegenwart*, ed. Heinz Geffcken (Berlin: Müller, 1888).

Heimers, Manfred Peter, *Die Trikolore über München* (Munich: Buchendorfer, 2000).

Hertslet, Edward (ed.), *The Map of Europe by Treaty*, 3 vols (London: Butterworths, 1875).

Heyland, Karl, 'Occupatio bellica', in Julius Hatschek and Karl Strupp (eds), *Wörterbuch des Völkerrechts und der Diplomatie*, vol. 2 (Berlin: de Gruyter, 1925), pp. 154–71.

Heyningen, Elizabeth van, *The Concentration Camps of the Anglo-Boer* (Johannesburg: Jacan, 2013).

Hirth, Georg and Julius V. Gosen (eds), *Tagebuch des Deutsch-Französischen Krieges 1870–1871*, vol. 2 (Leipzig: Hirth, 1872).

Holland, Thomas, *The Laws of War on Land* (Oxford: Clarendon Press, 1908).

Holquist, Peter, 'The Russian Empire as a "Civilized State": International Law as Principle and Practice in Imperial Russia, 1874–1878' (Washington, DC: NCEER, 2006).

Houtte, Hubert van, *Les occupations étrangères en Belgique sous l'Ancien Régime* 3 vols (Ghent: Van Rysselberghe and Rambaut, 1930).

Howard, Michael, *The Franco-Prussian War: The German Invasion of France, 1870–1871* (London: Hart-Davis, 1962).

Hubatsch, Walther (ed.), *Freiherr vom Stein. Briefe und amtliche Schriften*, vol. 4 (Stuttgart: Kohlhammer, 1963).

Hunt, Michael, 'The forgotten occupation: Peking 1900–1901', *Pacific Historical Review*, 48 (1979), 501–29.

Hurst, Michael (ed.), *Key Treaties of the Great Powers 1814–1914*, 2 vols (NewtonAbbot: David & Charles, 1972).

Hüttenberger, Peter and Hansgeorg Molitor (eds), *Franzosen and Deutsche am Rhein 1789–1918-1945* (Essen: Klartext, 1989).

Hyman, Harold, *Era of the Oath: Northern Loyalty Tests during the Civil War and Reconstruction* (Philadelphia: University of Pennsylvania Press, 1954).

Hyman, Harold, *A More Perfect Union* (New York: Knopf, 1973).

Institut de droit international, 'Cinqième commission d'etude – réglementation des lois et coutumes de la guerre', *Annuaire de l'Institut de droit international*, 3 & 4 (1879 & 1880), part 1, 311–28.

Jelavich, Charles and Barbara Jelavich, *The Establishment of the Balkan National States, 1804–1920* (Seattle: University of Washington Press, 1977).

Jones, Gregg, *Honor in the Dust: Theodore Roosevelt, War in the Philippines*

and the Rise and Fall of America's Imperial Dream (New York: NAL, 2013).
Judd, Denis and Keith Surridge, *The Boer War* (London: Tauris, 2013).
Kanngiesser, Otto, *Geschichte der Eroberung der freien Stadt Frankfurt* (Frankfurt am Main: Keller, 1877).
Kebedgy, Michel, 'Les îles de la Mer Égee', *Revue générale de droit international public*, 20 (1913), 177–206.
Kielmansegg, Peter Graf von, *Stein und die Zentralverwaltung 1813/14* (Stuttgart: Kohlhammer, 1964).
Knell, Etienne, *La Bosnie et l'Herzégovine* (Paris: Rousseau, 1900).
Kolb, Eberhard, 'Der Pariser Commune-Aufstand und die Beendigung des Deutsch-Französischen Krieges', *Historische Zeitschrift*, 215 (1972), 265–98.
Kolb, Eberhard, 'Der schwierige Weg zum Frieden: Das Problem der Kriegsbeendigung 1870/71', *Historische Zeitschrift*, 241 (1985), 51–79.
Kolb, Robert and Sylvain Vité, *Le droit de l'occupation militaire* (Brussels: Buylant, 2009).
Koskenniemi, Martti, *The Gentle Civilizer of Nations* (Cambridge: Cambridge University Press, 2002).
Laguerre, J., *Les Allemands à Bar-le-Duc et dans la Meuse 1870–1873* (Bar-le-Duc: Comte-Jacquet, 1874).
D. Laizeau, *Récits de l'invasion 1870–1871* (Orleans: Puget, 1871).
Lameire, Irénée, *Théorie et pratique de la conquête dans l'ancien droit* (Paris: Rousseau, 1902).
Lane, Jack, *Armed Progressive: General Leonard Wood* (Lincoln, NB: University of Nebraska Press, 2009).
Lawson, Gary and Guy Seidman, *The Constitution of Empire* (New Haven: Yale University Press, 2004).
Lemas, Th., *Un département pendant l'invasion 1870–1871* (Paris: Fischbacher, 1884).
Leroy, Albert, *Le Havre et la Seine-Inférieure pendant la guerre de 1870–871* (Le Havre: Roquencourt, 1877).
Loening, Edgar, 'L'administration du Gouvernement-Général de l'Alsace durant la guerre de 1870–1871', *Revue de droit international et de législation comparée*, 4 (1872), 622–50, 5 (1873), 69–136.
Lone, Stewart, *Japan's First Modern War: Army and Society in the Conflict with China, 1894–95* (Basingstoke: Macmillan,1994).
Lorriot, Arthur, *De la nature de l'occupation de guerre* (Paris: Charles-Lavauzelle, 1903).
Louet, Ernest, *Expédition de Syrie* (Paris: Amyot, 1862).
Maccas, Léon, 'Salonique occupée et administrée par les Grecs', *Revue générale de droit international public*, 20 (1913), 207–42.
McCluskey, Philip, 'From regime change to *réunion*: Louis XIV's quest for

legitimacy in Lorraine, 1670–97', *English Historical Review*, 126 (2011), 1386–1407.

McIlwraith, Malcolm, 'The declaration of a protectorate in Egypt and its legal effect', *Journal of the Society of Comparative Legislation*, 17 (1917), 238–59.

McNair, Arnold D., 'Municipal effects of belligerent occupation', *Law Quarterly Review*, 57 (1941), 33–73.

McPherson, Edward (ed.), *The Political History of the United States of America during the Period of the Reconstruction, (from April 15, 1865 to July 15, 1870)* (Washington DC: Philp & Solomons, 1871).

McPherson, James, *Battle Cry of Freedom* (London: Penguin, 1990).

Magoon, Charles, *Reports on the Law of Civil Government in Territory Subject to Military Occupation by the Military Forces of the United States* (Washington DC: War Department, 1902).

Magoon, Charles, *Report of Provisional Administration from October 13th, 1906 to December 1st, 1907* (Havana: Rambla and Bouza, 1908).

Manuel de droit international à l'usage des officiers de l'armée de terre (Paris: Dumaine, 1877).

Martens, Fedor de, *Recueil des traités et conventions* (St Petersburg: Devrient, 1878).

Martens, Fedor de, *La paix et la guerre* (Paris: Rousseau, 1901).

Maslowski, Peter, *Treason Must be Made Odious: Military Occupation and Reconstruction in Nashville, Tennessee, 1862–65* (Millwood, NY: KTO Press, 1978).

May, Gaston, *Le traité de Francfort* (Paris: Berger-Levrault, 1909).

Mehrkens, Heidi, *Statuswechsel: Kriegserfahrung und nationale Wahrnehmung im Deutsch-Französischen Krieg 1870/71* (Essen: Klartext, 2008).

Meumann, Markus and Jörg Rogge (eds), *Die besetzte res publica: Zum Verhältnis von ziviler Obrigkeit und militärischer Herrschaft in besetzten Gebieten vom Spätmittelalter bis zum 18. Jahrhundert* (Berlin: Lit, 2006).

Mézières, Alf., *Récits de l'invasion: Alsace et Lorraine* (Paris: Didier, 1871).

Miller, Stuart Creighton, *"Benevolent Assimilation". The American Conquest of the Philippines, 1899–1903* (New Haven: Yale University Press, 1982).

Millett, Alan, *The Politics of Intervention: The Military Occupation of Cuba, 1906–1909* (Columbus, OH: Ohio State University Press, 1968).

Milner, Alfred, *England in Egypt* (London: Arnold, 1892).

Minger, Ralph, 'William H. Taft and the United States intervention in Cuba in 1906', *Hispanic American Historical Review*, 41 (1961), 75–89.

Minger, Ralph, 'Taft, MacArthur and the establishment of civil government in the Philippines', *Ohio Historical Quarterly*, 70 (1961), 308–31.

Mini, Fabio, 'Liberation and occupation: a commander's perspective', *Israel Yearbook on Human Rights*, 35 (2005), 71–100.

Molitor, Hansgeorg, *Vom Untertan zum Administré* (Wiesbaden: Steiner, 1980).

Mori, Jennifer, 'The British government and the Bourbon restoration: the occupation of Toulon, 1793', *Historical Journal*, 40 (1997), 669–719.

Nabonne, Bernard, *La diplomatie du directoire et Bonaparte: D'après les papiers inédits de Reubell* (Paris: La nouvelle edition, 1951).

Noyalas, Jonathon, *'My will is absolute law': A Biography of Union General Robert H. Milroy* (Jefferson, NC: McFarland, 2006).

Occupation of Mexican Territory (Washington DC: Government Printing Office, 1912).

Okey, Robin, *Taming Balkan Nationalism: The Habsburg 'Civilizing Mission' in Bosnia, 1878–1914* (Oxford: Oxford University Press, 2007).

Olson, Leonard, 'P.D. Kiselev and the Rumanian Peasantry: The Influence of the Russian Occupation on Agrarian Relations in the Danubian Principalities, 1828–1934', unpublished PhD thesis, University of Illinois, 1975.

Oppenheim, Lassa, *International Law: A Treatise*, 2 vols (New York: Longmans, 1906).

Ouvrard, Robert, *1809: Les Français à Vienne* (Paris: Nouveau monde, 2009).

Owen, Roger, *Lord Cromer: Victorian Imperialist, Edwardian Proconsul* (Oxford: Oxford University Press, 2004).

Parisot, Guillaume, 'De la négociation comme instrument d'occuption pacifiée et d'exploitation économique efficace pendant la guerre de 1870-1871', in Jean-François Chanet, Annie Crépin and Christian Windler (eds), *Le temps des hommes doubles* (Rennes: Presses Universitaires de Rennes, 2013), pp. 279–301.

Pellion, Jean, *La Grèce et les Capodistrias pendant l'occupation française de 1828–1834* (Paris: Dumaine, 1855).

Pena, Christopher, *General Butler: Beast or Patriot* (Bloomington: Ist Book Library, 2003).

Pérez, Louis, *Cuba between Empires 1878–1902* (Pittsburgh: University of Pittsburgh Press, 1983).

Pérez, Louis, 'Insurrection, intervention and the transformation of land tenure systems in Cuba, 1895–1902', *Hispanic American Historical Review*, 65 (1985), 229–54.

Petit, L.-M., *Histoire d'Épernay et de l'invasion 1870–1871* (Épernay: Villers, 1898).

Pfalz, Anton, *Die Franzosen in Wien im Jahre 1805* (Vienna: Deutsch-Wagram, 1905).

Phillips, W. Alison, *The War of Greek Independence 1821 to 1833* (New York: Scribner, 1897).

Pictet, Jean S., *Commentary: Fourth Geneva Convention* (Geneva: ICRC, 1958).

Pingaud, Albert, *Bonaparte: Président de la République Italienne*, vol. 2 (Paris: Perrin, 1914).
Pirenne, Henri, *Histoire de Belgique*, vol. 6 (Brussels: Maurice Lamertin, 1926).
Portes, René des, *L'expedition française de Rome* (Paris: Douniol, 1904).
Rambaud, Alfred, *Les Français sur le Rhin (1792–1804)*, 4th edn (Paris: Perrin, 1891).
Randall, J. G., *Constitutional Problems under Lincoln* (New York: Appleton, 1926).
Randolph, Carman, 'The Joint Resolution of Congress respecting relations between the United States and Cuba', *Columbia Law Review*, 1 (1901), 352–76.
Randolph, Carman, 'Some observations on the status of Cuba', *Yale Law Journal*, 9 (1900), 353–64.
Randon, Jacques, *Mémoires du Maréchal Randon*, vol. 2 (Paris: Lahure, 1877).
Rapisardi-Mirabelli, Andrea, 'La guerre italo-turque et le droit', *Revue de droit international et de législation comparée*, (1913), 523–72.
Rapport, Michael, 'Belgium under French occupation: between collaboration and resistance, July 1794 to October 1795', *French History*, 16 (2002), 53–82.
Rauch, Fedor von, *Mit Graf Waldersee in China* (Berlin: Fontane, 1907).
Report of Major-General E. S. Otis on Military Operations and Civil Affairs in the Philippine Islands 1899 (Washington DC: Government Printing Office, 1899).
Report of the Military Governor of Porto Rico on Civil Affairs (Washington DC: Government Printing Office, 1902).
Reynaud, Jean-Louis, *Contre-guerilla en Espagne (1808–1814): Suchet pacifie l'Aragon* (Paris: Economica, 1992).
Rivier, Alphonse, *Principes de droit des gens*, 2 vols (Paris: Rousseau, 1896).
Robin, Raymond, *Des occupations militaires en dehors des occupations de guerre* (Paris: Larose, 1913).
Rodogno, Davide, *Against Massacre: Humanitarian Interventions in the Ottoman Empire 1815–1914* (Princeton: Princeton University Press, 2012).
Rolin-Jaequemyns, G., 'Rapport de M Rolin-Jaequemyns', *Revue de droit international et de législation comparée*, 7 (1875), 447–511.
Romani, George, *The Neapolitan Revolution of 1820–1821* (Evanston, IL: Northwestern University Press, 1950).
Roth, François, *La guerre de 1870* (Paris: Fayard, 1990).
Rue, A. de la, *Sous Paris pendant l'invasion 1870–1871* (Paris: Furen and Jouvet, 1871).
Saunders, Myra, 'California legal history: the legal system under United

States military government, 1846–1849', *Law Library Journal*, 88 (1996), 488–522.
Sayyid, Afaf Lufti al-, *Egypt and Cromer* (London: Murray, 1968).
Schama, Simon, *Patriots and Liberators: Revolution in the Netherlands 1780–1813* (London: Collins, 1977).
Schmeller, Hans, *Die staatsrechtliche Stellung von Bosnien und der Herzogowina* (Leipzig: Wallmann, 1892).
Schwenk, Edmund, 'Legislative power of the military occupant under article 43, Hague Regulations', *Yale Law Journal*, 54 (1945), 393–416.
Scott, Winfield, *Memoirs of Lieut.-General Scott*, vol. 2 (New York: Sheldon, 1864).
Schroeder, Paul, *Metternich's Diplomacy at its Zenith 1820–1823* (Austin: University of Texas Press, 1962).
Schroeder, Paul, 'Bruck versus Buol', *Journal of Modern History*, 40 (1968), 193–217.
Schroeder, Paul, 'Austria and the Danubian Principalities, 1853–1856', *Central European History*, 2 (1969), 216–36.
Schroeder, Paul, *The Transformation of European Politics 1763–1848* (Oxford: Clarendon Press, 1994).
Sciout Ludovic, 'Le Directoire et la République Romaine', *Revue des questions historiques*, 39 (1886), 148–217.
Sciout, Ludovic, 'Le Directoire et la République de Berne (1797–199)', *Revue des questions historiques*, 51 (1892), 486–555.
Scott, Ivan, *The Roman Question and the Powers 1848–1865* (The Hague: Martinus Nijhoff, 1969).
Scott, James Brown (ed.), *The Proceedings of the Hague Peace Conferences: The Conference of 1899* (New York: Oxford University Press, 1920).
Scott, James Brown (ed.), *The Proceedings of the Hague Peace Conferences: The Conference of 1907*, 3 vols (New York: Oxford University Press, 1920–1).
Sefton, James, *The United States Army and Reconstruction, 1865–1877* (Baton Rouge, LA: Louisiana State University Press, 1969).
Serkis, Charles, *La Roumélie Orientale et la Bulgarie actuelle* (Paris: Rousseau, 1898).
Sorel, Albert, *L'Europe et la Révolution Française*, 8 vols (Paris: Plon, 1887–1904).
Spaight, J.M., *War Rights on Land* (London: Macmillan, 1911).
Spalaïkovitch, M.-J., *La Bosnie et l'Herzégovine* (Paris: Rousseau, 1899).
Spies, S. B., *Methods of Barbarism? Roberts and Kitchener and Civilians in the Boer Republics January 1900 – May 1902* (Cape Town: Human & Rousseau, 1977).
Stirk, Peter, *The Politics of Military Occupation* (Edinburgh: Edinburgh University Press, 2009).

Streit, Georges, 'La question crétoise', *Revue générale de droit international public*, 10 (1903), 222–82.
Stubbe da Luz, Helmut, *Okkupanten und Okkupierte*, 3 vols (Munich: Meidenbauer, 2004–5).
Suchet, Marshal, *Memoirs of the War in Spain*, vol. 1 (London: Colburn, 1829).
Surridge, Keith, *Managing the South African War 1899–1902* (Woodbridge: Boydell, 1998).
Suzanne Tassier, *Histoire de la Belgique sous l'occupation française en 1792 et 1793* (Brussels: Falk, 1934).
Thielemans, M. R., 'Deux institutions centrales sous le régime français en Belgique', *Revue Belge de philologie et d'histoire*, 41 (1963), 1091–135, 42 (1964), 399–4441, 44 (1966), 500–60.
Thierfelder, Rudolf, 'Die Verwaltung der besetzten französischen Gebiete 1870–1873', *Reich-Volksordnung-Lebensraum*, 4 (1943), 367–417.
Thiers, Louis, *Occupation et libération du territoire 1871–1875*, vol. 1 (Paris: Calman-Lévy, 1903).
Tignor, Robert, 'The "Indianization" of the Egyptian administration under British rule', *American Historical Review*, 68 (1963), 639–45.
Tignor, Robert, *Modernization and British Colonial Policy in Egypt 1882–1914* (Princeton: Princeton University Press, 1966).
Thimme, Friedrich, *Die inneren Zustände des Kurfürstentums Hannover unter der französisch-westfälischen Herrschaft 1806–1813* (Hanover: Hhn'sche, 1893).
Thomas, David Yancy, *A History of Military Government in Newly Acquired Territory of the United States* (Honolulu: University Press of the Pacific, 2002).
Tollefson, Harold, 'The 1894 British takeover of the Egyptian Ministry of the Interior', *Middle Eastern Studies*, 26 (1990), 547–60.
Umbreit, Hans, 'Towards continental domination' in Militärgeschichtliche Forschungsamt (ed.), *German and the Second World War*, vol. 5, part 2 (Oxford: Clarendon Press, 2000), pp. 5–292.
Vane, Charles (ed.), *Correspondence of Castlereagh*, vol. 4 (London: John Murray, 1853).
Varnava, Andrekos, *British Imperialism in Cyprus 1878–1915: The Inconsequential Possession* (Manchester: Manchester University Press, 2009).
Vattel, Emer de, *The Law of Nations* (Indianapolis: Liberty Fund, 2008).
Veve, Thomas, *The Duke of Wellington and the British Army of Occupation in France, 1815–1818* (Westport, CT: Greenwood, 1992).
Villefort, A., *Recueil des traités, conventions, lois, décrets et autres actes relatives à la paix avec l'Allemagne*, 5 vols (Paris: Imprimerie nationale, 1872–9).

Voigts-Rhetz, A. von (ed.), *Briefe von Voigts-Rhetz aus den Kriegsjahren 1866 und 1870/71* (Berlin: Rittler, 1906).

War Department, *Rules of Land Warfare* (Washington DC: Government Printing Office, 1917).

War Department, *The War of the Rebellion*, 128 vols (Washington DC: Government Printing Office, 1880–1901).

War Office, *Manual of Military Law* (London: HMSO, 1894).

War Office, *Manual of Military Law* (London: HMSO, 1907).

War Office, *Manual of Military Law* (London: HMSO, 1914).

Wheaton, Henry, *Elements of International Law* (Boston: Little, Brown and Co., 1863).

Wilson, James, *Under the Old Flag*, vol. 2 (New York: Appleton, 1912).

Wimpffen, Alfons, *Erinnerungen aus der Wallachei während der Besetzung durch die österreichischen Truppen in den Jahren 1854–1856* (Vienna: Gerold, 1878).

Winfield, P. H., 'The history of intervention in international law', *British Yearbook of International Law*, 3 (1922–3), 130–49.

Winthrop, William, *Military Law and Precedents* (Washington DC: Government Printing Office, 1920).

Wolff, Henry Drummond, *Rambling Recollections*, 2 vols (London: Macmillan, 1908).

Wood, Leonard, 'The existing conditions and needs in Cuba', *North American Review*, 168 (1899), 593–601.

Wood, Leonard, 'The military government of Cuba', *Annals of the American Academy of Political and Social Science*, 21 (1903), 153–182.

Index

Aegean islands
   Italian occupation of, 277–8
Aguinaldo, Emilio, 300–2, 306
Alexander I, 114
allegiance, 7, 11, 22, 30, 152–3,
   156, 164, 168, 177, 178, 235,
   237, 240, 272, 306
   temporary, 148
amalgame, 42, 75
American Civil War
   occupations during, 150,
   160–87, 193, 197, 221, 251,
   324
Ames, Adalbert, 175
Andrássy, Gyula, 260
Angoulême, Louis-Antoine de,
   112–13, 323
annexation, 13, 32, 45, 48, 54, 64,
   74–6, 80, 84, 116–17, 123–5,
   127, 142, 149, 153, 257, 260,
   262, 267–8, 277, 278, 288,
   293, 295, 307–9
   of Avignon, 41, 50
   of Belgium, 41, 45–6, 64
   of Boer Republics, 271–2
   of Bosnia-Herzegovina, 263
   of Comtat Vanaissan, 41, 50
   of Cyprus, 265
   of Geneva, 41, 46
   of Holland, 42
   of Ligurian Republic, 47
   of Nice, 41
   of Philippines, 300–1
   of Rhineland, 45, 47
   of Savoy, 41
   of Tripoli, 277
Anselm, Jacques de, 51
Ardagh, John, 243, 270
Ariga, Nagao, 275, 285
Ash, Stephen, 151–2
Austria
   French occupation of, 47, 78
   Prussian occupation of, 106,
   125–6
   territory occupied by: Bosnia-
   Herzegovina; Danubian
   Principalities; France; Naples;
   Papal; Piedmont; Schleswig-
   Holstein; States
authority, 14, 23–4, 33, 38, 41, 77,
   202, 213
   of the legitimate power, 7, 13,
   29, 112, 120–1, 130, 155,
   195, 199, 211, 213–14,
   230–1, 238, 241–2, 267,
   277
   of the occupant, 7, 10, 29, 52,
   67, 70, 72, 81–2, 84, 86, 87,
   89, 91, 113, 118, 120, 150–1,
   156–60, 164–5, 172, 174–5,
   177, 180, 197–8, 211, 230–2,
   233–5, 237–9, 246, 261, 266,

268–9, 273, 275, 296, 300–5,
319–20, 327
regulated by treaty, 88, 113, 264

Bacon, Robert, 295
Baring, Evelyn, 266–8, 293, 305
Barrot, Odilon, 121
Baty, Thomas, 11–12, 22–3
Baude, Georges, 235
Bazaine, François-Achille, 133–4, 189
Beernaert, Auguste, 230, 240, 241–2, 320
Belgium
  French occupations of, 51, 55–64, 116–17
Bell, James, 305
Belleville, Godefroy de, 79
belligerency, 8, 162, 183, 210–13, 308, 319
belligerent occupation, 90, 291, 322, 327–8
Bent, Charles, 153, 180
Benton, Thomas, 159
Benvenisti, Eyal, 322
Bernadotte, Jean-Baptiste, 77
Berthier, Louis, 71
Beugnot, Jacques Claude, 42
Beurnonville, Pierre de, 59
Beyer, Gustav von, 126–7
Bignon, Louis, 80
Birkhimer, William E., 179, 228
Bismarck, Otto von, 126, 128, 188–93, 197–8, 200, 209, 212–13, 215–16, 219, 254, 279, 324–5
Bismarck-Bohlen, Théodore, 197
Blair, Frank, 153
Blanc, Albert, 234–6, 240
blockade, 149, 161–2, 167, 182, 233–4, 250
Bluntschli, Johann, 197, 226, 229, 238–40, 247, 251, 321

Boer Republics
  applicability of Hague Regulations, 270–1
  British occupation of, 255–6, 270–3
Boneparte, Joseph, 42, 48, 82–4, 94
Bonaparte, Napoleon, 4–5, 39, 41–3, 45–8, 68–9, 104
Bosnia-Herzegovina, 319
  Austrian occupation, 260–3
  Ottoman sovereignty, 260–2
Brauchitsch, Heinrich von, 198–9, 201, 203–4, 209
Bray, Joseph, 216, 221, 228, 238, 241
Bremen
  French occupation, 78
Bremer, Paul, 1, 28
Brissot de Warville, Jacques-Pierre, 39
Britain
  territory occupied by: Boer Republics; Corsica; Crete; Cyprus; Egypt; France; Mexico; Sudan
Brooke, John, 292–3, 298–9, 325
Bruck, Karl von, 124
Brune, Guillaume, 71–3
Brussels Code, 228–39, 243, 245, 247, 257
Brussels Conference, 3, 9, 226–37, 239–40, 257, 289, 320–1
Buchanan, James, 149, 159–60
Buell, Don Carlos, 165–6, 183–4
Bulgaria
  Russian occupation of, 251, 257–60
Buol, Karl von, 123–4
Burián, Stephan, 260, 263
Burke, Edmund, 43
Burnett, Peter, 159
Burnside, Ambrose, 163

Index 349

Burrin, Philippe, 2–3
Butler, Benjamin, 164, 166–8, 171–2, 323
Bynkershoek, Cornelius van, 16–17

California
  American occupation of, 149–50, 152–3, 156–60, 175, 308
Calvo, Carlos, 229, 239
Cambon, Pierre-Joseph, 52
Cameron, Simon, 171
Capodistrias, Ioannis, 115
Carnot, Lazare-Nicolas-Marguerite, 45
Castlereagh, Robert Stewart, 86, 108–9, 114
Chaffee, Adna, 305
Chamberlain, Joseph, 271
Chamberlain, Joshua Lawrence, 151
Charles Felix of Savoy, 111
Chase, Salmon, 168
Cherkasskii, Vladimir, 258, 280
China
  applicability of Hague Regulations, 276
  Japanese occupations of, 255, 274, 276–7, 324
  multilateral occupation, 255, 275–6
Cisalpine Republic, 42, 46, 69–71, 75
Cispadane Republic, 46, 69
Clément, Jacques-Valère
Cleveland, Grover, 288
collaboration, 60, 72, 80, 155, 157–8, 200–1, 276, 286, 302, 305, 327
Concert of Europe, 104–7, 254, 279
Confederate States of America, 150–2, 161, 163–4, 167–9, 171–4, 176–7, 182, 326

conquest, 6–7, 10–25, 28, 31–3, 37, 40, 42, 45, 49–54, 60–1, 65, 69, 74–5, 78, 85–6, 88, 90–1, 104–5, 107–8, 111, 125–6, 128, 132–3, 135–6, 146–9, 160, 224–5, 247, 256, 231, 270–3, 275, 277–8, 300, 309, 311
  cession by treaty and, 13, 18–19, 289
  illegitimacy of, 13, 18–19, 49–51
  see also annexation
conservationist principle, 247, 251, 321, 323
contributions, 2, 53–4, 56, 62–4, 68, 73, 127, 202–5, 207, 210, 236
Coronini, Johann, 124
Corsica
  British occupation of, 85, 90
courts, 2, 9–10, 19, 22, 24, 85, 89–90, 146–8, 160–2, 166, 172–3, 175–7, 213–14, 238, 244, 300, 307–10, 327
  civil courts, 89, 135, 246, 264, 299
  indigenous courts, 63–4, 77, 126, 166–7, 194, 208–13, 222, 267–8, 302, 305
  international courts, 267
  military courts, 67, 90, 134–5, 154, 174–5, 179, 208–9, 232–3, 245, 309–10
Crete
  Greek occupation of, 269–70
  multilateral occupation of, 269–70
Crowder, Enoch, 296–7
Cuba
  American occupation of, 289–97
Custine, Adam Philippe, 43, 51, 55–7, 59, 63, 325

Cyprus
British occupation of, 263–5, 263, 319

Danton, Georges, 51–2
Danubian Principalities
Austro-Turkish occupation of, 123–5
Russian occupations of, 114, 117–19, 123–4, 321, 326
Russo-Ottoman occupation of, 123
Daru, Pierre, 81
Davis, George, 298–9
Davis, Jefferson, 161
Davout, Louis-Nicolas, 81
debellatio, 13, 32, 271, 285; *see also* conquest
Decaën, Charles, 76
Dejean, Jean, 75
Derby, Earl of, 230, 234
Despagnet, Frantz, 13, 32, 238
Diebitsch, Johann, 118
Diest, Gustav, 126–7, 143
Disraeli, Benjamin, 188
Dondukov-Korsakov, Alexander, 259
Dostoevsky, Fyodor, 259
Douglas, Stephen, 159
Ducrot, Auguste, 130
Duhamel, Alexander, 123
Duhesme, Guillaume, 82–3
Dumouriez, Charles François, 41, 43–4, 55–9, 325
Duncker, Max, 127
Durbach, C. F., 77

Eastern Rumelia, 258–9
Edwards, Henry Sutherland, 193, 206, 208
effective occupation, 6, 9–10, 29, 221, 233, 237–8, 245, 255–6, 271, 276, 302, 306, 320

Egypt
British occupation of, 5, 255, 265–9, 274, 283, 293, 298, 305–6, 319, 324
émigrés, 43, 131–2
Estrada Palma, Tomás, 295

Fabrice, Alfred von, 191, 211–12
Faipoult, Charles, 72
Falckenstein, Eduard von, 127
Farini, Luigi, 120
Favre, Jules, 189–90, 193
Ferdinand I of Naples, 137–8
Ferdinand VII, 111–13
Fiore, Pasquale, 13, 32, 251, 328
Florida
acquisition by the United States, 147–8, 178, 299–300
Folsom, J. L., 167
Foraker, Joseph, 294–5, 299–300, 307
foreign consuls, 127, 167, 263, 284
Forey, Élie, 132–4
Forster, Georg, 55, 59–60
Fouché, Joseph, 71
France
Allied occupation of, 86–9
German occupation of, 189–216, 218, 221, 225, 233
Spanish occupation of, 44
territory occupied by: Austria; Belgium; Bremen; Cisalpine Republic; Cispadane Republic; Crete; Hanover; Helvetic Republic; Hesse; Italian states; Ligurian Republic; Mexico; Munich; Naples; Parthenopian Republic; Prussia; Rhineland; Spain; Venice; Vienna
francs-tireurs, 189–90, 204–8, 221, 228, 326
Frankfurt am Main
Prussian occupation of, 127, 143

Frederick the Great, 20–1, 35
Frederick William II, 39
Frémont, John, 156, 159, 170–1
Fuad Pasha, Muhammed, 130, 144

Gambetta, Léon, 189–91, 201, 215
Garibaldi, Giuseppe, 122
Garran de Coulon, Jean Philippe, 46
Gazi Pasha, Mukhtar, 266, 268
Geneva Conference (1949), 8, 10
Geneva Conventions, 8, 10
  Art. 2, 8
Germany
  Allied occupation of, 85–6
  territory occupied by: France; Greece
  see also Prussia, territory occupied by
Gilinsky, Colonel, 241
Gillmore, Quincy, 179
Gladstone, William, 256, 267, 283
Gorchakov, Alexander, 227
Graber, Doris, 238
Grant, Ulysees S., 150–1, 158, 165, 174–5, 327
Granville, Lord, 265
Great Powers, 104–6, 114, 116, 243–5
  concept of, 136
Greece
  French occupation of, 114–15, 119
  German occupation of, 9
  territory occupied by: Crete; Salonica
Grenier, Paul, 76
Grey, Edward, 265
Grier, Robert, 146, 161
Grotius, Hugo, 15–17, 23, 33–4
guides, 204, 244, 274
  coercion of, 220–1
Gustavus Adolphus, 24

Hague Conference (1899), 3, 229–30, 240–3, 245, 270–1, 320
  Martens principle at, 243
Hague Conference (1907), 3, 230, 243–6, 320
Hague Regulations (1899), 270–2, 276
Hague Regulations (1907), 3, 10, 27, 244–5, 250, 321, 323
  Art. 3, 230
  Art. 9, 232
  Art. 10, 232
  Art. 42, 7, 10, 242
  Art. 43, 7, 29, 246–7, 250–1, 277
  Art. 45, 30
Hall, William, 10, 12, 21, 31, 229, 240
Halleck, Henry, 157–8, 162–5, 183
Hammer, Colonel, 233–4
Hanover
  French occupation of, 47, 76–80
  Prussian occupations of, 47, 77–8, 126–7
Harcourt, William, 267
Hautpoul, Alphonse de, 112
Hautpoul, Beaufort de, 129–31, 144, 323
Heffter, Wilhelm August, 6, 10, 29, 225, 229
Helvetic Republic, 46, 73–4
Henna, José, 298
Henry, Guy, 298–9
Hesse
  French occupations, 78–9, 126
  Prussian occupation, 126–7
Heyland, Karl, 7
Hoche, Louis Lazare, 41 74
Holy Alliance, 39, 91, 108–9
Horsford, Alfred, 231
hostages, 53, 61, 64, 83, 205, 207–8, 216, 236–7

Houtte, Hubert van, 21–2, 36
humanity
    invocation of, 15, 17–18, 40, 41, 141, 163, 169, 226, 232, 241, 243
Hungary
    Russian occupation of, 122
Hunter, Robert, 170–1
Hyman, Harold, 151–2

Inoue, Tetsujiro, 274
intervention, 52, 67, 70, 110–11, 113–14, 116, 121–2, 125, 128–31, 140, 266, 283, 288, 294–5, 329
    concept of, 107–9
invasion
    distinction from occupation, 10, 193, 216–17, 242–3, 245–6, 253
Iriarte, Francesco Suárez, 157–8
Italian states
    French Revolutionary and Napoleonic occupations of, 45–6, 68–72, 75–6
    see also Cisalpine Republic; Cispadane Republic; Ligurian Republic; Pathenopian Republic; Roman Republic
Italy
    territory occupied by *see* Tripoli

Japan
    territory occupied by: China; Korea
Jefferson, Thomas, 146, 178
Johnson, Andrew, 164–6, 168–9, 173–5, 177
Johnston, Joseph, 173
Jourdan, Jean Baptiste, 75
Juarez, Benito, 133
Jurien de La Gravière, Jean, 132

Kalckreuth, Friedrich, 60
Kállay, Benjamin, 263, 266
Kearny, Stephen, 152–4, 156–7, 180–1, 325–6
Kelly-Kenny, Thomas, 272
Kiselev, Pavel, 118–19
Kitchener, Herbert, 273, 305
Korea
    Japanese occupation of, 274
Kuropatkin, Aleksei, 229
Kutschera, Hugo von, 263

Labourdonnaye, Anne-François, 58
Lagrange, Joseph, 79
Lambermont, Auguste, 233–6, 320
Lameire, Irénée, 21–5, 35–6
Lansberge, Johan, 232, 320
Lanza, Count, 234
law of nature, 169, 189
law of occupation, 2–3, 10, 21, 24–5, 125, 214, 224–47, 270–1, 310, 321, 325–7, 329
League of Nations, 2, 18
Lee, Robert, 151
Leopold II, 39
Lesseps, Ferdinand de, 120
levée en masse, 189, 232–3
Lieber, Francis, 162, 183, 226, 247
Lieber Code, 162–3, 168–9, 171, 183, 226, 228–30, 290, 310
Ligurian Republic, 46–7, 70, 75
Lincoln, Abraham, 161–2, 164–5, 170–1, 173
Liprandi, Pavel, 119
Liverpool, Lord, 148
Lodge, Henry Cabot, 287
Loening, Edgar, 196, 221–2
Louet, Ernst, 130
Louis XIV, 42
Louis Napoleon, 105–6, 119, 121–2, 131, 188–9, 194

Index   353

Luxembourg
  Prussian occupation of, 198
MacArthur, Arthur, 302–5, 312, 315, 326
McKinley, William, 288–93, 198, 300–5
McNair, Arnold, 8–9
Madison, James, 147
Magoon, Charles, 246, 253, 296–7, 303, 317
Mahan, Alfred Thayer, 287
Mainz
  French occupation of, 43–4, 51, 55–7, 59–60, 327
Maison, Nicolas, 115
Mansfield, Lord, 19
Manteuffel, Edwin von, 127, 212–13
Martens, Fedor, 226, 238–44, 257–8, 280, 321
martial law, 7, 150–1, 171, 176, 179, 242, 270
Martignac, Jean-Baptiste, 112
Mason, Richard, 156–60
Massena, André, 71
Maximilian I, 133–4
Melzi d'Eril, Francesco, 75
Merlin de Douai, Philippe-Antoine, 40
Merlin de Thionville, Antoine-Christophe, 44
Merritt, Wesley, 300
Metternich, Klemens von, 43, 49, 105, 110–11, 117
Mexico
  American occupation of, 3, 149–60, 163, 176, 179–80, 327
  French occupation of, 128, 131–4
Miles, Nelson, 297–8
military codes, 228, 238, 244–6
military government, 84, 147, 150, 152, 158–60, 163, 165–7, 175, 180, 183, 196–7, 228, 246–7, 273, 294, 301, 303, 306, 310–11, 317, 320, 326
  defined, 7–8
military governors, 85, 87, 89, 126–7, 146, 160, 164–8, 173, 261, 190, 198, 308
  lack of clear duties, 165–6, 184, 272, 292, 298, 325–6
military occupation
  anxieties of the occupant, 63, 80, 87, 195, 326–7
  civil authorities of the occupant, 7, 52–4, 58–62, 65, 71–3, 77, 79–88, 164–5, 196–202, 258, 261, 263, 274–5, 296–7, 299–300, 302–5
  colonialism and, 5
  conflict between civil and military authorities of the occupant, 68–9, 71–2, 75, 86, 91, 120, 126–7, 130, 164–5, 273, 296–7, 303–5
  definition, 6–10, 290–1, 296, 300, 319–23
  difficulty of ending, 10, 31, 110–11, 113, 116, 121–2, 133–4, 188–92, 296–7, 206–7
  liberation and, 6, 50–2, 55–6, 59, 74–5, 81–2, 88, 91, 120, 257, 278, 329
  military discipline and, 55, 73, 77, 87–9, 153–5, 163–4, 192, 202
  myth of its illegality, 2, 29–30
  proclamations, 2, 56–7, 69, 72, 78–9, 120, 124, 126–7, 131–2, 138, 152–3, 156–7, 159, 163, 170–1, 194–5, 203, 207, 218, 221, 260, 271–2, 296–8, 301–2, 329
  regime transformation, 50–2, 55–8, 69–70, 76–8, 85,

117–19, 135–6, 175, 239–40, 246–7, 251, 264–5, 290–1, 293–4, 296–7, 299, 321, 323–4, 329
reliance on indigenous officials, 53–4, 57–60, 62–3, 79–80, 83, 166–7, 203–4, 230–1, 235–6, 238–42, 245, 261, 274, 276–7, 323
research on, 1–4
resistance to, 6, 8, 79, 82, 87, 94, 119, 126, 155–6, 194–5, 204, 208, 232, 243, 260–1, 264, 277, 301–2, 305–6
respect for existing laws, 54, 56, 64–5, 76–8, 126, 170, 197, 242, 257–8, 260, 264, 280, 291, 310, 321
see also contributions; effective occupation; multilateral occupation; oaths; occupation; pillage; taxation
Miller, Marcus, 301
Milner, Alfred, 267–8, 272–3, 294
Milroy, Robert, 163, 170, 172
Mini. Fabio, 2
missing reversioner, 293–4, 309–10, 317
Mitchel, Ormsby, 163, 169–70
Moltke, Helmith von, 59, 190, 202, 221, 237, 324–5
Montesquiou, Anne-Pierre, 50–1
Moreau, Jean-Victor, 47, 74, 76
Morgan, John, 168
Mortier, Éduard, 41, 77–9
Moynier, Gustave, 225, 228
multilateral occupation, 85–9, 111, 128, 130, 140–1, 255, 269–70, 275–6, 322–3
Munich
 French occupation of, 76
municipalisation of authority, 155, 199

Muñoz Rivera, Luis, 298–9
Murat, Joachim, 42, 75–6, 103

Naples
 Austrian occupation of, 110–11
 French occupation, 42, 46–8, 71–3, 75–6, 89–90
natural law *see* law of nature
Nelson, Samuel, 162
Netherlands
 French occupation of, 45–6, 64–8
Neumann, Leopold, 262
Nicholas II, 229
non-belligerent occupation, 8–9, 66–8
Nostiz-Walwitz, Hermann, 197

oaths, 7, 11, 22–4, 37–8, 80, 127, 167–9, 173, 201, 235, 240, 245, 262, 285
 iron clad test oath, 172–3, 175
 of allegiance, 11, 83, 150, 152, 168–9, 173–5, 235, 240, 262, 306
 of neutrality, 272–3
occupation
 relation to conquest, 6–7, 10–11, 23–5, 107–8, 111, 135, 224–5, 231, 239, 246, 247, 256, 309, 311, 321
Oppenheim, Lasa, 11–12, 21, 23, 31–2, 253
Otis, Elwell, 300–3
Ottoman Empire
 territory occupied by: Danubian Principalities; Thessaly
Oudinot, Charles, 120–1
Oxford Code, 228, 230, 237–41
Oyama, Iwao, 275
Oyré, François, 59

Pahlen, Pyotr, 118
Papal states
  occupations of, 70, 119–22
Parthenopian Republic, 46, 72
Pereira, Juan Solórzana, 16
Phelps, John, 164
Philippines
  American occupation of, 289, 296, 300–8, 311, 326
Philippovitch, Joesph, 261
Phillimore, Robert, 107
Pichegru, Jean-Charles, 65–6
Pictet, Jean, 8, 10, 31
Piedmont
  Austrian occupation of, 110–11
  French occupation of, 45, 75
pillage, 23, 36–7, 61, 64, 71, 73, 82, 127, 202–3, 206–7, 236–7
piracy, 161, 183
Platt, Orville, 294–5
Poland
  French occupation of, 81–2
Polk, James, 149, 159
Pope, John, 168–9
Poppé, N., 275
postliminium, 14, 33, 107, 170
Pretyman, George, 272
protectorates, 256, 267–9, 275, 279–80, 295
Prussia
  Austro-Prussian occupation of, 125, 142
  French occupation of, 47–8, 67–8, 80–1, 284
  territory occupied by: France; Frankfurt am Main; Hanover; Hesse; Luxembourg; Schleswig Holstein
Puerto Rico
  American occupation of, 281, 296–300, 307–8
Pufendorf, Samuel, 14, 18, 34
Putbus, Wilhelm, 192

raillement, 42
Ramel, Dominique, 65
Randolph, Carman, 309
Rapinat, Jean-Jacques, 73
refugees, 68, 131, 166, 260, 273
reprisals, 40, 79, 122, 203, 206, 210, 213, 232, 236
requisitions, 2, 54–5, 59, 61–5, 73–6, 85, 87, 118, 127, 194–5, 202–4, 206, 236
Reubell, Jean-François, 46, 66, 69, 73
reunion, 41, 59–1, 54, 60–1, 64, 74–5, 90, 116
Reyneval, Alphonse de, 120
Rhineland
  French occupation of, 41, 43–4, 59, 62–3, 65–8, 74, 77
Riley, Bennet, 159
Rivier, Alphonse, 13, 32
Roberts, Frederick, 271–3
Robespierre, Maximilien, 39, 44, 60, 95
Robin, Raymond, 8, 21, 76, 222, 322
Rolin, Eduard, 241
Rolin-Jaequemyns, Gustave, 197, 229, 237
Roman Republic, 71–2
Rome
  French occupations of, 46, 71–2, 89–90, 119–22
  Neapolitan occupation of, 89–90
Roosevelt, Theodore, 295–6, 306
Root, Elihu, 290, 293–4
Rosecrans, William, 164–5, 168
Rosemberg-Gruszcynski, E. R., 209
Rostolan, Louis de, 121
Roth, François, 193
Russell, John, 121, 123, 129

Saint-Cyr, Laurent Gouvion de, 83
Saint-Vallier, Charles de, 212–13

Saliceti, Antoine-Christophe, 68–9
Saligny, Alphonse Dubois de, 132–3
Salisbury, Marquess of, 256
Salonica
  Greek occupation of, 278
Sauviac, Joseph, 65–6
Savoy
  French occupation of, 50–1
Schauenbourg, Alexis, 73
Schleswig-Holstein
  Austro-Prussian occupation, 142
Schurman, Jacob, 302–3
Schwarzhoff, Julius Gross von, 243
Schwartzkoppen, E. von, 198
Scott, Winfield, 153–5, 157, 181
Seward, William, 167
Shafter, William, 291–2
Shellabarger, Samuel, 174, 176
Shepley, Heorge, 164, 166, 184
Sheridan, Philip, 189, 325
Sherman, William Tecumseh, 152, 165–7, 173, 184, 186
Shubrick, Robert, 156
Sieyès, Emmanuel, 66
Simon, Johann
sister republics, 46–7, 66–9, 71, 74–6, 93
Skobelev, Mikhail, 259
Sloat, John, 156
Smith, Jake, 305, 326
Sorel, Albert
Souham, Joseph
sovereignty, 5–7, 11–12, 15–24, 28, 34, 36, 52–3, 64, 68, 77–8, 85–6, 88–90, 95, 104–5, 123, 125, 128–9, 135, 145, 148, 178, 213–14, 218, 225, 234–5, 238–9, 246, 255–6, 261–3, 268–9, 278, 280, 288–9, 293, 295, 301–2, 304–5
  of the people, 52, 159
  suspended, 135, 148, 238–9, 241–2, 246
  see also missing reversioner
Spaight, John, 257
Spain
  French occupations of, 3–4, 27, 42, 48–9, 81–4, 87, 89–90, 94, 110–14, 119, 155, 323
Spooner, John, 303–4
Sprague, Peleg, 162
Stanhope, F. W., 173
Stanley, Edward, 164–5
Stanton, Edwin, 165
Stein, Heinrich vom, 85–7, 89–91, 322–3
Stevens, Thaddeus, 173–4
Stieber, Wilhelm, 201
Stockton, Robert, 156–7
Stolypin, Arkady, 259
subjugation, 4, 13–14, 18, 21, 83–4, 271, 306, 326; *see also* conquest
Suchet, Louis-Gabriel, 4, 83–4, 326
Sudan
  British occupation of, 268–9
suzerainty, 128–9, 135, 144, 256, 258, 268, 270, 278, 280, 295
Switzerland
  French occupation of, 46–7, 72–3
Syria
  French occupation of, 5, 128–31

Taft, William, 295–7, 303–5, 314, 326
Talleyrand, Charles, 42, 75
taxation, 2, 52, 54, 58, 69, 79, 88, 202–3, 214, 240–1, 272, 291
Terry, Alfred, 187
Thessaly
  Ottoman occupation of, 270
Thiers, Adolphe, 191, 212–13
Thouvenal, Edouard-Antoine, 128
Tocqueville, Alexis de, 120
Toulon

British occupation of, 44, 85
treason, 74, 153, 161, 169, 173, 199, 205, 240, 242, 244–5, 277, 327; *see also* collaboration
treaties
  Adrianople (1829), 117
  Amiens (1802), 47
  Balt Liman (1849), 123
  Basel (1795), 43, 45, 67
  Berlin (1878), 254, 257–62, 269
  Campo Formio (1798), 46
  Frankfurt (1871), 191, 211–13, 328
  Ghent (1814), 49
  Guadalupe-Hidalgo (1848), 149–50, 157–8
  Hague (1795), 66–7
  Leoben (1797), 45–6
  London (1827), 114
  London (1867), 188
  Lunéville (1801), 47, 93
  Nikolsburg (1866), 125
  Paris (1815), 87
  Paris (1899), 293, 295, 298, 301, 304, 310
  Peking (1860), 128
  Pressburg (1805), 47
  San Stefano (1878), 257
  Schönbrunn (1809), 48
  Tilsit (1807), 80
  Tolentino (1797), 45
  Tsien-Tsin (1858), 128
Tripoli
  Italian occupation, 277
Trochu, Louis, 190
Trouvé, Joseph, 71
Truesdail, William, 165, 184
Turpie, David, 288
United States of America

occupations by: American Civil War; California; Cuba; Mexico; Philippines; Puerto Rico

Vattel, Emer de, 18–19
Vedel, Peter, 236
Veljkovitch, Voislave, 242
Venice
  French occupation of, 46, 76
Veramendi, Manuel Reyes y, 155, 157
Verriére, Nicolas, 57
Vest, George, 289–90
Vienna
  French occupation of, 53, 78, 80
Villeneuve, Jerome Petion de, 50
Viogts-Rhetz, Konstantin von, 9, 189, 198, 202, 214, 231–6

Waldersee, Alfred von, 275
Warsaw, Grand Duchy of *see* Poland
Werder, Karl Friedrich von, 195, 205
Weyler, Valeriano, 273
White, Edward, 308–9, 320
Wilson, James, 276, 292–4, 297–8, 322
Winfield, P. H., 107
Winthrop, William, 228
Wood, Leonard, 290, 293–4, 296, 299, 306, 309, 322, 324, 326
Wright, Horatio, 169

Yugolslavia
  German occupation of, 9

Zheltuken, Peter, 118

EU Authorised Representative:
Easy Access System Europe Mustamäe tee 50, 10621 Tallinn, Estonia
gpsr.requests@easproject.com

Printed and bound by CPI Group (UK) Ltd, Croydon, CR0 4YY
18/01/2026
02037285-0006